Power Tools for
Technical
Communication

Power Tools for

Technical Communication

FIRST CANADIAN EDITION

David A. McMurrey

Wendy Wilson

Fanshawe College

George A. Tripp

Fanshawe College

THOMSON

NELSON

Australia   Canada   Mexico   Singapore   Spain   United Kingdom   United States

THOMSON

NELSON

Power Tools for Technical Communication
First Canadian Edition

by David A. McMurrey, Wendy Wilson,
George A. Tripp

Associate Vice-President, Editorial Director:
Evelyn Veitch

Acquisitions Editor:
Mike Thompson

Marketing Manager:
Sandra Green

Developmental Editor:
Natalie Barrington

Permissions Coordinator:
Nicola Winstanley

Copy Editor/Proofreader:
Cathy Witlox

Indexer:
Edwin Durbin

Production Coordinator:
Susan Ure

Design Director:
Ken Phipps

Interior Design Modifications:
Katherine Strain

Cover Design:
Eugene Lo

Cover Image:
Comstock Images

Compositor:
Nelson Gonzalez

Printer:
Transcontinental

Library and Archives Canada Cataloguing in Publication

McMurrey, David A.
   Power tools for technical communication/David A. McMurrey, Wendy Wilson, George Tripp—1st Canadian ed.

Includes index.
ISBN 0-17-625183-9

1. Technical writing—Textbooks.
I. Tripp, George A., 1945-
II. Wilson, Wendy, 1946- III. Title.

T11.M324 2006   808'.0666
C2006-900652-0

Preface

Whether you are a student or an instructor of technical writing, you'll want to read the following. It shows you how to use this book and discusses its main concepts and organization.

WHAT'S THIS BOOK ABOUT—WHO'S IT FOR?

This book is for students and teachers in introductory technical-writing courses—courses that are required in the technical majors such as the following:

Academic Majors Commonly Requiring Technical Writing

Aerospace engineering	Kinesiology
Air conditioning technology	Landscaping
Automotive technology	Legal assistant programs
Building construction technologies	Medical laboratory technology
Commercial arts	Nursing
Consumer electronics technology	Occupational therapy
Criminal justice	Office administration
Diagnostic medical imaging (radiology, sonography)	Pharmacy technology
Emergency medical (paramedic) technology	Physical fitness technology
Engineering—all kinds!	Physical therapy
Engineering design graphics	Quality assurance
Fire protection technology	Semiconductor manufacturing technology
Geomatics	Space science
Heating and refrigeration technology	Surgical technology
Industrial supervision	Waste water treatment
Information records management	Welding technology
International business	

The focus of this book is on people pursuing their own study programs and students coming to introductory technical-writing courses from other majors. Therefore, this book doesn't say much about issues such as workplace culture, professional ethics, and other such currently popular issues.

These are best left to the faculty in students' majors. For example, professionals in the healthcare field are far better positioned to address the culture and the ethics of workplaces such as hospitals, clinics, medical agencies, and the home-healthcare setting.

Instead, this book focuses on writing—technical writing. It focuses on design, format, style, structures, and applications of technical writing. It focuses on strategies and tools you can use to produce excellent technical documents in any of the common delivery methods. "Documents" refers to all manner of technical reports, proposals, instructions, and user guides, as well as business letters, memos, and e-mail containing technical material. "Delivery methods" refers not just to printed documents, but to oral-presentation delivery and delivery over the World Wide Web.

Instead of forcing you into a theory-now writing-later approach, this book groups topics by type (as shown in the following table), making it easier for you to construct your own preferred sequence. Like a hypertext in print, the chapters in this book can be used in practically *any* order you wish. Few technical-writing instructors or students use their textbooks in the published order anyway.

Topics Covered in *Power Tools*
(chapter numbers are shown in parentheses)

Part I: Practice Projects	Part I: Real-World Projects	Part II: Document-Design Tools	Part III: Document-Delivery Tools	Parts IV–V: Project-Development Tools
Description (1)	Site, accident, trip, field reports (1)	Headings (7)	Informal reports (1, 14)	Audience and task analysis (17)
Process (2)	Product specifications (1)	Lists (8)	Business-letter reports (2, 14)	Team writing (20)
Cause–effect (3)	Instructions (2)	Notices (9)	Memo reports (1)	Organization at **http://www.powertools.nelson.com**
				Sentence style at **http://www.powertools.nelson.com**

Continued

Topics Covered in *Power Tools—continued*
(chapter numbers are shown in parentheses)

Part I: Practice Projects	Part I: Real-World Projects	Part II: Document-Design Tools	Part III: Document-Delivery Tools	Parts IV–V: Project-Development Tools
Comparison (4)	Recommendation, evaluation, feasibility reports (4)	Tables (10)	Formal reports (14)	Grammar, usage, punctuation (B, C)
Definition (5)	Background reports (5)	Charts (10)	Oral reports (15)	Transitions at **http://www.powertools.nelson.com**
Classification (5)	Proposals (6)	Illustrative graphics (11)		Mechanics: abbreviations, symbols, numbers (A)
Persuasion, argumentation (6)	Progress reports (6)	Highlighting (7)		Topics at **http://www.powertools.nelson.com**
	Inquiry, complaint, adjustment letters (12)			Narrowing at **http://www.powertools.nelson.com**
	Résumés, application letters (13)			Outlining at **http://www.powertools.nelson.com**

HOW DO YOU USE THIS BOOK?

This book is *not* designed to be read or used from cover to cover. It is *not* set up to be read in the order that the chapters are listed in the table of contents. It's *not* designed to take you on a lengthy lock-step tour of theory and concepts before you get to do any actual writing.

Chapter sequences. Instead, this book is designed so that you can sequence chapters according to what you need to study, what you are ready to study, and which technical-writing projects you are interested in. Conceptual issues such as audience or page design are much more meaningful in the context of a writing project in which you use those concepts. When you are engaged in an actual technical-writing project, bookish issues like audience, transitions, organization, headings, lists, graphics, and collaboration all of a sudden have immediate relevance. However, if you studied audience six weeks ago, you are not likely to remember much about it or put it into practice effectively.

Project approach. Instead of forcing you into a long march through theory, this book enables you to design your study program to incorporate increasingly challenging projects. Select projects that are interesting and relevant. If you have already studied description, process, comparison, and definition, skip those portions of the chapters and move right into workplace projects such as instructions, proposals, and background reports. To supplement those projects, select the nonproject chapters that go best with them. For example:

- Course startup: about technical writing (Introduction) and workplace writing (Chapter 20).
- Audience analysis (Chapter 17) with definition writing (Chapter 5).

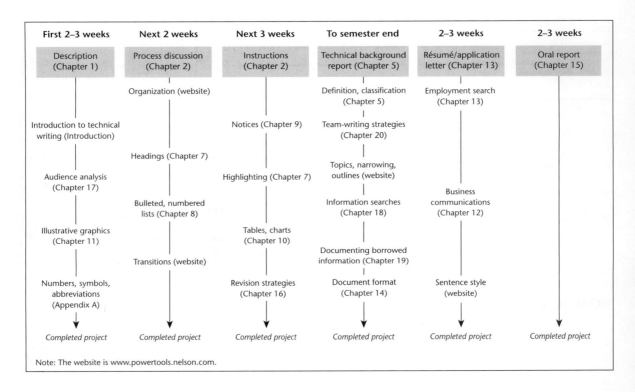

First 2–3 weeks	Next 2 weeks	Next 3 weeks	To semester end	2–3 weeks	2–3 weeks
Description (Chapter 1)	Process discussion (Chapter 2)	Instructions (Chapter 2)	Technical background report (Chapter 5)	Résumé/application letter (Chapter 13)	Oral report (Chapter 15)
	Organization (website)		Definition, classification (Chapter 5)	Employment search (Chapter 13)	
Introduction to technical writing (Introduction)		Notices (Chapter 9)	Team-writing strategies (Chapter 20)		
	Headings (Chapter 7)		Topics, narrowing, outlines (website)		
Audience analysis (Chapter 17)		Highlighting (Chapter 7)		Business communications (Chapter 12)	
	Bulleted, numbered lists (Chapter 8)		Information searches (Chapter 18)		
Illustrative graphics (Chapter 11)		Tables, charts (Chapter 10)			
	Transitions (website)		Documenting borrowed information (Chapter 19)		
Numbers, symbols, abbreviations (Appendix A)		Revision strategies (Chapter 16)	Document format (Chapter 14)	Sentence style (website)	
Completed project	*Completed project*	*Completed project*	*Completed project*	*Completed project*	*Completed project*

Note: The website is www.powertools.nelson.com.

FIGURE P-1

Ideas for interlacing chapters of this book. The six projects shown above use almost all of the chapters in this book and take up 14 to 16 weeks in total. In each, you begin with a project—something that addresses a real or realistic need or problem in the workplace. For additional ideas, see the instructor's manual or the textbook website at **http://www.powertools.nelson.com**.

- Graphics (Chapter 11) with descriptions (Chapter 1).
- Lists and notices (Chapter 9) with instructions (Chapter 2).
- Information search (Chapter 18) and documentation of borrowed information (Chapter 19) with the formal technical report (Chapters 5 and 14).
- Tables, graphs, and charts (Chapter 10) with recommendation reports (Chapter 4).

No doubt you'll find many other combinations and sequences that fit your learning or teaching needs. That's one of the main reasons that chapters in this book are grouped rather than sequenced. For additional ideas on combining and sequencing chapters, see Figure P-1.

All theory—no play. If you've ever looked in technical-writing textbooks, you've noticed that the common sequence of chapters looks like what is shown in Figure P-2. You've got to learn *all* the basics before you can start practising an art or skill, right? Yes indeed, if you are studying something such as medical procedures. For example, you don't get to "revise" if,

COMMON CHAPTER SEQUENCING: OTHER TECHNICAL-WRITING BOOKS

Chapters in this book corresponding to the following topics are indicated in parentheses:

1. *Technical writing*—About the subject and the field (Introduction).
2. *Audience*—The essential focus of all technical writing (Chapter 17).
3. *Workplace context*—Use and importance of technical writing in a broad range of fields, professions, occupations, and disciplines (Introduction and Chapter 20).
4. *Qualities of good technical writing*—Importance of direct, succinct, readable writing (Introduction).
5. *Ethics*—Ethical problems in technical writing and professions in general (throughout).
6. *International communication*—Considerations for writing for audiences in other cultures (references in Chapter 12).
7. *Page design and graphics*—Page layout, typography, headings, lists, illustrations (Part II chapters).
8. *Arrangement and organizational patterns*—Description, definition, process, general-to-specific, problem–solution, and others (Part I chapters).
9. *Information gathering*—Using the library and the Internet, as well as direct information-gathering methods (Chapter 18).
10. *Citing sources of borrowed information*—Using APA, MLA, IEEE (Chapter 19).
11. *Revision*—Substantive editing, copy editing, proofreading (Chapter 18).
12. *Applications*—Only after all of the above have been presented do you get to actually write documents such as instructions, reports, letters, memos (Part I chapters).

FIGURE P-2

Common chapter sequencing in technical-writing textbooks. Eventually, you get to write.

while trying to start an IV, you give your patient an embolism. However, you can practise activities like writing, cooking, painting, singing, composing, and sports in a safe environment, where it's okay if your first efforts aren't perfect or fully informed of all available theory. It's okay to "mess up." (Of course, cooking might be a problem—who wants to waste good food?) In these areas you learn a little, get some practice using what you just learned, and repeat the process again and again. If you try to swallow the theory whole, you'll gag—you won't remember much of it or put much of it into practice. It's like memorizing a whole box of German vocabulary cards without ever practising reading, speaking, or writing the language.

Workplace writing. This book acknowledges that most technical-writing students are not in workplace situations that provide good contexts for the writing projects discussed here. That's a problem because technical writing is all about workplace writing and solving workplace problems using the tools of technical writing. Faced with this dilemma, we try to find real situations in which descriptions, definitions, instructions, and other types of documents are needed. But more often we have to invent realistic situations. Sometimes that means starting with an interesting topic and working "backward" to a realistic workplace situation in which that topic would be featured.

Infrastructures. The first seven chapters of this book—Part I, "Project Tools for Technical Writers"—rely on the concept of infrastructure. The infrastructure of a society is its water, sewage, electrical, and gas systems; its system of roads and bridges, as well as mundane things like garbage collection, mail delivery, telephones, and so on. These are the backbone, the skeletal structure of a society. Without them, a modern society doesn't work. When they are working, we hardly notice them. They exist as if underneath—"infra" to—the surfaces of our society. Information structures such as description, classification, comparison, process, cause–effect discussion, and definition exist "underneath" the applications of technical writing—such as instructions, user guides, feasibility and recommendation reports, technical background reports, and other such technical documents. You rarely find a "pure" description or "pure" classification; instead, they are internal to the application—"infra." When these infrastructures inform a technical-writing application, they undergo a good many transformations: they lose the pure characteristics of organization and content described in Part I.

Infrastructures are important—they give you starting points, models, patterns with which to begin building technical documents. Infrastructures can be mixed and matched in an infinite variety of ways. For example, you can write a process discussion using the structure of a description; one by one, you can trace the events of the process through the components of the device. In the end, who cares whether we call it a process description or a physical description as long as it meets the needs of the audience and supports the purpose of the document?

WHAT'S IN THIS BOOK—WHAT'S DISTINCTIVE?

Obviously, the chapter organization of this book and its project approach are some of its most distinctive features. This book contains just about everything you expect to see in a technical-writing textbook, but there are some new features.

Topic boxes. Every chapter begins with a box of links to research for topics used in the chapter. Technical-writing courses are great opportunities to explore these areas. Where else can you explore such a broad range of science and technology?

Step-by-step "tools" approach. Everywhere, you'll find specific steps for using document-design "tools" such as headings, lists, tables, graphs, and charts. You'll see specific steps for thinking of projects, narrowing and outlining topics, checking organization and transitions, working in writing teams, developing instructions, planning recommendation reports, using presentation software (such as Microsoft PowerPoint), and more.

Student writing with annotations. Just about all of the examples in this book have student names associated with them. These examples give you a realistic sense of what can reasonably be expected of students in introductory technical-writing courses—people at the beginning of their careers, taking courses, often holding down jobs and taking care of families. And these examples are annotated—marginal comments point out key features in the examples.

Separate chapters on headings, lists, notices, and highlighting. Notice the page-design chapters in Part II. Elements like headings and highlighting, bulleted and numbered lists, tables, special notices, and graphics get their own chapters.

CHANGES TO THE CANADIAN EDITION

This textbook now has many added features for Canadian students and their instructors. Students from Fanshawe College in London, Ontario, have contributed their work, and we have added many Canadian examples, from the Niagara wine growing area to the Alberta wind farms. The section on research contains Canadian college and university library links and information on finding Canadian government documents. In fact, we were amazed at the wealth of resources provided by the federal government. A major theme through the book is the use of alternative fuels such as wind power, and government Web pages were the first place we looked for information on this topic. As much as possible, we have added Canadian research links at the start of each chapter. However, sometimes non-Canadian links were too tempting not to use—how could a grammar teacher not enjoy British author Lynne Truss's Eats, Shoots & Leaves website, for example?

ACKNOWLEDGMENTS

We would like to thank our colleagues in General Studies at Fanshawe College and the team at Thomson Nelson: Chris Carson, Mike Thompson, Susan Calvert, Cathy Witlox, and Nicola Winstanley, and especially Natalie Barrington, who guided us through the process of preparing the adaptation of this text.

We would also like to thank the reviewers who took the time to provide their feedback on this edition:

Jacqueline Ballhorn, Algonquin College
Treena Chobotar, Red River College
Brent Cotton, Georgian College
Sandy Dorley, Conestoga College
Anne Ward, Lambton College

We look forward to using this text ourselves, and welcome any input from instructors or students for future editions.

Wendy Wilson
Fanshawe College
wwilson@fanshawec.ca

George A. Tripp
Fanshawe College
gtripp@fanshawec.ca

Table of Contents

Quick Reference (inside front cover)

Preface   v

What's This Book About—Who's It For?   v
How Do You Use This Book?   vii
What's in This Book—What's Distinctive?   xi
Changes to the Canadian Edition   xi
Acknowledgments   xii

Technical Writing: An Introduction   1

What Is Technical Writing, or Technical Communication?   2
What Kind of Writing Is Technical Writing?   4
Who Are Technical Writers—Where Are They?   8
What Do Technical Writers Do?   9
Why Are There Technical-Writing Courses?   10
Technical Writers and Ethical Decision-Making   11
Workshop: Technical Communication   12
Practical Ethics: Association Guidelines   13

PART I.   Project Tools for Technical Writers   15

Chapter 1.   Description: Product Specifications and Informal Reports   16

How Do You Write a Description?   17
How Do You Write Product Specifications?   23
How Do You Write Informal Reports?   28
Workshop: Description   31
Technical Description: Technical Description: Workhorse Flashlight   33
Informal Report: Report on My Preliminary Investigation of Meeting the One-Tonne Challenge in a Heritage House   36

Chapter 2.   Processes: Instructions, Policies, and Procedures   40

What Is a Process?   41
How Do You Write about Processes?   42
How Do You Write Instructions?   46
How Do You Write Policies and Procedures?   51

Workshop: Process, Instructions, Policies, and Procedures   55
Process Document: Mission Overview: Deep Impact   57
Instructions: Finding and Installing Printer Drivers for the
    Canon BJC-5000   63

Chapter 3.   Causes and Effects: Primary Research Reports (Lab Reports)   67

How Do You Write about Causes and Effects?   68
How Do You Write Primary Research Reports?   75
Practical Ethics: Omission   77
Workshop: Causes, Effects, Primary Research Reports   80
Cause–Effect Discussion: The Effect of Climate Change on the
    Canadian Arctic   81
Primary Research Report: Bats Roosting in Deciduous Leaf Litter   83

Chapter 4.   Comparison: Recommendation, Evaluation, and Feasibility Reports   87

How Do You Write a Comparison?   88
What Are Recommendation, Evaluation, and Feasibility Reports?   93
How Do You Write a Recommendation Report?   94
Practical Ethics: Trusty Numbers   98
How Do You Write Feasibility and Evaluation Reports?   100
Workshop: Comparison and Recommendation Reports   102
Comparison: Comparison: Mars and Earth   103
Recommendation Report: Voice-Recognition Software:
    Recommendations for Medical Transcriptionists   105
Voice-Recognition Software: Appendixes   107

Chapter 5.   Definition and Classification: Background Reports   116

What Is a Definition and How Do You Write One?   117
What Is a Classification and How Do You Write One?   125
How Do You Write Technical Background Reports?   131
Workshop: Definition, Classification, Background Reports   134
Extended Definition: Molecular Manufacturing   137
Classification: Choosing a Solar Hot Water System in Canada   142

Chapter 6.   Persuasion: Proposals and Progress Reports   144

What Are the Tools for Persuasion?   145
How Do You Write Persuasively?   148
Practical Ethics: Biased Language   151
How Do You Write a Proposal?   152
How Do You Write a Progress Report?   157
Workshop: Persuasion, Proposals, and Progress Reports   162

Persuasive Technical Writing: It Is Time We Stopped Waging War
on the Earth   164
Memo Proposal: Proposal to Write a Feasibility Report on
Wind-Generated Power in Stand-Alone Residential Applications   168
Proposal Cover Letter: Proposal to Develop a Feasibility Report on
Wind-Generated Power in a Stand-Alone Residential Application
for CMNC355   173
Feasibility Proposal: Harnessing Wind Power for Home Use   175
Progress Report Cover Letter: Progress Report on the Feasibility
Report on Wind-Generated Power in a Stand-Alone Residential
Application   180
Progress Report: The Feasibility of Wind-Generated Power in a
Stand-Alone Residential Application   181

PART II. Document-Design Tools   189

Chapter 7. Headings, Highlighting, and Emphasis   190

What Are Headings: What Are They Good For?   191
How Do You Design Headings?   193
How Do You Use Headings?   195
How Do You Create Headings?   196
What Is Highlighting and Emphasis?   199
What Can Be Highlighted, and How?   201
How Do You Plan a Highlighting Scheme?   202
How Do You Add Highlighting and Emphasis?   205
Workshop: Headings and Highlighting   207

Chapter 8. Lists: Bulleted, Numbered, and Others   210

What Are Lists?   211
What Are Lists Good For?   213
Where Should You Use Lists?   214
What Are the Guidelines for Lists?   214
How Do You Create Lists?   216
Workshop: Lists   217

Chapter 9. Notices: Dangers, Warnings, and Cautions   219

What Are Notices?   220
How Do You Use Notices?   223
How Do You Write Notices?   224
How Do You Design and Create Notices?   225
Some Special Notices   228
Workshop: Notices   230

Chapter 10.   Tables, Graphs, and Charts   231

What Are They?   232
When to Use Which?   232
How Do You Design Tables, Graphs, and Charts?   235
How Do You Create Tables, Graphs, and Charts?   238
Workshop: Tables, Graphs, and Charts   244

Chapter 11.   Illustrative Graphics   248

What Should Be Illustrated?   249
What Are the Types of Illustrations?   250
How Do You Find or Create Illustrations?   253
Practical Ethics: Manipulating Photos   253
How Do You Format Illustrations?   255
How Do You Incorporate Graphics into Documents?   258
How about the Old-Fashioned Way?   259
Workshop: Graphics   260

PART III.   Document-Delivery Tools   263

Chapter 12.   Business Communications: Letters, Memos, and E-Mail   264

How Do You Write Effective Letters, Memos, and E-Mail?   265
How Do You Format a Business Letter?   267
How Do You Format a Memo?   270
How Do You Create a Letter or Memo Template?   272
What about E-Mail?   274
How Do You Write Problem Communications?   275
Practical Ethics: Murky Waters   277
Workshop: Business Letters, Memos, E-Mail   282
Complaint Letter: Complaint about Defective Digital Multimeter   284
Adjustment Letter: Compensation for Defective Camera   286
Inquiry Letter: Request for Information about Blackberry™ Communicators   288

Chapter 13.   Employment-Search Tools: Application Letters and Résumés   290

How Do You Get Started on a Job Search?   291
How Do You Write a Résumé?   293
How Do You Write an Application Letter?   301
Practical Ethics: Should You Tell the Truth on Your Résumé?   307
Workshop: Application Letters and Résumés   308
Application Letter: Application for Full-Time Position as System Support Specialist   309
Print Résumé   310

Chapter 14.   Formal Reports: Design, Format, Abstracts   312

Designing Technical Documents   313
Formal Reports and Other Technical Documents   313
Practical Ethics: Anecdotal Evidence   320
Summaries and Abstracts   322
Workshop: Document Design and Format   324

Chapter 15.   Oral Presentations: Preparation, Visuals, and Delivery   336

How Do You Plan an Oral Presentation?   337
How Do You Prepare Visuals for an Oral Presentation?   342
Practical Ethics: Biased or Slanted Graphics   343
How Do You Use Presentation Software?   345
How Do You Deliver an Oral Presentation?   347
How Do You Evaluate Oral Presentations?   348
Workshop: Oral Presentations   350

PART IV.   Tools for Project Development   351

Chapter 16.   Reviewing and Revising   352

First Pass: Audience, Purpose, Content   353
Practical Ethics: Universal Language   355
Second Pass: Design and Format   355
Third Pass: Style, Grammar, Mechanics   357
Workshop: Reviewing and Revising   359
An Instruction to Review and Revise:
    How to Change the Oil on a Cummins Diesel   360

Chapter 17.   Audience and Task Analysis   365

Who Reads Technical Documents?   366
Why Do They Read? What Are Their Tasks?   367
How Do You Identify Tasks?   370
How Do You Write for an Audience?   374
How Do You Revise for an Audience?   376
Workshop: Audiences and Tasks   377

Chapter 18.   Finding Information: Print, Internet, Informal Sources   380

How Do You Search for Information?   381
What about the Internet?   385
What about Encyclopedias and Other Reference Books?   388
What about Books?   389
What about Magazine, Journal, and Newspaper Articles?   390
What about Government Documents?   394
What about Brochures and Other Product Literature?   395
What about Informal, Unpublished Sources?   396

What about Surveys and Questionnaires?   397
Workshop: Information Search   398

Chapter 19.   Citing Sources of Borrowed Information   400

Intellectual Property and Plagiarism   401
Name–Year System (APA)   402
Practical Ethics: Plagiarism   403
Name–Page System (MLA)   405
For Additional Information   407
Workshop: Source Documentation   408

Chapter 20.   Managing Team Projects   409

How Do Industry Writing Teams Work?   410
Practical Ethics: Groupthink   413
How Do You Team-Write a Technical-Writing Project?   415
Workshop: Teams   420

PART V.   Writing Tools: Mechanics and Style   A-1

Appendix A.   Abbreviations, Symbols, and Numbers   A-2

Abbreviations, Acronyms, and Initialisms   A-3
Symbols   A-7
Numbers   A-8
Workshop: Mechanics   A-11

Appendix B.   Punctuation: Commas, Semicolons, Colons, Hyphens, Dashes, Apostrophes, and Quotation Marks   B-1

Introductory, Compound, Series, and Nonrestrictive Commas   B-2
Semicolons   B-8
Colons   B-9
Hyphens   B-10
Dashes   B-15
Apostrophes   B-16
Quotation Marks   B-18
Workshop: Punctuation   B-19

Appendix C.   Grammar Favourites   C-1

Fragments   C-2
Comma-Splice Sentences   C-4
Pronoun-Reference Problems   C-5
Parallelism Problems   C-6
Workshop: Grammar   C-8

Index.   Index-1

Technical Writing: An Introduction

Topics covered in this chapter include

- technical communications;
- audience analysis;
- ethics.

TECHNICAL COMMUNICATIONS

Search for local chapters of the Society for Technical Communication (**http://www.stc.org**), the largest professional organization of technical communicators.

AUDIENCE ANALYSIS

A Winnipeg-based technical writer has a site that includes information on audience analysis at **http://www.docsymmetry.com**.

ETHICS

The Independent Computer Consultants Association has a Code of Ethics posted for its members at **http://www.icca.org/ethics.asp**. For ethical issues related to various workplaces, you can go to the Workopolis website at **http://www.workopolis.com** and search for Working Wounded or Workplace Ethics 101.

When you have completed this chapter, you will be able to

- understand what it means to be a technical communicator;
- work with the different audiences for a technical communication;
- respond appropriately to some of the ethical dilemmas facing a technical writer.

If you are just getting started with technical writing, you probably have the same questions that are addressed in this introduction:

- What is technical writing?
- What kind of writing is technical writing?
- Who are technical writers and what do they do?
- Why are there technical-writing courses?

From the outset, however, understand that the point of this book, and of technical-writing courses, is not to turn you into a full-time professional technical writer. If you are interested in that—great! Take a look at the resources in the box on page 1. The technical communication profession is a good one—plenty of interesting work, lots of new technology, plenty of rewards, and, oh yes, pretty good pay and benefits. As we plunge deeper and deeper into the high-tech revolution, technical writers will be more in demand and their work will be more diverse and interesting.

Although this book certainly can give you a good start in a technical-writing career, its purpose is to show you some skills, techniques, concepts, and examples that will be valuable no matter what field, profession, or occupation you enter.

WHAT IS TECHNICAL WRITING, OR TECHNICAL COMMUNICATION?

Professional technical communicators prefer the term "technical communication," because the profession involves much more than writing. It involves communicating technical information through whichever communication tools do the job best. These tools include not only writing but graphics, animation, video, and audio. Thus, even though "technical communication" is a mouthful, it more accurately describes what professionals in this field do. The following offers pieces of a definition of technical communication:

- communicates technical information;
- has a specific purpose;
- is geared to the needs of a specific audience;
- occurs in a specific workplace situation;
- uses the communication tools that work best.

Consider this definition part by part in the following table:

Defining Technical Communication

Communication	This definition uses *communication* rather than *writing* because technical communicators use not only words but pictures, animation, sound, and video to present information.
Technical	The term *technical* refers to computers, electronics, and any body of knowledge, any craft, or any expertise not commonly understood. Thus, *technical* can refer not only to mechanical engineering but to carpentry, plumbing, auto repair, hairstyling, gardening, cooking, welding, nursing, massage therapy, restaurant management, acupuncture and acupressure, music recording, accounting, commercial graphics, and many other fields, as well as to the fields we commonly think of as "technical," such as brain surgery, electronics, and—yes—rocket science.
Information	*Information* in the technical world includes user guides (how to operate something), reference manuals (details on a process, concept, or the functions of a product), quick-reference guides, installation guides, troubleshooting guides, recommendation reports, background reports, progress reports, proposals, research reports, and so on. Business letters, memos, and e-mail also may contain technical material.
Specific purpose	What is provided is information—but it's information with a specific purpose for a specific set of readers. The purpose can be informative (what is this thing?), instructive (how do I use this thing?), or persuasive (I recommend we use this thing!). Technical communication is rarely literary (no sonnets in user guides) or expressive (no blowing off steam about the kludgy product).
Specific audience	Audiences of technical communication are not only rocket scientists and brain surgeons but ordinary people who may be "out of their depth" or "in over their heads." The users of technical information range from beginners to seasoned veterans. The most interesting challenges are those in which you must convey technical information to novices. That's why it's often best not to be an expert on a science or technology topic when you are writing for beginning and intermediate readers.
Needs	Audiences of technical writing have specific needs for information. They may need background on a topic, instructions for equipment, or recommendations on which product to purchase. They may need to know the structure or operation of equipment, or the causes or effects of a phenomenon. They may need a recommendation on which product to purchase or an evaluation of how well a program is working.
Specific situation	Most technical writing occurs within a specific framework in which a customer or client expects (and may even be paying for) the information. The information has direct professional, business, or industrial applications. It solves a workplace problem, responds to a need, or addresses an opportunity.
Tools	Technical communicators use a variety of communication methods to convey their message: words, sounds, images, and video. This information appears in print, online, and on-screen. Technical writers may find themselves using FrameMaker to develop a printed book, ForeHELP to develop online helps, Dreamweaver to develop a website, Photoshop to create images, After Effects to create animation, and audio and video tools to create tutorials that run on a DVD.

WHAT KIND OF WRITING IS TECHNICAL WRITING?

It's too easy to pass off technical writing as factual, objective writing with lots of numbers and symbols. From the preceding, you already know that technical communication is not just informative or instructional but also seeks to convince or persuade.

Technical Texts

Research reports. One of the classics of technical writing has long been the scientific research report. Traditionally, this type of report stays totally emotionless, uses exact words, loads sentences with statistical detail, interprets or speculates only in specially marked parts of the report, and uses all passive voice in an effort to sound objective.

The number of dead birds found on mortality plots did not differ from reference plots at $P = 0.05$ but did differ at $P = 0.10$ ($G = 2.982$, 1 df, $0.05 < P < 0.10$). While habitat type (i.e., agricultural vs. CRP) did not influence the number of dead birds found on mortality plots ($G = 0.53$, 1 df, $P > 0.05$; Table 1), end turbines (turbines at the end of a turbine string) were associated with a disproportionate number of dead birds ($G = 5.05$, 1 df, $P \leq 0.05$; Table 1). The seasonal mortality pattern did not differ from random at $P = 0.10$ ($G = 7.04$, 3 df, $0.50 < P < 0.10$). Mortality was higher than expected by chance in spring.

Source: Osborn, Robert G., et al. "Bird Mortality Associated with Wind Turbines at the Buffalo Ridge Wind Resource Area, Minnesota." *American Midland Naturalist* 143 (2000): 41-52.

User guides. Another of the "classics" of technical writing is the user guide—in other words, instructions. Unlike the scientific research report, user guides have become personal, direct, helpful, and friendly.

Choosing the right search terms is the key to finding the information you need.

Start with the obvious—if you're looking for general information on Hawaii, try *Hawaii.*

But it's often advisable to use multiple search terms; if you're planning a Hawaiian vacation, you'll do better with *vacation Hawaii* than with either *vacation* or *Hawaii* by themselves. And *vacation Hawaii golf* may produce even better (or, depending on your perspective, worse) results.

Source: The Essentials of Google Search. <http://www.google.com/help/basics.html>.

Online helps. Online helps are those windows of quick reminders or quick helps you get when you press the Help button on most software applications. Helps differ from user-guide information in that they are shorter, serving more to remind than to teach. This difference is subtle, but compare this FTP help information to the search engine user-guide information just above: helps are shorter and less explanatory.

Transferring Files or Folders

To transfer files or folders:

1. Select the files or folders on the source system.

2. Open the folder to which you want to transfer files on the destination system.

3. Select the file transfer mode.

Continued

Technical Texts cont'd.

4. Transfer the files using the left and right arrow buttons located between the list boxes.

Click the left arrow button to transfer files from the remote to the local system.

Click the right arrow button to transfer files from the local system to the FTP site.

Adapted with permission from Michael Caldwell, former technical-writing student at Austin Community College.

Technical-support writing. With increasingly high-tech products going to nontechnical consumers, addressing consumer problems via telephone and e-mail has become an employment growth area. This writing is primarily internal: technical-support people write problem–solution summaries and add them to a database that other technical-support people can use. (And increasingly, these same problem–solution databases are made available online to consumers.)

Problem: The battery pack cannot be fully charged in 3.5 hours by the power-off charging method.

Action: The battery pack might be overdischarged. Do the following:

1. Turn off the computer.
2. Make sure that the over-discharged battery pack is in the computer.
3. Connect the AC adapter to the computer and let it charge.

If the battery pack cannot be fully charged in 24 hours, use a new battery pack.

Reference information. Reference information is encyclopedia-style information, typically presented in tables or alphabetically. It doesn't teach you how to use something; it tells you what the settings, features, modes, and variables are and what their effects are. In the example to the right, the reference information explains the function and format of one of many Perl command-line options. The complete set of options is arranged alphabetically. In contrast, user guides take a step-by-step, hand-holding approach.

-v Option

The -v option specifies which version of Perl is running on your machine. When the Perl interpreter sees this option, it prints information on itself and then exits without running your program. For example:

```
$ perl -v test1
```

produces output similar to the following:

```
This is perl, version 5.001

Copyright (c) 1987-1994, Larry Wall

Perl may be copied only under the terms of
either the Artistic License or the GNU
General Public License, which may be found
in the Perl 5.0 source kit.
```

Adapted with permission from Red Hat, Inc.

Continued

Technical Texts cont'd.

Consumer literature. Government agencies and non-profit organizations often find themselves in the business of conveying technical information about environmental issues, regulations, and product safety concerns. This material is distributed to the public—in other words, consumers.

Information like that in the example here is indeed technical, but it is presented in such a way that ordinary citizens not only understand it but feel obligated to comply with it.

Environmental Impacts

Across Canada, we will feel and see the effects of climate change:

- **Nunavut.** Summer melting of glaciers may lead to wide-scale flooding. If the Greenland Ice Sheet melts, it contains enough ice to raise the global sea level by six to seven metres.

- **Western Arctic.** Thawing of permafrost, or permanently frozen ground, could impact buildings and roads constructed for those solid conditions. Meanwhile, seasonal forest fire danger levels are predicted to increase in the Yukon and Northwest Territories.

- **British Columbia.** Of greatest concern are "debris flows"—watery slurries of mud, gravel, and boulders that travel at high speeds down steep mountain stream courses during heavy rains. Warmer winters may increase insect pests while wetter springs may delay planting.

- **Prairies.** Hotter and longer summers result in increased evaporation, and less surface water is available for use. Forty percent of the rural population of Saskatchewan relies on groundwater.

- **Ontario.** A warmer climate and longer frost-free seasons may permit the spread of new diseases from warmer climates, such as Lyme disease, malaria, and West Nile virus.

- **Quebec.** The freshwater portion of the St. Lawrence River may see a deterioration in water quality, loss of wetland habitats and reduction in biodiversity. Droughts would mean less water available for consumption, agriculture, and recreation, and more conflicts over use.

- **Atlantic.** Highly sensitive to the effects of sea-level rise, this portion of Canada will experience such effects as increased erosion, rapid migration of beaches, and flooding of coastal freshwater marshes.

Source: http://onetonne.gc.ca, Government of Canada Climate Change, 2005. Reproduced with the permission of the Minister of Public Works and Government Services, 2005.

Continued

Technical Texts cont'd.

Consultant technical writing. Consultants regularly get involved in technical writing—in some cases, it's their primary work-getting tool and their primary work output. Consider proposals: they seek approval or contracts to do work and are typically loaded with technical information. Consider recommendation and feasibility reports: they advise recipients to take one course of action or another and pile on plenty of technical information to support that advice.

Accuracy. Accuracy is the most significant consideration; without it, the program is useless. Dragon Systems' NaturallySpeaking scored highest on all of the accuracy tests performed by *PC Magazine* and was unequivocally selected as the Editors' Choice. In their tests, the average accuracy was 91% and at times was considerably greater [1].

Average accuracy for L&H Voice Xpress was 87% [2]. Accuracy for IBM's ViaVoice tested at 85% [14], and Philips FreeSpeech98 was 80% [15].

Although Dragon Systems' NaturallySpeaking is considerably more expensive, its accuracy, speed, ease of use, and flexibility justify the extra expense.

Adapted with permission from Dr. Pat Roach, former online technical writing student.

Marketing literature. Technical writers also get involved in marketing literature—product brochures and specifications, for example. This field is often called "marketing communication," or "marcom" for short. Marketing people, product planners, and technical writers team up to develop promotional literature for their products. In marketing-oriented technical writing, you see all the common inducements, promotion, and language that you would expect to see in any written advertisement.

Red Hat Linux 6.1

for Intel (x86), Alpha, and SPARC® platforms

Release 6.1 takes ease of installation to a new standard for Linux, and provides the workstation, server, and customer service features that are important to you. Red Hat delivers third party applications for personal productivity, all of the Internet server favourites such as Apache, SAMBA, and SendMail, and fast FTP access to updates from priority.redhat.com.

New Features:

- New, easier installation
- High availability clustering
- Enhanced systems management with LDAP integration
- Easy connection to the Internet with the new PPP Dialer
- Choice of KDE or GNOME default desktop

Adapted with permission from Red Hat, Inc.

Continued

Technical Texts cont'd.

Technical journalism. You've probably read plenty of newspaper and magazine articles on science and technology topics. The writers of this material are also "technical writers," although they may prefer the term "technical journalists." This form seeks to entertain as much as to inform. If you write about nanotechnology for *Omni* (a popular mainstream magazine devoted to science and technology topics), you want readers to go "Gee—wow!" as much as to feel more informed.

Notice in this example how the technical journalist highlights the human element and the excitement brought on by the impact of this discovery.

When Kary Mullis was a second-year grad student at Berkeley he wrote a paper called "The Cosmological Significance of Time Reversal," about how half the matter in the universe is going backwards in time. He sent it to *Nature* and they published it immediately, attributing it to a "Dr. Mullis." In 1983, 10 years after receiving his doctorate in biochemistry, a 39-year-old Mullis sent *Nature* another paper about a technique called polymerase chain reaction (PCR) that essentially amplifies DNA, enabling scientists to make millions of copies of a DNA molecule in an incredibly short time. *Nature* rejected it. Then *Science* rejected it. Over the next 10 years, however, the science world became convinced that PCR was the biggest advancement in molecular biology in decades. In 1993, Mullis was awarded a Nobel Prize in chemistry for an invention that shed new light on the quest to decode DNA.

From the moment he conceived of PCR, while gliding along the highway through the mountains of Northern California, Mullis knew the epic implications. He describes his revelation in his book, *Dancing Naked in the Mind Field*: "PCR was a chemical procedure that would make the structures of the molecules of our genes as easy to see as billboards in the desert and as easy to manipulate as Tinkertoys. . . ."

Adapted with permission from www.feedmag.com.

WHO ARE TECHNICAL WRITERS—WHERE ARE THEY?

Many people work part-time as technical writers—some are not even aware of it. Maybe even you are a technical writer and don't know it!

Part-time technical writers. Plenty of ordinary people in a wide variety of professions and occupations do part-time technical writing. They must routinely convey information about their expertise to others—often to others who are not experts. How these part-timers convey that technical information has much to do with the success of a project or the well-being of an organization or a community, not to mention their own professional and financial well-being. Communities, organizations, projects, and individuals cannot be successful without successful communication, including successful technical communication. Just about every technical profession involves a good measure of technical writing. That's one big reason why there are technical-writing courses.

Full-time professional technical writers. There are plenty of full-time professionals who consciously describe themselves as "technical writers" and "technical communicators." The classic technical writers work in places like Dell, IBM, Hewlett-Packard, Microsoft, Adobe, Research in Motion, and Nortel, where they develop user guides, online helps, and Web pages for hardware and software products. However, technical writers also work in plenty of noncomputer companies such as Boeing, Lockheed, Caterpillar, and General Motors. Look around: any expensive, complex equipment has a user guide or reference manual associated with it.

Academic, government, research-oriented technical writers. Plenty of technical writers work in government agencies and academic institutions. Good examples are technical writers at Manitoba Conservation, who write brochures, guides, and reports concerning environmental issues for the public. They also get involved in developing research reports, grant proposals, and other such materials.

Freelance technical writers. Lots of technical writers work freelance, usually specializing in a particular industry such as computers, aerospace, heavy machinery, or medicine. They work right alongside the full-timers doing similar tasks, but only for a set period of time or set project.

Technical journalists. Some technical writers double as journalists. They write magazine and journal articles about various aspects of science, technology, medicine, health, and other such areas. As mentioned earlier, they often bring out the excitement of new developments in science and technology.

WHAT DO TECHNICAL WRITERS DO?

What do technical writers do? The answer is obvious—they write! Right? Actually, studies of full-time technical writers show that they write for only about one-fourth of the time they spend on the job.[1] The rest of the time is taken up in research, project meetings, and interviews with developers and engineers. They spend time sending and answering e-mail and working with prototypes of products they are documenting. If they are not documenting a product, they may be spending their time gathering and analyzing data for reports and interviewing the experts.

Experts are important to technical writers. Technical writers cannot maintain the same level of expertise as product developers, engineers, and research scientists. Instead, they rely on those people for information and reviews. Technical writers are a different kind of expert: they are experts in communication, document design, usability, and audience analysis. In this respect, when you study technical writing you play a role like that of the full-time technical writer. You start with a workplace requirement and

---

[1] Price, Jonathan, and Henry Korman. *How to Communicate Technical Information*. Redwood City, CA: Benjamin/Cummings, 1993.

you carefully analyze your audience. You are probably not an expert on your topic so you must find information, interview experts, and do other sorts of research—just like a technical writer.

WHY ARE THERE TECHNICAL-WRITING COURSES?

The need for technical-writing courses should be obvious by now.

Employer demands. Leaders in every field, profession, and occupation demand good writing skills in their employees. Such skills are critical to the success and well-being of communities, organizations, professions, projects, and individuals. General writing skills are one thing, but the skills you get in a technical-writing course are more directly focused on scientific and technical needs. That's why most technical majors require technical-writing courses.

Vital tool for any professional. Engineers, for example, tell us that they spend 20 to 40 percent of their work time writing memos, letters, e-mail, reports, and proposals. They also say that this percentage increases as they are promoted. And finally, they say that they wish they had had more writing courses in college.[2] In one survey, more than half of the graduates in technically oriented majors (for example, engineering, science, nursing) said that the ability to write well is of "great" or "critical" importance, and nearly all said that the ability to write well is important.[3] In another survey of graduates in a range of professional fields, three-fourths of the respondents rated writing as "very important," the highest rating possible.[4]

Powerful tool for other courses. Don't delay your technical-writing course until the very last semester. Technical-writing skills are valuable in writing projects you do for other courses. Knowing how to prepare a report, use headings and lists, construct tables and graphics, control highlighting, and make the finished product readable and professional looking—these are invaluable skills in academic courses as well as in the workplace.

Chance to explore science and technology. Practicality aside, a technical-communication course can be one of the most stimulating of your academic career. Where else can you explore topics like the ones sprinkled throughout this book—extraterrestrial intelligence, global warming, electronic game design, wind energy, solar power, recycling, time travel, computer viruses, cloning, fractals, human expeditions to Mars, photovoltaics, brain research, nanotechnology, and so on? Where else are you challenged to explain how a light bulb works, how an acoustic speaker produces sound, how a photovoltaic device generates electricity from the sun, how a CD-ROM holds over 600 megabytes of sound or data, how a television

---

[2] Beer, David, and David McMurrey. *Guide to Writing as an Engineer*. New York: Wiley, 1997.
[3] Anderson, Paul V. "What Survey Research Tells Us about Writing at Work." *Writing in Nonacademic Settings*. Ed. Lee Odell and Dixie Goswami. New York: Guilford, 1985. 3–85.
[4] Roth, Lorie "Education Makes a Difference: Results of a Survey of Writing on the Job." *Technical Communication Quarterly* 2 (1993): 177–184.

produces colour and images on screen, how a computer adds two simple numbers, or why the sky is blue?

TECHNICAL WRITERS AND ETHICAL DECISION-MAKING

As a technical writer you will occasionally find yourself having to make a decision based on ethics rather than on scientific information. Sam Dragga, a technical-communications scholar, asked 48 technical communicators how they made moral choices and found that, for them, the process was "fluid and dynamic" rather than defined by critical thinking techniques or codes of conduct. Dragga reported that "while simple or unimportant issues may be decided individually according to conscience, complicated and critical issues are usually discussed with trusted colleagues or supervisors."[5] In other words, no textbook or theory on ethics can prepare you for every ethical situation, but at least you won't have to face these situations alone.

Regardless of your future profession, you will be confronted with ethical decisions. In fact, you've probably already made numerous decisions on the job that call for ethical judgments without even realizing it. Have you ever taken a pen from work to use at home? Have you ever used e-mail or surfed the Web on company time? More than likely you didn't have any problem determining whether your behaviour was ethical or not, if you even stopped to question yourself.

But what you consider good behaviour might be unethical or wrong in another person's eyes. What then?

Academics and philosophers have struggled with these questions for years, proposing many different models to help people determine what is ethical and what isn't. The following list, which uses the acronym **AUTHOR** to help you remember it, outlines some useful rules:

The ethical writer is

Accurate
- Uses facts, statistics, and language correctly and precisely.

Unbiased
- Writing does not contain bias; arguments are not unfairly slanted.

Trustworthy
- Keeps company and personal information private.

Honest
- Gives credit where due and does not violate copyright. Does not use statistics and images to create false impressions.

---

[5] Dragga, Sam. "A Question of Ethics: Lessons from Technical Communicators on the Job." *Technical Communication Quarterly* 6 (1997): 2, 162.

Open
- Considers all options and does not start with preconceived solutions.

Reliable
- Honours commitments and submits work in a timely fashion.

Scattered throughout this book are boxes titled "Practical Ethics." These are intended to promote discussion. We have not provided answers.

WORKSHOP: TECHNICAL COMMUNICATION

Here are some suggestions for exploring technical communication in the workplace:

1. *Interview professionals.* Interview professionals in your field concerning the amount of writing they do, the types and purposes of the writing they do, the importance of that writing, and any recommendations they may have for you or your technical-writing instructor. Consider designing a questionnaire that you can send to professionals or fill out as you interview them.

2. *Analyze an organization chart for written work.* Get together with two or three other students in your field or major, draw up an organization chart typical of companies or agencies in your field, and identify the kinds of writing that employees located at various areas in that organization do. Identify who writes what to whom, and the purposes and characteristics of that writing. Don't forget to identify writing that stays within an area of the organization and writing that travels outside of the organization (for example, to customers or the public).

3. *Analyze samples of technical writing.* Find two or three examples of technical writing that are dramatically different—in terms of content, approach, intended audience, technical level, design, and so on. Define the audience, purpose, and situation of these examples.

4. *Compare technical writing for different audiences.* Find two technical documents on the same subject—one written for experts, the other written for novices (people untrained or inexperienced in the subject matter). Identify what the novice version does to help readers understand the subject matter; identify what the expert version *doesn't* do.

5. *Analyze a technical document from another field.* Find a technical document, written for an expert audience, in some field that you know little or nothing about. Identify what the writer could do to

Practical Ethics: Association Guidelines

 Many professional associations and employers have established ethical guidelines for their members or employees. The Society for Technical Communication (STC) is an association of technical writers in a variety of different fields that provides opportunities for education and networking. The following ethical guidelines can be found on the STC website, http://www.stc-va.org:

Legality: We observe the laws and regulations governing our profession. We meet the terms of contracts we undertake. We ensure that all terms are consistent with laws and regulations locally and globally, as applicable, and with STC ethical principles.

Honesty: We seek to promote the public good in our activities. To the best of our ability, we provide truthful and accurate communications. We also dedicate ourselves to conciseness, clarity, coherence, and creativity, striving to meet the needs of those who use our products and services. We alert our clients and employers when we believe that material is ambiguous. Before using another person's work, we obtain permission. We attribute authorship of material and ideas only to those who make an original and substantive contribution. We do not perform work outside our job scope during hours compensated by clients or employers, except with their permission; nor do we use their facilities, equipment, or supplies without their approval. When we advertise our services, we do so truthfully.

Confidentiality: We respect the confidentiality of our clients, employers, and professional organizations. We disclose business-sensitive information only with their consent or when legally required to do so. We obtain releases from clients and employers before including any business-sensitive materials in our portfolios or commercial demonstrations or before using such materials for another client or employer.

Quality: We endeavour to produce excellence in our communication products. We negotiate realistic agreements with clients and employers on schedules, budgets, and deliverables during project planning. Then we strive to fulfill our obligations in a timely, responsible manner.

Fairness: We respect cultural variety and other aspects of diversity in our clients, employers, development teams, and audiences. We serve the business interests of our clients and employers as long as they are consistent with the public good. Whenever possible, we avoid conflicts of interest in fulfilling our professional responsibilities and activities. If we discern a conflict of interest, we disclose it to those concerned and obtain their approval before proceeding.

Professionalism: We evaluate communication products and services constructively and tactfully, and seek definitive assessments of our own professional performance. We advance technical communication through our integrity and excellence in performing each task we undertake. Additionally, we assist other persons in our profession through mentoring, networking, and instruction. We also pursue professional self-improvement, especially through courses and conferences.

From www.stc-va.org. Reprinted with permission from the Society for Technical Communication.

---

enable you to understand that document, noting things like definitions, historical background, examples, and so on.

6. *Discuss an ethical problem.* Form six groups and have each group take one of the letters in **AUTHOR**. Imagine a situation that might arise related to that letter. Then have each group lead a class discussion on its issue. For example, imagine as a technical writer you are privy to information that might affect the company business. To find some situations online, search for Workplace Ethics 101 on Workopolis at **http://globecareers.workopolis.com**.

7. *Summarize your findings.* As directed by your technical-writing instructor, select one of the preceding workshops and summarize your findings in a memo to your technical-writing class. Better yet, meet with two or three other students, consolidate your findings, and team-write the memo.

PART I

Project Tools for Technical Writers

CHAPTER 1

Description: Product Specifications and Informal Reports

Topics covered in this chapter include

- the Kyoto Protocol;
- solar cars.

THE KYOTO PROTOCOL

Alternative energy sources are in the limelight, especially with global warming and the controversy surrounding the Kyoto Protocol. Most communities in Canada have developed plans for the "One-Tonne Challenge." If you search the Web for your community's name and "one-tonne challenge," you will find the plan in your area.

SOLAR CARS

Many educational institutions have developed fuel-efficient cars. For example:

University of Waterloo Midnight Sun VIII
http://www.midsun.uwaterloo.ca/www

Fanshawe College race car
http://www.fanshawec.on.ca/news/2002/sae.asp

Search "solar car" and the name of a school for more examples.

When you have completed this chapter, you will be able to

- use description as a tool in your technical documents;
- write descriptions of technical objects;
- write product specifications.

Many applications of technical writing rely on description as an essential infrastructure. As you know from the Preface, an *infrastructure* in this context is a special combination of content and organization that enables a technical document to do its work. A *description* is a special combination of physical, quantifiable details with part-by-part organization. The applications covered in this chapter—product specifications and informal reports—commonly use description as their infrastructure.

This chapter shows you how to write descriptions and then how to construct product specifications and informal reports with description built in as the infrastructure.

Note:
- If you are new to this book, see "How Do You Use This Book?" in the Preface.
- For additional examples of the documents discussed in this chapter, see **http://www.powertools.nelson.com**. On this website you will also find an additional example of technical writing: a bid specification for the construction of single-storey purple-martin birdhouses.

HOW DO YOU WRITE A DESCRIPTION?

Before getting into the details of new-product specifications and informal reports, take a moment to review description, the essential infrastructure used in these documents. In this context, *description* means the presentation of physical, quantifiable details about some object. Physical details include colour, shape, size, texture, materials of construction, ingredients, weight, height, width, depth, and so on. Quantifiable details are those you can count or measure, such as the number of trees on a vacant lot, the number of inhabitants of a city, or a distance between geographical locations.

One of the best, most organized ways to present this physical, quantifiable detail is the *part-by-part approach* (see Figure 1-1). Think of the simple wooden pencil. You can describe the lead, the wooden barrel, the

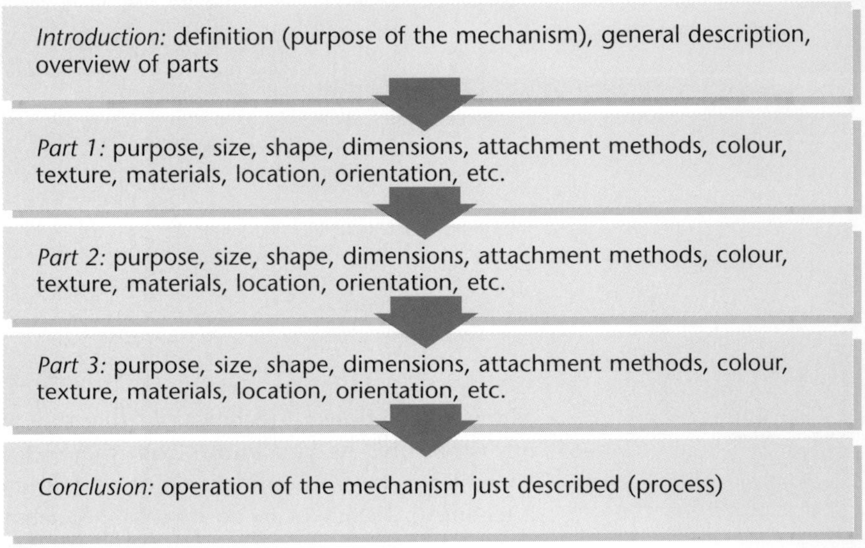

Introduction: definition (purpose of the mechanism), general description, overview of parts

Part 1: purpose, size, shape, dimensions, attachment methods, colour, texture, materials, location, orientation, etc.

Part 2: purpose, size, shape, dimensions, attachment methods, colour, texture, materials, location, orientation, etc.

Part 3: purpose, size, shape, dimensions, attachment methods, colour, texture, materials, location, orientation, etc.

Conclusion: operation of the mechanism just described (process)

FIGURE 1-1

Part-by-part description. Describing part by part enables you to take a more organized approach to description. Describe each part in one or more sentences or in one or more paragraphs.

eraser, and that metal clip that holds the barrel and eraser together. Describe each of these parts separately in a sentence or two, or even a whole paragraph.

Of course, there are other ways to organize a description. Sometimes the thing you want to describe does not divide as neatly into parts as does the wooden pencil. For example, describing a vacant lot for real estate purposes might work better with the *characteristics approach*—location, dimensions, vegetation, structures, soil, and so on.

The following steps walk you through the important phases in writing a simple description using the part-by-part approach. To get a sense of how the steps work in a writing project, we follow a single example through all of the steps.

1. **Find a simple project involving description.** Try finding a situation in which specific readers need a description. For example, insurance adjusters need flood damage descriptions and real estate investors need property descriptions. But why would anyone need descriptions of bottle openers, corkscrews, sunglasses, coffee cups, or wooden pencils? One possibility is product specification. In manufacturing, marketing specialists need descriptions for advertisement planning; manufacturing specialists, for planning the manufacture of the product; financial specialists, for planning production costs and projected revenues. (Having trouble thinking of a topic? See **http://www. powertools.nelson.com**.)

Imagine that you've decided to describe a bow saw—the kind of saw used to cut tree limbs. It has very coarse teeth that quickly rip through wood. Why is this description needed? Let's use the product specification idea: your company is developing a new bow saw. All interested parties in the company need to do their respective planning work in relation to this new product. They all need a description of the product for their marketing, manufacturing, financial, packaging, and distribution planning.

2. **Define the purpose and audience for the project.** The next step is to clarify the purpose and audience. (See Chapter 17 on analyzing audiences and adapting to them.) If you've found a real or realistic situation for a description, then your audience and purpose are almost defined already.

For this bow saw description, picture an audience of marketing, manufacturing, financial, and distribution planners. Marketing people need information for advertisements and catalogues. Manufacturing people need to know dimensions and materials of construction. Financial planners need information for projecting manufacturing costs and potential revenues. Distribution planners need information such as size, dimensions, and weight to plan packaging and distribution. To simplify matters, let's write the bow saw description for manufacturing planners only.

3. **Research the thing you are describing.** Early in a project, you may need to research the object you've chosen to describe. In particular, you'll need part names and various specifications. The website listed below provides resources that contain labelled pictures of thousands of objects. These resources explain the processes by which equipment works and you'll find plenty of terminology about parts and construction.

Brain, Marshall. How Stuff Works: **http://www.howstuffworks.com**

If you searched the Web for "bow saws," you'd probably be surprised at how much information you'd find. Much, of course, is advertisement. Still, you can find some nice images to borrow (legally for academic purposes, if you cite the source), as well as dimensions and other specifications.

4. **Plan and develop graphics.** Try to visualize the graphics needed in your description. Use the strategies in Chapter 10 and Chapter 11 to plan the drawings, diagrams, photos, and charts you need to include.

A good graphic for the bow saw description is obviously a labelled drawing of the bow saw itself, and perhaps also a close-up of the saw blade, showing the teeth. Because specifications are important for this description, label the drawing with various measurements (lengths and widths of the parts of the bow saw).

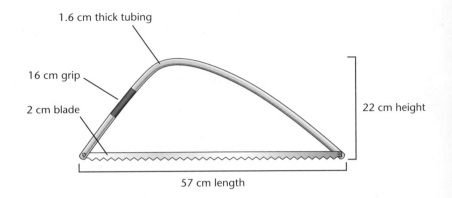

5. **Identify the parts and subparts.** Make a list of the parts whose descriptions best meet the needs of your audience. For this practice description, try to discuss at least four parts of the item. Omit unimportant parts such as electrical cords. Don't forget to list important subparts. For example, a description of a mechanical pencil would include details on the subparts of the lead-advancing mechanism.

> How many parts does this bow saw have? Two? Three? First, there is the saw blade with its jagged teeth. There is also the C-shaped handle—or should it be called the frame, or the brace? You'll have to research that one. This particular bow saw has a plastic or rubber grip on part of the handle.

6. **Plan the overall description.** You'll also need an overall description of the object. Think of that wooden pencil. Describing the parts is not enough; you still need to describe characteristics that the part-by-part descriptions cannot address, such as the overall length and the overall weight. The overall description may also need a definition of the thing you are describing.

> The overall description of the bow saw must include its fully assembled weight, length, and height. Define it according to how and why the bow saw is useful.

7. **Plan the description of each part.** One of the next steps is to decide the order in which to describe each part and whether to spend a few sentences or an entire paragraph on each part.

> In this sample description, describe each part in a separate paragraph:
> - *Saw blade*—explain its purpose; provide details on its length, height, and width; its materials of construction and colour; and precise details about the saw teeth.
> - *Handle*—explain its purpose; describe its length, shape, colour, materials of construction, and its diameter; include details as to where and how much it angles and where and how much it tapers. Also explain how the saw blade is attached.

■ *Grip*—explain its purpose, and then describe the grip in terms of its materials of construction, length, thickness, colour, and method of attachment to the handle.

8. **Sketch out the headings you'll use.** If your description is going to be more than two or three paragraphs, use headings (see Chapter 7). If you describe each part in one or more separate paragraphs, create a heading to identify each part.

   For the description of the bow saw, let's use "Saw blade," "Handle," and "Grip" as the headings to introduce the description of these parts.

9. **Select the sources of description.** One problem with practice descriptions is that they fail to provide enough descriptive detail. Use the sources of description listed in the table on page 22 as a way of thinking of that extra detail. These sources are like tools you can use to develop a description to its fullest.

   This bow saw description obviously does not need to draw on all of these sources of description. Include details as to its size, shape, colour, finish, texture, weight, methods of attachment, materials of construction, and pattern (in the handle or of the teeth). Anything else?

10. **Plan an introduction.** Introductions must indicate the *topic* and *purpose* of the document and provide an overview of what will be discussed. Also included must be an *audience identifier* to help readers decide whether the information is suited to their needs, interests, and knowledge level. Descriptions should also include a list of parts to be described and an *overall description*.

    Imagine that you've written a short paragraph on each of the parts of the bow saw, along with the overall description. For the introduction, indicate the topic, audience, and purpose—an informative description to enable manufacturing planners to develop plans to manufacture the bow saw. Define the bow saw and discuss its uses. Indicate that you are about to provide a part-by-part description and list the parts to be described. Because the overall description is brief, include it in the introduction.

11. **Consider the format.** For this simple project, you don't need the elaborate report formats shown in Chapter 14. Instead, use the format of the sample description of the flashlight at the end of this chapter. Use a descriptive title centred at the top of the page and second- and third-level headings. Use lists, illustrations, tables, and citations of your borrowed information sources, as necessary.

    This bow saw description is an initial overview of the product idea, not likely to require more than two pages. Let's use the memo format, with "Working description of the new bow saw product" in the subject line. Use headings,

Sources of Description

Source of description	Comments
Purpose	How is the item used? What are its applications?
Size	How big or small is it? Can you compare its size to something familiar?
Shape	How is it shaped? Can you compare its shape to something familiar?
Colour	What are its colours?
Texture, finish	How does it feel to the touch—rough, smooth, grainy, wavy? How does it look—shiny, glossy, dark, dull?
Dimensions	What are its length, height, width, depth?
Weight	How much does it weigh?
Materials of construction	What materials are used in its construction—wood, steel, aluminum, cardboard?
Ingredients	If it is something that is mixed, what are the ingredients?
Methods of attachment	How are the different parts attached—glued, welded, bolted or screwed on, nailed in?
Location, orientation of parts	What's the orientation of the parts to each other—above, below, to the left, to the right, within?
Age	How old is it?
Temperature	Is temperature an important descriptive detail?
Moisture content	What's the percentage of water content?
Amount	How many are there?
Capacity	How much can it hold?
Volume	What are the various measurements of volume related to it?
Smell, odour	What does it smell like?
Pattern, design	Does it have a certain pattern or design associated with it?

subheadings, lists, graphics, and tables in this memo just as you would in any report.

12. **Review and revise your rough draft.** Use the strategies in Chapter 16 to systematically review and revise your description. Use the top-down approach described in Chapter 16: start by reviewing for audience, purpose, and situation; then move on to content, organization, and transitions; then work with headings, lists, tables, and graphics;

Purpose: This description begins with the overall purpose of the thing to be described.

Sources of description: Notice the different sources used here: output (in watts and voltage); construction components (arrays, subarrays, panels, cells); orientation (southerly direction and 40° tilt); quantities (100 kw, 3,000 panels, 10 cells, 3 panels); dimensions (cm); other components (inverters, transformers, feed lines, meters); financial details and percentages.

Illustration: Wouldn't it help to have a diagram that illustrated the relationships of the panels, arrays, subarrays, sections, and cells here?

Churchill High School is actually located in Winnipeg, Manitoba. However, it does not use this photovoltaic system (http://www.wsd1.org/churchill).

Churchill High School in Winnipeg, Manitoba, uses a system of solar photovoltaic flat-plate panels to generate its electricity needs. Currently, this system produces 100 kw, but could produce considerably more with some simple modifications. The Churchill photovoltaic system is made up of more than 3,000 panels. Each panel contains 10 photovoltaic cells. The photovoltaic array is made up of separate subarrays of photovoltaic modules deployed in rows on a southerly facing slope. Each subarray is made from 3 stand-alone (but electrically integral) sections called panels, supported by a portable mechanical jack. Although the panels can be manually tilted to follow the path of the sun, they have been put in a stationary position that optimizes their exposure to the sun. Each panel measures 740 cm by 235 cm and contains 10 photovoltaic cells. The power generated by these panels is transmitted at 4160 v from the inverters and a step-up transformer to the main 4160 v utility feed line into the school. Separate meters are used to measure power bought from or sold to the local utility. At the optimum tilt angle—about 40 degrees—the array provides about 14% of the annual school load. This amounts to annual energy savings of between $8,000 and $16,000.

FIGURE 1-2

Description using the part-by-part approach. Although this description is a single paragraph, you can see where the description of each part begins and ends.

then sentence style and technical style; and finally, grammar, usage, spelling, and punctuation problems.

Understanding the essential infrastructure (description) will enable you to write heavily detailed but well-organized technical documents such as those discussed in the next sections of this chapter.

HOW DO YOU WRITE PRODUCT SPECIFICATIONS?

Specifications describe purchaser requirements for products, projects, and services. If a local garden store hired you to build birdhouses that it would sell, the store owner would give you specifications as to the dimensions, materials, and construction of those birdhouses. As shown in Figure 1-3, some specifications are just tables of numbers and words, requiring little actual writing.

Specifications not only describe the physical characteristics of something. They also specify *operational* characteristics: how the thing will run or work, how it will hold up under certain kinds of wear and tear, and so on. Specifications like these can also be captured in table form, as Figure 1-4 shows. Some specifications are performance or operationally oriented

Although Canada officially uses the metric system, in practice most building construction materials still use the imperial system. Check the entire project before deciding on which system to use.

Specifications: Chickadee Birdhouse	
Type of bird	Chickadee
Floor	5-1/2″ × 4″
Front	8″ × 5-1/2″
Sides (2)	8″ × 5-1/2″
Back	11″ × 5-1/2″
Entrance hole	1-1/8″ centred 1″ below the top of the front piece
Material	Ash
Construction	Brass screws (not nails or glue)

FIGURE 1–3

Specifications for a birdhouse. Some specifications do not require writing, just tables of numbers and words, as in these specifications for a chickadee birdhouse.

Notice that the designers use dual measurement systems depending on the component being described. Again, remember to check the requirements of the entire project.

SAE Competition Race Car Formula One Style Specifications (developed by students in the Fanshawe College Mechanical Design Program)	
Chassis	Monocoque style, chrome-moly 4130 round steel tube 1 inch
Suspension	Nitrogen gas charged gas shocks
Body	2024-T3x0.032 skin Fibreglass mat polyester resin
Drive train	610 cc Kawasaki Fuel Injected
Speed	135 kph racing speed
Dimensions	Maximum width 2 feet Maximum height 2 feet 6 inches Length 110 inches
Weight	610 pounds dry
Array area	18 square feet
Peak output	35 HP

FIGURE 1–4

Specifications for an SAE competition race car. Notice that the specifications for speed and output are operational characteristics. The rest are construction specifications. Although many universities are building solar cars, others are still interested in efficient gasoline-powered vehicles.

Source: Information provided by John Queenan, Coordinator, Mechanical Design, Fanshawe College, London, Ontario (http://www.fanshawec.on.ca/news/2002/sae.asp).

only. That is, they specify how the product or service should perform but say nothing about its materials, constructions, dimensions, or other such details.

Precise, clear writing is critical in specifications. If the product is not built "to spec" or if the product or service does not perform "to spec," someone could be headed for a lawsuit. That's one reason why specifications have a particular style, format, and organization and why some technical writers spend their whole careers as specification writers. If specification writing is so specialized, why consider it here? It's an excellent challenge to your ability to describe with great precision. Here are some characteristics to notice about specifications:

- Use decimal-style numbering for sections and each individual detailed specification.
- Use exact numbers for measurements and other such details. Use numerals rather than words for numbers.
- Include operational specifications as well as physical ones, as necessary.
- Use "shall" to indicate requirements.
- Use precise language that cannot be interpreted in multiple ways. In other words, avoid ambiguity.
- Use a terse writing style. Incomplete sentences and omission of understood words are acceptable. (A great chance to use fragments!)
- Be careful with pronouns such as "it," "they," "which," and "that." Make sure there is no doubt of what pronouns refer to and what modifiers modify.
- Make sure your specifications are complete in terms of their expected purpose: for example, be sure to specify the grade and thickness of wood for those birdhouses.

The following walks you through the most important steps in writing a simple set of specifications. To get a sense of how these steps work in an actual writing project, we'll follow another example throughout.

1. **Find a project requiring specifications.** When you study technical writing, you must often "work backward" from a topic you want to write about to the reasons for writing about it and the people for whom you write. If you can find someone in need of specifications, great! For example, your next-door neighbour may want a deck. Write the specifications, capturing the exact design and dimensions your neighbour wants. However, if your neighbour already has a deck, find a simple object for which someone might require specifications. Simple things like cabinets, shelves, gardens, fences, woodsheds, or doghouses work just fine.

   Imagine you want to write construction specifications for that chickadee house with the dimensions shown in Figure 1-3. These will be design and construction specifications like those in the sample specifications shown at **http://www.powertools.nelson.com**.

2. **Define the purpose, audience, and situation.** Specifications provide excellent practice in adjusting your writing to a specific audience, purpose, and situation. The customer has specific requirements as to what the product or service should be and how it should work. It's your job to capture those physical and operating characteristics in your specifications.

> Why write specifications for a chickadee birdhouse? Imagine that you work at a wildlife centre whose owner wants to sell all sorts of wildlife products, such as birdhouses. She wants you to write specifications for chickadee birdhouses as well as other products to be sold at the centre. She will then send out these specifications to craftspeople who will bid on the construction work for these wildlife shelters. Thus your specifications capture your boss's ideas as to the design of these products and enable craftspeople to bid on these building projects.

3. **Write the scope and definitions sections as necessary.** A *scope statement* defines what you will specify, what you will not specify, and who will have which roles and responsibilities. A *definitions section* establishes the meanings of any terms that you use in a specialized way. If these sections are short enough, they can be consolidated into the introduction; otherwise, they can be grouped into a section of their own.

> In the scope and responsibilities section, define what the contractor must do and what happens if the contractor must deviate from the specs. In the definitions section, explain who the "contractor," "bidder," "client," and "owner" are. Ensure that the contractor knows what you mean by such terms as "wood," "screws," and "glue."

4. **Provide a general description of the product or service.** Include an overall description of the product or service. In the design section, the part-by-part description cannot address overall specifications such as overall length, width, height, and other details. These are addressed in the overall description.

> Let's provide a brief description of the completed chickadee house: how tall, wide, and deep it is; where the entrance hole is located; and so on. If possible, supply a labelled drawing as well.

5. **Write a materials section, if needed.** Consider including a section specifying requirements for materials to be used. What kind of wood, hardware, nails, screws, glue, paint, plastic, and so on will be neces-

sary? If these materials are easy enough to specify in the design section, you can dispense with a separate materials section.

In these specifications, be sure to "spec out" the materials you expect the contractor to use. What type of wood? What type of fasteners? If wood screws, what type and size? If glue must be used, what type or brand?

6. **Write the design section.** The design section contains the most excruciatingly detailed and precise writing you may ever do. In this section, you proceed part by part, specifying dimensions, clearances, materials of construction, attachment methods, and so on.

Now comes the hard part. In the design section, you'll wear out the word *shall.* Use the same approach that you see in the sample specs shown at **http://www.powertools.nelson.com**. Each main part is introduced, and its specifications and its attachment to other parts are explained. Notice that each sentence uses decimal numbering. If several statements must be made about an individual part, those statements are indented and given lower-level decimal numbering.

7. **Write an operating characteristics section, if needed.** The type of specifications discussed here are primarily for the design and construction of a product. But even this type must include requirements for operation. For example, how much load can the product bear? If some part slides in and out, should it slide smoothly without binding? Certain characteristics cannot be specified physically with numbers, dimensions, materials, and so on. You must state *operational requirements* instead.

Fortunately, the specifications for the chickadee birdhouses need no operating instructions. The craftspeople will bang these birdhouses out and then the wildlife centre will sell them. Purchasers will need to know how to set up the birdhouses, where to place them, and how to clean them periodically; but those are instructions, and that's another chapter (Chapter 2 to be precise).

8. **Write the introduction for your specifications.** In an introduction to specifications, you can state the purpose of the document, the product or service to be described, the recipient or customer of these specifications, and any administrative details such as cost or project dates relating to the project.

In a simple introduction, state who owns the specifications as well as the design and the finished chickadee houses. Also provide an overview. For example, state that these specifications contain scope and responsibilities statements, definitions, materials requirements, design specifications, and inspection requirements.

9. **Consider the format.** See the various report formats shown in Chapter 14. Typically, specifications are a separate formal document with a cover letter or memo attached to the front.

   Write the chickadee house specifications as a separate document. Use headings, subheadings, lists, graphics, and tables in this document just as you would in any other technical document. Attach a simple cover memo, addressed to the owner of the wildlife centre, stating that the specifications she requested are attached and that she should let you know if she finds any problems with them.

10. **Review and revise your rough draft.** Use the strategies in Chapter 16 to systematically review and revise your specifications. Use the top-down approach described in that chapter: start by reviewing for audience, purpose, and situation; then move on to content, organization, transitions; then headings, lists, tables, graphics; then on to sentence style and technical style; and finally, grammar, usage, spelling, and punctuation problems.

HOW DO YOU WRITE INFORMAL REPORTS?

If you browse a big stack of technical-writing textbooks (and there are plenty), you'll see a category of reports loosely called "informal," made up of things like site reports, inspection reports, accident reports, field trip reports, investigation reports, and so on. These informal reports are rather similar: they have description as their primary infrastructure; and they are usually written internally. But before starting, consider these distinctions:

■ **Site and inspection reports.** A site or inspection report is a description of a site: a building, a lot, a facility, equipment, and so on. It provides objective details important to a particular audience; for example, Realtors. If it evaluates whether the property is a good investment, it is a recommendation or evaluation report, discussed in Chapter 4.

■ **Accident reports.** The accident report takes the site report several steps further. Not only does it describe something (in this case, an accident), it may also delve into the causes of that accident. In this case, you use the strategies for discussing causes and effects discussed in Chapter 3. Discussing causes and effects naturally forces you to write about *processes*: event-by-event discussions of how the accident occurred. See strategies for discussing processes in Chapter 2.

■ **Trip reports.** Trip reports can be the least descriptive, and they overlap the other informal reports discussed here. If you went to a professional conference or industry exposition you might be expected to turn in a summary of your observations (along with the expense report). Plenty of description would be needed, and the report might read more like a narrative (in which case, you'd use the strategies for writing about processes, presented in Chapter 2).

■ **Investigative, analytical reports.** Another type of informal report not only describes and considers causes, problems, and solutions but also includes some research to determine whether those causes or solutions are in fact the most likely or the most effective. In this case, the report uses the strategies of the primary research report, presented in Chapter 3.

Here are the essential steps and considerations for writing an informal report.

1. **Find a project for an informal report.** Use the definitions of the different informal reports to get some ideas. For example, you could go inspect a building, a vacant lot, some equipment, a wrecked car, or flood damage.

   Imagine that you work for the police department and have been assigned the task of describing a car accident and doing some preliminary speculations as to the causes.

2. **Identify and analyze the audience, purpose, and situation.** Work backward to define an audience and situation. For example, if you inspect a vacant lot, you might be working for a real estate investment company. If you inspect flood or tornado damage, you might be doing so for an insurance adjustment company.

   Your audience is the police department and, potentially, insurance representatives and those involved in the accident. Each of these sets of readers has different interests and needs. Each group uses different language, although the special terminology used by the police and insurance agents is likely to be similar and nearly unintelligible to the third group—those involved in the accident. Your report must be understood by all three audiences.

3. **Do the necessary research and investigation.** A nice thing about informal reports is that you get out of the house, the dorm, or the library. Take your camera, tape measure, and notebook to the site and record as much detail as you can—whatever is relevant to your audience, purpose, and situation.

   How do you reconstruct the accident? You use police accident reports, visit the scene of the accident, and conduct interviews. You may need to review city traffic ordinances in case the accident falls into a grey area between multiple laws.

4. **Identify the things you must describe.** For most descriptions, you must use the part-by-part or characteristics approach. How does that work in terms of a building, for example? Describe the location and the surroundings; then the exterior, breaking that down into roof, siding, windows, doors, and so on; then the individual rooms; and

finally, infrastructural things such as plumbing, electrical, and heating and cooling systems.

> You must describe the location where the accident occurred and the damage to the vehicles. You may also need to describe the injuries received by those involved.

5. **If narration is needed, discuss the events step by step.** You may need to provide a brief narration of what you did or what happened. For example, if you went to an exposition or took a tour of a facility, describe what you saw event by event.

> In the accident report, attempt to reconstruct and then narrate the accident step by step. This will be a challenge: you'll get different information from the people involved. You might even need to interview witnesses to the accident for their perception.

6. **If causal discussion is needed, identify the related causes.** Your job may be more than just a site description. You may have to determine what caused the problem at that site; for example, damage caused by a flood, fire, mudslide, or structural collapse. If so, describe the damage in one section. In another section, either (a) compare the possible causes, attempting to determine the primary one, or (b) carefully walk through the obvious cause step by step, event by event.

> Obviously, determining the causes of the car accident will be an important part of your work on this project. Ultimately, who was at fault and why?

7. **If primary research is needed, set up and collect data from your research.** Instead of speculating on the causes or solutions, you may have to confirm your viewpoint through experiments. If so, design the report like a primary research report: discuss your experimental method, data, conclusions, and recommendation. See Chapter 3 for discussion and examples.

> This accident report doesn't seem to require primary research, but don't dismiss the possibility outright. What if the accident occurred at a tricky intersection at which many other accidents have occurred? If so, interview locals to see what they think. Perhaps run some informal experiments to see if you have any problems at the intersection. Observe traffic at the intersection to see if a high rate of near-accidents occurs.

8. **Organize and rough-draft your informal report.** Once you've identified all the pieces of information that must go into your informal report, find a way to organize it. The best plan may be to start with objective descriptive and narrative information and then move on to interpretive discussion such as causes and effects.

In this accident report, create a section that narrates the accident neutrally, without interpretation, and then describes the damage. Then summarize the different perspectives on the accident from the different parties involved, including witnesses. End with your view of what happened and why it happened.

9. **Consider the format.** Chapter 14 shows that you can design an informal report for e-mail or as a memorandum or a business letter. It can be a separate report with a cover letter or memo, an oral report, or it can be posted on the World Wide Web. The informal report at the end of this chapter is a self-contained memo written from one member of an engineering consulting firm to another. If the description is more than three pages, consider using a cover memo or letter and making the report a separate, attached document.

In the accident report, use the business letter format; this communication goes to different people in different organizations. After the introductory paragraph, use "Accident: Events and Damage" as the heading for objective narration of the accident and the objective description of the damage. To introduce the summary of the different viewpoints, use "Different Perspectives" as the heading. For your interpretation and conclusion, use "Conclusions" as the heading. Throughout, use lists, graphics, and tables in this letter just as you would in a report.

10. **Review and revise your rough draft.** Use the strategies in Chapter 16 to systematically review and revise your informal report. Use the top-down approach described in Chapter 16: start by reviewing for audience, purpose, and situation; then moving on to content, organization, transitions; then headings, lists, tables, graphics; then on to sentence style and technical style; and finally, grammar, usage, spelling, and punctuation problems.

WORKSHOP: DESCRIPTION

Here are some additional ideas for practising the concepts, tools, and strategies in this chapter:

1. *Identify parts.* The part-by-part approach is one of the keys to writing detailed, well-organized descriptions. See how many parts you can name for one or more of the following objects:

Bicycle without gears or hand brakes	Flower	Molly bolt
Ordinary pliers	Ant	Spray bottle
Classroom desk-chair	Reading glasses	TV remote

2. *Plan the sources of description.* For one or more of the objects for which you just listed parts, make a list of the sources of description you would use to describe those parts.

3. *Identify sources of description.* Take a look at the following description and list the sources of description you see.

   ```
   The CheapTech BikeLite is simply a battery-powered
   light source that can be attached to a bicycle for
   visibility when riding at night. As it uses light-
   emitting diodes (LEDs) to provide its light, it
   is small (about 7 x 5 x 4 cm) and light enough
   (approximately 60 g including the battery) to be
   detached and slipped into the rider's pocket when not
   in use. The BikeLite consists of two major parts:
   the LED unit, which contains five LEDs together with
   the necessary electronics and battery; and the
   mounting bracket, which is used to fix the BikeLite
   on to a bicycle frame. The LED unit is detachable and
   is fixed to the bracket using a plastic clip. If
   required, the clip can also be used to fix the unit
   to a belt or other article of clothing.
   ```

4. *Write a brief description.* Take a look at the instructions and specifications for creating any of the following, and write a detailed description of the completed item:

   House for American robins and barn swallows:
   http://www.npwrc.usgs.gov/resource/tools/ndblinds/robin.htm
   House for house wrens, black-capped chickadees, white-breasted nuthatches:
   http://www.npwrc.usgs.gov/resource/tools/ndblinds/houswren.htm
   Other nesting structures or feeders:
   http://www.npwrc.usgs.gov/resource/tools/ndblinds/ndblinds.htm

   Made available by the U.S. Geological Survey's Northern Prairie Wildlife Research Center.

5. *Plan a site or accident report.* Imagine that you must write a site or accident report on one of the topics listed below. What are the parts or characteristics you'd use for the descriptive sections of that report?

Hurricane damage	Tornado damage	Flood damage
Vacant lot	Used automobile	Rental property
Potential office space	Street needing repair	Technology exposition

TECHNICAL DESCRIPTION

Title: The title for this description is bold, centred, a few point sizes larger than the regular text. Notice that the title is not just "Workhorse Flashlight" but includes the fact that this is a "technical description." Make sure your titles capture both the topic and focus of the information that follows.

Notice that there is no Introduction heading. In a short document like this, it ought to be obvious that the paragraph following the title is introductory.

Introduction: The introduction to this technical description does two essential things: (a) provides a general description of the flashlight and (b) provides a list of its parts, which doubles as an overview of the sections to follow.

In-sentence list: This is an example of an in-sentence list. Notice that lowercase letters are used and that the letters are enclosed on both sides with parentheses. (See Chapter 8 for more on lists.)

Figure title: Notice the figure title. It is centred below the figure and italicized, making it distinct from regular text and headings. Don't just number figures—include a descriptive title as well.

Second-level heading: Because this is a short document, first-level headings are not necessary. (For more on headings, see Chapter 7.)

Third-level heading: These are used for the two paragraphs describing the subparts of the body of the flashlight.

TECHNICAL DESCRIPTION
Workhorse Flashlight

The Workhorse is a hand-sized plastic flashlight that fits into most automobile glove compartments. The Workhorse's overall length is 15 cm, with a diameter of 5 cm at the head of the flashlight, tapering to 3.2 cm in diameter at the battery compartment. The cylindrically shaped body of the Workhorse is made of matte black, high-impact plastic, ribbed for a secure handgrip. The Workhorse Flashlight consists of two major parts: (a) the body, containing battery compartment and switch; and (b) the bulb assembly, containing the reflector, the bulb, and the connector. The flashlight is powered by two 1.5-volt, C-size batteries. (See Figure 1 for an illustration of the fully assembled flashlight.)

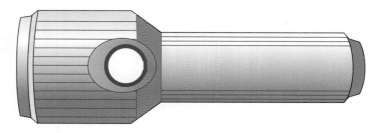

Figure 1. *Fully Assembled Flashlight*

Body

The body of the Workhorse Flashlight is 14.3 cm, with a diameter of 5 cm at the screw, or head end, tapering to 3.2 cm at the battery compartment. The interior of the screw end is threaded, allowing for connection with the bulb assembly. (See Figure 2 for an illustration of the complete flashlight assembly.)

Battery compartment. The battery compartment holds the batteries, the power source for the flashlight. The compartment is cylindrical, 8.9 cm long and 3.2 cm in diameter, with a coiled metal spring on the interior of the closed end, and 0.6 cm wide strip of gold-coloured metal running along one interior side of the compartment. The compartment holds two 1.5-volt C batteries, in a stacked position, with the negative end of the lowermost battery in contact with the spring and the positive end of the lowermost battery supporting the negative end of the uppermost battery. The open end of the battery compartment closes with the insertion of the bulb assembly.

Switch. The switch turns the flashlight on and off. It is located on the body of the Workhorse 3.8 cm from the screw end. The switch is made of white plastic, designed to be activated with the thumb of the hand holding the flashlight. When the switch is pushed forward, toward the larger end of the flashlight, the light turns on. When the switch is returned to the original position, the light turns off.

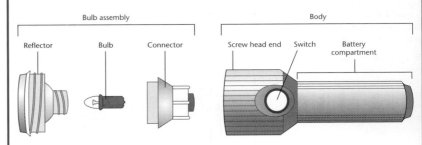

Figure 2. *Components of the Workhorse Flashlight*

Bulb Assembly

The bulb assembly of the flashlight consists of the reflector, the bulb, and the connector. When fully assembled, the bulb assembly is 5 cm long, with a diameter of 5 cm at the reflector end, reducing to 2 cm at the contact end of the connector. The bulb assembly completes the flashlight by screwing into the end, or head end, of the body of the flashlight.

Reflector. The reflector magnifies and projects the light generated by the battery-powered bulb. When viewed from the larger end, the reflector consists of a transparent flat plastic cover over a chrome-coloured reflective plastic concavity with a central hole. The elements are permanently attached together and housed in matte black plastic. The reflector screws into the connector on one end, and the midsection of the reflector provides the main screw for attachment to the flashlight body.

Bulb. The light source for the Workhorse is a glass bulb, 1.3 cm long, permanently fused onto a cylindrical metal base 1.3 cm long and 1 cm in diameter. The bottom of the metal base has a protrusion, providing the electrical connection between the bulb and connector. The bulb itself contains a metallic filament, one-half the length of the glass portion of the bulb, surrounded, at a point halfway up the length, by a clouded white plastic-like material.

Connector. The connector connects the reflector and bulb to the battery power source. The connector is made of black plastic, ringed with a metallic collar 1 cm wide. The closed end of the connector is mounted with a 2.1 cm gold-coloured metal strip. The metal strip facilitates the connection between the bulb and the batteries. The open end of the connector is threaded to allow joining with the bulb and reflector.

When fully assembled, the Workhorse Flashlight is a sturdy, easily held tool providing light sufficient for regular outdoor and emergency use. The compact size makes the flashlight easily portable, and batteries and bulb are readily accessible for replacement.

Many thanks to Mary Bailey, former technical writing student at Austin Community College for this technical description and permission to adapt it here.

Third-level headings. Notice how the subsections of the bulb-assembly description are introduced by third-level headings. (See Chapter 7 for more on headings.)

Sources of description: Consider the different types of descriptive detail used here: contents (subparts), length, diameter, width, shape, attachment methods, colour, materials of construction, relationship of the parts, location.

With the description complete, the concluding paragraph focuses on function and use.

INFORMAL REPORT

Howitt Home Improvements
Specializing in the One-Tonne Challenge
357 Elmira Road North
Guelph, Ontario N1K 1S5

Memo header: Notice the standard date, to, from, and subject labels. Notice, too, the inner alignment of the text following those labels. Use tabs to create this alignment, not spaces.

Subject line: Notice how specific the subject line is. This helps readers decide whether to read the memo and how to file it. It also helps to retrieve it when readers look for it in a big stack of memos.

Introduction: Notice how brisk and to the point this introduction is. It provides some brief background on the reason for this memo and then states its purpose.

Style and tone: Obviously, these are people who work closely together—thus, the direct, personal, informal tone.

Table: This writer summarizes details of the heritage house efficiently, using a table. Don't forget that you can use headings, tables, lists, and illustrations in business letters and memos just as much as you can in formal reports. (For designing and creating tables, see Chapter 10.)

Memo

To:	John Howitt, Manager
	Howitt Energy Consultants
From:	Michael Carrier, HVAC Specialist
CC:	Almonte Heritage Foundation
Date:	May 6, 2006
Subject:	Report on my preliminary investigation of meeting the One-Tonne Challenge in a heritage house

---

I have just returned from my inspection trip to the heritage house project in Almonte, Ontario. Our team met with the Almonte Heritage Foundation, which is renovating the building, on March 25, 2006. I interviewed the main historical and architectural team and completed my inspection of the building. I have prepared my preliminary recommendations. The following is a brief summary of my findings and recommendations.

Brief Description of Existing Structure

As you will recall from our previous discussions, the building has been designated as a historical structure by Parks Canada. In our proposals to make changes to the structure to meet the One-Tonne Challenge, we must be careful to retain all of the important historical features of the building. The characteristics of the building include the following:

Internal usable	297 m^2
External usable	654 m^3
Appliances	Typical refrigerator, freezer, range, range hood, microwave, toaster, dishwasher, sump pump, washing machine, dryer. These are obvious updates.
Occupancy	4 people
Utilities	Municipal water, natural gas water heater, furnace.
Building structure	Limestone masonry construction

Walls and insulation	The interior walls are plaster and lath applied directly to the interior surface of the limestone structure
Floors	Pine flooring throughout
Windows	Single-pane glazed wood-framed with no provision for storm windows
Roof/ceiling	Slate roofing
Electrical	60 ampere service installed in early 1960s with aluminum wiring
Water	Galvanized steel, noninsulated piping for hot and cold water
Lighting	Standard incandescent bulbs throughout
Heating system	A converted coal-fired "octopus" furnace with gravity feed now serves the building
Foundation	Fieldstone foundation. Partially completed basement with crawl space

For more detail, the Parks Canada report of January 2004 outlines the structure of the building.

General Guidelines for Modifications to Heritage Buildings

Older homes being retrofitted deserve special consideration. Whether the home is 50, 75, or 100 years old, it represents a part of our architectural heritage. Maintaining the durability of the structure is especially important. Homes over 50 years old may incorporate unusual construction details and materials that make it necessary to improvise and adapt standard retrofit methods. Retrofitting will require sensitivity to the design, materials, and special features of the home. Changes to the building's appearance should be minimized; the emphasis should be on repairing, rather than replacing, building components.

Although there are bound to be some sacrifices in energy efficiency, a little more planning and care can do a lot to make older homes more comfortable, durable, and energy efficient. Extra care at the planning stage involves assessing the home from several aspects.

Specific Recommendations

Using the general guidelines, I am making the following preliminary recommendations for modifications to the existing building to meet the One-Tonne Challenge:

Headings: Notice the use of headings in this memo. They enable readers to skip uninteresting sections and go to the information they want. For example, the particular recipient of this memo would probably remember every detail of the prototype. (For more on headings, see Chapter 7.)

Air sealing: Comprehensive air sealing is one of the least obvious and most effective retrofit projects for older homes.

Heating system: A total tune-up of the heating system is another inexpensive, effective, and invisible measure for older homes. In this case, the heating system should be replaced with a modern gas-fired hot water system.

Insulation: Preserving the structure is especially important; take extra care to provide a vapour barrier and air barrier when insulating. You can often re-insulate basements and attics without affecting the appearance of the house. Since there is no chance of blowing insulation into the wall cavity, the attic and basement insulation upgrade will be especially important. Adequate attic ventilation may be provided with power vents in the soffits.

Windows: Windows are one of the most important aspects of a home's originality. Careful weather-stripping of older, single-pane, wood-frame windows will do much to improve their energy efficiency. However, in this case the original wooden windows have deteriorated past the point of repair. Custom-made windows that resemble the originals should replace the existing wood frames. To avoid the labour of storm removal and replacement, the new windows should be triple-pane gas-filled units.

Doors: Preserving the original doors is important to the overall appearance of an older home. Careful weather-stripping will improve their performance. As with windows, avoid aluminum storms. A better alternative is to restore the enclosed vestibule that is found in most older homes.

Wiring: The wiring service should be upgraded to 200 amperes and the aluminum wiring replaced with copper. Any of the older knob and tube wiring should be completely removed.

Water: The galvanized steel water piping should be replaced with copper pipes. The hot water pipes should be insulated.

Lighting: The existing incandescent bulbs should be replaced with "look-alike" fluorescent units.

Summary

Once these changes have been made, another air leakage and energy audit will be completed to ensure that the building meets the requirements of the One-Tonne Challenge.

Throughout the modifications, a representative of the Almonte Heritage Foundation will be consulted to ensure compliance with the guidelines.

I will keep in touch with the contractors and the heritage people as the project progresses and inform you of any important developments.

Source: From "Keeping the Heat In," http://oee.nrcan.gc.ca/residential/personal/home-improvement/heritage.cfm?attr=4 © Minister of Natural Resources Canada, 2005. Reproduced with permission.

CHAPTER 2

Processes: Instructions, Policies, and Procedures

Topics covered in this chapter include

- NASA's exploration voyage to Mars;
- Canada's Deep Impact mission;
- installing printer drivers.

NASA MARS EXPLORATION
NASA
http://www.NASA.gov

The Canadian Encyclopedia (search for "NASA")
http://www.thecanadianencyclopedia.com/index.cfm

CANADA'S DEEP IMPACT MISSION
Canada has its own space agency, as well. Canadian scientists are involved in a variety of satellite programs and, of course, with Canadarm.

The Canadian Space Agency
http://www.space.gc.ca/asc/eng/default.asp

Also, look at these sites:

Canadian Satellites
http://www.space.gc.ca/asc/eng/satellites/default.asp

Canadian Science and Technology Museum
http://www.sciencetech.technomuses.ca/english/index.cfm

When you have completed this chapter, you will be able to

- use processes as a tool in writing technical documents;
- write instructions or procedures for users;
- plan and write policies and procedures.

Instructions and policy-and-procedure documents both have process at their core. A *process* is a series of actions or events that accomplishes something. Photosynthesis is a natural process occurring in plants. The cycle of seasons is another process. In addition to natural biological processes, there are mechanical processes; for example, the way a combustion engine works, the way a solar cell produces electricity, and so on.

As you know from the Preface, most technical documents are based on one or a combination of *infrastructures*—elemental structuring principles that enable those technical documents to do their job. The infrastructure essential in instructions and policy-and-procedure documents is the process. To enable people to understand processes and procedures, you must break the event or action into its units: its steps, phases, or events.

This chapter shows you how to write about processes and then how to build processes into the infrastructure of instructions and policy-and-procedure documents.

Note:
- If you are new to this book, see "How Do You Use This Book?" in the Preface.
- For additional examples of the documents discussed in this chapter, see **http://www.powertools.nelson.com**.

WHAT IS A PROCESS?

Before getting into instructions and policy-and-procedure documents, take a moment to learn or to review the idea of process, that essential infrastructure used in these kinds of technical documents. The worlds of science and technology are fascinated by how things happen; in other words, processes. **A process is a series of events or actions that occur over time and that accomplish something.** Processes occur in the natural and mechanical worlds; these processes are for the most part repetitive or repeatable; for example, photosynthesis or mitosis. Processes also occur in the human social world. Although many of these are repeated, you can also treat one-time-only events, such as the first walk on the moon, as processes. Other processes are plans, such as the expeditions to Mars, that haven't happened yet. The *step-by-step approach* is key to writing about processes: you must carefully discuss each step, phase, action, or event in a process.

As Chapter 3 on causal discussion explains, discussions of processes and discussions of causes and effects are often hard to differentiate. In fact, it's almost impossible to discuss causes and effects without discussion of process, the events within which the causes and effects are working. To avoid splitting hairs, let's say that the discussion of a process is organized by the steps, phases, or events and that the main focus is the narration of the events within that process.

HOW DO YOU WRITE ABOUT PROCESSES?

Let's walk through the most important steps in writing about processes. To provide a sense of how these steps work in an actual writing project, we'll follow an example through each of the steps.

1. **Find a project involving discussion of a simple process.** Try to find a situation in which a specific group of readers needs an explanation of a noninstructional process. It's easy to think of encyclopedia-style processes such as those involving automotive technology, electronics, computers, agriculture, medicine, and natural phenomena. You can find plenty of processes around your house, garage, or yard, but why would anyone want one of those processes discussed? (For more ideas on topics, see **http://www.powertools.nelson.com.**)

   Instead of all the usual processes explained in any encyclopedia—mitosis, photosynthesis, water cycle, gestation of an embryo—how about a process discussion that people you know will actually use? Perhaps a process-oriented discussion of NASA's plans to put human beings on Mars and the activities planned while there?

2. **Define the purpose and audience for this project.** The next step is to clarify the purpose and audience for your process discussion. (See Chapter 17 for audience-analysis strategies.) If you've started with a real set of readers in a real situation, this step is easy.

   As often happens when you are studying technical writing, you must work backward from a topic that interests you to the situation in which a document involving that topic is needed. Who wants to read about NASA's plans for a human expedition to Mars and why? If you had searched the World Wide Web for this information in early 2000, you wouldn't exactly have gone into orbit with the fragmented, highly technical material you found. But NASA takes a keen interest in making good information available to the public, which will build excitement for its projects. As a member of the Mars Society, you are concerned about the quality of information that is currently available about the expedition. You recognize the need for good information about the expedition. Your purpose is primarily informative, though a persuasive aim lurks in your project to get people enthusiastic about the Mars expedition and to support it.

3. **Do some research.** To write about even a simple process, you may need to do some research to gather information on the process you are writing about. The following website focuses directly on processes:

Brain, Marshall. *How Stuff Works* <**http://www.howstuffworks.com**>.

If you did some searching on Mars, and the human exploration of Mars in particular, you'd find plenty of material. As of the year 2000, the information was quite formal: lots of passive voice and a general "personless" style of writing. It would be a challenge to present this information in a way that would be understandable and interesting to the target audience, another example of why technical writers are so necessary.

4. **Plan and develop graphics.** Early in this project, try to visualize the graphics your process discussion will need. Use the strategies in Chapter 10 and Chapter 11 to plan the drawings, diagrams, photos, and charts you may need.

Graphics will be a fun part of this project. NASA provides plenty of photos of Mars, the stages of the expedition, diagrams of the trajectories, timelines, and much more. It's certainly legal for you to use these materials for academic purposes; just remember to cite your sources (where you found the material). For a process manual—or anything—being published, request permission to use the source's graphics. Downloading, importing, sizing, cropping, and positioning graphics in your documents can be challenging; see Chapter 11 for these techniques.

5. **Identify the main steps or phases in the process.** With your topic, purpose, and audience defined, identify the important steps in your process.

If you succeed in disentangling NASA's information on the Mars expedition, you'll see that the expedition is tentatively designed around six launches. The first three put supplies, equipment, and shelter in place. Systems for producing oxygen, fuel, power, and even food will be functioning by the time people arrive. The plans for growing food on Mars are worthy of a technical report in their own right, not to mention the plans for scientific analyses of conditions on Mars. The best way to structure this discussion is to have a section for each launch, in other words, each main phase.

6. **Discuss each step or phase separately.** Now you're ready to begin writing the actual process discussion one step at a time. If your readers want only a paragraph on the entire process, spend no more than a sentence per step. If they want more detail, explain each step in one or more full paragraph(s).

Each section will discuss when that launch begins and ends and what it accomplishes. You could probably write a separate report on each launch, but your readers want just an overview. How long will it take for a launch to get to Mars? How will the nuclear power plant be set up, checked out, and made operational? And just what do they plan to grow on Mars? In any case, spend a sentence or two per launch; or, if you've got more room, spend a paragraph per launch. Notice how each step is represented as a separate paragraph in the diagram in Figure 2-1.

Introduction: definition of the process (noninstructional), overview of the steps or phases

Step 1: definition or overview of the step; events occurring in the step; causes and effects related to these events

Step 2: definition or overview of the step; events occurring in the step; causes and effects related to these events

Step 3: definition or overview of the step; events occurring in the step; causes and effects related to these events

Conclusion

FIGURE 2-1
Step-by-step process discussion. Discuss each step or phase in a sentence—or, better yet, a paragraph—of its own.

7. **Identify any other necessary sections.** Once you've written, or at least planned, the discussion of the process phases, consider what nonprocess information readers may need in order to understand the process better. Do they need background or conceptual information before getting into the process itself?

It won't work to dive right into the first launch. Consider the possibilities: where will they land; why was that site chosen; why is the expedition being planned in the first place; what are the goals; will it really happen, or will there be public opposition to such an expensive project?

8. **Sketch out the headings you'll use.** If your process discussion takes more than two or three paragraphs, use headings (see Chapter 7). If you discuss each step in one or more separate paragraphs, create a heading to identify each step.

   For the discussion of the Mars expedition, you'll want to use a descriptive heading to introduce each of the phases of the expedition.

9. **Plan an introduction.** It's best to write, or at least plan, the essential parts first—steps, phases, or events—followed by the supplementary materials like those mentioned in Step 4. Only then should you write or plan the introduction. In it, indicate the topic, purpose, and intended audience, and provide an overview of what you'll cover.

   For the Mars expedition, get phrases such as "NASA's plans for the human exploration of Mars" into the first few lines. Find a clever way of implying that the discussion is aimed at a high school-level audience, but without specifically saying so. Finally, indicate that you plan to discuss the purpose, schedule, and activities for each launch.

10. **Consider adding a conclusion.** Good possibilities for conclusions might be to discuss the causes or effects of the process or to give a description of the end result produced by the process.

    For a conclusion to this discussion of NASA's plans for the human exploration of Mars, one obvious concern might be whether these plans will ever be carried out. Addressing this issue briefly and generally would be a good way to finish up. Another possibility would be a brief, general discussion of the outcomes of the expedition. What will we discover there? What will we get for all those billions of tax dollars?

    Take a look at the single paragraph process discussion in Figure 2-2. Even though it's only one paragraph, you can see exactly how each step begins and ends, as well as the introduction and conclusion.

11. **Consider the format.** For a simple project, you are not likely to need the elaborate report formats shown in Chapter 14. Instead, use the format you see for the process example at the end of this chapter. Begin with a descriptive title centred at the top of the page, and use second- and third-level headings. Use lists, notices, illustrations, tables, highlighting, and documentation (citations of your borrowed information sources) as necessary.

12. **Review and revise your rough draft.** Use the strategies in Chapter 16 to systematically review and revise your process discussion. Use the top-down approach described in that chapter: start by reviewing for audience, purpose, and situation; then move on to content, organization, and transitions; then check headings, lists, tables, and graphics;

In 1999 NASA outlined its plan for future missions. This process description summarizes these plans.

The process here is the sequence of planned expeditions to Mars. Each expedition is like a step. Notice that the individual expeditions are discussed one by one in order.

Notice the strong transition words ("begin," "following," "next step"): they alert readers that a new step or phase is about to be discussed. (For more on transitions, see Chapter 18.)

This discussion would be more readable if it used a numbered list for each of the expeditions, and possibly an italicized label using the name of the spacecraft.

In the first decade of the next millennium, Mars will be the destination for a number of expeditions currently planned by the United States, Russia, and Japan. Because of the relationship of the orbits of Mars and Earth, the optimum launch "window" for expeditions to Mars occurs every 26 months. NASA hopes to launch spacecraft to Mars during every available window between now and 2005. The sequence of missions will begin in 1999 with the launch of Mars Polar Lander to be launched January 3, 1999, and to land on Mars December 3, 1999. It will carry a microphone for listening for sounds on the Martian surface. Following the Polar Lander will be the March and April 2001 launches of the Mars Survey Orbiter and Lander, respectively. The Orbiter will orbit Mars for three years, analyzing the planet's surface and measuring the radiation environment; the Lander will study soil and atmospheric conditions on the surface of Mars. The next step will be the Mars Surveyor to be launched in 2003, which will feature a lander and a rover. The rover will travel 10 km, searching for organic materials and signs of life using a sampling arm to gather Martian rock and soil. The lander will be equipped with an imaging system, radiation monitors, and instrumentation to study the physical and chemical properties of the soil gathered by the rover. Sometime between July and August 2005, the Mars Surveyor will be launched. Its purpose will be to gather samples collected and stored by the Mars Surveyor 2001 or 2003 missions and bring them back to Earth. NASA has not targeted a human expedition to Mars until 2012.

FIGURE 2–2

Sample process discussion. The sequence of expeditions to Mars planned by NASA are steps in the process, that process being the exploration of Mars.

then examine sentence style and technical style; and finally, review for grammatical, spelling, and punctuation problems.

HOW DO YOU WRITE INSTRUCTIONS?

Instructions (or procedures) show people how to do something step by step. **They provide step-by-step explanations of how to do things, operate things, repair things, or construct things.** The reader of the instructions is actually performing the task as he or she reads them. The following sections walk you through the important steps for developing instructions.

1. **Find a project for instructions.** Find a smallish device around your apartment or house that needs instructions. Look for a simple software application in need of a user guide. If you are interested in taking on something more complex but don't want to write 150 pages,

select essential tasks, or perhaps a set of advanced tasks, from an application.

Imagine that you are charged with the task of writing a set of instructions for the typical toy watch with the LED display and two buttons. Admittedly, such watches do not come with instructions. You're expected to fumble around until you figure it out. Our user-friendly toy watch company will eliminate the fumbling and provide simple instructions!

2. **Define the purpose and audience.** The next step is to decide on a purpose and an audience for this process discussion.

Is the audience for these instructions a five-year-old, or is it really parents? If grown-ups read the manual only as a last resort, we certainly can't expect preschoolers to read it. As is the practice with instructions, assume an eighth-grade reading level. Picture an audience with lots of little distractions, under pressure to make the watch work before somebody starts crying.

3. **Define the tasks.** When you write instructions, you must perform a *task analysis*. Identify the common tasks that readers want to perform with the mechanism. See Chapter 17 for details on task analysis.

The tasks for the toy watch are simple:
- Set the time, which actually has these subtasks: setting the hour, setting the minute, setting AM/PM.
- Set the date, which has these subtasks: setting the month, setting the day of the month, and setting the year.
- Make it glow in the dark.
- Change the battery? Not likely—the battery will outlast the toy watch.

4. **Do some research.** When you write instructions, much of your research is hands-on: you observe yourself performing the tasks so that you can write about them. Research into print materials may also be necessary; for example, you may need to research organic pest-control methods for a backyard-gardening manual.

In this case, your only research will be to confirm your understanding of how to set the time and date on the toy watch. Be aware of the mistakes you make; your readers will probably make the same ones. Include them as notes in your instructions. You could research how LEDs work, but neither the kids nor their parents will be interested.

5. **List the equipment and supplies needed.** For some instructions, you must list the equipment (tools such as screwdrivers, rulers, hammers, scissors) and the supplies (consumables such as tape, nails, ingredients) that readers will need to gather. Present this list before the procedure, under its own heading with a lead-in such as "Before beginning, gather the following items."

The only items people will need in order to use the toy watch are the toy watch itself and maybe a pencil to press the buttons. These are so incidental you don't need a list.

6. **Plan the special notices.** Notices are those specially formatted warnings, cautions, and dangers commonly found in instructions. They keep people from hurting themselves, damaging equipment, or ruining the procedure, and they defend manufacturers from lawsuits. See Chapter 9 for details.

   For the toy watch instructions, there are some obvious notices: don't submerge it in water, don't throw it or stomp on it, and don't eat it. But consider the "gotchas" you experienced when you were learning how to use the watch yourself. For example, after you set the time or date, you needed to keep pressing the MODE button until you returned to the full display of date and time. Also, you now know you needn't worry about leaving the watch glowing in the dark all night: it automatically turned off after 10 minutes.

7. **Plan the highlighting scheme.** Instructions commonly use special effects like bold, italics, and alternate fonts to cue readers about the meaning and context of elements such as button names, displayed information, and text that readers must type. Use special effects carefully, consistently, and with restraint. To plan a highlighting strategy, see Chapter 7.

   Even the toy watch instructions need some highlighting. For the three buttons— MODE, SET, and ☺ (glow)—you could use some combination of small caps, bold, or sans serif font (such as Arial, to contrast with the Times New Roman used in regular text). You could highlight instances in which you refer to something displayed in the LED. Perhaps you could find a font resembling the typical design of LED numbers and letters or just use a font like Courier New, which looks typewritten.

8. **Plan and develop graphics.** Illustrations are important in instructions. They show readers locations of buttons, knobs, dials, and components. They show the orientation of hands in relation to the components as well as before-and-after views. Illustrations show the essential objects and the essential actions involved in the procedure. Use the strategies in Chapter 11 to plan the drawings, diagrams, and photos you may need to include.

   The toy watch instructions need only a few illustrations. The most important will be a diagram of the watch with the MODE, SET, and ☺ (glow) buttons labelled. Consider one or more diagrams illustrating the LED when you are setting the date or time. For example, when you press the MODE button once, the LED displays a blinking numeral for the hour.

9. **Plan the terminology.** Readers are dismayed when different words are used to refer to the same thing. In the computer world, "hard drive," "hard file," and "fixed disk" all refer to the same thing, sometimes even within the same document! The same happens with "display," "screen," and "monitor." "Press," "depress," "hit," "strike," and "mash" have all been used to refer to the simple action of pressing a key on a keyboard. Avoid making up words, using inappropriate words, and using words above the appropriate reading level. Can you guess what "deiconify" refers to? What's happening when a computer "warps," "barfs," "relinquishes," "disengages," or "actuates" something. Define any specialized or potentially unfamiliar terminology (see Chapter 5).

> With the toy watch instructions, let's stick with "press" as the verb for the buttons (not "push" or "poke"). Should you refer to the LED as the "screen," "display," or "window"? Use the word parents will most likely recognize, but avoid "LED." Call the three buttons "buttons" and not "keys" or "switches." When something shows up in the LED, say that it "is displayed" rather than "appears" or "shows." Even though the glow button is labelled with the ☺ symbol, call it the GLOW button.

10. **Identify the main headings.** For instructions, plan the headings (see Chapter 7 for the format and style for headings).

> For these instructions, you need three main headings: "How to Set the Date," "How to Set the Time," and "How to Illuminate the Watch Face." You could use gerund phrasing, "Setting the Time"; or you could use imperative phrasing, "Set the Time." But use just one of these styles of phrasing; keep headings parallel in phrasing (see Appendix C). For instructions, use task-oriented phrasing for headings: headings like "Time," "Date," or "Glow" don't convey that a procedure is about to be discussed.

11. **Plan or write the step-by-step procedures.** If you've done all of the preceding, you're more than ready to start writing. It's a good strategy to plan or write the step-by-step procedures first. That way, you can determine what other noninstructional information is needed. When you write procedures, use numbered lists for sequential steps. For nonsequential steps, use bulleted lists. For example, troubleshooting steps are nonsequential: readers try different ways to fix a problem, but in no necessary order. (See Chapter 8 on lists.) In your procedure section, begin each task with a task-phrased heading. Introduce the numbered or bulleted list of steps with a lead-in sentence.

> For example, create a heading such as "Setting the Time." Beneath it, use a lead-in such as "To set the time," followed by the step-by-step procedure. For each step in the procedure, use imperative phrasing: "Press the MODE button";

"Press the SET button." Supply additional explanatory detail as necessary; for example, "Press the MODE button until the hour number blinks."

12. **Develop and supplement each step as necessary.** Complex instructions typically need more than numbered steps. Some require background and theory before the procedures become meaningful. In researching the steps, you may have used a custom-colour tool on a computer. You pushed three little sliders until you got the colour the way you wanted it. If the readers don't know the theory as to how colours are created using red, blue, and green or how saturation and hue influence the process, they might spend a whole day pushing those sliders around.

In some instructions, it's important to give readers before-and-after views of the project or equipment they are working on. For example, what should the computer screen look like before you press the Compile button; what should it look like after? Provide readers with information so that they can determine whether they've completed the task correctly. For example, how thick should the pancake batter be once you've mixed in all the ingredients?

Lucky for you, the toy watch requires no assembly and no theory! However, explain that in normal operation the colon between the hour and minute numerals blinks every second. When readers want to change the hour, they should press the Mode button until they see just the hour numeral flashing on the LED. These before-and-after views help readers know whether they are performing tasks correctly.

13. **Write an introduction.** Introductions to instructions must accomplish several important tasks: identify the procedure to be explained; indicate the knowledge, experience, and skills required to be able to understand the instructions; and provide an overview of what will be explained. (This overview doubles as a *scope* statement, indicating what will not be covered.)

The instructions for the toy watch hardly need much introduction. Picture a title, "Using the Warrior Princess Watch," followed by an introductory sentence such as "Anyone can set the date and time on the Warrior Princess Watch by following these easy instructions:" Despite its simplicity, this introductory sentence does identify audience skills needed as well as provide an overview.

14. **Consider adding a conclusion.** Instructions need little in the way of conclusions. However, some possibilities include telling readers how to get additional information if they have a problem or what other interesting things they might try next.

If any conclusion is needed, it might be some comments about changing the battery, a technical support number, or perhaps a policy concerning malfunctioning watches. And, of course, if Marketing requires it, you may have to add a customer-cordiality note such as "Have fun with your Warrior Princess Watch!"

15. **Consider the format.** Instructions are formatted depending on how they will be used. For simple procedures that employees must follow, a memo or e-mail might work. For equipment instructions, laminating and posting them right next to the equipment might be a good idea. If the instructions are like directions that come with a product, design them like a small booklet complete with front and back covers and a table of contents.

   If you want to turn the instructions for the Warrior Princess Watch into a user guide, include a front cover with the name of the watch and the words "Operating Instructions." Include a trademark symbol and product and document numbers. On the back cover, include something like "Printed in Canada" and a publication date.

16. **Review and revise your rough draft.** Use the strategies in Chapter 16 to systematically review and revise your instructions. Use the top-down approach described in that chapter: start by reviewing for audience, purpose, and situation; then move on to content, organization, transitions; then headings, lists, tables, graphics; then sentence style and technical style; and finally, grammar, usage, spelling, and punctuation problems.

HOW DO YOU WRITE POLICIES AND PROCEDURES?

Policy-and-procedure manuals are another essential workplace document that use process as the essential infrastructure. In the following, you get an introduction to these manuals, their function in the workplace, and their contents and design.

About Policies and Procedures

Organizations use policy-and-procedure documents to record their rules and regulations: attendance policies, substance-abuse policies, workflow procedures, and so on. Once recorded, the policies and procedures are there for everybody in the organization to refer to, and these documents become the means of settling most disputes within the organization. To distinguish between these two terms, *policies* are rule statements. Policies are like laws; for example, most organizations have antiharassment policies, which mimic actual government-legislated laws. *Procedures,* on the other hand, are the step-by-step methods of carrying out those policies. Of course, some policies do not require procedures. If the organization has a no-smoking policy, that's all that need be said. However, a procedure is needed for handling the situation if someone were to break that policy.

Plan a Policy-and-Procedure Document

Writing a brief policy-and-procedure document is another good way to build your technical-writing skills. Keep in mind that the following does not give you the whole story. Here are some good resources for full coverage of policy-and-procedure manuals:

- Business Owner's Toolkit. *Small Business Guide,* available at **http://ww.toolkit.cch.com**
- University of Virginia. *Office of Environmental Health and Safety: Policies and Procedures.* **http://keats.admin.virginia.edu/polproc/home.html**
- Stephen Page. *Establishing a System of Policies and Procedures,* a self-published book available at **http://www.companymanuals.com**
- Simon Fraser University. *SFU Policies and Procedures.* **http://www.sfu.ca/~extrel/sfupolicynew**

The following walks you through the main steps in developing a simple policy-and-procedure document.

1. **Find a situation or organization needing policies and procedures.** A surprising number of small organizations lack policy-and-procedure manuals. Check your workplace to see if any such manual exists. There are also plenty of other inventive ways to find a situation in which you can write a relatively brief manual.

   Imagine that you live in an apartment with three other students. Some of you have had bad experiences with these situations in the past, and as a group you are determined not to repeat them. You want to set up policies for things like loud music, parties, drugs and alcohol, cooking, cleaning, groceries, and so on. As a group, you want to draft a set of policies and procedures that all agree to and will abide by.

2. **Identify the general policies the organization needs.** All organizations, no matter what their business, have general policies such as those relating to sexual harassment, discrimination, smoking, drugs, alcohol, and absenteeism.

   Your apartment policy-and-procedure document will contain lots of policies. You and your apartment mates want to state policies on smoking, drugs, alcohol, loud music, television, parties, and general slovenliness. Violating certain policies will be grounds for getting kicked out of the apartment. Violating other policies will earn the culprit ingenious forms of punishment!

3. **Identify the technical policies the organization needs.** Some organizations must define policies relating to their specific work and the associated technology. For example, healthcare agencies have precise policies and procedures on how their healthcare professionals must wash their hands, dispose of syringes, draw blood, and so on. Software development companies have precise policies and procedures on how to protect the confidentiality of new products under development.

> As mentioned earlier, your apartment policy-and-procedure document is likely to include all general policies. However, if the four of you have a small business that you run from the apartment, then you might need technical policies. For example, you might run a typing, formatting, and résumé-writing service. You'll need policies and procedures on how you take in work, how you complete it, and how you ensure its quality.

4. **State the purpose for each policy.** Typically, it's not enough just to state the policy. You must also explain its purpose, its justification, and its importance.

> The reason for the no-drugs policy is that everyone could be arrested just because one individual has them hidden away in a closet. The groceries, cooking, and cleaning policies ensure that everyone pitches in. The "quality assurance" policy specifies a series of steps to ensure that your résumé work is satisfactory to customers and is free of "bugs."

5. **Plan or write the procedures for each policy, as needed.** As mentioned earlier, not all policies need procedures. For example, you don't need a procedure to tell people how to follow the no-smoking policy. But plenty of policies do require step-by-step procedures. Organizations want policies carried out a certain way. If it's a step-by-step procedure, use numbered lists. If it's a list of things to try or to consider, use bulleted lists. Be sure to use the style and format for lists presented in Chapter 8.

> Consider the procedures for the policies on groceries, cooking, and cleaning. Menus must be planned, all must chip in to buy food, people have to cook, others have to clean up, and policies are needed for when individuals are absent. Apartment-cleaning procedures need to be developed. What will be done? How will it be done? When will it be done? (Who's going to scrub the potty?)

6. **Write the definitions for each policy–procedure section, as needed.** As you write policies and procedures, you'll notice that certain words and phrases are essential and must be defined carefully. For example, if the policy states "no smoking on premises," you must define what you mean by "premises." These definitions need to be placed before the procedure and after the policy.

As you develop your apartment policies and procedures, you'll find that plenty of terms must be defined. For example, what constitutes loud music? A certain number on the volume dial? How do you define messy? Or do you use a different term altogether?

7. **Cross-reference other policies.** As mentioned above, policies mimic laws. In some cases, they are based on existing federal, provincial, or local laws. When that's the case, reference the law.

Your apartment policies-and-procedures document may not need cross-references. Of course, if you are pre-law, you'd cite the statutes on possession of drugs or city bylaws regarding noise levels. If you are in nursing school, you might want to cite health-related dangers of letting strange life forms grow in the refrigerator, the toilet, or the bathtub.

8. **Review and revise your rough draft.** Use the strategies in Chapter 16 to systematically review and revise your policies and procedures. Use the top-down approach described in that chapter: start by reviewing for audience, purpose, and situation; then move on to content, organization, transitions; then headings, lists, tables, graphics; then on to sentence style and technical style; and finally, grammar, usage, spelling, and punctuation problems.

Considerations like these provide the nucleus of a policies-and-procedures document. If you are writing one for real, be sure to study some of the full-length published sources mentioned previously.

Design a Policy-and-Procedure Document

If you've developed or rough-drafted the information in the preceding, you're more than ready to write or complete your policy-and-procedure document.

Special design requirements. You'll need to consider special design work for your policy-and-procedure document as follows:

■ Begin each policy (including its purpose, definitions, procedures, and cross-references) on a new page.

■ Use decimal-style numbering. This makes it easier to refer to specific sections of the policy-and-procedure document.

■ Include dates at the end of each policy section. For example, note the date reviewed, date revised, or date effective. That way, people in the organization can tell whether a policy is up to date.

Packaging possibilities. Design your policy-and-procedure document according to how your organization will use it:

- *Formal bound document with cover letter or memo.* The common way to design such a document is to print it out, put it in a ring binder, and give a copy to each employee. The ring binder enables you to issue change pages, rather than reprinting and redistributing the whole thing.
- *Web page policy-and-procedure document.* Since 2000, organizations have been publishing their policy-and-procedure manuals on the World Wide Web, specifically, on their intranets. Doing so saves time, paper, and money. Of course, employees must have ready access to computers and get used to using an online version of the manual. Also, the online manual must be designed well.

Regardless of the packaging you choose, use headings, lists, tables, and graphics just as you would in any other technical document.

WORKSHOP: PROCESS, INSTRUCTIONS, POLICIES, AND PROCEDURES

Here are some additional ideas for practising the concepts, tools, and strategies in this chapter:

1. *Identifying noninstructional processes.* Choose any three of the following topics and define as many processes associated with them as you can:

Real estate prices	Weather	Blood pressure
Sleep	Trees	Batteries
Marriage	Divorce	Cameras
Radios	Automobiles	Breakfast
Autumn	Employment	Painting or drawing
Gardening	Education	Cooking
Cats	Dogs	

2. *Identifying instructional processes.* Choose any three of the preceding topics and define as many instructional processes associated with them as you can.

3. *Defining noninstructional phases.* For those noninstructional processes you defined in Exercise 1, define as many of the phases as you can.

4. *Defining instructional tasks.* For those instructional processes you defined in Exercise 2, define as many of the tasks as you can.

5. *Defining instructional steps.* For any of the tasks you previously defined, identify as many of the individual steps as you can.

6. *Analyzing instructions and user guides.* Find several examples of instructions and user guides and compare them according to their use of numbered and bulleted lists, phrasing of headings, format and content of notices, use of highlighting, graphics, and other such detail.

7. *Defining policies and procedures.* Choose one of the following situations and define up to a half dozen policies; then define the procedures for each of those policies:

Employees' use of the World Wide Web during regular workday hours

Students living in an off-campus co-op

Employees' use of office telephones for private calls

Telephone-help-desk employees' interactions with customers

Students' use of computers in college computer labs

Employees holding parties on company property

Receptionists' interactions with customer phone calls and office visits

Students visiting the tutoring lab at school

PROCESS DOCUMENT

Mission Overview: Deep Impact

Deep Impact is the first mission ever to attempt impact with a cometary nucleus in an effort to probe and discover the secrets that lie beneath its surface. Scheduled for launch in January 2005, Deep Impact will fly directly to its encounter with comet Tempel 1, making no planetary flybys along the way. The voyage will take about six months.

The mission has been designed as the most expedient way to accomplish the project's primary scientific objective—to observe close-up the internal composition of a comet. The mission is part of NASA's Discovery program, aimed at launching many small, relatively low-cost missions that perform focused science with fast turn-around times, and are joint efforts with industry, small business, and universities.

Mission Phases
Six mission phases have been defined to simplify descriptions of the different periods of activity during the mission. These are the (1) launch, (2) commissioning, (3) cruise, (4) approach, (5) encounter, and (6) playback phases.

Launch
Deep Impact will be launched from Space Launch Complex 17B at Cape Canaveral Air Station, Florida. The launch period opens on Jan. 8, 2005, and continues through Jan. 28. Two instantaneous launch windows occur each day. On Jan. 8, the first is at 1:40 p.m. EST, with a second window 39 minutes later.

The spacecraft will be launched on a variant of the Delta II launch vehicle known as a Delta 7925. This version of the Delta II uses a first-stage rocket with nine solid-fuel boosters and a second-stage rocket with a restartable engine. It is topped by a Star 48 solid-fuel upper-stage booster.

Process: Processes can be repetitive events occurring in nature or in society. You can treat future events as processes, such as the plan for the Deep Impact mission.

In-sentence list: The overview is presented in a six-item in-sentence list in the introduction. Notice that both opening and closing parentheses are used. (For more on lists, see Chapter 8.)

By the time you read this, the Deep Impact mission will have completed its probe and we will know the results.

Headings: In this relatively short document, second-level headings are used to mark off the main phases of the Deep Impact mission. The third-level heading indicates events within a phase. (See Chapter 7 for more on headings.)

Transitions: Notice how many words and phrases throughout this document alert us to where we are in the process: "At the moment of liftoff"; "Seconds later"; "After achieving this parking orbit"; "About one minute after"; and so on. This document very carefully guides us through the events, alerting us to their interrelationships, sequencing, and timing. (For more on transitions, see Chapter 20.)

Hyphens: Throughout this document, hyphens are used in compound modifiers. For example, "spin-stabilized," "push-off," "167-kilometre-high," and "first-stage" are hyphenated when placed before nouns. A good test for hyphens is to see whether the phrase can be misread. For example, in "spin-stabilized stage," is it a "spin that is stabilized" or is it a "stage that is stabilized"? Obviously, it is the second, and you need to join "spin" and "stabilized" with a hyphen to avoid momentary confusion. You want your technical writing to be as immediately understandable as possible. (For more information on hyphens, see Appendix B.)

Launch Events

At the moment of liftoff, the Delta II's first-stage main engine ignites, along with six of its nine solid-fuel boosters. The remaining three solids are ignited in flight following the burnout of the first six. The spent booster casings are then jettisoned in sets of three. The first-stage main engine continues to burn for 4.4 minutes, when it shuts down.

Seconds later, the Delta's first and second stages are separated, and approximately 5 seconds later, the second stage is ignited. The Delta's payload fairing, or nose cone, is jettisoned approximately 5 minutes into flight. The rocket's second stage continues to burn until a 167-kilometer-high (90-nautical-mile) circular parking orbit is achieved. The second stage shuts down just under 10 minutes after liftoff.

After achieving this parking orbit, the Delta rocket and Deep Impact spacecraft will coast for approximately 17 minutes before reaching the proper position to depart from Earth orbit. At this point the Delta's second-stage engine is restarted and burns for almost 2 minutes. After a brief coast lasting 50 seconds, the Star 48 upper stage with attached Deep Impact spacecraft is spun up to about 60 rpm to stabilize the vehicle for the third-stage burn. Three seconds later, the second stage separates from the upper stage. Thirty-seven seconds after separation of the second and third stages, the Star 48 spin-stabilized third stage is ignited. The burn lasts for approximately 87 seconds.

Approximately 4-1/2 minutes after burnout of the third stage, a yo-yo despin system is used to decrease the spin rate of the third-stage/spacecraft stack from about 60 rpm to nearly 0 rpm. A few seconds later, the spacecraft is separated from the spent third-stage motor. Pyrotechnic actuators and push-off springs on the launch vehicle release the Deep Impact spacecraft on its trajectory to comet Tempel 1.

About one minute after third-stage separation, the spacecraft's solar array will be deployed, and the spacecraft will rotate to point it at the Sun in about 5 minutes.

Audience: To promote the space program, NASA makes lots of information available to the public. Since the audience is the general public, plenty of the details need extra explaining.

In order to assess the health of the spacecraft and respond to any anomalies, mission controllers plan to establish communications with the spacecraft as soon as possible after separation from the third stage. The Delta's upper stage sends the spacecraft out of Earth orbit over southern Africa, so the spacecraft is headed east over the Indian Ocean when it separates from the launch vehicle. The first opportunity for contact with NASA's Deep Space Network is via the tracking complex near Canberra, Australia. The first downlink from the spacecraft is expected 11 to 15 minutes after separation, depending on the launch date and time.

Commissioning Phase

Quotation marks: Quotation marks are used around "commissioning phase" because it is an unusual phrase and because it is defined at that point. The writer could have used italics instead (but not both italics and quotation marks) to highlight this phrase at its point of definition.

The phrase "commissioning phase" is used to describe the period after the spacecraft is stabilized in flight until 30 days after launch. This is a time of initial operation, checkout, and calibration for the spacecraft and payload. Thrusters will be fired in one initial trajectory maneuver to correct for any errors in the flight path remaining from the launch.

During this phase, the spacecraft's scientific instruments will be tested using the Moon as a calibration target. The spacecraft's autonomous navigation system will be tested using the Moon and Jupiter as practice targets.

Cruise Phase

Future tense: Future tense is often abused—that is, used unnecessarily—in technical writing. However, in this context, there is no other choice. When this document was written, these events were still in the future. Notice that the present tense is used to describe the events occurring during the phases.

Cross-references to illustrations: Notice that direct cross-reference is made to figures, even if the figure occurs on the same page. This is standard good practice: draw the readers' attention to illustrations, tables, and charts and give them a clue as to what they contain and how they are related.

The cruise phase begins 30 days after launch and ends 60 days before the cometary encounter. As the spacecraft flies toward the comet, the mission team will conduct scientific calibrations, an encounter demonstration test, ground operational readiness tests, and a second trajectory correction maneuver. In addition, some initial observations of comet Tempel 1 will be attempted. (See Figure 1 for the trajectory.)

Illustration: This illustration was in the original file made available by NASA on the Internet. To get it into another document, just take a screen capture of the page on which it occurs and then crop it to the desired size. Remember to cite the source of your graphics, and if your document is to be published, permission should be requested from that source. (For more on screen capture, cropping, and graphics in general, see Chapter 11.)

Placement of illustrations: Place illustrations just after the point where they are relevant. If an illustration won't fit, bump it to the top of the next page, fill in the remaining white space with text, and set a cross-reference to the illustration (but do not include a page reference).

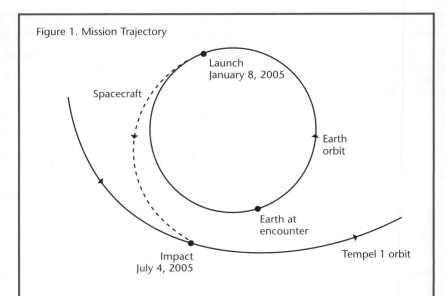

Figure 1. Mission Trajectory

Approach Phase

The approach phase extends from 60 days before to five days before encounter. Sixty days out roughly coincides with the earliest time that the team expects the spacecraft to be able to detect comet Tempel 1 in its high-resolution camera. This milestone marks the beginning of an intensive period of observations to refine knowledge of the comet's orbit. Regular scientific observations will be used to study the comet's rotation, activity, and dust environment.

Comet Encounter

The encounter phase begins five days before and ends one day after the impact with comet Tempel 1. This brief but very intense period includes two final targeting maneuvers, leading up to release of the impactor and its dramatic collision with the comet's nucleus. After releasing the impactor, the flyby spacecraft will execute a deflection maneuver so that it does not also collide with the comet; the maneuver will also slow it down enough to make observations after the impact and before flying past the nucleus.

The flyby spacecraft then observes the impact event, the resulting crater and ejected material, before transmitting these data to Earth.

Dual Measurements: Many technical documents, like this one, are written for international audiences. That means offering both British and American versions, as well as international metric versions of the measurements.

Introductory-element commas: Appendix B is adamant about punctuating any introductory element, no matter how short, with a comma. For example, "After releasing the impactor directly in the path of the oncoming comet" is an introductory element. So is "Throughout the Deep Impact Mission."

Numbers: As you would expect, this document contains plenty of numbers. For numbers that are both exact and essential, use digits. However, if a number begins a sentence, write it out. (For more information on numbers versus digits, see Appendix A.)

Passive voice: Notice how much this document uses the passive voice. In this context, it is the most efficient and effective way to write. For example, "The impact...has been scheduled" is a passive-voice sentence. Little would be gained by rephrasing the sentence to read "NASA engineers have scheduled the impact...." In every instance of the passive voice in this document, we know who the agent of these activities is—people back on the planet Earth.

Both the Deep Impact spacecraft and comet Tempel 1 are in curved orbits around the Sun. However, the comet is traveling substantially faster in its orbit than is the spacecraft so the comet actually runs over the spacecraft at a relative velocity of 10.2 kilometers per second (about 22,820 miles per hour).

After releasing the impactor directly in the path of the oncoming comet, the flyby spacecraft fires its thrusters to change course, safely passing by the nucleus with adequate time to observe the impact and resulting crater. This deflection maneuver is designed to make the spacecraft miss the cometary nucleus by 500 kilometers (311 miles). This distance was chosen to provide a survivable path through the comet's inner coma dust environment while still allowing a sufficiently close view of the crater by the spacecraft's high-resolution camera. The spacecraft will be protected by dust shields and oriented in a way to allow its cameras to continue taking pictures throughout the approach until it comes to within about 700 kilometers (420 miles) of the comet's nucleus. At this point, the spacecraft will stop taking pictures and fix its orientation so that its dust shields protect it as much as possible during the closest pass by the comet.

The kinetic energy released by the collision event will be 19 gigajoules, which is about the equivalent of the amount of energy released by exploding 4.5 tons of TNT. This in turn is about the amount of energy used in an average American house in one month.

Encounter Timing

The impact with the comet on July 4, 2005, has been scheduled during a 55-minute window in which Deep Space Network complexes in both California and Australia can track the spacecraft. Besides allowing for fully redundant coverage by these two ground stations, the timing also permits the event to be observed by the major observatories at Mauna Kea on the island of Hawaii (where it will still be the evening of July 3). Another consideration in the encounter timing was to provide an optimal opportunity for observations by two NASA spaceborne observatories, the Hubble Space Telescope and the Spitzer Space Telescope.

Final section: Although the primary focus of this document is outlining the six phases of the mission, the reader may want a feeling of a wrap-up statement. This description of a promotional contest and what will happen to the spacecraft when the mission is completed satisfies that desire.

Playback Phase

The playback phase begins one day after impact and continues until the end of mission, 30 days after the cometary encounter—or Aug. 3, 2005. Wrapping up the primary mission, data taken during the impact and subsequent crater formation will be transmitted to Earth. Backward-looking observations of the departing comet will be continued for 60 hours after the impact to monitor changes in the comet's activity and to look for any large debris in temporary orbit around the nucleus.

Nom de Plumes to Help Make Cometary Plume

Space fans worldwide may celebrate July 4, 2005, as the day their names reach a comet. The Deep Impact project sponsored a "Send Your Name to a Comet" campaign that invited people from around the world to submit their names via the Internet to fly onboard the Deep Impact impactor. A mini compact disc bearing the names of more than half a million space enthusiasts is onboard Deep Impact. The mini-CD will melt, vaporize, and essentially be obliterated—along with everything else aboard the impactor—when it collides with comet Tempel 1.

Source: National Aeronautics and Space Administration. "Deep Impact Launch Press Kit." January 2005. 17 Jan. 2005 <http://www.jpl.nasa.gov/news/press_kits/deep-impact-launch.pdf>.

INSTRUCTIONS

Finding and Installing Printer Drivers for the Canon BJC-5000

These instructions guide home users through the process of finding and installing printer drivers for a Canon BJC-5000 printer. The instructions apply to the Windows 2000 operating system. They are written for a user with intermediate computer skills.

The process involves three steps: finding the drivers, downloading them, and installing them on your computer. You will need to have an Internet connection and you may need your Windows 2000 Installation CD.

You may need to perform this operation again in the future if, for some reason, your printer drivers become corrupted and the printer no longer prints.

A. Finding your driver on the Internet

In the first step, you connect to the Internet and search for the drivers on the Canon website.

1. Connect to the Internet as you normally would.

2. *Double-click* the Internet Explorer icon on your Desktop.

3. *Click* in the **Address Bar** and select the text displayed.

4. *Type* www.canon.ca and press **Enter.**

5. *Click* **English** (Figure 1).

   The next page displays a grey menu bar at the top of the screen.

Figure 1: Canon Website

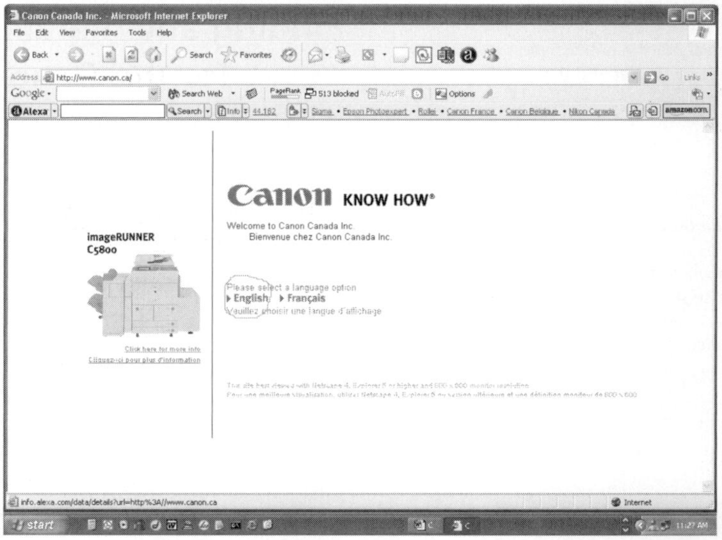

Actions and responses: Notice that the responses to an action are not included as items in the numbered lists.

6. *Click* **Downloads.**

   The next page has two columns. One says "Consumer Products" and the other says "Office Products."

7. *Click* **Click Here** on the **Consumer Products** side of the page (on the left side of the page).

   This page displays a list of drop-down menus listing the different products that Canon offers.

8. *Select* **BJC-5000** from the drop-down menu underneath the text "Bubble Jet Printer."

Section overview: Following each second-level heading and before the steps, these sentences provide an overview of the actions in the section. They also prevent you from having stacked headings—two or more consecutive headings with intervening text.

Highlighting: These instructions use italics and bold in an industry-standard way. Italics are used for user actions and bold is used for interface buttons, etc.

B. Downloading the driver to your computer

Now that you have found the drivers, you download them to your computer.

1. The page in step 8 above displays another list of options. Under the "Download Drivers" heading at the top of the page, *click* **Click Here to Download Drivers.**

   After you click on the link, a new browser window will open.

Figure titles: Notice that each figure in these instructions has a figure title left-aligned above the figure. These identify the contents of the figure and make reference to the figure easy.

2. *Click* the option at the top for **Printer Driver for Windows 2000** (Figure 2).

Figure 2: Choosing the Driver

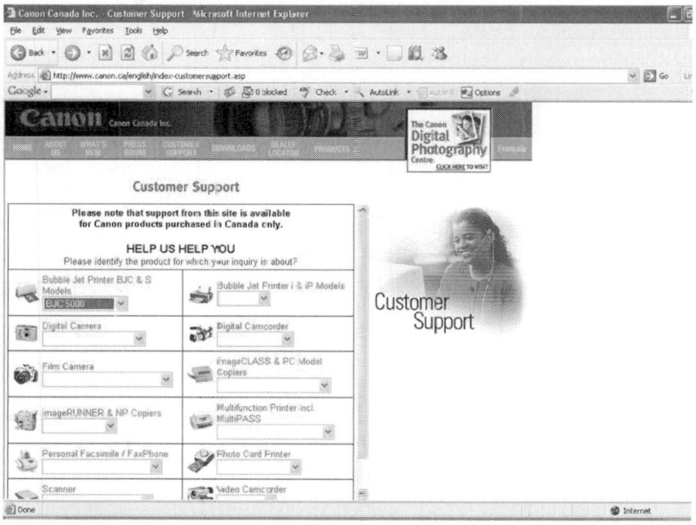

The page that is shown has a disclaimer, as well as an executable file at the bottom (**BJC-5000W2K.EXE**).

3. *Click* this link to begin the download.

The download may take several minutes depending on your Internet connection.

4. *Click* **Open** in the File Download window, in Figure 3.

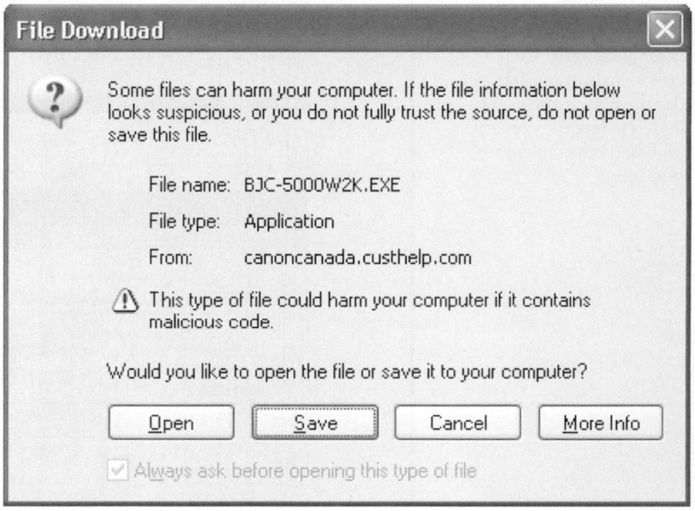

Illustrations: Create screen captures like these in Windows by pressing PrtScn and pasting the images into your document. Most software applications provide sizing and cropping tools to shape the image as necessary.

Figure 3: Download the File

File Download

? Some files can harm your computer. If the file information below looks suspicious, or you do not fully trust the source, do not open or save this file.

File name: BJC-5000W2K.EXE

File type: Application

From: canoncanada.custhelp.com

⚠ This type of file could harm your computer if it contains malicious code.

Would you like to open the file or save it to your computer?

Open   Save   Cancel   More Info

☑ Always ask before opening this type of file

Caution notices: Any warning, caution, or danger notices would be inserted in the text *before the action* indicated and formatted in some way to make them stand out from the instructions.

C. Installing the drivers

Once the file has downloaded, the application runs automatically.

When the application has finished unpacking the entire driver, installation instructions developed by Canon will open. Follow these instructions carefully and there should be no problems.

Once the operation is complete, print a test page.

Final section: Although the operations in these instructions are being performed at the user's home, the reader may want a feeling of a wrap-up statement. The document offers a user-test and an alternative troubleshooting option.

If there is difficulty with either the installation or the drivers, contact me at my office or by telephone at 519-555-8603.

Adapted from an assignment by student Rob Dykeman. Screenshots used courtesy of Canon Canada Inc.

CHAPTER 3

Causes and Effects: Primary Research Reports (Lab Reports)

Topics covered in this chapter include

- global warming and weather changes;
- ladybugs and aphids in the Niagara region;
- bats.

GLOBAL WARMING AND WEATHER CHANGES
Government climate change
http://www.climatechange.gc.ca

The Green Lane, Environment Canada's Internet resource site
http://www.ec.gc.ca/envhome.html

APHIDS IN THE NIAGARA WINE DISTRICT
Search for Niagara + aphids + ladybugs on Google.

BATS
Canadian Wildlife Federation
http://www.cwf–fcf.org

Caving Canada's Canadian Bat Resources
http://www.cancaver.ca/bats/index.htm

When you have completed this chapter, you will be able to

- use cause and effect organization;
- differentiate between causes and effects;
- organize and write primary research reports.

A *primary research report* is a report in which you gather your most important information directly from primary resources, such as the field or the laboratory, rather than from published documents. While you summarize published information in the "literature" section of a primary research report, the most important information comes from surveys, samplings, questionnaires, tests, and experiments—original data that you generate, collect, and analyze. Because the primary research report focuses on why certain things happen, its infrastructure is some combination of causes and effects.

This chapter shows you how to write about causes and effects and then how to construct primary research reports in which you incorporate causes and effects as the infrastructure.

Note:

■ If you are new to this book, see "How Do You Use This Book?" in the Preface.

■ For additional examples of the documents discussed in this chapter, see **http://www.powertools.nelson.com**.

HOW DO YOU WRITE ABOUT CAUSES AND EFFECTS?

Before getting into the details of primary research reports, spend some time thinking about how to discuss causes and effects, which are central to the primary research report.

Defining types of causes and effects.   Defining causes and effects can be bewildering. Some create a telescoping effect, with one cause or effect leading to another and still another. Or the situation may have alternative causes associated with it that are controversial.

■ *Telescoping causes.* Sometimes defining causes and effects only leads to additional causes and effects. Consider the sinking of the Titanic. What caused it? The mighty ship ran into an iceberg, which tore a big gash in its side. But why did it run into an iceberg? Was it a problem with the course, with the navigator, or with the lookouts? Why did the gash cause it to sink? After all, it was supposedly unsinkable. Notice how one question leads to another, just like a telescope being extended further and further.

■ *Alternative causes.* Some cause–effect discussions force you to consider competing alternative causes. Did the navigators of the Titanic plot a course through waters known to be filled with dangerous icebergs, thinking that the ship was invulnerable? Was the general attitude of the builders, owners, or crew nonchalant? Consider the example of global warming and the greenhouse effect. Some people refuse to accept the notion that the average temperature of our planet has risen and continues to rise. Others refuse to accept the notion that human activities are the primary cause of that temperature increase. Scientists debate over a host of causes, attempting to prove which are primary.

▪ *Hypothetical, projected effects.* Another important form of cause–effect discussion has to do with predicted effects, results, or consequences. Predicted effects are based on current conditions: if this situation continues, that is going to happen. The perfect example is the Y2K problem that worried our technology-dependent society as year 2000 approached. Everything from no effect at all to disruption and chaos equal to the Great Depression and nuclear war was predicted because of the change of four little digits. It quickly became evident that nothing was going to happen.

Discussing causes and effects.　What happens when you actually write about causes and effects? Providing details on causes and effects is largely a matter of the following:

▪ *Explaining processes (step-by-step events).* A causal discussion of the Titanic might discuss step by step how the ship set sail, how its course was charted when it hit the iceberg, and how the ship slowly filled and then broke in half and sank. Causes and effects would be emphasized throughout.

▪ *Providing descriptions (physical, visual, quantifiable details).* This same discussion might also include descriptions of the iceberg, the gash in the hull, and so on. The global warming discussion might include information about the CO_2 that has been produced and how it traps radiation in the atmosphere.

▪ *Making comparisons, particularly to the familiar.* Help readers understand causes and effects by comparing them to something familiar. For example, the greenhouse effect—the much-debated primary cause of global warming—is often compared to the way a closed automobile warms up by trapping heat.

▪ *Discussing examples.* For certain causal discussions, reviewing examples helps. If you were focusing on the causes and effects of the extreme weather we have been experiencing in Canada, you might recount examples of bad storms such as the 1998 icestorm in Quebec or the Toronto snowstorm of 1999.

▪ *Emphasizing keywords and transitions.* Also important in discussing causes and effects is emphasizing specific causes and specific effects. Phrases such as "The main cause of," "Another cause of," and "One of the most noticeable effects of" are cues to readers. Equally important are transitions. Words like "because," "as a result of," and "in turn" help readers see the connections between the causes and effects. Take a close look at Figure 3-1 to see how causes and effects are carefully named and how transitions emphasize these relationships.

Introduction: This discussion focuses on the effects of the increase of just a few degrees in average global temperature. Notice that the last sentence of the introduction provides an overview of the effects ("impacts") to be discussed.

The scientific community is in increasing agreement that the next century will see traumatic environmental change. The United Nations Intergovernmental Panel on Climate Change (IPCC) is predicting an average global temperature increase of 1 to 3.5 degrees Celsius in the 21st century. This increase could have dramatic effects on land, water, and air.

Effect-by-effect discussion: Notice that this cause–effect discussion takes up one effect per paragraph, one at a time.

■ *Impact on land.* The current boundaries of year-round farming temperatures are moderate. But the lands today considered the bread baskets of the world are left with reduced crop yields. Because higher average temperatures will cause moisture in the soil to evaporate at higher rates, scientists are predicting reduced crop yields. As already witnessed by the growth of the Sahara Desert, deserts are also expected to expand because of the increase in average global temperatures.

Bulleted list: Bulleted-list items help differentiate the individual effects discussion. (Bullets are used rather than numbers because these effects are not in a required sequence.)

■ *Impact on water.* Increased temperatures will result in increased melting of polar icecaps, which will in turn cause the world's oceans to rise between 15 and 95 centimeters over the next century, according to IPCC projections. This means that a low-elevation area like Bangladesh will stand to lose over 20 percent of its usable land, and the city of New Orleans, for example, could be underwater. Rising waters will increase coastal erosion, heighten the damaging effects of hurricanes, and contaminate water supplies that coastal cities and farms depend on.

Labels: Each of these bulleted items starts with a label that identifies the topic of the item, like a mini-heading. Notice that the label is not a grammatical part of the rest of the bulleted item.

■ *Impact on atmosphere.* Scientists are uncertain what will happen to the atmosphere as average global temperatures increase. Because of the increase in cloud cover, resulting from increased evaporation, temperatures are likely to decrease. However, those same clouds also have the effect of trapping heat, which increases the planet's average temperature.

Source: Adapted from UNEP and WMO. *Common Questions about Climate Change*, 1997. Available on the Internet at www.gcrio.org. UNEP. *Climate Change: Information Kit.* July 1999. Available on the Internet at www.unep.org.

FIGURE 3-1

Short cause–effect discussion. Notice that this example discusses the effects ("impacts") one at a time, each in its own paragraph. Notice, also, how the bulleting and labelling make the individual effects more distinct.

Let's step through the important phases in writing cause–effect discussions. To give you a sense of how these steps work in an actual writing project, we'll follow a single example throughout.

1. **Find a simple project involving the discussion of causes, effects, or both.** It's easy enough to think of complex exercises such as why the sky is blue; what causes earthquakes, tornadoes, or tsunamis; why the sound of a large speeding vehicle is so shrill when it is approaching;

or how acoustic speakers reproduce sound. How about starting with a real or realistic problem in the workplace? To write a simple cause–effect discussion, think of some specific situation that fits one of the following:

■ Define and discuss the causes of a problem.
■ Define and discuss the effects of that problem.
■ Define and discuss the solutions to that problem.

(Having trouble thinking of a topic? See the textbook website for an expanded list of topics at **http://www.powertools.nelson.com.**)

Assume that you must write the cause–effect section for a technical background report on global warming. This section has two parts: the first discusses the causes of global warming; the second discusses the effects. You are not going to get into solutions, at least not in this section. You are just exploring the basic mechanism of global warming.

2. **Define an audience and purpose.** The next step is to decide on an audience and purpose for this cause–effect discussion. Who are your readers? Why do they need this information? What, if anything, can you assume about their background on the topic? (See Chapter 17 for strategies to use in analyzing audiences and adapting your writing to them.)

Assume you are writing for an audience of investment advisers—individuals who advise investors about long-range investments. Obviously, these people need to know whether the global warming threat is just a gloom-and-doom scare or a no-nonsense reality. These investment advisers are not scientists or environmentalists. They are nonspecialist readers who need technical detail served up in a way that they can understand. Your purpose is to present the arguments for the global warming theory. Elsewhere in the report, you may get into the standard arguments against this theory.

3. **Do some research.** For even a simple cause or effect, you may need to do some research.

If you did some research on global warming, you'd find lots of information, like the links at the beginning of this chapter. Activist groups such as the World Wildlife Federation and the Environmental Defense Fund believe that global warming is a serious threat. They have websites presenting their points of view. But the other side of the issue is well represented also—for example, by the Cooler Heads Coalition, the National Consumer Coalition, and the Instant Experts Guide from the Heartland Institute.

4. **Plan and develop graphics and tables.** Early in this project, visualize the graphics this cause–effect discussion will need. Use the strategies in Chapter 11 to plan the drawings, photos, and charts you may need to include.

Graphics for a global warming report might include a diagram of the earth showing how radiation is trapped in the atmosphere. You might also need a line graph depicting rising global temperature averages over the past century or a table showing how much our production of carbon dioxide (CO_2) has dramatically increased over the past century.

5. **Identify the causes.** With your topic, purpose, and audience defined, figure out the causes that must be discussed.

   For global warming, a variety of causes are cited, with human activities, of course, being the most debated. Practically any article, report, or book on this topic will show that among the most commonly cited causes are fuel combustion leading to increased CO_2; ranching, farming, and landfills leading to increased methane; land clearing leading to reduced consumption of CO_2; and heavy harvesting of marine organisms leading to increased plankton (CO_2 producers) in the oceans.

6. **Identify the effects.** With your topic, purpose, and audience defined, figure out the effects that must be discussed. Remember that the problem–solution discussion is practically the same as the cause–effect discussion.

   In this project, the effects of global warming are obviously, first and foremost, an overall rise in average global temperature ($-17^\circ C$ in the past century). Effects variously cited include a rise in sea levels (10 to 25 cm in the past century), reduction of glaciers and polar icecaps, and an increase in water temperature that has affected fish stocks on both coasts of Canada.

7. **Identify relationships between the causes and effects.** Once you've listed the causes and effects, think about how they are related. Does one cause lead to an effect that, in turn, becomes the cause of another effect? Are there multiple causes that have varying degrees of force?

   Some alleged causes of global warming precede others: melting of glaciers and the polar icecap obviously precedes the rise in sea levels. The causes also vary in terms of their force and in terms of controversy. The same is true for effects: some are more powerful; some are more controversial. The cause–effect section in this global warming report must make these relationships clear.

8. **Discuss the causes and effects.** Take a rigorously organized approach to your discussion of the causes and effects. Discuss each one separately, in a sentence or two or in a paragraph or two (which is illustrated in Figure 3-2). As mentioned earlier, discussing causes and effects usually involves description, step-by-step process discussion, examples, and comparisons.

Introduction: explanation of the problem; overview of the causes to be discussed	*Introduction:* explanation of the problem; overview of the effects to be discussed
Cause 1: discuss how this cause is the main cause or a contributing cause; explain this cause using description or process	*Effect 1:* discuss how this effect is the main effect or an important one; explain this effect using description or process
Cause 2: discuss how this cause is another cause or a contributing cause; explain this cause using description or process	*Effect 2:* discuss how this effect is another main effect or an important one; explain this effect using description or process
Cause 3: discuss how this cause is another cause or a contributing cause; explain this cause using description or process	*Effect 3:* discuss how this effect is another main effect or an important one; explain this effect using description or process
Conclusion	*Conclusion*

FIGURE 3-2
Cause–effect discussion. Here are two possibilities for structuring a cause–effect discussion. The idea is to discuss one cause or effect at a time. There are other possibilities; for example, a chain reaction in which one effect turns into a cause that, in turn, leads to another effect.

In this global warming report, use statistics to explain how the global temperature increase can be demonstrated. Do the same with increased sea levels. Perhaps provide comparisons of glaciers, sea levels, and temperatures a century ago and today. You might include a step-by-step discussion of how CO_2 traps heat in the atmosphere, if you believe that your bottom-line–minded investor audience would want this technical discussion. In any case, keep the discussion of the causes and effects separate. Be heavy-handed with the transitions between the causes and effects. For example, use the phrase "Another cause considered important in the global ..."

9. **Sketch out the headings you'll use.** If you discuss each individual cause or effect in one or more paragraphs, create a heading for each one (see Chapter 7).

   For the global warming report, use a second-level heading to introduce the causes and another second-level heading to introduce the effects. Use third-level headings to introduce the discussion of the individual causes or effects.

10. **Plan an introduction.** Introductions must indicate the topic and purpose of the document and provide an overview of what will be discussed. In the case of causal discussions, provide an overview of the causes, effects, or both that you are about to discuss. Do the same if

you plan to discuss problems and solutions or conditions and symptoms, which are causal discussions as well. Another element to consider is the *audience identifier*, which helps readers decide whether the information is suited to their needs, interests, and knowledge level.

Imagine you've written the main text for this cause–effect section on global warming. Go back now and plan the introduction. Perhaps start with a warning: most of this part of the report is controversial; the goal is simply to present the theory. Perhaps provide a quick review of how global warming is defined. Be sure to indicate that causes will be discussed first and then effects. It may be heavy-handed to list the causes and effects here. Just the words "causes" and "effects" should be enough.

11. **Consider adding a conclusion.** You can summarize the main points to refocus your readers, state a conclusion, or provide some general closing thoughts.

For this conclusion, you might want to remind readers that most of what you've just presented is rather warmly debated (no pun intended). You might also point out that this field changes constantly. For example, a recent study indicated that receding glaciers are not necessarily proof of global warming. You might also review a list of major related questions about which scientists simply do not have a clue.

12. **Consider the format.** For this simple project, you don't need the elaborate report formats shown in Chapter 15. Instead, use the format you see in the cause–effect discussion of schizophrenia at the end of this chapter. Begin with a descriptive title centred at the top of the page, and use second- and third-level headings. Use lists, notices, illustrations, tables, highlighting, and documentation (citations of your borrowed information sources) as necessary.

13. **Review and revise your rough draft.** Use the strategies in Chapter 16 to systematically review and revise your cause–effect discussion. Use the top-down approach described in that chapter: start by reviewing for audience, purpose, and situation; then move on to content, organization, and transitions; then headings, lists, tables, and graphics; then sentence style and technical style; and finally, grammar, usage, spelling, and punctuation problems.

HOW DO YOU WRITE PRIMARY RESEARCH REPORTS?

Primary research reports are often called "empirical" research reports because they contain data gathered directly from experiment and observation rather than information gathered from printed or in-person sources. This section discusses the primary research report and then shows you how to plan, write, and design one. Because the primary research report seeks to determine why something happens or what will happen as a result, cause–effect discussion is its essential infrastructure.

The following sections guide you through contents and organization of the primary research report as well as the typical phases in its development.

1. **Build a team.** Primary research reports are good opportunities to work as part of a team. These types of reports are commonly developed by teams, because the tasks required by most primary research reports take a lot of work.

2. **Find a project requiring a primary research report.** Throughout, this book emphasizes writing projects that solve real or realistic workplace problems. Primary research reports certainly do that, but they also venture into the realms of pure knowledge, where there is no immediate practical problem to be solved. However, someday someone may find practical applications for that knowledge. As you search for a project, or for people needing some research done, remember that you're not limited to the traditional lab experiment. You can also do field research, involving surveys and questionnaires.

   Imagine you work for a small private winegrower in the Niagara region of Ontario. In fall of 2001, an infestation of Asian ladybugs invaded Ontario and had a devastating effect on the wine of that year when the droppings of bugs contaminated the wine with pyrazine, causing it to have a nasty aroma. Some of the 2001 crop had to be dumped. The infestation was caused when hot dry weather caused a jump in the numbers of aphids, or tree lice, which the ladybugs feed upon. Now with a hot summer predicted, a new infestation threatens. Your boss has asked you to find out the best way to control aphids. You'll run an experiment testing several methods of aphid control, collect the data, and write him a report.

3. **Define an audience and purpose.** As with any technical-writing project, begin by developing an in-depth understanding of the situation requiring a report and of the needs, interests, and knowledge levels of the readers. Readers of primary research reports expect this sequence: problem, background, method, data, discussion, and conclusions. They also expect details that enable them to visualize or even do your experiment.

Your boss does not have a scientific background and wants a report that lays everything out for him in layman's terms. He is not a specialist in areas like botany, entomology, or chemistry. He is looking for a practical solution to his ladybug/aphid problem and likes the research format because it details specific conditions like weather, geography, people, and success rates.

4. **Describe the problem and the background.** One of the first things to do, either in the introduction or in a separate section of its own, is to discuss the situation that has led to the research. For example, research may be lacking for your topic, or there may be conflicts in existing research. Explain this at the beginning of a primary research report.

   In your primary research report, you'll include a background section in which you first discuss the details of your aphid/ladybag problem, then the difficulty of determining how to control it, and finally, the lack of good information on this problem.

5. **Describe the purpose, objectives, and scope.** Toward the beginning of this type of report, discuss what you intended to do in the research project—what were your objectives? Also, explain the scope of your work—what were you not trying to do?

   Your purpose is to discuss several methods of controlling aphids and ladybugs. Because of the bad PR that would come from heavy insecticide use, you limit your experiment to organic control methods.

6. **Plan the review of literature.** After you've established the basis for the project, summarize the literature relevant to it. Summarize the theory and research directly relevant to your project. Show how it contradicts itself or is inadequate.

   On the Internet, in your local library, in farm and garden stores, and from other winegrowers in your area, you discover a wide range of ideas about how to keep the aphid population down, thereby depriving Asian ladybugs of their food supply. For example, some farmers plant such things as dill, fennel, coreopsis, and brightly coloured flowers near crops, and this may be an option for vineyards. There is also an organic method involving sabadilla. Summarize this literature and the opinions in a separate "literature review" section.

7. **Describe the materials, equipment, and facilities.** Remember that one of your goals in writing this type of report is to enable readers to visualize or even repeat the research you performed. Therefore, you must discuss the equipment and facilities you used. Describe it in detail, providing brand names, model numbers, sizes, and other such specifications.

Practical Ethics: Omission

 It is quite common—and even beneficial—to quote experts in technical documents. It is also quite common to condense a quote to fit the length and requirements of your report. You need to zero in on the shortest, most relevant statement the expert made and weed out anything extraneous. When you do this, it's important to let your readers know that you aren't using a full or complete quotation by using an ellipsis (…) to indicate exactly where words or phrases have been omitted.

According to the Modern Language Association (MLA), "Whenever you wish to omit a word, a phrase, a sentence, or more from a quoted passage, you should be guided by two principles: fairness to the author quoted and the grammatical integrity of your writing. A quotation should never be presented in a way that could cause a reader to misunderstand the sentence structure of the original source."[1]

When you are writing any type of technical document, you have to decide not only what portions of a quote to include, but also which facts to include. As a writer, part of your job is to sort through all the information available on a topic and to provide your audience with only what they need to know. It can be tempting to provide only the information you *want* to, but there are some ethical implications to doing so.

Imagine that Valentine's Day is nearing and you have to write about chocolate. As you browse the Internet for information, you find several reports that chocolate, similar to red wine, may reduce the risk of heart disease. If you write an enthusiastic report on the health benefits of chocolate without also pointing out the health risks associated with high-fat foods, you are not being fair to your audience.

Consider other situations in which you have an ethical obligation *not* to omit certain facts. You are a statistician hired by a drug company to report the results of a drug study to Health Canada. Do you omit some of the side effects, or downplay the risks, in order to get the drug approved? Let's say the drug is approved by Health Canada, side effects and all, and you are in charge of publicity. What information will you include and what will you omit in the ad campaign aimed at doctors or the general public?

Another place to be careful about what you omit is the bibliography. Obviously, you cite resources that support your claims, but it's also important to include those sources that contain contrary information.

Being careful about what you omit not only makes your documents fair and balanced, but it's also a sign of professionalism.

[1]Gibaldi, Joseph. *MLA Handbook for Writers of Research Papers.* New York: Modern Language Association of America, 1999: 85.

For this project, you'll enlist the help of several other small winegrowers who are interested in reading the report. Each will try a different method on a small area of vines and, at the same time each day, will take note of the number of aphids and/or ladybugs. You'll compare soil samples and measure the amount of direct sunlight each row of vines gets each day. You'll try to ensure that each planting is roughly the same in terms of soil, sunlight, and type of grape. Describe all of these efforts in a separate section of the primary research report.

8. **Explain your theory, methods, and procedures.** To enable readers to repeat your project, you must also explain the procedures or methods you used. Use the step-by-step format for this discussion. If you are testing a theory or basing your research on a theory, explain that as well.

This section will read like a log of what you and your fellow researchers noted each evening when you checked the vines for aphids and ladybugs, right through to the actual cultivation of the grapes and the first tasting of the wine. As for theory, you can discuss the strategy used in each control method; for example, one method will be more aggressive, involving spraying the vines with an organic compound, whereas another will be more passive, involving a co-planting.

9. **Present the results, findings, and data.** Critical to any primary research report is the data that you collect. You present it in tables, charts, and graphs (see Chapter 10), as well as in regular paragraphs. In any case, you don't interpret the data at this point. Just present it, without trying to explain it.

   How are you going to collect statistical data for this experiment? Count dead aphids? Test the wine for contamination? Unfortunately, one area of your vineyard had to be left as a "control" area—in other words, no methods were used to control aphids and ladybugs. You decide to count aphids on three separate plants once a week and record your results. You can present the raw data in tables and perhaps use line graphs to show the comparisons between the control group and the other groups more dramatically.

10. **Write the discussion, conclusions, and recommendations.** In primary research reports, you interpret or discuss your findings in a section separate from the one for data. This is the time to explain your data, interpret it, make recommendations, and state ideas for further research.

    Now you get to interpret your results and make recommendations. Which control method worked best? Why did it work best? Can you identify conditions that may have "skewed" or distorted your findings? Based on your findings, how strong of a recommendation can you make for the winning aphid/ladybag control method?

11. **Format the list of information sources.** Ideally, a primary research report builds upon or adds to a body of knowledge. Your primary research report rests on top of all the work done by other researchers on the same topic. For that reason and others, you must list the sources of information you used or consulted in your project.

    Create citations for each of the information sources that you used to research this project. In your relentless pursuit of the aphid, you consulted books, journal articles, agricultural reports, the Internet, local farm and garden stores, and fellow winegrowers. Make a citation for each of these that you in some way refer to, summarize, or quote.

12. **Plan the appendixes.** Create an appendix for your report for such things as the information sources, large tables of statistics, large illustrations or other kinds of graphics, or any other information that might be useful to readers but that doesn't fit in the main text. (See Chapter 14 for appendix format.)

    In the appendixes of this report you might provide a map showing the locations of the vineyards in your experiment and diagrams of each one. If the data tables are too big for the body of the report, put them in an appendix as well.

13. **Write the introduction.** In the introduction to a primary research report, briefly state the problem your research addresses, the purpose of your research, perhaps the limitations of your findings, and an overview of the contents of the rest of the report.

    In the introduction to the aphid research report, briefly refer to the ladybug problem and the difficulty of finding a good solution (but keep it brief; you'll have a background section that goes into the details). State that this report presents findings, conclusions, and recommendations along with procedures. Perhaps mention also the scope of your report—that it's not rigorous experimental science.

14. **Plan the format.** Traditionally, a primary research report is written as an article to be published in a journal. The example primary research report at the end of this chapter uses that format. However, if you were doing this research for a client or employer, you could enclose the report within a business letter or memo. As Chapter 14 shows, you could make the report an attachment to a cover letter or memo, or you could integrate the report with the letter or memo into one self-contained whole.

    Because you and your boss intend to share your report with other winegrowers who have assisted you with the research, you decide to format the report as a report integrated into a letter. You use a word-processing program to create a mail merge so you can add different contact information to each letter report.

15. **Review and revise your rough draft.** Use the strategies for reviewing and revising in Chapter 16 to systematically review and revise your primary research report. Use the top-down approach described in that chapter: start by reviewing for audience, purpose, and situation; then move on to content, organization, and transitions; then headings, lists, tables, and graphics; then on to sentence style and technical style; and finally, grammar, usage, spelling, and punctuation problems.

WORKSHOP: CAUSES, EFFECTS, PRIMARY RESEARCH REPORTS

Here are some additional ideas for practising the concepts, tools, and strategies in this chapter:

1. *Identifying causes.* Consider one or more of the following topics or situations and identify the possible causes—either sequential, telescoping, or controversial.

Sneezing	Ulcer	Heart attack
Red colour of Mars	Lightning	Wind
Tsunami	Headache	Migraine
Stopped-up sink	Common cold	Overdraft at the bank
Overheated car engine	Car air conditioner not cooling	Solar eclipse

2. *Identifying effects.* Consider one or more of the preceding topics or situations, and identify the potential effects—either sequential, telescoping, or controversial.

3. *Experiments and surveys.* Consider any one of the following experiments or surveys. How would you structure the primary research report on that experiment? What would be the main sections and what would they contain?

Best varieties of tomatoes for your backyard garden

Most effective organic methods of pest control in backyard gardens

Online learning versus traditional classroom learning

Effects of free ridership on the use of mass transportation

Effects of melatonin on sleep behaviours

Dvorak keyboard versus the standard QWERTY keyboard

Productivity and in-house fitness/recreational facilities for employees

Fundraising efforts of the Terry Fox Foundation

CAUSE–EFFECT DISCUSSION

The Effect of Climate Change on the Canadian Arctic

Scientists have noticed that temperatures in the Arctic are increasing ten times as fast as they are anywhere else on the globe (DiManno A4). This temperature increase has been attributed to global warming. Causes of global warming may include increasing consumption of fossil fuels, which have led to the so-called greenhouse gases. While the causes are still being debated, it is clear that something is going on in the Arctic. Global warming may not be the cause, but climate change is evident and demonstrable. Some things affected by climate change, which has seen the permafrost melt, the polar icecaps retreat, and the ocean levels rise, are as follows:

- Vegetation
- Animal habitats
- Marine transportation
- Indigenous communities

Changes already documented in these areas have led scientists to predict further changes to come. Some possible changes are outlined below:

Changes in Vegetation
The tree line will move northward and forests will replace tundra. Tundra vegetation will change to desert. Insect outbreaks will increase, as will the number of forest fires. Forest fires will be followed by invasions of non-native species. However, a longer growing period may move agriculture northward (Hassol 11).

Disappearing Animal Habitats
Certain species are dependent on the polar ice for survival. These include polar bears, seals, and some seabirds. Land animals such as caribou will be affected by loss of access to food sources, breeding grounds, and

migration routes. Other species will move northward, bringing new diseases such as West Nile virus. While northern freshwater fisheries are likely to suffer, some fisheries will become more productive (Hassol 10).

Alterations in Transportation Routes

Thawing ground may improve marine transportation in the Arctic, and possibly even lead to new passages to Europe. However, land transportation will be disrupted when frozen roads disappear earlier in the spring. Loss of transportation will affect mining, oil, and forestry, although, to compensate, offshore extraction of oil and gas may become more accessible (Hassol 10).

Disruption of Indigenous Communities

Approximately 4 million people live in the Arctic, about 10% of whom are indigenous people. In the Canadian Arctic, however, indigenous people make up 50% of the population. Indigenous people will be affected by the loss of hunting. Safety during travel will also be affected as the ice thins. Scientists have compared their own results with the knowledge and observations of indigenous people when studying the effects of climate change, adding further validity to the findings of both (Hassol 11).

Conclusion

Although there may be some positive effects that come from climate change in the Canadian Arctic, overall the changes are expected to be catastrophic. The changes are expected to affect more than just the Arctic area, as rising sea levels bring changes across the globe. The rapidly changing Arctic climate has sent scientists to a state of high alert, and this may be the best result for the future of our planet.

Works Cited

DiManno, Rosie. "In a Cold Arctic Sweat." *Toronto Star.* 6 Aug. 2005: A4.

Hassol, Susan Joy. "Impacts of a Warming Arctic." *Arctic Climate Impact Assessment.* Cambridge, UK: Cambridge University Press, 2004.

PRIMARY RESEARCH REPORT

Primary research report: This example reports on research done to verify that bats roost on the ground in the winter. As you'll see, it's essentially a series of observations made during prescribed burns in a forested area. Source: "Bats Roosting in Deciduous Leaf Litter." *Bat Research News*, 40(3) (1999): 74–75.

Introduction and background: In a longer research report, you'd see a separate background section with its own heading. It would summarize the current knowledge about the topic, present the research question, and perhaps discuss the rationale for attempting to find answers for it.

In this case, the report is brief; an elaborate literature review is not needed. This introduction quickly refers to existing research ("recent surge of information …"), poses the research question ("little is known …"), and then states the purpose of this report ("Herein, we report …").

Writing style—point of view: While this report certainly has the atmosphere of traditional research-reporting style, notice that it is comfortable with the contemporary first-person style ("Herein, we report …," "We made 10 observations …," "On 16 February, we conducted …"). Even so, this report still contains lots of passive voice, and rightly so, because we are more interested in the bats! But notice the reference to "researchers"— that's a little confusing. Same people?

Bats Roosting in Deciduous Leaf Litter

Christopher E. Moorman,[1] Kevin R. Russell,[1] Michael A. Menzel,[2] Stephen M. Lehr,[1] Justin E. Ellenberger,[1] and D. H. Van Lear[1]

Despite the recent surge of information concerning characteristics of roost sites used by tree-roosting bats during summer (for example, Crampton and Barclay, 1998; Menzel et al., 1998), little is known about roost sites used by bats during winter. During summer, some tree-roosting bats roost within the canopy of hardwood trees (Menzel et al., 1998). However, once leaves fall, deciduous trees may no longer be adequate as roost sites. Herein, we report observations that further support claims concerning use of litter on the forest floor by bats in winter.

Observations

We made 10 observations of bats in winter flying from deciduous leaf litter in three upland hardwood stands in the South Carolina Piedmont. The three stands were located on the Clemson University Experimental Forest ca. 4 miles N of Clemson, South Carolina. All observations were made in stands comprised predominately of mixed oaks (*Querus*) with lesser amounts of yellow poplar (*Liriodendron tulipifera*), hickory (*Carya*), and red maple (*Acer rubrum*). The understory was sparsely vegetated with isolated mountain laurel (*Kalimia latifolia*), red buckeye (*Aesculus sylvatica*), and American holly (*Ilex americana*). Depth of the litter layer in the three stands was ca. 7 cm.

A single bat was flushed from leaf litter on 5 January 1999, as several researchers walked near its location. Nine other observations were made while conducting low-intensity strip-head fires in 6 1-ha [hectare] plots within the three stands. All burns were conducted on clear days. Bats roused during prescribed burns flew as the strip fires approached, and

[1]Department of Forest Services, Clemson University, Clemson, SC 29634
[2]Division of Forestry, West Virginia University, Morgantown, WV 26506

Modifier problem: The traditional research-writing style makes it easy to create dangling and misplaced modifiers. For example, the words "one bat was flushed while raking fire lines" suggest that the bat was doing the raking. To fix this one, rewrite it as "one bat was flushed while the fire lines were being raked."

Numbers: Notice the contrasting use of numbers as words and as digits throughout this report. Any numerical value that is both exact and essential is displayed as a digit. Thus "5 " is used with "m"; "10" with "observations"; "7" with "cm"; "4" with "miles." But notice that words are used in "three upland hardwood stands" and "two plots." Although these are exact values, the writers don't view them as essential or critical enough to display as digits.

Content and organization: Although this is a brief and rather informal report, it still has the structure of the research report: it begins with a research question and literature review, provides details on observations, and begins discussing and concluding only in the final section. Throughout, related research is cited. Notice how carefully these writers avoid drawing conclusions or speculating on causes or effects in "Observations."

one bat was flushed while raking fire lines. Two or more of the researchers viewed each bat. Once bats were roused, they flew over the roost site for several seconds and disappeared into the canopy of smoke created by the fire. Because bats flew out of sight, some observations could have been on the same individual.

On 16 February, we conducted a prescribed fire at two plots bisected by a small perennial stream. The aspects and slope gradients of the two plots were 105° SSW and 280° WNW and 40% and 15%, respectively. At the time of the burn, ambient temperature was 18°C, and the minimum temperature the night previous was 2°C. Two bats flew from the forest floor of the SSW-facing slope, and three bats were flushed from the WNW-facing slope. One of the bats on the WNW-facing plot flew from a location within 5 m of where the first bat was flushed on 5 January, suggesting that the individual may have returned after researchers left the area.

On 25 February, we conducted a second prescribed fire at two plots bisected by a different biennial stream. The aspects and slope gradients of the two plots were 45° NE and 216° SSW and 32% and 23%, respectively. Ambient temperature during the prescribed burn was 14°C, and minimum temperature the previous night was 0°C. Two bats were roused from the SSW-facing plot, but no bats were observed while burning the second plot.

On 23 March, a third prescribed burn was conducted at two plots bisected by a third small stream. Aspects and slopes of the two plots were 20° NNE and 210° SSW and 30% and 26%, respectively. While burning, ambient temperature was 22°C, and minimum temperature during the previous 24 hours was 4°C. One bat was flushed when fire lines were raked on the SSW-facing slope, and a second bat flew from the forest floor on the NNE-facing slope as the fires approached.

Latin abbreviations: Notice the use of "et al." It's Latin for "and others"; "al." is an abbreviation for "alia." "ca." stands for "circa" in Latin, or "about." Even though these are non-English words, their use is so common in this context they are not italicized. Although Latin abbreviations are generally not used, in this scientific context, they are standard, for example, "i.e." and "e.g." are other commonly used Latin abbreviations.

Source citations: This report uses American Psychological Association (APA) style. If you want to see details on Saugey et al., 1998, go to the literature-cited section at the end of this report: you'll see the title of the article and of the journal in which it appeared as well as dates. (Notice that if the author name is stated in the regular text, it can be omitted in the parenthetical citation.)

Documentation style: This report, published in *Bat Research News*, uses APA style. You can see that the in-text citations include names and years in parentheses. Notice that italics are not used on book and journal names but instead on species names only. That's the way these researchers want it!

Discussion and Conclusions

Although we were unable to make definitive identifications, we suggest the bats were eastern red bats (*Lasiurus borealis*). All were relatively large (i.e., larger than *Myotis*), and those seen up close were reddish. Saugey et al. (1989) also reported seeing bats "smoked" from their hibernation sites during a prescribed winter burn in Arkansas, and they believed the bats were eastern red bats resting in leaf litter on the forest floor. In 1993 and 1994, a female and male eastern red bat were radiotracked to a single site in hardwood-pine leaf litter on the forest floor (Saugey et al., 1998). Past reports were from the central United States, but our data indicate possible use of leaf litter by eastern red bats is more widespread geographically and may occur throughout the species' range.

Oak leaves dominated the litter layer of the plots prior to burns. No bats were flushed from up-slope portions of the stands, which typically contained fewer hardwoods and more pines (*Pinus*). Because of their color, insulatory properties, and resistance to decay, sites with well-developed hardwood litter, especially oak litter, may provide important wintering sites for eastern red bats. However, prescribed fires typically eliminate much forest-floor debris, including leaf litter and small woody debris. Therefore, fire likely renders the burned area temporarily inadequate for ground-roosting bats. Although prescribed fire traditionally has been used for pine management, recent research (Brose and Van Lear, 1998; Brose et al., 1999) indicates that fire is an essential ecological process in management of upland oaks during the regeneration phase. In light of our observations, further investigation of bat use of forest-floor debris is warranted, especially in areas where prescribed burning or other silvicultural manipulations are common.

Acknowledgements

We thank S. K. Cox, S. Perry, D. B. Vandermast, J. Albiston, and many undergraduates for assistance during prescribed burns. Prescribed fires were conducted for a project funded by McIntire–Stennis through Clemson University.

References

Brose, P. H., & Van Lear, D. H. (1998). Response of hardwood advanced regeneration to seasonal prescribed fire in oak-dominated shelterwood stands. *Canadian Journal of Forest Research*, (28), 331-339.

Brose, P. H., Van Lear, D. H., & Cooper, R. (1999). Using shelterwood harvests and prescribed fire to regenerate oaks on productive upland sites. *Forest Ecology and Management*, (113), 125–141.

Crampton, L. H. & Barclay, R. M. R. (1998). Selection of roosting and foraging habitat by bats in different-aged mixed wood stands. *Conservation Biology*, (12), 1347–1358.

Menzel, M. A., Carter, T. C., Chapman, B. R., & Laerm, J. (1998). Quantitative tree roosts used by red bats (*Lasirius borealis*) and Seminole bats (*L. seminolus*). *Canadian Journal of Zoology*, (76), 630–634.

Saugey, D. A., Heath, D. R., & Heidt, G. A. (1989). The bats of the Quachita Mountains. Proceedings of the Arkansas Academy of Science, (43), 71–77.

Saugey, D. A., Vaughn, R. L., Crump, B. G., & Heidt, G. A. (1998). Notes on the natural history of *Lasirius borealis* in Arkansas. Journal of the Arkansas Academy of Science, (52), 92–98.

Source: Moorman, Russell, et al. "Bats Roosting in Deciduous Leaf Litter." *Bat Research News*, 403, 1999: 74–75. Reprinted with permission.

CHAPTER 4

Comparison: Recommendation, Evaluation, and Feasibility Reports

Topics covered in this chapter include

- voice-recognition technologies;
- fuzzy logic;
- Mars compared to Earth.

VOICE-RECOGNITION TECHNOLOGIES
Click through the Yahoo Directory:

Business and Economy/Shopping and Services/Computers/Software/Voice Recognition. Note the categories on the "Voice Recognition" page as well. Click **Text to Speech** for more hits.

FUZZY LOGIC
National Research of Canada (search for "fuzzy logic")
http://iit-iti.nrc-cnrc.gc.ca

MARS AND EARTH
Canada in Space
http://www.canadainspace.ca

The Canadian Space Agency
http://www.space.gc.ca

The Mars Society
http://www.marssociety.ca

When you have completed this chapter, you will be able to

- use comparison effectively;
- see that the point-by-point method is preferable to the whole-to-whole method;
- organize and write recommendation, evaluation, and feasibility reports.

Recommendation, evaluation, and feasibility reports are a loosely differentiated set of reports that compare carefully gathered information to pass judgment on products, properties, plans, or personnel. As you know from the Preface, most technical documents are based on one or more *infrastructures*—elemental structures that enable reports to do their job. The infrastructure essential to recommendation, evaluation, and feasibility reports is *comparison*. To make an intelligent choice from a set of options (such as products, properties, plans, organizations, or personnel), you have to compare those choices against a set of requirements and against each other.

This chapter shows you how to write comparisons and then how to construct recommendation, evaluation, and feasibility reports with comparison incorporated as the infrastructure.

Note:
- If you are new to this book, see "How Do You Use This Book?" in the Preface.
- For additional examples of the documents discussed in this chapter, see **http://www.powertools.nelson.com.**

HOW DO YOU WRITE A COMPARISON?

Before getting into the details of recommendation, evaluation, and feasibility reports, take a moment to review comparison—the essential infrastructure used in these types of reports. Although comparisons can be structured in a variety of ways, the *point-by-point approach* is usually the most effective. It forces you, the writer, to compare items systematically, one *point of comparison* at a time. For example, in a comparison of three speech-recognition software applications, you might first discuss the accuracy of the three applications, then the ease of use, then the cost, and so on.

The opposite of the point-by-point approach is the *whole-to-whole approach*. It usually produces uneven, inconsistent, and incomplete comparisons. In the whole-to-whole approach, it's too easy to discuss one option, then the next, then the next, without ever directly comparing those options fully. (These two approaches are illustrated in Figure 4-1.)

Let's walk through the important steps in writing comparisons using the point-by-point approach. (See the example of a point-to-point comparison in Figure 4-2.) To give you a sense of how these steps work in an actual writing project, we'll follow a single example throughout.

1. **Find a situation requiring comparison of two or more items.** Try to find a workplace situation in which a document containing a comparison is needed. The comparison can be *informative,* to help readers understand the things being compared. For example, in the early days of the personal computer, word-processing applications were commonly compared with the typewriter. Comparisons can be

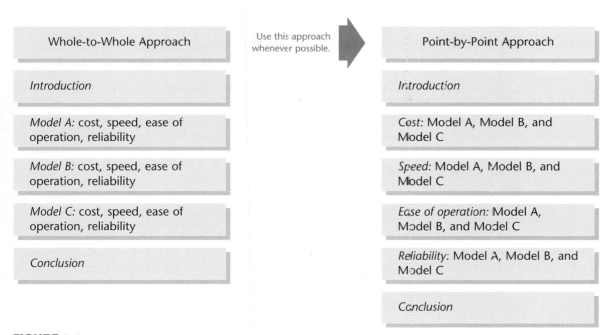

FIGURE 4-1

Different approaches to comparison. The whole-to-whole approach forces readers to make comparisons for themselves and easily becomes disorganized. The point-by-point approach systematically compares each item against one category, or point of comparison, at a time.

evaluative, to help readers decide whether to purchase, fund, implement, or continue something. Recommendation, feasibility, and evaluative reports are covered later in this chapter. (Having trouble thinking of a topic? See **http://www.powertools.nelson.com.**)

Imagine that you are part of a team developing a "white paper" on voice-recognition software for a provincial ministry. The ministry is considering the use of this software for its disabled employees. One part of the project is to compare voice-recognition software to something familiar to help ministry bureaucrats understand this software. Your comparison will be used in the "basics" section. The white paper will go on to discuss how the software works, how well it works, and other such issues.

2. **Choose what to compare.** You may already know what you are going to compare; for example, you might compare CD-ROMs to DVDs. However, if you want to compare something unfamiliar to something familiar, you may have some brainstorming to do. For example, what familiar item could you use for a comparison to superstrings (that strange concept with which physicists hope to develop the Grand Unified Theory)?

These paragraphs compare classical ("binary") logic and "fuzzy" logic.

Note how the two kinds of logic are compared, first, by how they deal with sets; second, by how they process data; and, third, by how they are or can be used in applications.

Notice that both kinds of logic get mentioned in each of the three paragraphs.

Notice the strong use of transition words that emphasize that a comparison is being made.

One of the essential theories that makes technologies like voice-recognition software possible is fuzzy logic and fuzzy sets, an idea developed by Lotfi Zadeh in the mid-1960s.

The essential distinction between classical logic and fuzzy logic has to do with sets and membership in sets. In classical logic, an individual item either is or is not a member of a set. For example, a certain tree is either a member of the set of tall trees or not. In contrast, fuzzy logic offers a method for expressing the extent to which an individual item belongs to a set. Thus, fuzzy logic can state that a certain tree belongs "partly" to the set of tall trees and that that tree can be described as "fairly tall."

Fuzzy-logic systems process data in a markedly different way than do systems based on binary logic. Binary logic is limited to two values—1 or 0 (yes or no)—in expressing the possibility that an event will occur. On the other hand, fuzzy logic can express that possibility in varying degrees of truthfulness or falsehood ("maybe," "probably," "most likely," "not likely," "no way!"). In other words, fuzzy logic provides a system for expressing the probability of an event.

Applications that use fuzzy logic reach far beyond the capabilities of those that use classical binary logic. Starting out in the 1980s as an experimental technology, systems using fuzzy logic became commercially viable in the 1990s. While systems using conventional binary logic had reached a dead end in areas such as speech and handwriting recognition, fuzzy-logic systems have enabled dramatic strides in these areas. Fuzzy systems are now used in camcorders, washing machines, and air conditioning systems, among others things. They are also used in Japan to control subways.

FIGURE 4-2

Short comparison. This example uses the point-by-point approach to compare classical, binary logic to "fuzzy" logic.

Just what can you compare voice-recognition software to? At first, you think you could compare training and using voice-recognition software to training a dog. Fetch! Exit! But that might not play well with ministry bureaucrats. Then you realize that this software is not merely about converting spoken words to text but about interpreting and acting on requests. It's very much like interacting with a human assistant—and that's the analogy you decide to use.

3. **Define a purpose and audience.** The next step is to zero in on a purpose and an audience for this comparison. (See Chapter 17 for strategies to use in analyzing audiences and adapting your writing to them.) To keep this practice comparison simple, use an informative purpose and a nonspecialist audience. Either help readers understand both things being compared, or use an analogy to something familiar to help readers understand one of them.

The audience for your comparison is bureaucrats who are clueless about voice-recognition software. These readers are executives, though, in positions to approve the acquisition of this software for hundreds of disabled employees. These officials have enough basic familiarity with computers to write documents. You know that they are interested in performance, results, and costs, and they are only minimally interested in technical details about how this software works. Your immediate purpose is to inform: these readers need to gain a reasonable level of understanding from your comparison. You also have another purpose lurking quietly in the background: you want those bureaucrats to get interested in and even excited about this software.

4. **Do some research.** To write even a simple comparison, you may need to do some research.

If you did some searching on voice-recognition software, you'd find advertisements from the major manufacturers of the software such as IBM, Dragon Systems, and others. However, you'd also find some interesting articles from *Scientific American* as well as general-discussion materials available from the manufacturers themselves. The technology is still relatively new in 2006 and they must establish its credibility. You'd also find literature from places like MIT and AT&T Bell Labs.

5. **Identify the points of comparison.** With your purpose and audience defined, choose the points of comparison that meet the needs of the readers and enable a good discussion of the things being compared. Identify three, four, five, or more points of comparison—enough to bring out the comparison fully.

You can compare how voice-recognition systems and human assistants take in and interpret requests, how they must clarify those requests if something's amiss, select the correct domain of knowledge (for example, weather forecasts or flight schedules), formulate queries, communicate the results of queries, and so on.

6. **Plan how to write each comparative point.** Now you're ready to plan the actual comparison. Plan to spend one or more sentences, or a whole paragraph, comparing the items according to *one point of comparison at a time*.

Consider the paragraph on clarifying requests. You can compare how a human assistant might ask, "Did you say Toronto or Trenton?" to how voice-recognition software would need the same capability. Another comparative paragraph would discuss selection of domains. If you asked, "When's the next flight to Vancouver?" how would the software know to check flight schedules as opposed to weather forecasts? You can compare how a human assistant would do this to how the software does it

7. **Plan and develop graphics.** Early in this project, visualize the graphics your comparison will need. Use the strategies in Chapter 10 and Chapter 11 to plan the drawings, diagrams, photos, tables, and charts you may need to include.

   Illustrative graphics for voice-recognition software may be hard to come by. You can show the basic setup: a microphone, a computer, and screen captures of the interface of the software. To help people understand the software, you might provide a flowchart of how speech is processed. Tables might be useful to present data on the performance of this software—comparing different software packages, in particular.

8. **Sketch out the headings you'll use.** If your comparison is more than two or three paragraphs, use headings (see Chapter 7). If you use one or more paragraphs to discuss individual points of comparison, create a heading for each one.

   Your points of comparison resemble the phases in the operation of voice-recognition software. You can use a heading for each point of comparison: "Input," "Interpretation," "Clarification," "Queries," "Action," and "Communication." Perhaps you can use a continuous example, such as asking a human assistant or the voice-recognition software about the next flight to Vancouver.

9. **Plan an introduction.** Save the introduction until after you've planned or drafted the main text of the comparison. In the introduction, indicate the purpose: to compare. List the items to be compared and the points of comparison you'll use, and provide some idea as to why the comparison is needed.

   In this introduction, indicate that you are going to provide a "nontechnical" overview of voice-recognition software by comparing it to interaction with a human assistant. Provide a general comparison: that using voice-recognition software is much like interacting with a human assistant.

10. **Consider adding a conclusion.** If your comparison doesn't "feel" complete after the final point of comparison, consider adding a summary that refocuses your readers, enabling them to finish reading with the right perspective.

    An obvious candidate for the conclusion would be to discuss the limitations of voice-recognition software—how it's *not* like a human assistant.

11. **Consider the format.** For this simple project, you are not likely to need the elaborate report formats shown in Chapter 14. Instead, use the format you see for the comparison of Mars and Earth at the end of this chapter. Begin with a descriptive title centred at the top of the

page, and use second- and third-level headings. Use lists, notices, illustrations, tables, highlighting, and documentation (citations of your borrowed information sources) as necessary.

12. **Review and revise your rough draft.** Use the strategies in Chapter 16 to systematically review and revise your comparison. Use the top-down approach described in that chapter: start by reviewing for audience, purpose, and situation; then move on to content, organization, and transitions; then headings, lists, tables, and graphics; then sentence style and technical style; and finally, grammar, usage, spelling, and punctuation problems.

WHAT ARE RECOMMENDATION, EVALUATION, AND FEASIBILITY REPORTS?

Out in the real world you are not likely to find people who use the names of these types of reports with as much precision as we do here. The names—recommendation, evaluation, and feasibility reports—are interchangeable for most professionals. But making the following distinctions may help you to get a sense of the range of this important type of report:

■ *Recommendation report*—Compares two or more options (products, properties, plans, organizations, or personnel) against requirements and then recommends one option (the one that best meets the stated requirements), several options (the ones that meet the requirements but in different ways), or none.
■ *Evaluation report*—Compares individual products, plans, programs, properties, organizations, or personnel against requirements and makes an evaluative judgment—whether it met its expectations, or whether it is "good" or "useful."
■ *Feasibility report*—Makes an evaluative judgment as to whether a project is possible or worthwhile. Its essential task is to tell readers whether a project is "feasible"—whether it is technically, socially, economically, administratively, or environmentally possible or practical.

These reports are essential tools for consultants. Consultants typically study a problem and recommend a solution. They usually get their jobs by submitting proposals (covered in Chapter 6). When they get a contract, they do the research and, generally, submit one of the types of reports presented in this chapter.

HOW DO YOU WRITE A RECOMMENDATION REPORT?

Comparison is the essential infrastructure of recommendation, evaluation, and feasibility reports. It forces you to identify key requirements, which you translate into points of comparison and discuss one at a time. It forces you to give equal time to each item being compared and to state how each item meets the requirements. Writing these reports with comparison as the infrastructure shows readers how you reached your conclusions and recommendations. If they are skeptical, readers can use your comparative information to reach different conclusions and make their own decisions.

The following example walks you through the typical phases in developing this type of report. (Be sure to look at the recommendation report on voice-recognition software at the end of the chapter, which illustrates most of the sections discussed in the following.)

1. **Find a situation in need of a recommendation report.** The classic situation is an individual or organization making an expensive purchase decision. Try to find just such a situation, or invent a realistic one. In this type of report, you start with a problem or need and two or more products, services, or programs that might help. You compare those options and recommend one.

   Imagine that a professional organization of medical transcriptionists has commissioned you to study voice-recognition software. You might have to do a *feasibility study* as to whether this software is practical in terms of its usefulness, accuracy, and cost. You might have to do a *recommendation report* comparing different voice-recognition software packages against your clients' requirements. Or you might have to do an *evaluation report* in which you research some organization currently using voice-recognition software to determine whether it is working. In any case, the medical transcriptionist organization is paying your fee: you do the work they require.

2. **Define the audience and purpose.** As with any technical-writing project, you begin by developing an in-depth understanding of the situation requiring a report and of the needs, interests, and knowledge levels of the readers of that report. For a recommendation, evaluation, or feasibility report, study the problem or the opportunity that the audience is considering. Study these readers' goals and their requirements for reaching those goals. Understand their level of knowledge and experience in relation to the potential project and its technical aspects.

   This medical transcriptionist organization wants a recommendation as to which software application to use, apparently having made up its collective mind to use this software. You recognize that its members want to know how the software works, how well it works, how easy it is to learn and use, whether its benefits justify its cost, and so on.

3. **Build a team?** Recommendation reports, like primary research reports and proposals, are good opportunities to work as part of a team. Typically, there's more work to do than one individual can handle.

> Writing on voice-recognition software will be no small project. You will have to research how this technology works, gather information about individual software products, review how this software is used in business and industry, collect evaluative information on how it performs, and more. You may have to reduce your coverage severely or put together a team of one or two others to share the workload.

4. **Describe the problem or opportunity.** In a recommendation, evaluation, or feasibility report, you focus on situations involving problems in need of solutions and opportunities for improvement. You must explain the situation that brought about the report; for example, an administrative decision, an organizational problem, or a request for proposals. Describe the project in your report in order to demonstrate your understanding of it and to reassure readers that you understand their situation. This section of your report also provides dates, names of individuals and organizations, contract numbers, and so on.

> In this voice-recognition project, medical transcriptionists want to solve the problems of slow, expensive, inaccurate medical transcription. They seek improvements in the efficiency and accuracy of their work. They want to know whether the software really works and which software package is the best for their needs. You might describe their current operations—how much manual transcription costs, how much time it takes, how much inaccuracy there is—in very specific statistical detail.

5. **Define the requirements and priorities.** In this type of report, you must research your readers' requirements and summarize them. Because you systematically compare the options one requirement at a time, you must have a section stating those requirements and their rationale. In the requirements section, include the following:

   ■ *Numeric requirements.* Some requirements are based on numbers; for example, costs, weight, height, and so on: "The maximum cost for the option is $2,000."
   ■ *Yes/no requirements.* Other requirements are simply a yes/no; does the option have a certain feature or not? For example, "The option must have on-screen editing capabilities."
   ■ *Rating-based requirements.* Still other requirements rely on ratings by experts or typical users: "The option must have an ease-of-use rating of at least 4.0 on a 5.0 scale."

It's not enough just to define requirements. You must also establish *priorities*. These help you decide in cases where there is no clear cut best choice among options, as is usually the case. For example, how will you decide if one option has the lowest cost while another option has the best functions?

For this voice-recognition project, include requirements such as cost maximums, minimum ease-of-use ratings, and percentage-based efficiency improvements. State these requirements in specific statistical, yes/no, or ratings-based terms. Because accuracy is still the biggest issue in this emerging technology, define it as the top priority, ahead of cost and ease of learning and use.

6. **List and describe the options.** Discuss options that may solve the problems, exploit the opportunities, or meet the requirements. Explain how you narrowed the field of options to the ones you actually compare. Consider discussing each option. In a recommendation or feasibility report, this discussion can be a separate section.

In the voice-recognition example, present the candidates just after the requirements section. Explain why you excluded other voice-recognition software packages. Explain how these candidates meet the minimal requirements presented in the requirements section.

7. **Consider including technical background.** For some reports, you must provide some technical background. That way, readers can understand related concepts and terminology as they are mentioned later in the report. Avoid including technical background that readers don't need. If you write the background section late in the project, you'll know which concepts, theory, and terminology readers need help with, and you can write the section accordingly.

In this report on voice-recognition software, it might not be a bad idea to discuss some theory: important aspects of human speech, techniques for sampling and recognizing speech, training methods used to accustom software to an individual's voice, and so on. Without this background, readers may have trouble understanding the comparative discussion. However, write this background after the comparison so that you focus strictly on background necessary for understanding the comparisons.

8. **Plan and write the point-by-point comparisons.** If you've done everything up to this point, you are ready to compare the options against the requirements and determine the best choice. The essential element, the heart of this type of report, is the comparison section. The point-by-point approach is critical in providing a systematic presentation of the strengths and weaknesses of the options being compared. (In the voice-recognition report at the end of this chapter, the heading "Points of Comparison" introduces the comparison.) To write an individual comparative section, be sure to do at least the following:

■ Begin by stating the point of comparison and the related requirement.
■ Compare and contrast the relevant details of each option related to the point of comparison. If one option is significantly less expensive, discuss reasons why that might be so. Explain whether the differences are significant.
■ State which is the best option for the point of comparison. State this conclusion overtly; don't leave it to readers to figure out, no matter how obvious it may seem.

In the comparisons section of this recommendation report, compare the software products by their accuracy, speed, ease of use, cost, and so on. In the processing speed comparison, state how fast each product can process human speech. Consider factors that might distort those speeds; for example, discuss whether one product takes more processing time but achieves greater accuracy. After this discussion, state a conclusion as to which product has the best speed. Qualify that statement if other factors make a difference. Follow this same pattern in each of the other comparative sections.

9. **Create a summary of conclusions.** Once you've finished the comparisons, copy the conclusions into a separate list of conclusions. Review these conclusions, apply the requirements and priorities you established earlier, and determine the overall best candidate. If you can't pick a winner, you may have to redefine your requirements and priorities. The list of conclusions is important for readers: they can scan it for the key facts and conclusions. (In the voice-recognition report at the end of this chapter, the conclusions summary is introduced by the heading "Executive Summary.") In a list of conclusions, state the following:

■ State the important *primary conclusions*, those that you reach in each of the comparative sections. For example, one option may be the least expensive; another may have the highest ease-of-use rating. These are primary conclusions.
■ Also state *secondary conclusions*, those that apply the readers' requirements and priorities to conflicting primary conclusions. Primary conclusions "conflict" when they point to different options as the best choice. One option may be the cheapest; another may be the easiest to use. What to do? Ideally, you've defined a priority that will help you decide.
■ And last, state a *final conclusion*—that is, which option is the best choice based on the requirements and priorities. Remember that although an option may be the best choice, it may not necessarily be the one that you would recommend. One option may be the "best" among the options compared, but it might meet so few of the requirements that you could not recommend it.

Practical Ethics: Trusty Numbers

 Take out your driver's licence and notice all the numbers on it. Besides the official licence number, there's your birth date, address, and height. These numbers are obviously concrete—either you stand 155 cm or you don't. Not all numbers are so easily established. In fact, when it comes to using numbers for advertising or conveying data, numbers can be manipulated to appear more informative and credible than they actually are. Take a look at the following claims and try to determine what might be wrong with them.

"9 out of 10 dentists surveyed prefer Granite brand toothpaste."

"Our herbal supplement improves memory by 14 percent."

"This modem speeds up Internet connections by 16.13 percent."

So what's wrong with these claims? Perhaps nothing. But then again, maybe they've been treated to a sleight-of-hand in order to convey something that isn't true.

For instance, it's important to know the context of any survey. If an independent organization surveyed 3,000 randomly selected dentists, had a 90 percent response rate, and found that 9 out of 10 preferred Granite toothpaste, the claim is credible. But if the Granite Corporation sent out 100 questionnaires to which only 10 dentists responded, then its claim is questionable at best.

The problem with the herbal supplement claim is that memory is a difficult thing to measure. Before you believe the claim, what questions would you want answered? For starters, how was memory improvement tested? What other factors were considered? Who conducted the research? Has the scientific community established a credible way to test memory? Is it possible to quantify memory improvement with a percentage? It can be misleading and even unethical to use precise numbers for something that is not really quantifiable.

Then there's the modem claim. The fact that two digits are used after the period in 16.13 percent indicates a high degree of accuracy and impressive performance. This is not problematic unless the speed can be measured only within ±2 percent.

Being an informed consumer means recognizing suspicious numbers. Being an ethical communicator means that the numbers you offer your audience will be trustworthy; they must be presented within their proper context, used to define something quantifiable, and applied accurately.

In the conclusions section for this recommendation report, repeat the key conclusions occurring in the comparison section; for example, which product had the best processing speed and best accuracy, was the least expensive, and so on. Those are the primary conclusions, as discussed earlier. Next, develop the secondary conclusions, indicating that you value the product with the best accuracy as opposed to the one with the lowest price. End with the final conclusion; that is, which voice-recognition software product is the best of the ones compared. Remember that this final conclusion is not necessarily a recommendation. Voice-recognition technology may not be mature enough to provide any real advantage for your readers.

10. **Create a summary table.** For most reports of this type, it helps to include a *summary table*, which is a table that summarizes all the key comparative information about the options. See the summary table in the voice-recognition report at the end of this chapter. Also, see Chapter 10, which discusses the basics of table design. Providing the summary table gives readers a different view of the same information

presented in regular paragraph form; it's another way of ensuring that readers get your message.

In this voice-recognition software report, design a table with rows for the four software applications compared and columns for the comparisons. One column might be for cost; another for requirements; another for ease-of-use ratings; another for accuracy; and so on. This design enables readers to compare vertically.

11. **Write the recommendation section.** Although it may seem totally obvious, you must state your recommendation and the main conclusions that support that recommendation in a separate section of the report. Introduce the recommendation with a readily identifiable heading so that readers can find it as soon as they open your report.

In the report on voice-recognition software, you can state which software product you recommend and then review the three or four most important reasons why. These reasons will summarize the most important conclusions. Consider writing a conditional recommendation: for example, if the readers expect to use the software often for critical projects, they should purchase the most powerful software (which is also the most expensive). If not, they should purchase the less expensive product.

12. **Format the list of information sources.** As with any professional writing project, indicate the sources of information you used to develop this report. Include not only printed sources (including product brochures) but Internet sources and informal, unpublished sources such as interviews. List them at the end of the report.

The information sources for this voice-recognition software report include the individuals you interviewed at the client's location, current users of the software, product specifications and brochures, manufacturers' sales representatives, magazine articles, and books on voice-recognition technology in general.

13. **Create any necessary appendixes.** Create an appendix for such things as information sources, large tables, large illustrations, or any other useful information that doesn't fit in the main text. In fact, you can move your background, descriptions, and comparisons to appendixes. That way, readers will see your conclusions and recommendations as soon as they open your report. (This approach is known as the "executive format" and is illustrated in the example recommendation report at the end of this chapter.)

In this example, you could include product specifications and brochures in one appendix, full-length examples of transcriptions in another, and detailed technical background in still another.

14. **Write an introduction.** Save your recommendation report's introduction to write when you are finished with the rest of the report. An

introduction is like a road map, and the process of writing is like finding your way—you can't create the road map until you've found your way. When you write the introduction, remember to indicate the topic, the purpose, and the intended readers—stating individuals' names or organization names, or both. Review the intended readers' needs for the information as well as their knowledge and background.

For the introduction, nothing is wrong with a straightforward, businesslike approach stating that the following is a report on voice-recognition software for medical transcription. For background, mention that this technology has advanced far enough that it now offers affordable recognition with reasonable accuracy. Perhaps mention that medical transcription is one field that needs such a solution. Continue by indicating the organization that commissioned the report, and indicate the purpose of the report. Include a quick in-sentence list of the report's contents: requirements, technical background, comparisons, conclusions, and recommendations.

15. **Consider the format.** Chapter 14 shows that you can design a recommendation report as a memorandum, a business letter, or a separate document with a cover memo or letter. The recommendation report on voice-recognition software at the end of this chapter is a separate document with a cover business letter.

Make this recommendation report a formal report with a transmittal letter attached to the front. It contains enough pages that the business-letter format won't work.

16. **Review and revise your rough draft.** Use the strategies in Chapter 16 to systematically review and revise your recommendation report. Use the top-down approach described in that chapter: start by reviewing audience, purpose, and situation; then move on to content, organization, and transitions; then headings, lists, tables, and graphics; then sentence style and technical style; and finally, grammar, usage, spelling, and punctuation problems.

HOW DO YOU WRITE FEASIBILITY AND EVALUATION REPORTS?

If you studied the preceding sections on how to structure a point-by-point comparison and how to develop a recommendation report, you already know how to write feasibility and evaluation reports. In these types of reports, you use comparison just as much as you do in recommendation reports.

Feasibility Reports

As explained earlier, a feasibility report tries to forecast whether a program or project will be feasible. *Feasibility*, in this context, focuses on whether a program or project is possible, practical, or both:

■ *Technical feasibility*. Does the voice-recognition software really work? Does it give us the advantages we need or solve our problem? Will it really save substantial time, money, and headaches?
■ *Financial feasibility*. Can we afford the software? Will it pay for itself in the proper amount of time? Are the advantages it brings worth the expense?
■ *Social feasibility*. Will employees use the software? A better example in this case might be a municipal recycling program. Will people participate?
■ *Administrative feasibility*. Is the idea legal? Does it conflict with existing regulations? Is there administrative capacity to handle it?

Obviously, individual feasibility studies needn't cover all these categories. For a feasibility report on whether a provincial ministry should use voice-recognition software, we must show whether it really works, provides significant advantages, is easy to learn and use, and is affordable. A feasibility report looks to the future and attempts to project whether an idea will work. Logically, the feasibility report precedes the recommendation report. A feasibility report tells us whether the plan will work and meet the needs. A recommendation report shows which option best meets the needs. (In everyday practice, these two kinds of reports are often combined and may be called practically anything—even proposals.)

If you understand point-by-point comparison, you know how to structure a feasibility report: compare aspects of the program or project category by category against the requirements. If it meets enough of the requirements, the right requirements, or the right combination of requirements, it's feasible.

Evaluation Reports

Whereas feasibility reports attempt to tell the future—will the program or project work?—evaluation reports study existing programs or projects to determine whether they are working. Requirements are essential for both types of reports. A feasibility report determines whether a program or project *will* meet a set of requirements. An evaluation report determines whether a program or project *is* meeting its requirements.

WORKSHOP: COMPARISON AND RECOMMENDATION REPORTS

Here are some additional ideas for practising the concepts, tools, and strategies in this chapter:

1. *Points of comparison.* To ensure that you understand the idea of point-by-point comparison, develop at least four points of comparison for one or more of the following topics:

Internet service providers	Cordless or cellular phones	Collies and Irish setters
Minivans (for the family)	Garden irrigation systems	Shampoos and conditioners
Lawn sprinklers	Tomato varieties	Microwave ovens

2. *Recommendation, evaluation, and feasibility reports.* To ensure that you understand recommendation, evaluation, and feasibility reports, develop a project for each type of report using one or more of the following topics:

Cellular phones for employees	Speech-recognition software for visually impaired employees
Underground lawn irrigation systems	Software for correcting usage and punctuation errors for case-worker staff
Notebook computers for all seventh graders	Electric vehicles for college maintenance and security
Home-schooling using the Internet	Tax incentives for installing devices that save on utilities (water, wastewater, gas, electricity)
Solar power for a residence	
Program for free city-bus riding	

3. *Automobile recommendation.* Imagine that you are going to write a recommendation report on automobiles for people just like you. What would you use as your points of comparison? What would your requirements and priorities be?

4. *Feasibility of a new technology.* Think of some new or emerging technology, and imagine that you must write a feasibility report on it for some local government or business organization. How will you determine its feasibility in technological, social, administrative, or other terms?

5. *Evaluation of a program.* Think of a program that is currently running in local or regional government; for example, free bus service or city-wide recycling. Imagine that you have been hired to evaluate that program and write a report containing your findings and conclusions. What would you use as your requirements? How will you decide whether the program is working?

COMPARISON

Notice that the introduction makes it sound like this comparison occurs within a larger report. The topic of that report is most likely NASA plans for a manned mission to Mars.

Introduction and overview: Notice the strong overview sentence occurring in the introduction. It isn't exactly the style of writing you'd find in *People* magazine, but it gets the job done. People need to know what they are about to read—a road map of the topics about to be discussed.

Illustration: Notice that this illustration does not have a title. Because its content is obvious and because this is a short document, no title is needed.

Abbreviations: Notice in these paragraphs that abbreviations that do not spell a word are not punctuated with a period. Notice too that they are not written against the number they modify (written "solid"). Thus, you'd say that the polar radius of Mars is 3,375 km (not 3,375km).

Point-by-point comparison method: Notice that this comparison does not have one big paragraph on Mars followed by another big paragraph on Earth. Instead the two planets are compared point by point: size, radius, orbit, length of year, temperature, atmosphere, length of day, and so on.

Table discussion: Notice how the second paragraph repeats some of the detail in the first table. This kind of repetition is common and acceptable: you give readers two views of important information— one in the form of a table, another in regular text.

Dual measurement style: Notice the standard presentation of measurements: the first is in standard international metric and the second, in parentheses, is in imperial.

Comparison: Mars and Earth

Any manned expedition to Mars must take into account the basic features of the planet *in comparison with* those of Earth. The following compares the two planets according to size, density, orbits, distances from the Sun, climate, atmosphere, and seasons.

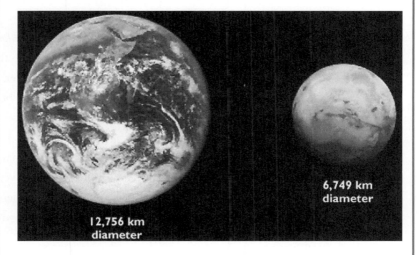

12,756 km diameter

6,749 km diameter

Size. Mars is *smaller than* Earth in terms of its mass, volume, and equatorial radius. Mars is *just over half* the size of Earth, its equatorial radius being 3,397 km to Earth's 6,379 km. Because it is approximately one-and-a-half times *farther from* the Sun, the martian orbit is *longer than* Earth's and Mars is *cooler than* Earth. The martian year is 687 Earth days.

Temperature and atmosphere. The surface temperature on Mars is from −17° C (1° F) to −107° C (−178° F), although temperatures can reach as high as 27° C (81° F) and as low as −143° C (−225° F). The atmosphere of Mars is composed chiefly of carbon dioxide (95.3%), nitrogen (2.7%), and argon (1.6%). The atmospheric pressure is *less than* 1/100th that of Earth, as shown in the following table:

Capitalization: Notice that not only Mars but Earth and Sun are capitalized. When the context is planets and astronomy in general, you capitalize names of all the "heavenly bodies."

	Mars	Earth	Ratio (Mars/Earth)
Mass (1,024 kg)	0.6419	5.9736	0.107
Volume (1,010 km³)	16.318	108.321	0.151
Equatorial radius (km)	3397	6378	0.533
Polar radius (km)	3375	6356	0.531
Mean density (kg/m³)	3933	5520	0.713
Surface gravity (m/s²)	3.69	9.78	0.377

Headings: This comparison uses third-level headings to indicate the start of each new comparative point. (See Chapter 7 for more on headings.)

Transitions: Comparisons need a lot of transition words, such as those highlighted in this example.

Orbit and seasons. Mars has seasons *similar to* those of Earth. The tilt of its rotational axis (axial inclination) to the plane of its orbit about the Sun is *about the same as* Earth's. However, *unlike* Earth, the strongly elliptical shape (eccentricity) of Mars's orbit means that the seasons on Mars are also affected by varying distances from the Sun. Because of Earth's almost circular orbit, our seasons result simply from the tilt of the Earth's rotational axis. *In contrast*, martian seasons are *about double the length* of those on Earth. However, a day on Mars is *roughly the same* length as a day on Earth: 24 hours, 37 minutes, and 23 seconds—or 1.026 Earth days, as shown in the following table:

Column alignment in tables: Notice the alignment in these tables: numerical data is right (or decimal) aligned and then centred within the column. Textual data is left aligned. (For more on tables, see Chapter 10.)

Footnotes in tables: Notice the use of explanatory footnotes in this table. You could put this information in the column headings with Earth and Mars, but that would balloon those two cells and create an awkward table.

Seasons	Earth[1]	Mars[2]
Spring	93	171
Summer	94	199
Fall	89	171
Winter	89	146

[1] Measured in terms of the Northern Hemisphere.
[2] Measured in terms of Earth days.

RECOMMENDATION REPORT

Voice-Recognition Software: Recommendations for Medical Transcriptionists

Executive Summary

From business, medical, and legal perspectives, the creation and maintenance of accurate, complete records are crucial. The primary downside to such thorough record-keeping includes: (1) the time required for dictation, (2) the costs in finding and hiring a competent medical transcriptionist, (3) the necessary delays between dictation and actual availability of the transcribed records, and (4) the time needed to proof and correct the transcriptionist's output.

Conclusions

To date, the weakest link in speech-recognition technology has been accuracy. This technology is rapidly advancing, and current software has significantly improved within the last year. Can a voice-recognition software program eliminate some of the problems occurring in conventional medical transcription? The following conclusions, along with the recommendation that follows, will help answer this question:

1. All of the programs specify system requirements that are well within the parameters of existing computer systems.
2. All of the programs integrate with Microsoft Word 97.
3. All of the programs can be installed by the average user with reasonable ease.
4. Dragon Systems' NaturallySpeaking Medical Suite is by far the most expensive voice-recognition program. Whereas it is $1,243, including one year of technical support, the other three programs are all under $200, exclusive of support.
5. Philips does not include a microphone with its software as do the other three software companies, but purchasing a microphone does not increase the total cost appreciably. Dragon Systems' microphone

Recommendation report: This report compares various voice-recognition software applications on the market and then recommends one over the others. Notice that it is not a feasibility report: it does not consider the overall practicality and effectiveness of this software.

Executive report design: Notice that this report starts with an executive summary made up of the key conclusions and recommendations. The background on voice-recognition software and product comparisons are considered appendixes, available if the executive readers want to read that detail. (This report would be bound and have a transmittal letter attached to the front cover. See Chapter 14 for more on report design.)

Primary conclusions: The first eight conclusions repeat what is stated in the product comparisons (in the appendixes). In fact, these conclusions are in the same order as the sections in which they are stated.

Secondary conclusions: With the primary conclusions stated, this writer moves on to the business of weighing cost against performance. One would expect more secondary conclusions here. For example, the writer could state that FreeSpeech98, despite its low cost, would simply be of no use in the environment the writer is considering.

Recommendation: In the "Conclusions" section, the writer has not made a recommendation; all she has done is reach a conclusion as to the best product of the four compared. In this "Recommendation" section, the writer puts her professional standing on the line by recommending one of the products.

Page break: Notice that the executive summary ends with a full page break to mark the boundary between it and the appendixes.

is considered more usable than the other microphones tested by *PC Magazine*.

6. Dragon Systems' NaturallySpeaking has accumulated a lengthy list of awards; no awards were found for the other three programs.

7. Dragon Systems' NaturallySpeaking Medical Suite with Add-On Vocabularies is easily customizable for most practices' needs for specialized medical vocabularies and medical forms.

8. Dragon Systems' NaturallySpeaking technology is the most accurate of the four programs tested.

9. Although Dragon Systems' NaturallySpeaking is considerably more expensive, its accuracy, speed, ease of use, and flexibility justify the extra expense.

Recommendation

Dragon Systems' NaturallySpeaking Medical Suite is strongly recommended for its superior accuracy, powerful customization features, and industry recognition and awards. No other product comes close, and its strong advantages justify its considerably higher price. Once the program has been customized, and the user has dictated for several weeks and become familiar with the software, acceptably accurate transcription and instantly available medical records should be possible with NaturallySpeaking Medical Suite, solving some of the record-keeping problems faced by most medical practices.

Introduction: When you write the introduction, be sure to identify the situation, indicate the purpose, and provide an overview of what's to come, as this introduction does.

Background: This report rightly includes background on voice-recognition software. At the time this report was written, people did not know much about this technology. Also, this background section introduces key concepts and terminology to be used in the rest of the report.

Documentation: The bracketed numbers are citations of borrowed information. Go to the end of this report to see what source number 11 is. This style of indicating the source of borrowed information is the "number system." Variations of it are used in the Council of Biology Editors and Institute of Electrical and Electronics Engineers (IEEE) styles.

Voice-Recognition Software: Appendixes

With the recent, widely advertised breakthroughs in voice-recognition software, many medical practices are considering its use for their transcription work. The expense, error rate, and record-completion delays associated with conventional transcription work have stimulated a search for better ways of accomplishing these essential record-keeping tasks. The following report reviews the capabilities and requirements of this new software and makes recommendations as to the best voice-recognition software on the market.

Several voice-recognition products currently exist in the marketplace, and viable choices are greater in number than they were only a few years ago. Rapid changes have been fuelled by the ever-increasing power and plummeting prices of desktop systems. Though room for improvement still exists, accuracy has advanced tremendously in a stunningly short time.

Voice-Recognition Software: Background
The first software-only dictation product for personal computers, Dragon Systems' DragonDictate for Windows 1.0, using discrete speech recognition technology, was released in 1994. Discrete speech is a slow, unnatural means of dictation, requiring a pause after each and every word [11].

Two years later, IBM introduced the first continuous speech recognition software, its MedSpeak/Radiology. These systems had five-figure price tags and required expensive personal computers. Continuous speech technology allows its users to speak naturally and conversationally, relieving much of the tedium of discrete speech dictation [11].

Power devourers. With all of the complex selections and tremendous flexibility demanded of voice-recognition software, it is small wonder that considerable computer muscle is required to run these programs. To take fullest advantage of current speech-recognition programs, a personal computer with a minimum of a 300-MHz Pentium II processor is recommended. A separate 16-bit SoundBlaster-compatible card is also advisable because the sound cards that are bundled as part of a personal computer's motherboard can produce inferior results with voice-recognition software [4].

Realistic reminders. Voice-recognition technology has advanced impressively over the last year, with programs variously offering smarter speech-recognition engines, larger active vocabularies, integration with the most popular word-processing programs, and improved accuracy. This report sorts through these features to find the most accurate program and the best value available and to determine if the accuracy supplied is acceptable at this time [4]. It is essential to remember the following:

- While voice-recognition software has made enormous strides, it is not perfect. Dictated records, particularly in the first few weeks of use, must be sufficiently proofed while on-screen.
- Because medical and legal requirements for obstetric and gynecologic records are exacting and extensive, considerable dictation is required. Dictation using voice-recognition software is like many other things: practice makes all the difference. Tests by PC Magazine Labs showed that increased experience with dictation and with the software significantly increased accuracy [3].
- Be prepared to invest a few weeks of dictation time and practice with the software in order to see enhanced accuracy.

Stringent demands. Much is demanded of speech-recognition programs. Accuracy is critical and speed is essential to any effective program. Added to these challenges is the enormous variation that exists among individual human speech patterns, pitch, rate, and inflection. These variations are an extraordinary test of the flexibility of any program. Voice recognition follows these steps:

1. Spoken words enter a microphone.
2. Audio is processed by the computer's sound card.

Numbered list: All of the preceding lists have been bulleted because the items were in no required order. Here, the items are in a required order—specifically, the sequence of phases by which voice-recognition software processes human speech. (For more on lists, see Chapter 8.)

3. The software discriminates between lower-frequency vowels and higher-frequency consonants and compares the results with phonemes, the smallest building blocks of speech. The software then compares results to groups of phonemes, and then to actual words, determining the most likely match.

   Contextual information is simultaneously processed in order to more accurately predict words that are most likely to be used next, such as the correct choice out of a selection of homonyms such as merry, marry, and Mary.

4. Selected words are arranged in the most probable sentence combinations.

5. The sentence is transferred to a word-processing application [11].

Voice-Recognition Software Requirements

Based on stated preferences and system specifications, the following requirements have been established for this study:

- Because the goal is to save time and effort while enhancing results and decreasing the salary overhead incurred with a medical transcriptionist, continuous speech recognition software is preferred, rather than the slower, more unnatural and lower-priced discrete speech recognition software also on the market.
- The application must run on a Pentium-powered personal computer using Windows 95 and be capable of integration with Microsoft Word 97.
- The software program must be easily and successfully installed by any intermediate-level computer user in the office.
- The program must be one that can be learned and customized reasonably quickly by nearly anyone in the office.
- The cost limit is $1,500.

Points of Comparison

The voice-recognition software programs compared are Dragon Systems' NaturallySpeaking 3.0 Preferred Edition, IBM ViaVoice 98 Executive, L&H Voice Xpress Plus, and Philips FreeSpeech98. Discussion of Dragon Systems' NaturallySpeaking will also include its Medical Suite.

Bulleted lists: Notice how often this writer uses bullets in this report. To emphasize the study's requirements, she creates five bullets. Notice also that this, as well as every other list in this report, is introduced by a lead-in punctuated with a colon.

In-sentence list overview: The points of comparison are listed here using an "in-sentence" list. The third-level headings that follow are in the same order as the items in this list. Notice the format: the lead-in is a complete sentence and is punctuated with a colon, both opening and closing parentheses are used, and semi-colons are used between the items because the items have their own internal commas. See Chapter 8 for more on lists.

Point-by-point comparisons: Typically, the best way to approach a recommendation report is to use comparison, and the best way to structure a comparison is the point-by-point approach. The points of comparison here include microphones, accuracy, cost, and so on. It would not work well to have separate sections on the Dragon System, the ViaVoice, the Voice Xpress, and the FreeSpeech in which all details for each option were discussed.

Italics for magazine and journal names: It's standard to italicize the names of magazines and to put the articles within those magazines in quotation marks.

Eight categories of comparison will be made in order to effectively evaluate these competing programs: (1) accuracy; (2) minimum system requirements; (3) capacity to manage a specialized medical vocabulary and medical records; (4) integration with Microsoft Word; (5) ease and speed of installation, customization, and use; (6) industry ratings and awards; (7) inclusion of microphones; and (8) cost.

Industry ratings and awards. Only one of these products refers to and lists awards on its website: Dragon Systems' NaturallySpeaking. None of the other three products has any such mention anywhere on its site, nor do any awards or industry recognition show up on multiple Web searches for the products. Dragon Systems' website lists over fifty awards, some of which are listed here:

- "Editors' Choice," *PC Magazine*, October 1998; this particular article is referenced several times in this report [1,7].
- "The 12 Best PC Products on the Planet: Input Device Category." *PC/Computing: Time Capsule*, August 1998 [7].
- "World Class Award: Best Voice Recognition Software." *PC World*, June 1998 [7].
- "The Best New Products/Software." *BusinessWeek*, January 1998 [7].
- "The Best of 1997/Cybertech." *Time Magazine*, January 1998 [7].
- "5 Star Rating." *PC/Computing*, November 1997 [7].

While industry recognition and journalistic evaluations are not the only considerations, Dragon Systems boasts an impressive list of awards and ratings by prestigious periodicals.

Inclusion of microphones. As previously noted, a microphone is necessary for the capture of spoken words. Here's how the products compare:

- Dragon Systems ships with a XVI Parrott 10-3 microphone; *PC Magazine* notes that it is usable, comfortable, and performs well [5].

- IBM's ViaVoice and L&H Voice Xpress Plus both provide an Andrea NC-80 microphone, which *PC Magazine* states is not as comfortable as the XVI Parrott 10-3 [5].
- Philips FreeSpeech98 does not include a microphone; it recommends its own SpeechMike at an extra cost of $69.95 [5].

None of these are make-or-break details, but Dragon Systems has a slight edge in the reviews provided by *PC Magazine*.

Dragon Systems made an enormous stride in June 1997, when it released NaturallySpeaking, the first general-purpose, continuous speech software program. Much more affordable than earlier programs, it brought the realm of continuous speech recognition to a much wider range of users. Two months later, IBM released its competing continuous speech software, ViaVoice [10].

Accuracy. Accuracy is the most significant consideration; without it, any program is useless. Dragon Systems' NaturallySpeaking scored highest on all of the accuracy tests performed by *PC Magazine* and was unequivocally selected as the Editors' Choice. In these tests, the average accuracy was 91% and at times was considerably greater [1].

Average accuracy for L&H Voice Xpress was 87% [2]. Accuracy for IBM's ViaVoice tested at 85% [14], and Philips FreeSpeech98 was 80% [15].

At first glance, these percentages, particularly the top two, may not seem significantly different. Consider, however, that for every 1,000 words, an accuracy rate of 87% means that 130 words must be corrected. An accuracy rate of 91% represents an average of 90 errors per 1,000 words, while an 80% rate means that 200 out of every 1,000 words must be corrected.

Thousands of words are dictated daily in this industry. Time is scarce and precious. Medicolegal conditions mandate that records must be

Pronouns and corporate nouns: Notice the use of "it" to refer to "Dragon Systems." Our tendency is to use "they," which creates a pronoun-reference problem. Another, more striking example of this problem is to refer to "IBM" as "they," "them," or "their."

Discussion of the comparative data: Notice that the writer doesn't merely throw out the numbers and move on. She explains how differences of 4 or 5 percentage points have a great impact on the effectiveness of this software.

Individual conclusion: Notice the overtly stated conclusion here at the end of the section on accuracy, even though it's obvious from the numbers above. State these conclusions even if they seem totally obvious to you.

Tables: Notice the design of this table:

Instead of dragging all this information through the regular text, the writer presents it far more economically in the form of a table.

- The table title spans all columns, and the source of the table is indicated in brackets at the end of the title.

- The column headings occur in the first row and are italicized.

- The column headings and the cells are left aligned. To some book designers, the columns for RAM and hard disk look bad. They'd prefer centring those columns under the headings. However, left alignment is common in table design, and it's certainly easier!

- This table is structured for vertical comparison, which is preferable according to conventional table-design wisdom. You scan downward to see how the products compare in terms of RAM requirements. However, if you had eight or more comparative categories, the table would fit better on the page if the four products acted as columns—in other words, turning the table 90 degrees.

exhaustively thorough and accurate. Under these rigorous circumstances, every percentage point counts, and Dragon Systems' NaturallySpeaking yields the highest accuracy.

Minimum system requirements. All four programs run on Pentium-powered personal computers utilizing Windows 95, 98 or NT 4.0 and require 16-bit SoundBlaster-compatible sound cards. Random access memory (RAM) requirements for software running under Windows NT are higher for all of these programs [5]. However, only the RAM required for Windows 95 is listed in the table below, as it is the operating system used in most practices. It is important to recall that, as noted earlier, significantly greater system resources are recommended to optimize performance. Given the sufficient system resources, none of these software programs should present a problem for existing systems.

Comparison of Minimum System Requirements [5]

Software	*CPU*	*RAM (MB)*	*Hard Disk (MB)*	*L2 Cache*
Dragon	Pentium/133MHz	32	180	None
ViaVoice	Pentium/166MHz	40	180	256 KB
L&H	Pentium/166MHz	32	130	None
Philips	Pentium/166MHz	32	150	None

Capacity to manage a customizable, specialized medical vocabulary. Medicine in general, and each medical specialty in particular, has its own complex, specialized vocabulary, and the ability to manage that vocabulary is critical:

- Dragon Systems' NaturallySpeaking offers a so-called Medical Suite targeted to medical professionals and specified as an alternative to transcription. Marketing materials state that an extensive vocabulary of thousands of words, including medical procedures, terms, drugs, diagnoses, and symptoms, is included. The software allows creation of multiple vocabularies for specialty customization, if desired [8].

- IBM offers add-on VoiceType Vocabularies for use with ViaVoice. The medical vocabularies available are for Emergency Medicine Dictation and Radiology Dictation. No other specialty customization is available [13].

- L&H Voice Xpress and Philips FreeSpeech98 do not offer medical vocabularies, either as add-ons or bundled with the software [9,12].

Two of the four companies offer a product that provides medical terminology. IBM's emergency room and radiology add-on software is not applicable to the dictation needs of obstetric and gynecologic practices. Dragon Systems' NaturallySpeaking Medical Suite offers the same voice recognition technology as the previously mentioned NaturallySpeaking Preferred Edition, with the addition of extensive customizable medical terminology that can be tailored to specialty practices.

Integration with Microsoft Word. All four programs integrate with Word 97 and can therefore be used with existing word-processing software [5].

Ease and speed of installation, customization, and use. Each of the four programs uses "wizards" to install and configure hardware, and all programs support macros for frequently used phrases:

- Dragon Systems' NaturallySpeaking uses its wizard to "train" the system to recognize the user's voice within 4 minutes. Material is provided so that about 30 minutes of reading aloud will improve accuracy [5]. Electronic medical documents can be analyzed automatically to "learn" new specialized terms and proper names. Its CommandWizard feature enables any user to create medical-specialty macros. Commonly used and required medical forms, electronically stored, can be called up readily with the user being prompted to fill out each section of a form [8].
- IBM's ViaVoice also trains the system by means of reading from selected texts for about 30 minutes, and its wizard adjusts microphone and speaker volume levels [5].
- L&H Voice Xpress Plus directs the user to read chapters of a book, and in *PC Magazine's* tests, about 75 minutes was required for the process [5].

Quotation marks: The word "wizards" is in quotation marks because, at the time this report was written, this was a strange usage. The same is the case for the word "train." It's an odd and unfamiliar idea to think of "training" a software product.

- Philips FreeSpeech98 directs the user to read selected text for about 15 minutes; ten training topics are available for the user's review [15].

Installation of all of the programs appears straightforward, and the initial basic "training" is not excessively time consuming for any of the products. Although all provide macros, the medical customization features of Dragon Systems' product are considerably greater. Though they will initially require more time and document input, accuracy is increased, and for this reason, Dragon's software is recommended in this comparison.

Cost. Highly significant price differences exist among these programs:

- The Dragon Systems' NaturallySpeaking Preferred Edition tested by *PC Magazine*, October 1998, retails for $179 when purchased directly from Dragon or through resellers. However, NaturallySpeaking Medical Suite, preferable for medical practices, is $995. An add-on Medical Specialty Vocabulary is available for $49. One year of 800-number telephone support for all products is an additional $199, for a total cost of $1,243, exclusive of tax and shipping costs, for the Medical Suite [6].
- IBM's ViaVoice 98 Executive software program costs $150, and the medical specialty add-ons are $240. However, because these add-ons are for emergency medicine and radiology, they are of no use to many practices [13].
- L&H Voice Xpress Plus is $70 [5].
- Philips Free Speech98 costs $39 and does not include a microphone. A Philips SpeechMike can be ordered for $69.95, for a total cost of $108.95, exclusive of tax and shipping costs [5].

L&H offers the best price by far. IBM and Philips are roughly in the same ballpark. Dragon Systems' Preferred Edition is more expensive at $200, but not significantly so. The only medical software program customizable to a wide range of practices is Dragon Systems' Medical Suite, which, at $1,243, is over ten times the cost of Philips' software, though it includes one year of technical support.

References: This section lists all the information sources this writer directly drew on to create this report. The format of this list is the number system; it loosely follows CBE style. Although the references are alphabetized here, in some styles you list them in order of their first occurrence in the text.

Publication and access dates: Notice that both the date these Web pages were published and the date this writer accessed them are shown. When you cite Internet sources of information, cite the date of publication that you find on the source. Typically, Web pages have a publication date somewhere, often at the bottom. Also, you must indicate the date you accessed the source, as is done here.

No author: If you cannot find an author name, you can use the organization name, as is done here with Berkeley Voice Solutions and Dragon Systems. If it doesn't even have an organization name, use the title of the page.

Italics and quotation marks: Notice that the names of magazines are italicized and the titles of articles are in quotation marks.

References

All references are found online.

1. Alwang, Greg. "Editors' Choice." *PC Magazine Online*. October 20, 1998. http://www.zdnet.com/pcmag/features/speech98/edchoice.html Accessed 23 October 1998.
2. Alwang, Greg. "L&H Voice Xpress Plus 1.01." *PC Magazine Online*. October 20, 1998. http://www.zdnet.com/pcmag/features/speech98/rev3.html Accessed 23 October 1998.
3. Alwang, Greg. "Performance Tests." *PC Magazine Online*. October 20, 1998. http://www.zdnet.com/pcmag/features/speech98/perftest.html Accessed 23 October 1998.
4. Alwang, Greg. "Speech Recognition: Finding Its Voice." *ZDNN*. October 2, 1998. http://www.zdnet.com/zdnn/stories/zdnn_display/0,3440,350879,00.html Accessed 23 October 1998.
5. Alwang, Greg. "Summary of Features." *PC Magazine Online*. October 20, 1998. http://www.zdnet.com/pcmag/features/speech98/features.html Accessed 23 October 1998.
6. Berkeley Voice Solutions. "Products and Services." http://www.pcvoice.com/products.html Accessed 21 October 1998.
7. Dragon Systems, Inc. "Dragon NaturallySpeaking Awards." http://www.dragonsys.com/news/awards.html Accessed 21 October 1998.
8. Dragon Systems, Inc. "Dragon NaturallySpeaking Medical Suite." http://www.dragonsys.com/products/medical.html Accessed 21 October 1998.
9. Lernout & Hauspie. "L&H Online Store." http://www.storefront.zbr.com/LHS-store Accessed 21 October 1998.
10. Munro, Jay. "Speech Technology Timeline." *PC Magazine Online*. March 10, 1998. http://www.zdnet.com/pcmag/features/speech/sb1.html Accessed 23 October 1998.
11. Munro, Jay. "Watch What You Say." *PC Magazine Online*. March 10, 1998. http://www.zdnet.com/pcmag/features/speech/intro1.html Accessed 23 October 1998.
12. Philips. "Philips Speech Processing." http://www.speech.be.philips.com Accessed 21 October 1998.
13. Provantage. "IBM VoiceType Dictation Vocabularies." http://www.provantage.com/FP_09907.htm Accessed 21 October 1998.
14. Stinson, Craig. "IBM ViaVoice 98 Executive." *PC Magazine Online*. October 20, 1998. http://www.zdnet.com/pcmag/features/speech98/rev2.html Accessed 23 October 1998.
15. Stinson, Craig. "Philips FreeSpeech98 " *PC Magazine Online*. October 20, 1998. http://www.zdnet.com/pcmag/features/speech98/rev4.html Accessed 23 October 1998.

Source: Many thanks to Dr. Pat Roach, former online technical-writing student, for writing this recommendation report and for permission to adapt it here.

CHAPTER 5

Definition and Classification: Background Reports

Topics covered in this chapter include

- nanotechnology;
- solar energy.

NANOTECHNOLOGY

There are many Canadian websites dealing with the emerging nanotechnology field. These include the following:

National Institute for Nanotechnology, University of Alberta, and National Research Council Canada
http://www.nint.ca/english.cfm

Industry Canada. Advanced Materials and Nanotechnology
http://strategis.ic.gc.ca/epic/internet/inamn-mpn.nsf/en/home

Innovation in Canada
http://www.innovation.gc.ca/gol/innovation/site.nsf/en/in02362.html

Other interesting material is available at these sites:

Ralph C. Merkle's nanotechnology site at Zyvex: "Nanotechnology"
http://www.zyvex.com/nano

NanoApex
http://www.nanoapex.com/links.php?cat=146

Ethical Issues in Nanotechnology
http://www.ethicsweb.ca/nanotechnology

SOLAR ENERGY

The Canadian government actively promotes all sorts of alternative energy programs, including solar energy and wind power, mentioned in other chapters. For a comprehensive guide to renewable energy in Canada, consider the following site: http://www.canren.gc.ca/default_en.asp.

When you have completed this chapter, you will be able to

- write synonym definitions, formal sentence definitions, and extended definitions;
- classify a subject, divide it into categories, and create a classification report;
- write a technical background report.

If you've skimmed the chapters of Part I, you know that instructions show people how to do something; recommendation reports recommend one thing over another; and proposals attempt to convince readers to approve a project.

Background reports, on the other hand, are less easy to define. They also solve real workplace problems and respond to real workplace needs. They do so by focusing on a *topic*—a subject matter—in a way that meets a specific audience's needs. Definition and classification, the two infrastructures for this chapter, are essential in writing background reports.

This chapter shows you how to write definitions and classifications and then how to use them as infrastructures for technical background reports.

Note:

- If you are new to this book, see "How Do You Use This Book?" in the Preface.
- For additional examples of the documents discussed in this chapter, see **http://www.powertools.nelson.com**.

WHAT IS A DEFINITION AND HOW DO YOU WRITE ONE?

The technical and scientific worlds are loaded with unfamiliar terminology. For all those unfamiliar words, an important tool is the definition. But defining a technical term is not always as easy as stating its synonym. Sometimes, a formal sentence definition, a full paragraph, or even an entire report may be necessary. In everyday use, definition means any sort of description or explanation. In this book, however, *definition* means the explanation of the meaning of a potentially unfamiliar word. As you can see in the following table, technical and scientific fields are loaded with such words.

Synonym Definitions

You can use a synonym—a simple, familiar word—to provide a quick on-the-spot definition of a potentially unfamiliar term. In these examples,

Field	Unfamiliar terms
Computers	Cache, bus, DRAM, binary, ASCII, file, FTP, Internet, client, server, virus, emulator, multitasking, parallel computing, relational database, terabyte.
Medicine	AIDS, HIV, pseudomonas, sickle cell anemia, asthma, hypertension, dyslexia, arthritis, PMS, schizophrenia, autism.
Economics	Recession, depression, inflation, venture capital, demand curve, amortization, M1, M2, M3, macroeconomics, microeconomics, hedging, monopoly.
Automotive technology	Drive train, disk brakes, cam, differential, fly wheel, fuel cell, power train, traction, planing, catalytic converter, desulfurization.
Agriculture	Hydroponics, organic, germplasm, floriculture, permaculture, viticulture, sustainable agriculture, desertification, terraforming.
Engineering	Stress, sheer, turbulence, intercalation compounds, optical tweezers, photonic devices, servo, composite, fibre optics, pneumatics, hydraulics, polymers.

notice how the following synonyms are introduced in parentheses or dashes, and clauses or phrases.

- One possibility of nanotechnology is "respirocytes" (artificial red blood cells) presented in an earlier issue of nanozine.com.
- Cryonics—freezing people for the future—involves replacing a human's blood and body water with chemicals to inhibit freezing damage and preserving them in liquid nitrogen (LN_2) at $-196°C$ ($-320°F$).
- An IBM research team from Zurich, Switzerland, created a fully functional abacus (an ancient device for calculation) that uses individual molecules as the "beads" for counting.
- The positional assembly required by nanotechnology requires molecular robotics—that is, robotic devices that are molecular both in size and precision.

Formal Sentence Definitions

You can use a full sentence to provide a more formal definition of a technical term. As illustrated in the following table, the *formal sentence definition* has a particular structure: it begins with the term being defined,

Raw materials		Formal Sentence Definition
Term	nanometre	A nanometre is a measurement that equals one billionth of a metre (3–4 atoms wide).
Category	measurement	
Differentiation	equals one billionth of a metre (3–4 atoms wide)	
Term	nanite	A nanite is a nanotechnology term for the microscopic combination of microscopic motors, gears, levers, bearings, plates, sensors, and power and communication cables with powerful microscopic computers.
Category	nanotechnology term	
Differentiation	for the microscopic combination of microscopic motors, gears, levers, bearings, plates, sensors, power and communication cables with powerful microscopic computers	
Term	fractals	Fractals are geometric figures, just like rectangles, circles, and squares, possessing special properties that Euclidean geometrical figures do not have.
Category	geometric figures	
Differentiation	just like rectangles, circles, and squares, possessing special properties that Euclidean geometrical figures do not have	

locates that term in a category, and then differentiates that term from the other members of that category.

Glossaries are home turf for formal sentence definitions—or should be. Use formal sentence definitions to write glossary entries such as in the following examples:

nanometre Measurement that equals one billionth of a metre (3–4 atoms wide).

nanite Microscopic combination of microscopic motors, gears, levers, bearings, plates, sensors, and power and communication cables with powerful microscopic computers. *See also* nanotechnology.

prion Microscopic protein particle similar to a virus but lacking nucleic acid; thought to be the infectious agent responsible for certain degenerative diseases of the nervous system. *See also* virus.

```
fractals  Geometric figures, just like rectangles,
circles, and squares, possessing special properties
that Euclidean geometrical figures do not have.
```

Extended Definitions

An interesting challenge for you as a technical communicator is the *extended definition*—a definition taking up one or more paragraphs. Some technical terms simply need extra discussion because the audience or situation requires it. Terms like *artificial intelligence, World Wide Web, distance education, El Niño, global warming,* and the *Big Bang theory* all seem to need extra discussion to become fully meaningful to some readers.

Take a look at the extended definition in Figure 5-1. Notice that it is made up of description, process, cause–effect, classification, and comparison—whatever it takes to convey a full sense of the term. These are the *tools for definition*; they are listed in the table in the following pages. To get a sense of how to write an extended definition, let's walk through the important steps and follow a sample project.

1. **Find a simple project requiring an extended definition.** Think of a practical situation requiring an extended definition. In past writing courses, you may have written definitions on things like freedom, democracy, socialism, home, happiness, and other such topics. That's *not* what we want here. For the technical-writing context, the term

Formal sentence definition: Start by carefully defining nanotechnology.	Nanotechnology is molecular manufacturing or, more simply, building things one atom or molecule at a time. A nanometre is one billionth of a metre (3 to 4 atoms wide). Utilizing the well-known physical properties of atoms and molecules, nanotechnology proposes the construction of nanosize devices possessing extraordinary properties. The trick is to manipulate atoms individually and place them exactly where needed to produce the desired structure. The anticipated payoff for mastering this technology is far beyond any human accomplishment so far. Technical feasibilities include self-assembling consumer goods, computers billions of times faster, extremely novel inventions (impossible today), safe and affordable space travel, medical nanotechnology (the virtual end to illness, aging, death), no more pollution, automatic cleanup of already existing pollution, molecular food syntheses (the end of famine and starvation), access to a superior education for every child on Earth, reintroduction of many extinct plants and animals, and terraforming here and throughout the solar system.
Supplementary definition: Define unfamiliar terms in the formal definition (or any preceding text).	
Process: Explain the basics of nanotechnology by focusing on the process: how it works.	
Causes and effects: Explore the impacts that nanotechnology could have on society.	

FIGURE 5-1

Short extended-definition. Notice how this extended definition briefly characterizes the process that nanotechnologists envision and then races headlong into the visionary effects of this idea on society.

need not have to do with engineering, electronics, or computers; but it must have some specialization, substance, or practicality about it. The following sample scenario shows you one way to do that. (Having trouble thinking of a topic? See **http://www.powertools. nelson.com.**)

> Imagine you've just heard an exciting news clip on CBC about something called "nanotechnology." You know it involves building things at the molecular level and that it will somehow revolutionize the world. Checking the Internet, you find a startling amount of information about it. But can you imagine a practical situation in which an extended definition of nanotechnology would be needed? Can you imagine a real-world problem that could be solved with a document that, in part, defined this word?

2. **Define a purpose and an audience.** The next step is to decide on a purpose and an audience for this extended definition. (See Chapter 17 for strategies to use in analyzing audiences and adapting your writing to them.)

> As a nonspecialist and beginner with this topic, you cannot expect to address researchers and experts. You need a nonspecialist audience that actively seeks this information. An audience of ordinary people with a casual interest in new technology won't work! But an audience with professional, governmental, business, or commercial interests will. Scenarios—such as a legislator considering a bill to fund increased research and development in nanotechnology, an investor considering investment in a start-up venture involving nanotechnology, or an association of nanotechnologists looking for a writer to explain nanotechnology to people in the right places—can give some context for an extended definition.

3. **Research the term.** Early on in this project, you may need to do some research on the term you've chosen to define.

> If you did a search on nanotechnology, you'd find items like the ones listed in the topic box at the beginning of this chapter. You'd see that at least three individuals seem to be the pioneers: Ralph C. Merkle, K. Eric Drexler, and Richard Smalley. All have websites. Corporations like IBM and Hewlett-Packard are involved in, and have Web pages devoted to, nanotechnology. Likewise, numerous universities have Web pages showing their research involvement in this field.

4. **Write a formal sentence definition.** It's a good idea to start an extended definition with a formal sentence definition, discussed in the preceding pages of this chapter. A good formal sentence definition can set up the rest of the extended definition—elements in the formal sentence definition will probably need further discussion.

For nanotechnology, find a way to define the term in one sentence. As Figure 5-1 shows, it's a manufacturing process that builds things atom by atom. If possible, squeeze in something about how nano assemblers must be "self-replicating" in order to build objects more efficiently. Can you also jam something about the revolutionary impact of this technology into this one formal sentence definition?

5. **Choose the tools for the extended definition.** Take a careful look at your formal sentence definition. Which of the definition tools does it seem to need? Think about the term itself. Which of the definition tools are most directly related to it? Which definition tools focus most on the key aspects of the term you are trying to define? (Figure 5-2 illustrates how these definition tools can work together in the paragraphs of an extended definition.)

In this example, you must explain the *process* of nanotechnological manufacturing. You'll need *comparison* to help readers to conceptualize a nanometre: if you blew up a baseball to the size of the Earth, the atoms would be the size of grapes. A discussion of the possibilities that nanotechnology raises is a discussion of its potential *effects. Classification* might be useful for exploring the potential social effects of nanotechnology in the fields of medicine, agriculture, space travel, manufacturing, and so on. This extended definition would need to consider *problems* as well—in other words, what's holding us back from realizing those visionary possibilities—as shown in table opposite.

Introduction: word to be defined; overview of discussion to follow
Process: you might start by explaining how something that is closely related to the term you are defining works
Description: you might follow by describing something closely related to the term you are defining
Classification: if some aspect of the term divides into categories—and if discussing those categories helps readers—discuss them!
Causes and effects: you can also discuss causes, effects, or both, related to the term you are defining
Conclusion

FIGURE 5-2
Extended definition—example. This diagram illustrates just one of many possibilities for structuring an extended definition. Each term will require its own combination of definition sources and its own sequence of those sources.

Tools for Extended Definition

Select the right combination of these tools to write extended definitions.

Extended definition tool	Description
Description	Provide descriptive detail about the term being defined (size, shape, dimensions, materials, ingredients, weight, density, location, methods of attachment, etc.).
Process	Explain the steps in one or more processes related to the term being defined.
Causes	Discuss causes related to the term being defined.
Effects	Discuss consequences, results, and effects related to the term being defined.
Problems	Discuss problems related to the term being defined.
Comparisons	Compare the term being defined to related or opposite things. Explore analogies involving the term.
Categories	Discuss the categories into which the term being defined can be divided; discuss the category to which the term being defined belongs.
Applications	Discuss the real-world uses of some aspect of the term you are defining.
Benefits, advantages	Discuss any benefits or advantages that are associated with the term you are defining.

6. **Plan and develop graphics.** In the early stages of this project, try to visualize the graphics your definition will need. Use the strategies in Chapters 10 and 11 to plan the drawings, diagrams, photos, and charts you may need to include.

> If you explore websites focusing on nanotechnology, you'll encounter some rather bizarre graphics: 3-D animations depicting how something can be built molecule by molecule, illustrations of molecular nano assemblers, arrangements of atoms and molecules to create "Buckyballs" and "Buckytubes," and so on.

7. **Organize the materials you'll use to write the extended definition.** Once you have a good idea of how to discuss the term you are defining, one of the next steps is to plan a sequence for that discussion. If you are uneasy about organizing the parts of a discussion like this, take a look at **http://www.powertools.nelson.com**. The following pattern frequently works:

Does this sequence for an extended definition of nanotechnology make sense? Start with the formal sentence definition, move on to an explanation of the manufacturing process, continue with a discussion of the applications of this technology, move on to the visionary projections of how nanotechnology will affect our society, then end with a discussion of what it's going to take to realize these visions.

8. **Sketch out the headings you'll use and the contents they'll introduce.** If your definition exceeds two or three paragraphs, use headings (presented in Chapter 7). For example, use a heading to identify each of the individual sources of definition.

   For this definition, how about these headings: "Nanotechnology Manufacturing Process," "Nanotechnology Applications," "Nanotechnology: Impact on Society," and "Conclusion: What It's Going to Take"? Under the first heading would be a paragraph on how nanotechnological machines will build things; under the second heading, a paragraph on the applications of this technology; under the third, speculation on the social impact. The final paragraph would discuss how much research and development will be needed to realize the visions surrounding nanotechnology.

9. **Plan an introduction.** The best time to write an introduction is *after* you've written the body of a document. Remember that the job of an introduction is to announce the topic and purpose, indicate the audience, provide an overview of the rest of the discussion, but introduce only a minimum of background.

   With the body of this extended definition planned, or even written, start thinking about the introduction. A perky journalistic approach for our serious-minded legislators won't work. Instead, let's start with something about the excitement and confusion over nanotechnology. Then state the formal sentence definition. Finally, indicate the purpose and provide an overview of what follows.

10. **Plan a conclusion.** You'll probably need some sort of ending sentence or paragraph for your extended definition.

    For a discussion like this, you can discuss a related subtopic but in a brief, general way. For example, a brief general discussion of the barriers to nanotechnology might be a good way to conclude this extended definition.

11. **Consider the format.** For this simple project, you are not likely to need the elaborate report formats shown in Chapter 14. Instead, use the format you see for the sample definition at the end of this chapter. Begin with a descriptive title centred at the top of the page, and use second- and third-level headings. Use lists, notices, illustrations, tables, highlighting, and documentation (citations of your borrowed information sources) as necessary.

12. Review and revise your rough draft. Use the strategies in Chapter 16 to systematically review and revise your definition. Use the top-down approach described in that chapter: start by reviewing for audience, purpose, and situation; then move on to content, organization, and transitions; then headings, lists, tables, and graphics; then sentence style and technical style; and finally, grammar, usage, spelling, and punctuation problems.

WHAT IS A CLASSIFICATION AND HOW DO YOU WRITE ONE?

Classification, like definition, is an important infrastructure for supplying basic information about a technical subject. Classification actually means two things: determining the class to which an item belongs and dividing a topic into categories.

Location within a Category

In one of its senses, classification means deciding to which category an individual item belongs. Within corporations, you have to decide whether a document is "for internal use only," "confidential," or "confidential-restricted." A company may develop a new computer: is it a laptop, a notebook, a palm-top, or a finger-top?

To write about which category an item belongs to, use comparison. Define the characteristics of each category, and then compare the characteristics of the item to those of the categories. In the end, declare the item a member of one category, or make up a new category.

Division into Categories

In technical documents, particularly technical background reports, a common strategy is to divide the subject into categories and to discuss each one separately (see Figure 5-3).

However, you must use only one *basis of classification*. Look at the examples in the table on page 127.

The following walks you through the important steps in writing a classification. To get a sense of how these steps work in an actual writing project, we'll follow an example through each of these steps.

Classification: This classification discusses three categories of devices essential to the theory of nanotechnology.

Overview: Notice that the introduction lets you know that three types of devices will be discussed.

The theory of nanotechnology relies on three essential types of devices to build almost any chemically stable structure atom by atom. These three devices are defined according to the role they play in the molecular-level manufacturing process.

■ *Assemblers.* One essential type of device in the theory of nano-technology is the "assembler." It possesses a submicroscopic robotic "arm" under computer control that enables it to hold and position reactive compounds in precise locations at which desired chemical reactions can occur. Thus, large, atomically precise objects can be built molecule by molecule through a sequence of precisely controlled chemical reactions. An essential characteristic of assemblers will be their ability to make copies of themselves. Vast armies of assemblers will be needed to build objects rapidly and cheaply.

Bulleted list: To make the discussion of the three categories distinct, the writer uses bulleted items with italicized labels.

■ *Molecular computers.* To direct the activities of assemblers, another essential type of device will be necessary: the molecular computer. With components a few atoms wide, though, a simple mechanical computer would fit within 1/100 of a cubic micron, many billions of times more compact than today's so-called micro-electronics. Even with a billion bytes of storage, a nanomechani-cal computer could fit in a box a micron wide, about the size of a bacterium. These molecular computers will be fast because, although their signals will move about 100,000 times slower than the signals in current computers, they will need to travel only 1/1,000,000 as far. Thus, these "nanocomputers" may be thousands of times faster than current microcomputers.

Transitions: Notice how much this writer repeats the words "type" and "essential." Notice also that key terms like "assembler" and "molecular computer" are used over and over again throughout. Synonyms would only confuse us!

■ *Disassemblers.* One last type of device that is essential in the theory of nanotechnology is the disassembler. While molecular computers will control molecular assemblers, providing the swift flow of instructions needed to direct the placement of vast numbers of atoms, disassemblers will help scientists and engineers ana-lyze things. Disassemblers will use enzymes and chemical reactions to break bonds and thus take anything apart, a few atoms at a time. Moreover, they record what it removes layer by layer.

Conclusion: This discussion ends with an overview of how these devices work together in the manufacturing process.

Assemblers, disassemblers, and nanocomputers will work together. For example, a molecular computer will direct the disassemblers to take apart an object and record its structure and then direct an assembler to use those recorded instructions in reverse to assemble perfect copies of that object.

FIGURE 5-3
Sample classification. This definition discusses types of devices one by one. Notice that the "principle of classification" is explained in the introduction.

Subject	Basis of Classification	Categories
Lasers	Potential for injury to humans (also based on watts)	Classes I, II, IIIa, IIIb, IV
Solar water	How water (or heating element) is circulated	Passive (gravity is used) and active (pumps are used)
Solar collectors	The design of the tubing through which water is circulated and heated	Flat-plate, evacuated-tube, and parabolic solar collectors
Solar cookers	How sunlight is focused and collected in the cooker	Box, parabolic, panel cookers
Schizophrenia	Commonly associated sets of behaviours	Paranoid, catatonic, disorganized, residual, undifferentiated
Diabetes	Dependency on insulin	Type I (insulin-dependent diabetes) and Type II (non–insulin-dependent diabetes)

1. **Find a simple project requiring a discussion of categories.** Try to find a practical situation in which you'd need to write about categories. To write a classification, you'll need to find a term that can readily be divided into categories, such as those shown in the preceding table. (Having trouble thinking of a topic? See **http://www.powertools. nelson.com.**)

   What's "categorizable" about nanotechnology? If you scan Web resources, you'll see lots of possibilities. Nanotechnologists divide human history into "bulk" and "molecular" technological methods. However, for an understanding of the fundamentals of nanotechnology, terms like "assembler," "disassembler," "replicator," and "meme" are essential and occur aga n and again in the literature on nanotechnology.

2. **Define a purpose and an audience.** The next step is to decide on a purpose and an audience for this classification. (See Chapter 17 for strategies to use in analyzing audiences and adapting your writing to them.)

   Imagine that this discussion will be a section in a technical report. But who wants such a report? Who's willing to pay thousands of dollars to research and write the report? What are their requirements in relation to this topic? Venture-capital investors are always a possibility; these executive-type readers need background to help them decide whether to invest. Federal and other government officials are another possibility; perhaps they need background in order to consider research-and-development funding. They don't have time to surf the Web all night or sort through stacks of books and articles that are way over their heads. That's for you to do!

3. **Research the topic.** Early in this project, you may need to do some research.

As the topic box at the beginning of this chapter shows, the World Wide Web is loaded with material on nanotechnology. But use caution! Some of it is wildly visionary. You can start by searching the Web using the term "nano-technology" with any of the major search engines. Also look at some "guide sites," and move on to some searches of online sources, such as Innovation in Canada (**http://www.innovation.gc.ca**) or Canadian Library Gateway (**http://collectionscanada.ca**). Also, use your local library to search for published magazine and journal articles on the topic.

4. **Plan and develop graphics.** Early on in this project, visualize the graphics for your classification. Use the strategies in Chapter 10 and Chapter 11 to plan the tables, charts drawings, diagrams, and photos you may need to include.

As you research nanotechnology, you'll see plenty of possibilities for graphics. Of course, because nanotechnology is a molecular thing, most of the illustrations are conceptual drawings. Conceptual drawings of nanotechnology processes and objects will be essential in helping readers understand this topic.

5. **Decide on a basis of classification.** Before dividing a topic into categories, find a good basis of classification, one that fulfills your readers' needs and presents the topic in the most informative way. To do this, you may need to draft several lists of categories until you find the most useful one.

In nanotechnology, terms like "assembler," "disassembler," "replicator," and "meme" occur constantly. Are these types of devices, or are they concepts? If they are concepts, there's no classification—it's not a set of categories. But as it turns out, the first three terms are indeed essential categories of nanotechnological devices. Their basis of classification is function—the job they do in the manufacturing process.

6. **Divide the topic into categories.** If you've learned enough about your topic from your initial research or know enough about it already, divide it into categories. Remember to apply only one basis of classification—the one you developed in the preceding step.

When you review your resources, you see that "meme," as it is used by the writers involved in this technology, is really not a category of nanotechnological devices. However, assembler, disassembler, and replicator are essential device types. Each has an important function in the business of nanotechnology.

7. **Write a formal sentence definition of the topic and each of the categories.** Start a classification with a formal sentence definition, discussed earlier in this chapter. Also define each of the categories. Put the definition of the topic in the introduction and the definitions of the individual categories in their respective body paragraphs.

   Nanotechnology is manufacturing at the molecular level. However, you need to explain this idea further before it begins making sense to readers. An assembler, as its name implies, is a molecular-sized device that assembles objects atom by atom. A disassembler, as its name also implies, is a device that disassembles objects in order to analyze their structure and contents. A replicator is a molecular-sized device that can build replicas of itself that do useful work.

8. **Use the tools for extended definition to discuss the categories.** Take a careful look at your formal sentence definitions; which of the definition tools do they suggest? Return to the list of extended-definition tools in the preceding pages and pick the ones you need.

   For example, in the paragraph on assemblers, you'll first need a *definition* of an assembler, then a discussion of the *process* by which it builds objects. Use an analogy to the process by which biological assemblers—cells—build objects. Consider discussing *effects*—the extraordinary impact that this new form of manufacturing could have on society. Problems—*causes*—that could hinder the progress of nanotechnologists will also be important. And finally, use plenty of *examples* throughout. (Figure 5-4 illustrates how these definition tools can work together in the paragraphs of a classification.)

Introduction: discuss or define the set to which the categories belong; provide an overview of the categories you'll discuss and the basis of the classification

Category 1: discuss this category using one or more of the definition sources discussed earlier in this chapter

Category 2: discuss this category using one or more of the definition sources discussed earlier in this chapter

Category 3: discuss this category using one or more of the definition sources discussed earlier in this chapter

Conclusion

FIGURE 5-4
Classification (discussion of categories). In this diagram, categories are discussed one at a time, each in its own paragraph. Each of those paragraphs uses the strategies for extended definition to discuss the category.

9. **Sketch out the headings you'll use.** For a classification of three or more paragraphs, use headings (see Chapter 7). If you discuss individual categories in one or more separate paragraphs, create a heading for each.

   For this classification, the headings will obviously be something like "Assemblers," "Disassemblers," "Replicators," and so on, followed by at least a paragraph on each.

10. **Plan an introduction.** Introductions, as you know, indicate the topic to be discussed; indicate the readers and situation the document is intended for; provide an overview of what is about to be discussed; and, only minimally, present background information (such as key concepts, definitions, or the importance of the topic). If you have a lot of background information, move it into a paragraph of its own following the introduction.

    For a separate document on nanotechnology, the introduction must define the term. If this definition becomes too long, you may have to move it to a second paragraph and just sketch a definition in the introduction. You'll also need to indicate the audience—investors or politicians—in the introduction as well as the purpose.

11. **Plan a conclusion.** For the final section, summarize (pull together the essential ideas you've discussed), conclude (draw some logical conclusion based on what you've been discussing), discuss some final point but at a general level, or use some combination of these methods.

    It might be useful to review the basic concepts previously discussed. After all, this topic will be rough going for many readers. A logical conclusion might comment on how soon we can expect nanotechnology to have an impact or whether it is a realistic possibility at all. A final-thought conclusion might discuss the problems that the future of nanotechnology faces, or perhaps the ethical questions it raises.

12. **Consider the format.** For this simple project, you are not likely to need the elaborate report formats shown in Chapter 14. Instead, use the format you see for the sample classification of solar collectors at the end of this chapter. Begin with a descriptive title centred at the top of the page, and use second- and third-level headings. Use lists, notices, illustrations, tables, highlighting, and documentation (citations of your borrowed information sources) as necessary.

13. **Review and revise your rough draft.** Use the strategies in Chapter 16 to systematically review and revise your classification. Use the top-down approach described in that chapter: start by reviewing for audience, purpose, and situation; then move on to content, organization,

and transitions; then headings, lists, tables, and graphics; then on to sentence style and technical style; and finally, grammar, usage, spelling, and punctuation problems.

HOW DO YOU WRITE TECHNICAL BACKGROUND REPORTS?

Technical background reports solve workplace problems by providing information on a topic, information for which readers have specific needs. For example, Hewlett-Packard made headlines in 1999 with its developments involving nanotechnology. Plenty of product planners sat up and wanted to know just what "nanotechnology" is. One way of delivering the information is the background report, for which you do the research and then summarize it for such clients. Its infrastructure is typically definition: to discuss a topic adequately, you must consider it from multiple angles such as description, process, classification, and so on.

Let's walk through the important steps in writing a technical background report and apply them to a sample project along the way:

1. **Build a team?** As with primary research reports and recommendation reports, technical background reports are great opportunities to work as a team. These reports take a lot of brainstorming and a lot of work.

2. **Find a project requiring a background report.** One of the hardest tasks in writing a technical background report for a technical-writing course is finding a real or realistic project. Something like "a report for anybody who happens to be interested in advanced manufacturing techniques" just won't work. Use the suggestions at **http://www. powertools.nelson.com** for developing practical technical-writing projects that solve real problems. Look around you for people and organizations or consider government officials; then think about new technologies and identify background information that would meet your audience's needs, help them make decisions, or help them solve problems.

   Imagine that you want to use your technical-writing course to find out about nanotechnology. The background report provides a good way to capture your findings in an introductory-type document. This report won't provide conclusions, recommendations, instructions, or other such information; it will just provide introductory, background information for readers to use according to their own needs.

3. **Analyze the audience and purpose.** Once you've found a situation involving a problem that can be solved, in part, by a background report, zero in on the audience. See Chapter 17 for strategies to use in identifying or inventing and then analyzing audiences. Zero in on the

purpose as well. To do all this, you may need to do some preliminary reading to become familiar with the topic.

> Who wants to read our technical background report on nanotechnology? Who would, in fact, pay us to write such a report? Investors perhaps? As of the year 2005, practical applications of nanotechnology were a long way off. Explore the following ideas:
> - What about government officials? Nanotechnology research and development will need a strong financial boost; other countries might get ahead of us. Imagine that you are a member of a legislative research team that has been directed to develop a background report on nanotechnology for politicians.
> - What about organizations promoting nanotechnology that need promotional literature? Obviously, they are the experts, but perhaps they are not the best people to write about it for general, nonspecialist readers.
> - What about marketing analysts and planners? They represent another possible set of readers.
>
> The legislative research team provides a good scenario. Politicians want to promote increased research and development in nanotechnology and bring that activity to their home province. The readers may be lawyers, career politicians, or educators—but they are not rocket scientists, nor are they nanotechnologists!

4. **Choose the "packaging" for the report.** Think about the design—the "packaging"—you'll use for this report. Will it be a memo report, business-letter report, online report, e-mail report, or formal bound report? See Chapter 14 for details on these options. For a report like this one, the format of the formal report, complete with cover letter and front- and back-matter elements, is probably the best choice. See sample excerpts from a report on alternative energy resources at the end of Chapter 14.

> This technical background report on nanotechnology will not be a short report, but neither will it run over 20 pages. Its primary audience is politicians who won't want lots of pages. A report this long will not work as a memo or letter report; it needs to be a formal report with a cover memo. The online format is not an option for our political readers; it must be a conventional printed, bound report.

5. **Narrow the topic for the report.** For practically any technical topic, you can write at least one large heavy book, if not multiple ones. But that's not what your readers want. They want you to do the legwork in the library, sift through all those books and articles to find the best ones, and then, in a nice tidy 20-page bundle, summarize the key information they need using words they can understand. See **http://www.powertools. nelson.com** for strategies to use in narrowing topics.

Remember that narrowing means chopping out topics that readers don't want and adjusting the level of detail to their needs. Our political readers need to know about nanotechnology, but not in excruciating technical detail. They need to know its likely applications and the impact on society. They also need to know how far research and development has progressed and how soon practical results will emerge. They will want to know where the research is, who the competition is, what the costs are, and what the likely payoff is.

6. **Use the infrastructures to develop a tentative outline.** Infrastructures include description, process, causes, effects, definition, classification, and persuasion. Each one requires certain kinds of content and certain kinds of organization, making them handy tools for developing outlines.

   To explain what "manufacturing at the molecular level" means, you'll need a *process* description—a step-by-step explanation of how things can be built atom by atom. You'll need to include *causes and effects*, as well—just what will be the impact on society? Lots of *definitions* will be in order—what does the prefix *nano-* mean? In fact the whole report will be essentially a big extended definition of nanotechnology. You may also need *description*—what will this equipment look like?

7. **Plan and develop graphics and tables.** As you research a topic, you'll see useful graphics and tables. Photocopy or download them and record complete bibliographic information for each one.

   - If the graphic is from a book, make a note of the author, title, page number, publisher, city of publication, and year.
   - If it's from an article, record the author, article title, magazine or journal name, date of the issue, volume and issue numbers (if applicable), and page number.
   - If it's from a Web page, record the author (if available) or organization, title of the page, URL, date you accessed the page, as well as the date of the last revision of the Web page.

   If you find that you must develop some of the graphics and tables yourself, get out your artist's beret, but also see Chapter 11 on illustrative graphics.

   For the nanotechnology project, you'll need flowcharts and diagrams of the manufacturing process. Tables will be good for showing expenditures on research and development as well as the projected impact on society.

8. **Set up a source list.** It's extremely annoying to have to go back and find bibliographic information on your sources. It takes time that you probably won't have, and inevitably you'll have trouble relocating some of your sources. Set up the sources list according to the format prescribed by the documentation style you are using.

9. **Review and revise your rough draft.** Use the strategies in Chapter 16 to systematically review and revise your definition. Use the top-down approach described there: start by reviewing for audience, purpose, and situation; then move on to content, organization, and transitions; then headings, lists, tables, and graphics; then sentence-style revision and technical style; and finally, grammar, usage, spelling, and punctuation problems.

WORKSHOP: DEFINITION, CLASSIFICATION, BACKGROUND REPORTS

Here are some additional ideas for practising the concepts, tools, and strategies in this chapter:

1. *Synonym definitions.* Rewrite the following sentences using the "raw materials" to create synonyms:

Base sentence:	One of the most important classes of disorders of the hematological system involves various types of anemia.
Raw material:	Anemia is a disorder of the red blood cells.
Base sentence:	Alzheimer's disease was first described in 1907 by Alos Alzheimer, a German physician.
Raw material:	Alzheimer's disease is defined as an adult-onset neurological disorder.
Base sentence:	Carbon dioxide is essential for photosynthesis.
Raw material:	Carbon dioxide is an odorless, colourless gas that constitutes about 0.035% of the atmosphere.
	Photosynthesis is the process by which the sun's energy is converted to forms usable by plants and animals.
Base sentence:	Canada produces 3.5 million tons of hazardous waste every year.
Raw material:	Hazardous waste can be defined as a substance that can cause serious, irreversible, or incapacitating illness as well as environmental damage if not handled properly.
Base sentence:	For example, gene therapy could provide medical treatment to eliminate sickle-cell disease.
Raw material:	Sickle-cell disease is a human genetic disorder involving red blood cells.

2. *Formal sentence definitions.* Use the following "raw material" to write formal sentence definitions:

Term	Raw materials
Solar collector	In a solar heating system; heats circulating water necessary for space heating; uses layers of glass to trap heat.
Salt marshes	Low coastal grassland frequently overflowed by the tide; develop when the rate of sediment deposition is greater than the rate of land subsidence.
Sickle-cell disease	Human genetic disorder; affects red blood cells; when red blood cells give up oxygen, they take on an elongated shape; elongated cells clog blood vessels and are less able to become reoxygenated.
Greenhouse effect	The trapping of solar radiation into the lower atmosphere; makes Earth's surface warmer than it would be otherwise; caused by carbon dioxide in atmosphere; blocks re-radiation of infrared heat back into space.
Hazardous waste	Can cause death or increase in serious, irreversible, or incapacitating illness; poses substantial threat to human health and the environment if improperly treated, transported, or disposed of.

3. *Tools for definition.* Take a look at the following extended definition and identify the tools for extended definition.

Salt marshes are defined as low coastal grassland frequently overflowed by the tide. They form in lagoons, estuaries, and other sheltered coastal positions. They develop when the rate of sediment deposition is greater than the rate of land subsidence. Sediment deposited on the marsh surface follows a simple distribution pattern: larger, heavier sand grains are deposited close to the low tide mark, while lighter silt particles are carried farther inland on the high tide. Mudflats form between the marshes and the sea, acting as a buffer and dissipating wave energy. Deep, branching drainage channels develop on the marsh, directing flood patterns and reducing the erosion from flood tides. The height of a salt marsh above sea level cannot exceed the level of the highest spring tide. If this limit is reached because of a drop in relative sea level, then the salt marsh will evolve into a brackish or

```
freshwater  marsh  and  eventually  become  coastal
scrub or woodland. Normally, salt marshes are cov-
ered  in  rooted  vegetation,  mainly  grass  species,
which are adapted to withstand periodic submergence
in saltwater. The plant roots anchor the surface of
the  sediment,  increasing  resistance  to  erosion  in
storm conditions. Plants on the marsh are distrib-
uted in characteristic zones, according to the level
of  salinity  and  frequency  of  submergence  that  they
are adapted to survive. Many salt marshes in Europe
are located in sparsely populated areas. In the past
they were often reclaimed from the sea to be used
for heavy industry and refuse disposal. The increas-
ing  recognition  of  the  importance  of  marshes  as  a
wildlife habitat has reduced the number of reclama-
tion and industrial schemes aimed at salt marshes.
```

4. *Division into categories.* Divide one or more of the following topics into categories, types, and classes. (If you can't think of categories, look these topics up in any general encyclopedia.)

Primates	Telescopes	Industrial robots
Trees	Cancers	Solar energy devices
Clouds	Rocks	Shells
Hurricanes	Earthquakes	Pollution
Computers	Basic electronic components	Telephones
Solar eclipses	Food	Trauma

5. *Background reports—using infrastructures.* Consider one or more of the following topics for technical background reports. Which infrastructures would you use, and what would be their contents?

Industrial waste disposal for a neighbourhood association	Hypoglycemia for school counsellors and advisers
Steroids for athletic coaches and trainers	Creationist theories for science faculty
Evolution theories for fundamentalist congregations	Fossils for the paleontology club
Loans for citizens	Energy-saving techniques for homeowners
Solar automobiles for college maintenance supervisors	

EXTENDED DEFINITION

Molecular Manufacturing

Since nanotechnology has seized popular imagination, it has been used loosely to refer to research where dimensions, quantities, and locations are around 1,000 nanometres. However, the "nanotechnology" that leaders like K. Eric Drexler, Ralph C. Merkle, and others are talking about refers to a process in which essentially every atom can be put in the right place at manufacturing costs not greatly exceeding those of the required raw materials and energy. This makes possible the manufacture of almost anything for which we can provide detailed atomic specifications. Because their concept of nanotechnology refers to manufacturing atom by atom and molecule by molecule, leading nanoscientists sometimes prefer the term "molecular manufacturing." The following further explores this new technology and its applications (Merkle, 2000).

Manufacturing Technologies: Current and Future

Merkle uses LEGO™ to explain the basics of molecular manufacturing. Common forms of manufacturing such as casting, grinding, and milling manipulate atoms in what he calls "great thundering statistical herds." In current manufacturing methods, we can "push the LEGO™ blocks into great heaps and pile them up," but we cannot fit them together the way we want at the molecular level (Merkle, 2000). If we had a manufacturing process that gave us that level of control, we could rearrange the atoms in a chunk of coal to make a diamond or the atoms in ordinary sand to make a computer or the atoms in dirt and water to make potatoes. This is what Merkle and others call "molecular manufacturing."

An example illustrating this contrast is lithography, the essential manufacturing process used to build computer chips. Continued improvements in lithography have enabled us to work with dimensions less than one micron. But despite the improvements in computer hardware capability that submicron lithography has made possible, this

Headings: Because this is a relatively short document, it does not use first-level headings (unless you consider the title a first-level heading). In fact, you can imagine this entire document as a background section in a longer report on molecular manufacturing. In any case, a heading like "Molecular Manufacturing: Essential Components" is a second-level heading, as defined in Chapter 7. Headings like "Positional assembly" are third-level headings.

manufacturing method will probably reach its fundamental limits in the first two decades of the 21st century. Merkle and others believe that nanotechnology will provide a "post-lithographic" manufacturing process. It will enable us to build inexpensive computer systems with "mole quantities of logic elements that are molecular in both size and precision" (Merkle, 2000).

Molecular Manufacturing: Essential Components

Merkle identifies two concepts essential to molecular manufacturing: positional assembly and self-replication.

Positional assembly. To get "the right molecular parts in the right places," some form of positional assembly is required. This implies robotic devices that are molecular both in their size and precision. The idea of such devices, as strange as it may seem, is not new. Richard Feynman, considered one of the founding theorists of nanotechnology, introduced this idea in "There's Plenty of Room at the Bottom," his famous 1959 presentation to the American Physical Society: "The principles of physics, as far as I can see, do not speak against the possibility of maneuvering things atom by atom" (Feynman, 1997). According to Drexler, "Just as today's engineers build machinery as complex as player pianos and robot arms from ordinary motors, bearings, and moving parts, so tomorrow's biochemists will be able to use protein molecules as motors, bearings, and moving parts to build robot arms, which will themselves be able to handle individual molecules" (Drexler, 1997).

Self-replication. For objects to be manufactured inexpensively and efficiently, self-replicating components are also needed. This idea was originally put forth by John von Neumann in the 1940s. Such a device would make copies of itself and manufacture the desired objects (Merkle, 2000). In *Engines of Creation,* Drexler foresees replicators whose components will include molecular "tape" to supply instructions, a reader to translate those instructions into arm motions, and several assembler arms to hold and move workpieces. Drexler calculates that such a replicator will add up to one billion atoms or so and, working at one million atoms per second, will copy itself in one thousand seconds (about fifteen minutes). Working singly, a replicator would need a century to stack up enough copies to make a "respectable speck." But with replicators making copies of themselves, the process would produce a ton of copies in less than a day (Drexler, 1997).

Molecular Manufacturing: Applications

When they discuss applications of molecular manufacturing, nanotechnologists such as Ralph C. Merkle, K. Eric Drexler, and Richard Smalley become downright visionary. Self-assembling consumer goods; computers billions of times faster; extraordinary inventions (impossible today); safe and affordable space travel; a virtual end to illness, aging, and death; no more pollution and automatic cleanup of already existing pollution; molecular food synthesis and thus the end of famine and starvation; access to a superior education for every child on Earth; reintroduction of many extinct plants and animals; terraforming on Earth and in the Solar System—these are the things they foresee (What is nanotechnology?, 2000).

Medicine. One of the most far-reaching applications is medical research. To treat disease, current medical technology uses techniques involving drugs, radiation, and surgery. These techniques are generally slow, tedious, and sometimes dangerous. Nanotechnological agents (often called "nanites") could perform the tasks of drugs, radiation, and surgery far better. Instead of relying on open heart surgery to remove a blockage in an artery, nanites could be inhaled and find their way through the body to the specified artery and pick apart the blockage without causing any harm. Some nanotechnologists believe that "nanomedicine" will enable people to live for indefinite amounts of time (Hunter, n.d.). According to one nanomedicine researcher, Robert Freitas, nanomedicine, which he defines as "the ability to direct events in a controlled fashion at the cellular level," will be "the key that will unlock the indefinite extension of human health and the expansion of human abilities" (Freitas, 2000).

Applications and effects: As an additional way of exploring the meaning of nanotechnology, this definition discusses applications and their effects on society. Thus, short definitions, comparison and contrast, as well as cause and effect have all been used to extend this definition.

Space exploration. Another area that will benefit from this new concept is space exploration and aerospace technology. Nanosystems could be used to manufacture the materials, fuel, and hardware needed in spacecraft. These materials would cost virtually nothing because nanites will be able to rearrange the molecules of any common substance into those of another. And these same processes can be used on other planets using common materials found there to create oxygen, food, and other substances needed to sustain human life. And if nanomedicine enables people to live practically forever, we'll need to settle other planets to keep from overpopulating Earth.

Computer industry. An area where nanotechnology may make its first practical impact is the computer industry. Nanosystems may enable the manufacture of computer chips with a cost of less than a dollar per pound, with operating frequencies of tens of gigahertz or more, with a size of roughly 10 nanometres per device, and with extraordinarily low energy requirements (or as Drexler puts it, "roughly the energy of a single air molecule bouncing around at room temperature") (Drexler, 1997).

Conclusion: When?

When asked how soon these scientific miracles may happen, nano-technologists are the first to say that they just do not know. However, *Wired* magazine in 1995 assembled some of the top minds in nano-technology and asked them to estimate when certain critical events in the advance of nanotechnology might occur. Their predictions for when we might see the first molecular assembler (a device for position assembly discussed previously) ranged from 2000 to 2025; for a nano-computer, 2010 to 2100; for cell repair, 2018 to 2050; for a commercial product, 2000 to 2015; for laws regulating nanotechnology, 1998 to 2036 (What is nanotechnology?, 2000).

Information sources: Occurring at the end is the list of information sources used to write this document. The style used here is APA. Notice that the items are alphabetized and that the second line is indented using the "hanging indent." And finally, these entries include both the publication date and the date the writer of this extended definition accessed them.

References

Drexler, K. E. (1997). Engines of creation: the coming era of nanotechnology. Retrieved Feb. 28, 2000, from http://www.foresight.org/EOC.

Feynman, R. P. (1959). There's plenty of room at the bottom: An invitation to enter a new field of physics. Retrieved Feb. 28, 2000, from http://www.zyvex.com/nanotech/feynman.html.

Freitas, R. A. (2000). Nanomedicine. Retrieved Feb. 28, 2000, from http://www.foresight.org/nanomedicine.

Hunter, R. (n.d.). Nanotechnology and its applications. Retrieved Feb. 28, 2000, from http://www.personal.psu.edu/dept/sci4/science/articles/nano.html.

Merkle, R. C. (n.d.). Nanotechnology. Retrieved Feb. 28, 2000, from http://www.zyvex.com/nano.

Merkle, R. C. (n.d.). How long will it take to develop nanotechnology? Retrieved Feb. 28, 2000, from http://www.zyvex.com/nanotech/howlong.html.

What is nanotechnology? (2000). Retrieved Feb. 28, 2000, from http://www.nanozine.com/whatnano.htm.

CLASSIFICATION

Choosing a Solar Hot Water System in Canada

Before deciding on a solar hot water system, you should become familiar with the various types of water heaters and their suitability for your needs. A variety of solar water heater designs are available for consumers. There are variations in collector styles and component arrangements, as well as different methods of freeze and overheating protection. If you are planning to use a solar water heater year-round in Canada, it must be protected from freezing in the winter and overheating in the summer. Solar water heaters that meet the Canadian Standards Association (CSA) International guidelines have automatic controls to prevent overcharging the solar heater (i.e., to prevent potential scalding water temperatures). The following report outlines the two situations that apply and then discusses the three common types of solar water heating systems for these situations.

Classes of Solar Water Heaters

Do we need a year-round or a seasonal solar water heater? This depends on when you will be using the residence where the solar heater is installed.

Seasonal solar water heaters. Seasonal heaters are designed for use in climate conditions not requiring freeze protection. Seasonal solar water heaters tend to be less expensive than solar water heaters sold for year-round use because they do not require equipment to protect the solar collectors and outside piping from extreme freezing temperatures.

Year-round solar water heaters. These heaters can withstand the extremely cold temperatures often experienced in Canada. These types are recommended if the residence is used throughout the year, and is in a climate requiring freeze protection. Year-round solar water heaters are more convenient and fail-safe because they can operate in all climate conditions. Because these solar water heaters operate all year, they

Types of water heaters: This document, which occurs in a larger buyer's guide for solar water heating systems in Canada, explains the two general classifications of solar water heaters and then presents the three common categories of heaters and their uses.

Introduction: Notice that the introduction begins with a general discussion of water heaters and then provides an overview of what is covered.

Second-level headings: This document uses two second-level headings (see Chapter 7): one for two general classes; the other for common types of systems.

No stacked headings: If there were no text between the second-level heading "Classes of Solar Water Heaters" and the third-level heading "Seasonal solar water heaters," we would have stacked headings on our hands! (See Chapter 7 for details.)

Basis of classification: Notice that the heaters are classified according to the type of freeze protection provided for the collectors.

Third-level headings: These headings are "run in" to the paragraph and use sentence-style capitalization. (See Chapter 7 for information about third-level headings.)

normally provide more solar hot water than a seasonal water heater. These products require maintenance comparable to conventional water heaters. Maintenance will ensure good performance and increase your energy savings.

Common Systems

The following are common system types (the first two can be freeze protected in the Canadian climate):

- "Antifreeze" systems use special fluic to transfer heat from the collector to a heat exchanger in the storage unit. These systems are fully freeze protected, prevent contamination of the hot water, and can operate in all climate conditions. Snow will slide off the collector as the sun begins to warm them. On days with heavy snowfall, performance can be increased by removing the snow from the collectors.

- Drainback systems automatically drain the collectors when they are not collecting solar energy or when the temperature of circulating water is 3°C or less. Make sure that the system's minimum temperature rating is appropriate for your climate.

- Thermosiphon systems do not have freeze protection, and are popular for cottages where water heating is needed only in the summer. These solar water heaters are often less expensive than models incorporating freeze protection.

Whichever system you choose, be sure to do your homework on its suitability for the location of the installation and the usage of the household.

Source: Adapted from Natural Resources Canada. "Solar Water Heating Systems: A Buyer's Guide." 2000. <http://www.canren.gc.ca/prod_serv/index.asp?Cald=138&Pgld=744>. Reproduced with the permission of the Minister of Public Works and Government Services Canada.

Discussing the categories: Notice that the paragraphs that discuss types in this document do so by explaining how they work (process), where they are used (comparison), and what's good and bad about them (causes, effects, and comparison).

Bulleted list: The three systems are presented in a bulleted list to emphasize them.

CHAPTER 6

Persuasion: Proposals and Progress Reports

Topics covered in this chapter include

- wind farms;
- recycling;
- environmental assessments.

WIND FARMS
Canadian Wind Energy Association
http://www.canwea.ca/en/CanadianWindFarms.html

Ontario Power Generation
http://www.opg.com

The David Suzuki Foundation
http://www.davidsuzuki.org

RECYCLING
Canada Recycling (Search for your city and add the words "waste management" to the search.)
http://www.recycle.nrcan.gc.ca

ENVIRONMENTAL ASSESSMENTS
The Canadian Environmental Assessment Agency
http://www.ceaa-acee.gc.ca/index_e.htm

Natural Resources Canada
http://www.nrcan-rncan.gc.ca

Parks Canada (Search there to find what happens when a project turns up an archaeological site.)
http://www.pc.gc.ca

When you have completed this chapter, you will be able to

- use persuasive techniques to organize your work and effect organization;
- create a logical argument;
- avoid logical fallacies in your writing;
- organize and write progress reports.

As you know from the Preface, most technical documents are based on one or a combination of *infrastructures*—elemental structures that enable those documents to do their job. The infrastructure essential in proposals and progress reports is *persuasion* (also known as *argumentation*). To convince people to hire you to do a project and to reassure them that the project is going well, you need persuasive strategies. This chapter reviews the common persuasive strategies and shows you how to write proposals and progress reports with those strategies built in.

Persuasion is certainly at the core of résumés and application letters as well as "problem communications" such as complaint, adjustment, and inquiry letters. However, this chapter is already splitting at its seams. For résumés and application letters, see Chapter 13, "Employment-Search Tools: Application Letters and Résumés." For problem communications such as complaint, adjustment, and inquiry letters, see Chapter 12, "Business Communications: Letters, Memos, and E-mail."

Note:
- If you are new to this book, see "How Do You Use This Book?" in the Preface.
- For additional examples of the documents discussed in this chapter, see **http://www.powertools.nelson.com**.

WHAT ARE THE TOOLS FOR PERSUASION?

Before getting into the contents, organization, format, and style of the technical-writing applications covered in this chapter, review some of the basics of writing persuasively (see Figure 6-1 for an example). If you remember Rhetoric and Composition 101, you know that several types of "appeals" are available for persuasive writing:

- *Logical appeal*. When you use reasons and arguments backed up by facts and logic to make your case, you are using the logical appeal. We normally think of the logical appeal as the only legitimate method of argument, but the "real world" shows us different.

Main assertion: The paragraph begins with a straightforward thesis that wind farms should be subject to assessments. The paragraph itself is intended to prove more than this, however, as it is a rebuttal of some environmentalists' view that wind farms should not be built at all.

Support: Relying primarily on an article by Dr. David Suzuki, this writer goes through a series of issues related to birds: the type of birds affected; a comparison with other high structures; and a reference to a situation in California.

Direct quotations: Notice that this writer quotes several pithy phrases from Suzuki's articles, quotations that carry some of the attitude and personality of the original author.

Documentation: Even if this writer had not quoted her source directly, she is still obliged to cite the sources of the information she has borrowed. Note that the format used here is APA.

Before a wind farm site is approved, it must be assessed thoroughly for its potential effect on birds. Environmental activists are fighting the construction of farms in Nova Scotia and Alberta because of the effect on birds, and because the farms spoil the natural landscape. In an article published in the *New Scientist* and in comments published on his website, Dr. David Suzuki says that while he thinks "windmills are beautiful," they, "…like any development, need to be sited properly and appropriately." For example, because wading species and ducks are the most likely to be affected, "estuaries and shallow shorelines could be risky sites for wind energy development." Some birds are killed when they fly into the turbines, but no more than are killed by flying into any other high structures such as skyscrapers or radio towers. He notes that in Toronto, "10,000 birds collide with the city's tallest buildings every year." If the windmills are properly sited, the risk to birds is much lower than the risk these high buildings pose. He also points to the fact that 7,000 windmills built on a migratory path for birds in Altamont Pass in California led to the death of only 0.2 birds per turbine per year. However, he comments that "right now, no one can say what sort of cumulative impact building hundreds of wind farms will have on bird populations." We need to do research and assess each situation specifically.

Source: Suzuki, D. (2005). The beauty of wind farms. *New Scientist, 2495,* 20.

FIGURE 6-1

Single-paragraph example of persuasion. This paragraph would be one of several paragraphs attempting to discredit the opposition to wind farms.

- *Emotional appeal.* When you attempt to rouse people's anger or sympathies in a persuasive effort, you are using an emotional appeal. A photo of a little girl fleeing from a burning village bombed by war planes or an oil-soaked seagull on a beach devastated by an oil spill are images that spark emotions like anger, horror, and sympathy; but they don't make a logical case for or against anything. These images may, however, capture readers' attention and cause them to pay more attention to the rest of your persuasive effort.

- *Personal appeal.* When you present your qualifications, experience, expertise, or wisdom, attempting to build readers' confidence, you are using the personal appeal. As with the emotional appeal, there is no logical justification for the personal appeal. It's like saying, "Trust me." Despite that, readers sometimes want to know who you are and what gives you the right to speak so authoritatively on a subject. Just as the emotional appeal can be used legitimately to get readers to pay attention and care about your message, the right amount of personal appeal can build readers' confidence in you—or at least a willingness to hear you out.

You may also have encountered the *stylistic* appeal—the use of language and visual effects to increase the persuasive impact. For example, a glossy, fancy design for a résumé can have as positive an impact as the content.

In your rhetoric and composition studies, you may also have encountered something called the Toulmin approach to persuasion. The complete system involves claims, grounds, warrant, backing, and rebuttal, but a particularly useful element is the *rebuttal,* and another known as the *concession.*

- *Rebuttal.* In a rebuttal, you directly address counterarguments that your persuasive opponents might bring up. You show how they are wrong, or at least how they don't affect your overall argument. Picture yourself face to face with your persuasive opponents. What arguments are they going to come back at you with? How are you going to answer those arguments? In a *written* persuasive effort, you must simulate this back-and-forth, debate-style argumentative process. Imagine your opponents' counterarguments (arguments they might put forth against your position) and then imagine your own rebuttals (your answers to those counterarguments).
- *Concession.* In a concession, you acknowledge that certain opposing arguments have some validity, but you explain how they do not damage your overall argument. Concessions build personal appeal: they make you seem more open-minded.
- *Synthesis.* Modern rhetoricians urge us not to view the persuasive process as a win–lose, all-out war. When people are entrenched, they shut out the arguments of the other side. Such rigidity prevents us from resolving the issue and getting on with our lives. Instead, the process of counterargument, rebuttal, and concession should be sincere and continuous until all parties reach synthesis—a middle ground where they drop their weapons and agree.

You should also be aware of the logical fallacies commonly found in persuasive efforts:

- *Hasty generalizations.* When you draw a conclusion based on too little evidence, you make a hasty generalization. For example, if you conclude that there is a big social trend to return to the '70s look because you see two or three pairs of bellbottoms and paisley shirts one day, you've drawn a hasty generalization based on a very limited, incomplete sample.
- *Irrelevant, ad hominem arguments.* When you base all or part of your persuasive effort on your opponent's character, behaviour, or past, that's an *ad hominem* argument (meaning "to the man" in Latin). If a middle-aged political candidate were attacked for smoking marijuana in university, that might be an irrelevant personal attack.
- *Bandwagon effect.* If you base all or part of your persuasive effort on the idea that "everybody's doing it," you're using the bandwagon effect.

Commercial advertisement commonly uses this tactic: everybody's buying the product—so should you!

■ *False causality.* If you argue that because one event came after another, the first event caused the second, you may be making an argument based on false causality. For example, imagine that your father joined IBM in 1984 as a regular employee and shortly thereafter the company began its historic slide to near-extinction. Imagine further that in 1995 he left the company, at which time the company began its remarkable comeback. Was it your dad who nearly brought the company to its knees? Did his departure save the company?

■ *Oversimplistic, either–or arguments.* If you reduce the choices to the choice you favour and a totally unacceptable choice, you are using an oversimplistic, either–or argument. Advocates for a nuclear power plant might argue that either we build the thing or we go without electricity.

■ *False analogies.* When you compare a situation to a simple object or process, that's an *analogy*. When you base an entire persuasive effort on an analogy, you may have problems. Some analogies are just wrong to begin with. And all analogies break down at some point. For example, arguments relating to global warming often use the analogy of how a car heats up when the windows are closed. The Vietnam War was justified using the analogy of how dominoes all topple over when they are lined up. Analogies can help readers understand, but not justify, an argument.

HOW DO YOU WRITE PERSUASIVELY?

Let's walk through the important steps in writing persuasively. For a sense of how these steps work in an actual writing project, we'll follow an example through each of the steps.

1. **Find a simple project requiring persuasive writing.** Finding a project for persuasion is like trying to pick a fight. Think of the main issues of the day—global warming, ozone-layer depletion, alternative fuels, mass transportation, pesticides, zero population growth, solar energy, cloning (bioengineering), abortion, effects of computer- and video-game violence, capital punishment, nuclear armaments, chemical warfare. Each of these topics has multiple issues that are hotly debated. Technical-writing courses are not the place for the common pro-and-con and letter-to-the-editor essays you may have written in past writing courses. However, these topics have a technical side that challenges your abilities as a technical writer, and several of the document types presented in this book use persuasion. (Still having trouble thinking of a topic? See **http://www.powertools.nelson.com.**)

Imagine that you are a member of a group fighting against a wind farm being built next to a provincial park. Generally, wind farms are seen in a positive light as they are a source of clean renewable energy. However, your group, while in favour of wind farms, does not want one built in that particular place as you believe it will spoil one of the most pristine scenic views in Canada. Your problem is persuading government officials who are considering allowing the farm to be built that there is another side to this story.

2. **Define a purpose and an audience.** The next step is to decide on a purpose and an audience for this persuasion. (See Chapter 17 for strategies to use in analyzing audiences and adapting your writing to them.)

   You have more than one audience for this task. As well as persuading government officials to change their views, you need to raise public awareness and overcome the halo effect of environmentalism. Your task has been made more difficult by an article written by Dr. David Suzuki, Canada's best-known environmentalist, who has come out in favour of building the windmills on that site (see earlier in the chapter). Appeal to these two audiences in distinctly different ways: for example, local businesspeople might want to know how placing the windmills in that spot will affect their pocketbooks (tourism might be hurt, for example). They want to be persuaded that the scenic beauty has intrinsic value. Government officials, on the other hand, while concerned about public opinion, need more scientific proof and suggestions as to where else they can realistically place the windmills.

3. **Do some research.** To write persuasively about a topic, you may need to do a bit of research.

   By searching on the Ministry of Natural Resources website, you might find Environmental Impact Guidelines. The Canadian Wind Energy Association's website might show you the current locations and capacities of wind farms. Another good source of information would be the Government of Canada Climate Change website. However, what you most need to find are reasons against building a wind farm in a tourist area, and for that, you might need statistics on the number of tourists who visit the affected area. For those statistics you might go to Canada Tourism at **http://www.CanadaTourism.com.**

4. **Plan and develop graphics and tables.** Early in this project, visualize the graphics your persuasive argument will need. Use the strategies in Chapter 10 and Chapter 11 to plan the tables, charts, diagrams, and other graphics you may need to include.

   The most important nontextual information will be tables of statistics about the environmental impact of wind farms on birds (how many are killed by the turbines), the noise pollution, and the effect on tourism. For greater impact, you can represent this table data as charts and graphs. Also, a graphical representation of the view, both unblocked and blocked, would add emotional impact to your argument.

5. **Identify the main logical arguments.** With your topic, purpose, and audience defined, identify the most important arguments.

> What are the logical arguments against building a wind farm in this spot? You can't expect to make converts with a NIMBY (Not in My Back Yard) argument, as that will persuade only people who actually live in your back yard. However, readers might be persuaded with arguments about noise pollution and major environmental impacts, especially on the bird population.

6. **Discuss each argument separately, providing plenty of support.** You must prove each logical argument, using supporting data, reasoning, and examples. You can't just baldly state that something costs less, works better, provides benefits, and is acceptable to the public. You've got to prove it!

> In your persuasive argument, you might use the argument that the sight of the wind turbines will deter tourists from coming to the area. How can you prove such forward-looking information? The best way would be to show the impact wind farms have had in other areas of the world. You might also quote news reports of people complaining that the noise of the wind turbines kept them awake at night.

7. **Consider emotional appeals.** At best, emotional appeals capture readers' attention and get them to care about the issue. At worst, they rouse strong emotions such as fear and anger, preventing readers from thinking clearly about an issue.

> What emotional appeals could you use to persuade readers that wind farms are not always the best option? You might draw an analogy to another situation where wildlife was harmed by construction. You might mention the loss of the caribou habitat from the building of the Alaska Highway. However, such emotional appeals, especially when analogies, should be used sparingly. Don't base your argument on something that might happen because it is "like" another situation.

8. **Consider personal appeals.** Like emotional appeals, personal appeals have no logical relevance to an argument. If you use the personal appeal, you attempt to build readers' confidence in you as someone who is knowledgeable and reliable. Citing years of experience and education is a common example of building a personal appeal.

> You will have your work cut out for you in this area, as you must address all the advantages of wind energy that the opposition can bring to bear. You can't deny the advantages, so the best thing to do is to downplay them, agree with them, and then give your reasons that these advantages will work best elsewhere.

Practical Ethics: Biased Language

 Nobody wants to be reduced to a stereotype, especially when it comes to race, age, religion, gender, or physical status. Stereotyping people isn't courteous, and from a practical writing standpoint, readers who feel they're being unfairly stereotyped simply won't listen to what you're trying to communicate.

There are very few instances in which it's even necessary to mention a person's nationality, disability, or religion. The authors of *The Business Writer's Handbook* point out that "identifying people by such categories is simply not relevant in most workplace writing. Telling readers than an engineer is Native American or that a professor is African-American almost never conveys useful information."[1] Mentioning this type of information has the added negative impact of implying that it's unusual for people of a certain background to hold these positions. This implication is both untrue and offensive.

If you work for a company that is expanding into new territory and you have to write an informative memo acquainting salespeople with the demographics of this territory, facts about culture, religion, and age might be relevant and necessary. In this case (and others like it), take the time to choose descriptive words that inform without being derogatory. Use *Native American* instead of *Indian*, *mentally handicapped* instead of *retarded*, *Christian* instead of *Bible thumper.*

Taking care to avoid biased language will go far in assuring that whatever you write will be received openly by a wide and diverse audience. It's only common sense.

[1] Alred, Gerald, Brusaw, and Oliu. *The Business Writer's Handbook.* New York: St. Martin's Press, 2000, p. 75.

9. **Address any counterarguments.** It's a good idea to address counterarguments—objections people might raise in relation to your argument. Imagine people out there saying, "But—but—but—!" Discuss their counterarguments and show how they are wrong, how they can be addressed, or how they are irrelevant to your main point.

> Instead of demanding that local government must block the construction of a wind farm in this area, begin by discussing the typical output of an average wind turbine. How many houses would one wind turbine power? What would happen when there was no wind? Is it actually worth destroying the beauty of the scenery to bring electrical power to 25 homes?

10. **Sketch out the headings you'll use.** If your persuasion is more than two or three paragraphs, use headings (presented in Chapter 7). If you present arguments one at a time in separate paragraphs, create a heading for each one.

> For this persuasion, you might have headings to introduce each of your main arguments; for example, "Impact on the Bird Population," "Actual Output of a Single Wind Turbine," and so on.

11. **Plan an introduction.** In an introduction to a persuasive argument, you cannot start out guns blazing and swords rattling. It's not necessary to state your main argumentative point right away. Instead, just

indicate the subject matter—not your main point about it. Your readers are more likely to hear you out.

> Imagine that you've written the main sections of this persuasion. You have logical appeals, counterarguments, and possibly some personal and emotional appeals as well. Instead of demanding that authorities not build the wind farm because it will spoil your view, begin with a quiet purpose statement saying that this document "looks at" or "investigates" the possibility of major negative impacts being incurred by the wind farm. Indicate that this document is for both government officials and ordinary citizens. Provide an overview, indicating that you will be discussing the environmental impact, including on flora and fauna, the possible effect on tourism in the area, and the noise factor for residents.

12. **Write a conclusion.** In a persuasion, the final section is often a "true" conclusion. If you have not yet overtly stated your main argumentative point, now's the time. When you do, summarize the main arguments that support it.

> While the introduction may be the place for quiet understatement, the conclusion is the place to pound home your main point. Come out and state vigorously why a wind farm should not be built near your provincial park, and summarize the main reasons why.

13. **Consider the format.** For this simple project, you are not likely to need the elaborate report formats shown in Chapter 14. Instead, use the format you see for the sample persuasion at the end of this chapter. Begin with a descriptive title centred at the top of the page, and use second- and third-level headings. Use lists, notices, illustrations, tables, highlighting, and documentation (citations of your borrowed information sources) as necessary.

14. **Review and revise your rough draft.** Use the strategies in Chapter 16 to systematically review and revise your persuasion. Use the top-down approach described there: start by reviewing for audience, purpose, and situation; then move on to content, organization, and transitions; then headings, lists, tables, and graphics; then sentence style and technical style; and finally, grammar, usage, spelling, and punctuation problems.

HOW DO YOU WRITE A PROPOSAL?

Proposals are useful tools to get interesting, useful, and financially or professionally rewarding projects approved or under contract. The following sections discuss just what proposals are, how persuasion fits in, and how to plan and design a proposal.

About Proposals

People use the word "proposal" loosely in ordinary conversation. However, *proposal* here refers to a document that seeks to get its writer or its writer's company hired or approved to do a project. In a proposal, you seek to convince readers that you (or your organization) can do the project successfully and that you are the best choice for the project. Obviously, the proposal is a persuasive and even competitive document. Consider the following situations:

- A software development company needs a user's guide written for the new software application it is producing.
- A government agency needs someone to train its employees to convert its information to a Web page.
- To proceed with a doctoral thesis, a graduate student must prepare a proposal for approval by her committee.
- To write their technical reports, students in a technical-writing course must write proposals for approval by their instructor.

The software company or the government agency might issue a request for proposals (RFP), compare the proposals received, select the best one, and contact the proposal writer to arrange a contract.

Plan a Proposal

The following walks you through the important steps in writing a proposal. To see how these steps work in an actual writing project, we'll follow an example through each of the steps.

1. **Build a team?** Proposals are good opportunities to work in teams. In the professional world, plenty of proposals are developed by teams. In technical-writing courses, team-written proposals can be effective: proposals take a lot of brainstorming to plan; team members who work well together generally out-brainstorm individuals; and proposals take a lot of work to write.

2. **Think of a project for a proposal.** If you know people wanting to install a local area network in their company and you have that expertise, you've got an ideal, "real-world" situation for a proposal. However, you may not be so lucky as to have tailor-made projects just begging for proposals. Instead, you may have to use your imagination. If you know of an ongoing project, back up to the beginning and write your own proposal. Think of companies, agencies, or individuals in need of projects and write a proposal for one of them. Think of an interesting topic, and then imagine a related project that would call for a proposal. See **http://www.powertools.nelson.com** for other methods of finding and narrowing topic ideas.

To get a sense of how to develop a proposal, imagine that you want to address wind energy somehow. There are plenty of possibilities, as the following examples demonstrate:

- You could research the feasibility of building a wind farm in your county. Would it work? Would the public accept it? How much would it cost? Would it pay for itself or even bring in revenue?

- You could develop a background report on wind farms for county council members who need in-depth information to help in their decision making.

- Consider this possibility: what about a case-study report in which you research several sites for their suitability as wind farms? Imagine that the provincial government has sent out an RFP requesting just such a study.

3. **Define the problem or situation.** Proposals offer to undertake a project that will help the customer solve a problem or take advantage of an opportunity. To convince the customer that you, the proposal writer, understand it, include a section discussing your perspective on the problem or situation. In terms of persuasion, this builds personal appeal—readers' confidence in you.

In this proposal project a group of environmentalists have asked you to do an environmental assessment of the proposed wind farm site. They hope to use the assessment as a tool to stop the construction of the site. The Canadian Environmental Assessment Agency (**http://www.ceaa.gc.ca**) provides funding for environmental assessments in certain situations—for example, for anyone "living or owning property in an affected area." Another possibility is if you "are planning to provide expert information relevant to the anticipated environmental effects of the project." Imagine that you decide that your first step will be to apply for a funding grant to pay for your time and the resources you might need to do the assessment.

4. **Describe a purpose and an audience.** To write a proposal that has a chance of winning the contract or gaining approval, carefully analyze the audience—the customers (the recipients of your proposal). Understand their technical level, and don't overshoot or undershoot it. Understand what they are looking for and what will convince them that your approach or your project is worthy of approval. See Chapter 17 for strategies for analyzing audiences.

While the environmental group will comprise part of your audience (they will want to know what you are asking for), your main audience will be the government funding agency. These readers will want to know that you have the qualifications to do the assessment, and that the assessment is worth doing. You will have to write in a technical, clear manner and have a precise knowledge of what your costs will be. The government is not likely (not anymore anyway) to throw money at you if it thinks you will not be spending it in a useful way.

5. **Describe your proposed project.** In your proposal, describe specifically what you propose to do. It's easy to get so caught up in "selling" your project that you neglect to explain what you actually propose to do (and not do).

> Your project will be to do a study of the effect on the bird population in the area, and to measure noise from a similar installation with the same population density. In the "proposal" section, be careful to state that you intend to focus on these two issues. You will also need to show clearly that you are not beginning from a particular standpoint, but that you want to find out the facts.

6. **Describe some combination of the results, benefits, and feasibility of your proposed project.** Proposals can be categorized as *solicited* and *unsolicited*. Solicited proposals are requested by the customer—for example, by means of an RFP. Unsolicited proposals have not been requested. They come in the mail or through the door unexpectedly. In an unsolicited proposal, you have to convince the customer that the proposed project should be done and that its results will be valuable. *Results* refer to what the customer will get from the proposed project. *Benefits* refer to the positive gains for the customer. *Feasibility* refers to the likelihood of those benefits (for some projects, you can't guarantee the benefits).

> As this proposal is unsolicited, you will need to sell yourself and the need for the assessment.

7. **Describe your method and plan.** Some proposals must describe the method and the process that the proposer intends to use in the project. Doing so gives the customer an opportunity to visualize how the project will proceed and to compare different proposers' plans.

> In this proposal, describe the procedures you'll use to do this research. Explain how you'll set up the study of the bird population in the area.

8. **Create a tentative schedule for your project.** Most proposals contain a timeline for the proposed project. Identify the major milestones and establish either completion dates or completion time frames for them. Including the schedule builds personal appeal: it shows customers that you are organized and professional.

> As you are proposing to do primary research for this study, you will draw on your own experience and should have a clear idea of how long an assessment would take you. However, you will also need to allow time to analyze your data and write the report itself. You will also need time to research other areas to see what the findings are before you begin your own assessment. You will also need to consult regularly with your clients, the environmental group. Block out the initial research time, the primary research time, and the report writing time. Allow yourself time to complete a first draft, let it sit for a bit, and then edit and

polish up the report. At this stage you are asking for funding to do the assessment, so if you ask too little from the government agency, you will find yourself working for a few dollars an hour. On the other hand, if you ask for too much time, you may not receive the funding as it will be clear that you are overcharging.

9. **List your qualifications for the project and references.** An important function of the proposal is to present your qualifications for the project. You can briefly list your education, training, and work experience; you can attach your résumé; or you can do both. References to past customers who have been satisfied with your work may also be useful, as may pictures and descriptions of your past projects. Again, this material builds personal appeal.

If you are a student in a technical-writing course, the qualifications section may be a problem. What qualifications do you really have for this project: good intentions, strong work ethic, Internet savviness, good technical-writing skills, low rates? Some instructors may encourage you to invent a realistic set of qualifications—even your own consulting firm complete with logo and stationery! Spend some time identifying or researching the appropriate qualifications for this project.

10. **List the costs, fees, and necessary resources for your proposed project.** Some proposals show how much the project will cost, what resources will be needed, and so on. "Break out" the costs and hourly rates for the different types of work, as well as the costs for other project expenses. Even an internal project has costs; estimate your total hours, resources you'll need, and so on.

What will be the costs for this project? Costs may include gas mileage for getting to the local library, photocopying, or ordering government reports. Online research may cost in terms of connect time; you'll likely be ordering reports and articles over the Internet as well. You might search commercial databases, which will mean start-up and usage fees. The most important cost you will identify will be for your own time. As a professional, you do not work for nothing, but the environmental group does not have the funds to pay for your time. It is, therefore, imperative that you persuade the government agency to pay for your time.

11. **Consider whether graphics or tables are needed.** Proposals are just as likely to need graphics and tables as any other technical document. In fact, including them will lend professionalism to your finished proposal. Maps, floor plans, sketches, flow charts, and other such graphics can be good ways to convey information in your proposal. You can use tables to show your costs and fees, statistics about the problem, or project results. (See Chapter 11 for ideas and strategies for graphics; Chapter 10, for tables, charts, and graphs.)

This funding proposal is not the final product and will likely not need as many graphic elements as your final report to the environmental group. However, you need to persuade the government agency that there is a need for the report, and that it should fund the work. You will, therefore, want to show the results of other similar assessments in different provinces, or even different countries. The best way to show this type of information would be with charts, such as pie charts. For emotional impact you might want to show photos of birds that have been killed by the turbines, although you should not overdo this type of persuasion.

12. **Include other necessary supporting information.** Certainly not all of the sections just described are needed in every proposal. Nor are they the only sections that may be needed; they are just the most common. Back away from this project occasionally, and imagine what your customer needs to approve your project or to select you to do the project. A proposal is a persuasive effort. What else would help convince your readers: a tentative outline of the final report; a sketch of the finished project; samples of what the finished project will look like?

13. **Consider the format.** Chapter 14 shows that you can design a proposal as a memorandum, a business letter, or a separate document with a cover memo or letter. The two proposals at the end of this chapter show a memo version and a report with a cover letter.

    This proposal is an external document, written from you to the government funding agency. Thus, it must be either a self-contained business letter proposal or one with a separate format and a cover letter. The format you choose may depend on the requirements of the government office; you will need to research what these are.

14. **Review and revise your rough draft.** Use the strategies in Chapter 16 to systematically review and revise your proposal. Use the top-down approach described there: start by reviewing for audience, purpose, and situation; then move on to content, organization, and transitions; then headings, lists, tables, and graphics; then sentence style and technical style; and finally, grammar, usage, spelling, and punctuation problems.

HOW DO YOU WRITE A PROGRESS REPORT?

Progress reports are another interesting example of persuasion, although they are a quieter form than the proposal. The following discusses what progress reports are, how they function within a project, as well as how to plan and design progress reports.

About Progress Reports

When you are involved in a lengthy, complex, or expensive project, you must write regularly scheduled progress reports summarizing the status of the project. These reports are essentially persuasive: they seek to convince readers that you are handling the project competently and progressing smoothly, or that you are addressing problems responsibly. If there are problems, you are letting your customer know about them up front, rather than hiding them. Your customer can see your efforts to solve the problems and can even get involved. If the project is going smoothly, your customer can feel satisfied with your work. Progress reports also help you defend yourself or your organization in case you get blamed for something that is not your fault. For example, if your technical documentation contained serious inaccuracies because developers wouldn't take the time to review it, you could have stated that in your progress reports.

The essential information in a progress report includes a summary of the work completed, the work in progress, the work coming up, and an overall assessment of the status of the project. It answers the customer's question, "How is it going?" It also enables you to go on record by saying, "These are our concerns." Progress reports also contain other information such as schedules, outlines, drawings, expense reports, and early data and conclusions—whatever is needed to convey a full sense of the status of the project.

Plan a Progress Report

The following steps guide you through the important considerations in writing a progress report. To see how these steps work in an actual writing project, we'll follow a single example through each of the steps.

1. **Find a project for which you can write a progress report.** If you are not involved in a project, finding a project for a progress report in a technical-writing course can be a problem. Consider this: write about your progress on your semester technical report, usually assigned early in the semester and due toward the end of the semester. Perhaps you are involved in a team design project in your major, or in a project at work. Perhaps you are an intern at a major corporation involved in developing a new release of a product: try interviewing managers and developers on the status of the project (not a bad way to get to know some key players if you want to get hired full time).

   Imagine that you've chosen to write a progress report on your semester technical report project to let your professor know how you are progressing. You're writing that the report you proposed, two versions of which are at the end of this chapter, is now nearly done. The progress report will give your professor a chance to evaluate your work and make sure you haven't headed off in the wrong direction.

2. **Analyze the audience; review your purpose and objective.** Remember that your goals are not merely to report on the status of the project but to maintain good relations with your customer and to protect yourself. Remember, as well, that the actual reader of your progress report may not necessarily be at your technical level. Project managers do not necessarily have the technical depth, but they pay the bills!

3. **Write a brief description of the project.** It's a good idea to include a descriptive overview of the project. That way your customers can see whether your idea of the project is the same as theirs. It also helps newcomers in the customer's organization understand what the project is about.

   In your description, say that your purpose is to provide homeowners with background information on wind energy as well as on environmental and cost issues. Mention when the report was assigned and what the delivery date is. You are not delivering your report to a government agency or professional body, but you should consider your professor to have the same status as these two customers. After all, he is the one who holds your future career in his hands.

4. **List of the main tasks in the project.** One good way to assess your progress is to create a task analysis of the project. List all the important tasks that you must complete in order to finish the project. Better yet, turn that list into a Gantt chart (as shown in Figure 6-2) that shows start and stop times for those tasks on an overall timeline.

Task	Sept. 25–Oct. 1	Oct. 2–Oct. 8	Oct. 9–Oct. 15	Oct. 16–Oct. 22	Oct. 23–Oct. 29	Oct. 30–Nov. 5	Nov. 6–Nov. 12	Nov. 13–Nov. 26
Prototype	▨							
Style guide		▨						
Graphics				▨				
Rough-draft phase			▨					
Rough-draft review					▨			
Style-guide update					▨			
Rough-draft revision						▨		
Final draft: edit/proof							▨	
Final-draft production								▨
Final-draft inspection								▨
Project upload								▨
Party at Julie's								▨

FIGURE 6-2

Gantt chart. Gantt charts are useful in projects where critical tasks must be complete before others can begin.

You know that the project requires that you do the following: search library databases, the Internet, and government documents. You also know you are expected to interview two or three experts in the field, including, possibly, other professors at your school. The project also includes writing the rough draft of the report, adding the graphics, running a table of contents and a list of figures, and deciding what should be moved to the appendixes. Set up a Gantt chart showing the expected start and completion dates of each major task in your project.

5. **List what you have completed, what you are currently working on, and what you have left to do.** Assess your project in terms of completed tasks, current tasks, and future tasks. Be as specific and detailed as you can be. Instead of saying that the questionnaire analysis took longer than expected, say that it required 21 hours over the projected 85.

   In your research for your feasibility study, imagine that you have completed your library database and Internet searches; however, you had requested interviews with manufacturers and installers and have not managed to complete these because the interviewees have not been available. You do have times scheduled and need to tell your professor that this is the case. You have completed the first draft of the report but have not yet added the graphics as you need to add the interviews first. These two tasks, and the final edit, are all you have left to do.

6. **List major concerns and problems related to the project.** Spend some time thinking about what is not going so well in your project, what the problems are, and what unexpected things have happened. Perhaps certain important information has not yet arrived. Find a diplomatic way to describe these problems in the actual progress report—if you want to maintain good relations with your customer (internal or external).

   Imagine that you've not found a contractor who has already installed the system you are going to recommend. You know you can't rely just on the manufacturer for information. Find a way to put a positive spin on this situation. Perhaps you found a homeowner who is using the system and is happy with it. You intend to contact the homeowner and ask her who installed her system.

7. **Summarize project expenses, hours, and resources used.** Progress reports don't necessarily include expense reports. Your customer will be the one to stipulate what is included. Obviously, money, time, and other resources consumed to date are an important indicator of project status. If you do include such details, present them as tables (see Chapter 10 for details on designing tables).

   So far, you and your group have worked 4 weeks and logged 390 hours. You've run up several hundred dollars of long-distance phone calls. You've purchased over a hundred dollars' worth of books, articles, and reports, and you've done nearly a hundred dollars' worth of photocopying.

8. **Summarize current outcomes, if applicable.** For some projects, you may want to give your customers a glimpse of current results. If you are running an experiment, show the data you've collected so far. If you are designing or building something, provide photographs, drawings, diagrams, or blueprints. If you are writing a report, show the current outline.

   In this project there is not much for your professor to glimpse. However, you might provide a brief summary of the wind turbine system you intend to use. Or you could provide a brief overview about what is necessary for the installation of a system. You will know you are successful if your professor starts to get interested in installing his or her own system.

9. **Write an overall, concluding summary of the project status.** If you've assessed your project in terms of work completed, work ongoing, work upcoming, expenses, resources used, and problems and concerns, you are ready to write a detailed, informed summary.

   In your summary, you can honestly state that the project is going smoothly and is on schedule—with the exception of that one concern about the interviews.

10. **Plan the introduction.** When you've rough-drafted or at least planned your progress report, it's time to write or plan the introduction. It may seem backward, but it's only then that you really know the topics you cover and the major points you make. In an introduction to a progress report, at least state the purpose of the document (to tell the customer about the status of the project) and provide an overview of what you'll cover.

    Keep the introduction to this progress report brief. State that this is a progress report to bring your professor up to date on the work your group has done on your feasibility report. Also state that you will describe the overall project, work completed, and work upcoming, and that you will assess the overall status of the report.

11. **Consider the format.** Chapter 14 demonstrates how to design a progress report as a memorandum, a business letter, or a separate document with a cover memo or letter. The progress report at the end of this chapter is a separate document with a cover business letter.

    A progress report to your professor should probably be considered an internal document. However, in this case we have shown you an example of an external document, which has a cover letter and a formal report format. Whichever type you choose, make the progress report neat, concise, and professional.

12. **Review and revise your rough draft.** Use the strategies in Chapter 16 to systematically review and revise your progress report. Use the top-down approach described there: start by reviewing for audience, purpose, and situation; then move on to content, organization, and transitions; then headings, lists, tables, and graphics; then on to sentence style and technical style; and finally, grammar, usage, spelling, and punctuation problems.

WORKSHOP: PERSUASION, PROPOSALS, AND PROGRESS REPORTS

Here are some additional ideas for practising the concepts, tools, and strategies in this chapter:

1. *Topics for persuasion.* Consider the following topics. What persuasive documents might be written involving these topics?

Internet privacy	Career planning
Gene therapy	Animal testing
Website design	Immigration

2. *Persuasive appeals.* For one of the persuasive projects you defined in the preceding item, make a list of the logical, emotional, and personal appeals you might use, along with any counterarguments you might have to address.

3. *Topics for proposals.* Consider the following topics. What sorts of proposals can you imagine for them? Who would be the recipients of these proposals?

Life in extreme environments	Climate changes
Computers and elementary students	Oceanic pollution
	Lack of city recreational areas
Sleep disorders	Speech-recognition software
Homeless people	

4. *Audiences for proposals.* Consider the following audiences. What sorts of proposals might they be interested in?

High school principals	City council members
Technical-writing professors	Political-party leaders
Senior citizens	Parent–teacher association

Board members for a battered women centre

Neighbourhood association members

Student council members

Department head for city planning

5. *Requests for proposals.* Consider the following organizations, agencies, and places. What sorts of requests for proposals (RFPs) might they issue?

Environment Canada

Partners in Art Education

Habitat for Humanity

Senior Citizens' Association

Ministry of Natural Resources

Department of Health and Social Services

City Council

City Planning Department

6. *Tasks and proposals.* Choose one of the following simple projects, and then list the major tasks that the project would include and that you would describe in a proposal.

Creating a program to encourage middle school students to plan to attend college

Obtaining computers for a disadvantaged school

Starting a community garden

Holding an International Day at your college

7. *Gantt charts.* For the task list you created in the preceding exercise, sketch a Gantt chart showing the start and end dates for each task in relation to the overall start and end dates for the project.

PERSUASIVE TECHNICAL WRITING

It Is Time We Stopped Waging War on the Earth

I am a Green and I have been one for most of my life. I don't hug trees, but I have planted 20,000 of them in a mistaken, but well-intended, attempt to make the land where I live go back to Gaia faster. I am also a scientist and my main contribution has been the Gaia theory, which sees the Earth actively sustaining its climate and chemistry so as to keep itself habitable.

I consider the Earth to have reached a state profoundly dangerous to our civilization. I am deeply concerned that public opinion, and consequently governments, listen less to scientists than they do to the green lobbies. These lobbies are well-intentioned, but they understand people better than they do the Earth. Consequently, they recommend inappropriate remedies and action.

The outcome is almost as bad as if the medieval plague had returned and we were earnestly advised to stop it with alternative, not scientific, medicine. Alternative green remedies, like wind turbines and bio-fuels alone, will not cure the Earth's sickness. This is why I recommend the appropriate medicine of nuclear energy as part of a sensible portfolio of energy sources.

Few of us would doubt that Rachel Carson's 1962 book, *Silent Spring*, crystallized green thinking, but few seem to remember that her concern was for birds, which she saw as the voices of the natural world. Her warning was about the living Earth and the imminent destruction of wildlife by the uncontrolled use of pesticides and herbicides. We greens care about the natural world. But many people in the politicized green movement live in cities. Their concerns are not about chemicals killing wildlife, but about the possibility that chemical residues in foodstuffs might poison themselves.

Persuasion in technical-writing courses: Technical-writing courses are not normally the place for editorial essays. However, the techniques of persuasion, which are used well in this essay, are worth studying. You should always be aware of when you have slipped from a logical to an emotional argument and be careful to use the emotional techniques sparingly. As well, facts and expert opinions need to be substantiated with documentation.

Personal appeal: The writer states his case after first giving his qualifications to do so. Not only is he a scientist, he is also a confirmed environmentalist, or "green." By telling us his qualifications, he identifies himself with the opposition before telling us his contrary opinion.

Rebuttal: The essay is written as an extended rebuttal of the common green arguments that the environment can be saved by green methods. The author frequently makes his case by using analogies and metaphors. In fact, the title itself uses a metaphor, which he extends through the piece. The earth is a living being, against which a war can be fought. A living being that can become "ill" and be "cured."

Concessions: The author refers to a seminal environmental text and acknowledges the importance of that work. Then he gently reminds the reader what the book was really about. He concedes that greens "care about the natural world" but points out that they have other issues that are important to them.

Emotional appeal: Although this paragraph contains facts, it really appeals to the emotions. Two million people die yearly in the developing world because we are too selfish to let them use DDT. You should be aware that even facts and statistics can be used to sway a reader's emotions.

By ignoring the Earth, we greens have made appalling errors. Greens persuaded the comfortable First World that chlorine-containing chemicals like DDT were carcinogenic. Soon, legislation banned its use and manufacture, denying the developing world the chance to combat malaria successfully. Now, two million die yearly of this disease. There's no proof DDT causes human cancer, yet the perception was enough for the public to support madly selfish legislation.

This mistake is nowhere near as harmful as green energy policy, which actually intensifies the global-warming crisis. An outraged Gaia responds to the harm we do by changing the environment to a state where we are no longer welcome.

What are these threats? Most of us know that winters are shorter and spring comes earlier. But, in the Arctic, climate change occurs more than twice as fast as in temperate latitudes, and torrents of summertime melt water now plunge from Greenland's kilometre-high glaciers. The complete dissolution of Greenland's icy mountains will take time. But, by then, the sea will have risen seven metres, rendering uninhabitable such low-lying coastal cities as London, Venice, Calcutta, New York, and Tokyo. The Arctic Ocean's floating ice is even more vulnerable. In 30 years, much of its white-reflecting surface may become dark sea that absorbs summer sunlight.

Logical appeal: Numbers are used here, and although they aren't specifically documented (this is an article, not a report), the sources are mentioned.

At the equator, the climatologist warns that a four-degree rise in temperature is enough to eliminate the vast Amazon forests—a great global air conditioner—in a catastrophe for their people and their biodiversity. The scientists behind the Intergovernmental Panel on Climate Change predicted in 2001 that global temperatures would rise between two and six degrees Celsius by 2100. But even this grim forecast could be an underestimate. Swiss meteorologists say the excessive heat of the 2003 summer in Europe was wholly different from any previous heat wave. More than 20,000 died from overheating; it was a warning of worse to come.

Personal appeal: This paragraph begins with an analogy, and moves to a prediction. Predictions by experts are acceptable, and in this case the expert is the author. As with any documented work, the reader must judge the credibility of the expert. Read James Lovelock's biography at Wikipedia.com and you will see he is well qualified to make the predictions he makes here.

The great Earth system, Gaia, is trapped in a vicious circle of positive feedback. Extra heat from any source, whether from greenhouse gases, the disappearance of Arctic ice, the changing structure of the ocean surface, or the destruction of tropical forests, is amplified. It is almost as if we had lit a fire to keep warm and failed to notice that the furniture had ignited. That leaves little time to put out the fire before it consumes the house.

Like a fire, global warming is accelerating and we have little time left to act. Seven years since Kyoto, little has happened. Those who construct models of such changes (I am one) predict that, somewhere between 400 and 600 parts per million of carbon dioxide, the Earth passes a threshold beyond which global warming becomes irreversible. We are now at 380 parts per million and could reach 400 ppm within seven years.

We must stop gaining energy from fossil fuels in a way that emits greenhouse gases to the air and we must do it in the next decade. Carbon sequestration is a grand idea but can we achieve it in time? Clean renewable energy sounds appealing, but in practice is ruinously expensive and little more use than trying to survive on a diet of canapés alone. Burning gas instead of coal also sounds good and green since it cuts carbon-dioxide emissions in half. But, in practice, it may be the most dangerous energy source of all, because natural gas is 23 times as potent a greenhouse gas as CO_2.

Conclusion: In his conclusion, the author states his case overtly, referring back to what he said in paragraph two. He softens his criticisms somewhat by referring to potentially irresponsible third parties (the United States and China). The article was published in a Canadian newspaper, and he can expect that his readers will accept this part of the argument.

We will do our best to avoid a catastrophe. But green concepts of sustainable development and renewable energy are beguiling dreams that can lead only to failure. I cannot see the United States or the emerging economies of China and India cutting back; soon they will be the main source of emissions. To retain civilization, our survivors will need Draconian energy saving, the self-restraint to stop burning fossil fuel, and a secure and reliable source of energy. There is no sensible alternative to nuclear energy. I believe this supply of electricity will give us the chance to survive through the difficult times to come.

Our civilization is energy-intensive and we cannot turn it off without crashing. We need something much more effective than the green ideology of the Kyoto agreement. We must stop thinking of human needs and rights alone. Let us be brave and see that the real threat comes from the living Earth, which we have harmed and is now at war with us. We have to remember we are a part of it and it is our home.

Source: Lovelock, James. "It Is Time We Stopped Waging War on the Earth." *The Times and Transcript* 28 Mar. 2005: D7. Reprinted with permission from the author.

MEMO PROPOSAL

Memo format: The memo format is appropriate here in that an instructor and students can be considered as members of the same organization, making it an internal communication.

Subject line: Notice that the subject line identifies the topic and purpose of the memo. If "proposal" were omitted, readers would wonder if the memo was going to discuss the entire topic.

Introduction: In a business-like manner, the introductory paragraph states the purpose of the memo, refers to the context (the instructor's assignment), and then gives a brief overview of the contents of this memo.

Report scope and purpose: The writers have decided on a topic for their report, but have not really focused on a scope and purpose. As you follow through the proposals, progress report and final report, you will notice that the purpose and scope become more and more clear. Here, the report is addressed to general readers who are interested in saving money—in other words, 95% of Canadians. Try to create a report that addresses a particular need for a limited group of people. You will find the report much easier to write if you do. Read the final report and you will understand the difference.

MEMORANDUM

TO: George Tripp, CMNC355 Instructor
FROM: Katie Mulder, Lee Pearsons, Kristen Schwartzentruber, Architectural Technology Division
CC: Dan Douglas, Program Coordinator
SUBJECT: Proposal to write a feasibility report on wind-generated power in stand-alone residential applications.
DATE: October 9, 2006

In September this year you requested that we prepare a group-written report in fulfillment of the requirements for CMNC355. The following is a proposal to conduct a feasibility study analyzing wind-generated power in a stand-alone residential application. This proposal contains an overview of the topic, an outline of the work we plan to do, our qualifications, and a projected schedule.

The proposed report will inform the reader of the need for and benefits of wind-generated power in residential applications. In our report we will compare the costs, benefits, and drawbacks of wind-generated power in stand-alone residential units located in Southwestern Ontario. The report will determine the feasibility of wind power compared to conventional energy sources.

We look forward to hearing your ideas on the scope of this feasibility report.

Need for Wind-Generated Power

As nonrenewable power sources such as oil, natural gas, and coal deplete, the costs of these resources increase. Wind power is boundless and will always remain a constant source of energy. Current studies have proven wind energy to be one of the most reliable and cost effective sources of natural power available. Tight budget restrictions of today often force consumers to look for such alternate sources of energy.

Benefits of Wind-Generated Power

In the report, we will document the following:

1. Wind as a renewable resource;
2. The cost effectiveness of wind-generated power compared to conventionally powered buildings;
3. The amount of energy produced by wind turbines;

4. Environmental benefits of wind power compared to conventional energy; and
5. Public health benefits resulting from the use of wind power rather than conventional energy sources.

Report Audience

We will address the report to professors George Tripp and Dan Douglas. However, we will target the report to general consumers interested in the use of alternate energy sources to save on energy costs, reduce pollution, and conserve nonrenewable resources.

Procedure

In writing this report, we will take the following steps to obtain information:

- Our first sources will be our textbooks and information that we can find at local libraries and in online library databases at the college.
- We will also search for information using the Internet, either with search engines or with addresses provided to us by others.
- We will also solicit interviews with experts, such as manufacturers and installers of wind-generation systems, as well as professors at the college.

Description of Final Report

The end product will consist of at least eight double-spaced pages for the written version, and a PowerPoint presentation for the class presentation. We will include graphics, charts, and digital photographs that we take ourselves. The report will include appendixes, including a glossary of unfamiliar technical terms.

Our Qualifications

As aspiring architectural technologists, we are aware of the importance of sustainable energy sources and the increasing costs of common energy sources. We have completed several courses relating to building science, building materials and methods, and zoning and building code requirements, so we understand the uses of energy within residential and small commercial buildings. We also have experience with determining how to maximize the energy efficiency of electrical systems within buildings. We are confident that our qualifications and knowledge will allow us to find the required technical information to write this report.

Work Schedule for Feasibility Report

We will deliver the report to your office on December 8, 2006. Here is our schedule for the project:

1. Conduct on-site interview   on October 13
2. Library research   through October 21
3. Correspondence   through October 21
4. Review correspondence received   finish October 28
5. Write preliminary draft   finish October 28
6. Produce graphics   finish November 4
7. Finalize preliminary draft   finish November 11
8. Deliver preliminary draft   on December 8

   All dates subject to change

Costs

There will be minimal costs involved in producing this study. We will have the cost of fuel for site visits and costs for printing, graphics, binding, and duplicating the report. We will borrow a digital camera from the college library for the photographs we intend to use, so no costs will be incurred for that.

List of Graphics

A list of graphics we plan to use is presented here:

1. Estimated Costs of Several Wind Turbines   Chart
2. General Assessment of Power Consumption   Graph
3. Noise Pollution Comparison   Graph
4. How a Wind Turbine Works   Diagram
5. Energy Output of a Wind Turbine   Graph

Tentative Outline
   I. Introduction
      A. History of Wind Energy
      B. How a Wind Turbine Works
  II. Environmental Impact
      A. Wind as an Inexhaustible Resource
      B. Public Health Benefits
      C. Noise Pollution
 III. Energy Production and Consumption
      A. Energy Produced by Turbine
      B. Energy Consumed by Building
      C. Production and Consumption Relationship

IV. Costs
    A. Monetary Costs
        1. Material and installation
        2. Maintenance
        3. Money savings
    B. Economical Development
        1. Land usage
        2. Ideal location
 V. Conclusion
    A. Summarize pros and cons
    B. Summarize costs
    C. Recommend action

Information Sources

As noted above, we have most of the basic theoretical knowledge required for this report. For the finer details, we can talk to instructors, use the library databases, contact provincial and local government experts, and search the Internet. We also have several contacts in the wind turbine manufacturing field through one of our group. We do not foresee any difficulties finding all the required information.

Working Bibliography

Documentation: Note that APA style is used in this list.

Canada. Environment Canada (2004). *The green lane.* Retrieved Sept. 30, 2004, from http://www.on.gc.ca

Canadian Wind Energy Association (2004). Retrieved Sept. 30, 2004, from http://www.canwea.ca

Gipe, Paul (1993). *Wind power for home and business: Renewable energy for the 1990s and beyond.* White River Junction, Vermont: Chelsea Green Publishing Company.

Marbek Resource Consultants, SGA Consulting for the Renewable and Electrical Division, Energy Resources Branch of Natural Resources Canada (2000). *Stand-alone wind energy system: A buyer's guide.* (Cat. No. M920175-199E).

McGowan, Jon C. (1997). Wind power. In *The Wiley encyclopedia of energy and the environment* (Vol. 2, pp. 1523–1534). New York: Wiley Publishers.

MSC Enterpriser (1998). *Wind energy basic information.* Canadian Wind Energy Association (CanWEA).

Potts, Michael (1993). *The independent home: Living well with power.* Post Mills, Vermont: Chelsea Green Publishing Company.

The Alternative Energy Store, LLC (2004). Retrieved Sept. 30, 2004, from http://www.shop.altenergystore.com

Feasibility of the Project

We do not anticipate problems in obtaining the information we need for this report or in completing the report by the given deadline.

The costs for this project, as stated above, are not a problem. This project will supply an excellent opportunity for education as it will allow us to combine our education with our interest in the environment. The future should definitely be green, and we would like to research this exciting alternative energy possibility.

Please contact me if you have questions regarding the report. My home phone number is 519-555-3333, and my e-mail address is astudent@rogers.com.

PROPOSAL COVER LETTER

Cover business letter: The writers chose to attach a cover letter to their proposal and make the proposal a separate document. If they had chosen to use a self-contained business-letter format, they would move the signature block to the end of the proposal, delete the title (on the next page), and then merge the contents of the paragraph in the cover letter and the introductory paragraph on the next page.

Contents: Notice the contents of this letter. It states the purpose of the document to follow, gives an overview of the contents of the document to follow, and provides contact information for the author. Notice that these same contents are repeated in the introductory paragraph for the proposal proper on the next page. That's because the writer can't be sure if this cover letter will remain attached once it gets to the recipient.

The A Team
Fanshawe College
1460 Oxford St. E.
London, Ontario N5Y 5R6

October 28, 2006

Mr. George Tripp, Professor
Fanshawe College
1460 Oxford St. E.,
P.O. Box 7005
London, Ontario N5Y 5R6

Re: Proposal to develop a feasibility report on wind-generated power in a stand-alone residential application for CMNC355.

Dear Mr. Tripp:

In response to your request for a group-written feasibility report in fulfillment of course requirements for CMNC355, we enclose the attached proposal report on wind-generated power for the home. The final report is due at the end of the semester and will be accompanied by an oral presentation in front of the class.

This report will provide you with an introduction to wind energy. It will compare the costs, benefits, and drawbacks of wind-generated power in a stand-alone residential unit located just north of London, Ontario. Through this technical report we will determine whether or not the installation of a wind turbine is feasible and realistic for this application. The feasibility will be determined as we compare it to the primary use of conventional energy sources.

As you will see in the proposal, we have already done some preliminary research on the Internet and in the library databases. We have also contacted manufacturers and installers and will conduct interviews with representatives of both groups. We look forward to learning more on the subject and hope to be able to educate you and members of the class on this topic with our presentation. If you have any questions or comments, please contact us at our college e-mail addresses or in the online class discussion forum.

Sincerely,

Katie Mulder   *Lee Pearsons*   *Kristen Schwartzentruber*

The A Team
Architectural Technology
Fanshawe College

FEASIBILITY PROPOSAL

Alternative format: This proposal is similar to the previous one, but reformatted to accompany a cover letter.

Harnessing Wind Power for Home Use

The following is a proposal to conduct a feasibility study analyzing wind-generated power in a stand-alone residential application. This proposal contains an overview of the topic, an outline of the work we plan to do, our qualifications, and a projected schedule.

The proposed report will inform the reader of the need for and benefits of wind-generated power in residential applications. In our report we will compare the costs, benefits, and drawbacks of wind-generated power in stand-alone residential units located in Southwestern Ontario. The report will determine the feasibility of wind power compared to conventional energy sources.

We look forward to hearing your ideas on the scope of this feasibility report.

Need for Wind-Generated Power

As nonrenewable power sources such as oil, natural gas, and coal deplete, the costs of these resources increase. Wind power is boundless and will always remain a constant source of energy. Current studies have proven wind energy to be one of the most reliable and cost effective sources of natural power available. Tight budget restrictions of today often force consumers to look for such alternate sources of energy.

Benefits of Wind-Generated Power

In the report, we will document the following:

1. Wind as a renewable resource;
2. The cost effectiveness of wind-generated power compared to conventionally powered buildings;
3. The amount of energy produced by wind turbines;
4. Environmental benefits of wind power compared to conventional energy; and

5. Public health benefits resulting from the use of wind power rather than conventional energy sources.

Report Audience

We will address the report to professors George Tripp and Dan Douglas. However, we will target the report to general consumers interested in the use of alternate energy sources to save on energy costs, reduce pollution, and conserve nonrenewable resources.

Procedure

In writing this report, we will take the following steps to obtain information:

- Our first sources will be our textbooks and information that we can find at local libraries and in online library databases at the college.
- We will also search for information using the Internet, either with search engines or with addresses provided to us by others.
- We will also solicit interviews with experts, such as manufacturers and installers of wind-generation systems, as well as professors at the college.

Description of Final Report

The end product will consist of at least eight double-spaced pages for the written version, and a PowerPoint presentation for the class presentation. We will include graphics, charts, and digital photographs that we take ourselves. The report will include appendixes, including a glossary of unfamiliar technical terms.

Our Qualifications

As aspiring architectural technologists, we are aware of the importance of sustainable energy sources and the increasing costs of common energy sources. We have completed several courses relating to building science, building materials and methods, and zoning and building code requirements, so we understand the uses of energy within residential and small commercial buildings. We also have experience with determining how to maximize the energy efficiency of electrical systems within buildings. We are confident that our qualifications and knowledge will allow us to find the required technical information to write this report.

Work Schedule for Feasibility Report

We will deliver the report to your office on December 8, 2006. Here is our schedule for the project:

1. Conduct on-site interview   on October 13
2. Library research   through October 21
3. Correspondence   through October 21
4. Review correspondence received   finish October 28
5. Write preliminary draft   finish October 28
6. Produce graphics   finish November 4
7. Finalize preliminary draft   finish November 11
8. Deliver preliminary draft   on December 8

  All dates subject to change

Costs

There will be minimal costs involved in producing this study. We will have the cost of fuel for site visits and costs for printing, graphics, binding, and duplicating the report. We will borrow a digital camera from the college library for the photographs we intend to use, so no costs will be incurred for that.

List of Graphics

A list of graphics we plan to use is presented here:

1. Estimated Costs of Several Wind Turbines   Chart
2. General Assessment of Power Consumption   Graph
3. Noise Pollution Comparison   Graph
4. How a Wind Turbine Works   Diagram
5. Energy Output of a Wind Turbine   Graph

Tentative Outline

I. Introduction

    A. History of Wind Energy

    B. How a Wind Turbine Works

II. Environmental Impact

    A. Wind as an Inexhaustible Resource

    B. Public Health Benefits

    C. Noise Pollution

III. Energy Production and Consumption

    A. Energy Produced by Turbine

    B. Energy Consumed by Building

    C. Production and Consumption Relationship

IV. Costs

    A. Monetary Costs

        1. Material and installation

        2. Maintenance

        3. Money savings

    B. Economical Development

        1. Land usage

        2. Ideal location

V. Conclusion

    A. Summarize pros and cons

    B. Summarize costs

    C. Recommend action

Information Sources

As noted above, we have most of the basic theoretical knowledge required for this report. For the finer details, we can talk to instructors, use the library databases, contact provincial and local government experts, and search the Internet. We also have several contacts in the wind turbine manufacturing field through one of our group. We do not foresee any difficulties finding all the required information.

Working Bibliography

Canada. Environment Canada (2004). *The green lane.* Retrieved Sept. 30, 2004, from http://www.on.gc.ca

Canadian Wind Energy Association (2004). Retrieved Sept. 30, 2004, from http://www.canwea.ca

Gipe, Paul (1993). *Wind power for home and business: Renewable energy for the 1990s and beyond.* White River Junction, Vermont: Chelsea Green Publishing Company.

Marbek Resource Consultants, SGA Consulting for the Renewable and Electrical Division, Energy Resources Branch of Natural Resources Canada (2000). *Stand-alone wind energy system: A buyer's guide.* (Cat. No. M920175-199E).

McGowan, Jon C. (1997). Wind power. In *The Wiley encyclopedia of energy and the environment* (Vol. 2, pp. 1523–1534). New York: Wiley Publishers.

MSC Enterpriser (1998). *Wind energy basic information.* Canadian Wind Energy Association (CanWEA).

Potts, Michael (1993). *The independent home: Living well with power.* Post Mills, Vermont: Chelsea Green Publishing Company.

The Alternative Energy Store, LLC (2004). Retrieved Sept. 30, 2004, from http://www.shop.altenergystore.com

Feasibility of the Project

We do not anticipate problems in obtaining the information we need for this report or in completing the report by the given deadline.

The costs for this project, as stated above, are not a problem. This project will supply an excellent opportunity for education as it will allow us to combine our education with our interest in the environment. The future should definitely be green, and we would like to research this exciting alternative energy possibility.

Please contact me if you have questions regarding the report. My home phone number is 519-555-3333, and my e-mail address is astudent@rogers.com.

PROGRESS REPORT COVER LETTER

Cover letter: This progress report begins with a cover letter, separate from the actual report itself.

Letter format: This letter uses the block format, in which all components start at the left margin. Notice the use of the subject line (Re:).

Contents: The cover letter identifies what is attached—a progress report. This letter reminds readers of the overall purpose of the project and briefly describes its contents. In the second paragraph, the writer mentions the purpose of the attached report and lists its essential contents.

Signature block: Notice the contents of the signature block: complimentary close, four lines for the signature, the typed name of the writer (in this case, the group name of the writers), organization name, and enclosure.

The A Team
Fanshawe College
1460 Oxford St. E.
London, Ontario N5Y 5R6

October 28, 2006

Mr. George Tripp, Professor
Fanshawe College
1460 Oxford St. E.,
P.O. Box 7005
London, Ontario N5Y 5R6

Re: Progress report on the feasibility report on wind-generated power in a stand-alone residential application.

Dear Mr. Tripp:

We are pleased to update you on the status of the proposed report. This report will provide you with an introduction to wind energy. It will compare the costs, benefits, and drawbacks of wind-generated power in a stand-alone residential unit located just north of London, Ontario. Through this technical report, we will determine whether or not the installation of a wind turbine is feasible and realistic for this application. The feasibility will be determined as we compare it to the primary use of conventional energy sources.

Attached is a status report of The A Team's work on the project. We are confident that our group will produce a report that serves your needs. If you have any questions or concerns, please contact one of our team members.

Sincerely,

Katie Mulder   *Lee Pearsons*   *Kristen Schwartzentruber*

The A Team
Architectural Technology
Fanshawe College

Enclosed: Progress Report

PROGRESS REPORT

The Feasibility of Wind-Generated Power in a Stand-Alone Residential Application

In September 2006 you requested that we research and write a feasibility report on a technical topic relating to our program, Architectural Technology. We are writing to inform you of our progress on the report, which is to be presented to you in class on December 8, 2006.

In this progress report, we have included a brief project description to confirm the purpose and scope of our feasibility report. We have also included overviews of the work completed, the work in progress, and the work still to be completed. Finally, we provide an overall assessment of the report's status.

Description of the Proposed Work

The purpose of our report is to determine the feasibility of installing a wind turbine to help power a conventional single-family home in either a city or rural area. The report can be used by a homeowner to compare the benefits and weaknesses of wind power to conventional energy sources available from the grid.

The scope of the report is limited by the requirements of the typical homeowner who needs to power such things as appliances, water heating, and lighting. We do not intend to cover broader uses, such as farming or small-business needs. We intend to document the following: (1) environmental impact of a stand-alone system, (2) energy production and consumption, (3) costs.

Audience

The intended audience is a homeowner interested in purchasing a stand-alone energy source. The report is geared toward a prospective buyer of a stand-alone wind energy system and his or her consultant. Given that the audience is already somewhat familiar with our subject, we will include brief background information on the way wind power works, the types of systems available for residential purposes (micro, mini, and small). Our main focus will be on the environmental impact, technical performance, and cost implications of the system.

Report Outline

The report will be organized in an easy-to-follow format and written in simple, clear language. Following is an updated outline for the feasibility study:

Projected outline: Notice that the outline is carefully designed and avoids some common problems: first- and second-level heads use initial caps on all the main words (but not prepositions or articles); third- and lower-level heads have initial caps on the first word only; there are no As without Bs, no 1s without 2s; alignment is carefully maintained; and the phrasing of items at the same level within the same section is carefully parallel.

I. Introduction
   A. Wind as a Source of Energy
   B. Harvesting the Wind: How a Wind Turbine Works

II. Environmental Impact
   A. Wind as an Inexhaustible Resource
   B. Public Health Benefits
   C. Noise Pollution
   D. Impact on Flora and Fauna

III. Energy Production and Consumption
   A. Energy Produced by Turbine
   B. Energy Consumed by Building
   C. Production and Consumption Relationship

IV. Costs and Materials
   A. Monetary Expenses
      1. Material and installation
      2. Operational costs
      3. Maintenance
      4. Money savings
   B. Economical Development
      1. Land usage
      2. Ideal location

V. Conclusion
   A. Summary of Pros and Cons
   B. Summary of Expenses
   C. Recommended Action

Timeline: Note that the team's schedule has changed since they wrote the proposal.

Bibliography: The method used here is APA.

Timeline

We will deliver the report to you in class on December 8, 2006. Here is our schedule for the project:

1. Complete preliminary draft   November 6
2. Produce graphics   November 10
3. Finalize preliminary draft   November 13
4. Deliver preliminary draft   December 8

Bibliography

We have found both paper and Internet sources. The printed sources we have located are as follows:

Gipe, P. (1993). *Windpower for home and business: Renewable energy for the 1990s and beyond.* White River Junction, VT: Chelsea Green Publishing Company.

Marbek Resource Consultants, SGA Consulting for the Renewable and Electrical Division, Energy Resources Branch of Natural Resources Canada (2000). *Stand-alone wind energy system: A buyer's guide.* (Cat. No. M920175-199E).

McGowan, J. C. (1997). Wind power. *The Wiley encyclopedia of energy and the environment* (Vol. 2, pp. 1523–1534). New York: Wiley Publishers.

MSC Enterpriser (1998). *Wind energy basic information.* Canadian Wind Energy Association (CanWEA).

Potts, M. (1993). *The independent home: Living well with power.* Post Mills, VT: Chelsea Green Publishing Company.

The Internet resources we have located are as follows:

The Alternative Energy Store, LLC. (2004). Retrieved Sept. 30, 2004, from http://www.shop.altenergystore.com

Canadian Geographic (2004). *Fuel for thought.* Retrieved October 13, 2004, from http://www.canadiangeographic.ca/Magazine/MJ03/Etcetera/fuelsQandA.asp

Canadian Geographic (2004). *Talking appliance energy*. Retrieved October 13, 2004, from http://www.canadiangeographic.ca/Magazine/MJ01/solar_homecosts.asp

Canadian Wind Energy Association (2004). *An introduction to stand-alone wind energy systems*. Retrieved Sept. 30, 2004, from http://www.canwea.ca

Canadian Wind Energy Association. (2004). *Stand-alone wind energy systems: A buyer's guide*. Retrieved Sept. 30, 2004, from http://www.canwea.ca

Krause, B. L. (n.d.). Wind turbine noise output evaluation. Retrieved June 5, 2005, from http://www.bergey.com

Northwest Seed (2004). *Wind energy benefits the local economy*. Retrieved October 13, 2004, from http://www.nwseed.org/news/news_archive/article2.pdf

NRG Systems, Inc. (2004). *Benefits of wind energy*. Retrieved October 13, 2004, from http://www.nrgsystems.com/facts/benefits.php

Ontario: Ministry of Agriculture and Food (September 2003). *Electricity generation using small wind turbines at your home or farm*. Retrieved October 13, 2004, from http://www.gov.on.ca/OMAFRA/english/engineer/facts/03-047.htm#availability

Ontario: Ministry of Energy (2004). *Wind energy*. Retrieved October 13, 2004, from http://www.energy.gov.on.ca

The British Wind Energy Association-Renewable Energy House (2004). *Benefits of wind energy*. Retrieved October 13, 2004, from http://www.bwea.com/energy/benefits.pdf

McIntyre, T. (2004). *Energy facts and figures*. Canadian Geographic. Retrieved October 13, 2004, from http://www.canadiangeographic.ca/Magazine/MJ01/solar_facts.asp

American Wind Energy Association (2002). *What do I need to know to purchase a residential wind turbine?* Retrieved October 13, 2004, from http://www.awea.org/faq/rsdntqa.html

Canada. Environment Canada (2004). The green lane. Retrieved Sept. 30, 2004, from http://www.on.gc.ca

List of graphics: Once again, this is a requirement from a technical writing course, although a paying client might want to know these details as well. Knowing what graphics will be included in the project gives the client one more way of visualizing the final product, and one more way of asking for changes.

Status of project: This is the main part of any progress report. Back in the introduction, the writers tell us they'll break this discussion into three areas. Here, they discuss the status of their work in each of these areas, and include the specific tasks that each member of the group has completed.

Graphics

The following graphics will be included in the report:

Wind energy system components	Diagram
Wind turbine sound measurements	Chart
Energy sector growth rates	Chart
Monthly wind speed measurements	Table
Annual energy consumption sample	Table
Turbines typical to our report	Pictures

Acquisition of Suitable Images (Ads and Graphics)

The graphics for this project are progressing nicely.

Work completed. We have the information for all of the graphics, and are currently organizing and formatting the information.

Work to be done. The graphics have yet to be incorporated into our report. We will be organizing them into their respective areas upon completion of the rough draft.

Compilation of Sources and Written Text

There is very much information to sort through in the preparation of this report. We have completed 80% of the information gathering and have written about 30% of the rough draft. Our project is on schedule and we will be finishing our feasibility study in time to prepare a formal presentation of our research.

Work completed. We have gathered the majority of information required and are organizing it into the corresponding categories of our report. Information has been obtained regarding the cost, materials, maintenance, environmental issues, energy consumption, and the history of wind energy. We have also researched different types of turbines and several manufacturers. We have chosen to use a Canadian manufacturer by the name of WestTech Energy in Kelowna, BC. WestTech manufactures a wind turbine called the 10 kW HAWT which is geared toward our application. The 10 kW HAWT (Horizontal Axis Wind

Turbine) will be used throughout our report as the typical wind energy source.

Work to be done. We have yet to complete our rough draft of the feasibility study. We have organized the outline of our report into the chosen topics of research and we are in the process of sorting our research into the respective topics. Once our rough draft is prepared, we will begin the editing of text and insertion of graphics into the report. As we are preparing the final draft we will begin to plan our formal presentation of the feasibility study.

Group Work Breakdown

So far we have worked as a group for most things we have done. All work is divided completely equally; one person types as the group discusses together what should be typed. The research was broken into sections and we focused mainly on our selected topics, while also obtaining information for the other topics if we came across any. Next week, we are individually doing more intense research on the selected areas of wind energy as outlined below. The purpose of this is to confirm the accuracy and level of technical information provided so far. We have decided that we will form the conclusion and final draft together.

Katie:

> Wind as a Limitless Resource
> Public Health Benefits
> Noise Pollution
> Land Usage
> Ideal Location

Lee:

> History of Wind Energy
> How a Wind Turbine Works
> Energy Produced by Turbine
> Energy Consumed by Building
> Production and Consumption Relationship

Kristen:

> Material and Installation
>
> Operational Costs
>
> Maintenance
>
> Money Savings

Overall Appraisal

The research we have done to date is very comprehensive and relates directly to our topic. The organization of research has yet to be done and once it is completed, our rough draft will be prepared. Our report will be complete and submitted on time and we do not foresee any obstacles in the future that will hinder the study's progression. Based on our research to date, we are confident that the pole-mounted WestTech 10 kW HAWT system, which is designed to provide all the power required by a single-family residence, will be a feasible and beneficial addition to a residential property.

PART II

Document-Design Tools

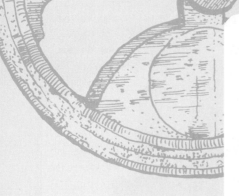

CHAPTER 7

Headings, Highlighting, and Emphasis

Topics covered in this chapter include

- sleep and dreams;
- alternative transportation fuels.

SLEEP AND DREAMS
For interesting information on this topic, try:

The Dreams Foundation
http://dreams.blogharbor.com

Dream Research, Sleep Disorders & Science of Dreams
http://www.dreams.ca/science.htm

A flashy Canadian site that compares dreams to movies and provides many interesting articles and much commentary is located at
http://www.dreamresearch.ca.

ALTERNATIVE TRANSPORTATION FUELS
Government of Canada's Climate Change website
http://www.climatechange.gc.ca/english/newsroom/1997/kyoto4b.asp

Environment Canada
http://www.ec.gc.ca/energ/fuels/fuel_home_e.htm

When you have completed this chapter, you will be able to

- design headings with appropriate level characteristics;
- use headings appropriately in your documents;
- create and apply heading styles with your word processor;
- run a Table of Contents page for your document;
- plan a highlighting scheme for your document;
- add highlighting and emphasis to your documents.

Now that just about everyone has powerful desktop-publishing software, we can all go wild with special typographical effects such as bold, italics, underscores, small caps, larger and smaller type sizes, different fonts, and even colours. In addition, the word-processing tools have amazing built-in programs that allow us to automatically change the entire document with a few clicks of the mouse. It is now easy to make our documents consistent throughout and to automatically generate tables of contents, lists of figures, and so on.

Using headings and developing a consistent system of highlighting and emphasis are similar in result, but we are going to address them separately.

WHAT ARE HEADINGS: WHAT ARE THEY GOOD FOR?

Headings are those titles and subtitles that you see inserted right in the running text of a document. They indicate the topic, purpose, or both, of the paragraphs that follow. Headings are one of the most powerful tools you can use in your technical, business, and scientific writing. They increase the readability, scannability, and the overall professionalism of your documents.

This chapter discusses the value of headings in technical writing and some basic design considerations for headings. It then shows you how to create and use headings. Included in this chapter are techniques for creating headings with Microsoft Word. All other word-processing packages have similar capabilities. You'll also learn how to create *styles*, powerful tools that ensure consistency and increase efficiency.

Headings indicate the topic and purpose of the paragraphs that follow. Actually, the best analogy for headings is that they are like outline items that have been pumped into the text at the appropriate points. For example, try to reconstruct the outline you'd see for the headings in Figure 7-1.

First-level heading: With this alphanumeric system, the level 1 heading is at the left margin with a leading Roman numeral. The Arial font, bold, 16 point contrasts with the body Times New Roman. The before spacing is set to 12 points and the after spacing is 24.

I. INTRODUCTION

The Alternative Transportation Fuels (ATF) R&D Initiative falls under the Efficiency and Alternative Energy (EAE) Program. The ATF Initiative of the EAE program is managed by the Transportation Energy Technology division of NRCan's CANMET Energy Technology Centre. The federal government has been active in alternative transportation fuels for more than twenty years. In 1990–91 approximately $3 million was allocated for the ATF R&D Initiative. In 1997, the EAE program's objectives were expanded and its funding was renewed.

Second-level heading: This heading is indented 0.5" with 12-point spacing before and 12-point spacing after. The font is Arial, bold, italic, 14 points. The second-level headings use title case (capital letters on the nouns, pronouns, verbs, adjectives, and adverbs).

A. Evaluation Objectives

This evaluation measured the cost effectiveness, relevance, and success of the ATF R&D Initiative. Overall management of the Initiative was also assessed, along with an examination of what other Initiatives exist in this area. The scope of the evaluation is restricted to projects that were funded in the 1997–2002 period. The following were measured and evaluated:

1. The Initiative's progress toward meeting its objectives to promote the development of alternative fuels technologies and standards and demonstrate the environmental benefits of alternative transportation fuels.
2. The extent to which the outcomes of the ATF R&D Initiative support the objectives of government to stabilize CO_2 emissions at 1990 levels, enhance the competitiveness of Canadian industry, and improve the environmental quality of life.
3. Current project management and accountability functions within the Alternative Transportation Fuels R&D Initiative.

Third-level heading: These headings are introduced by an Arabic numeral. They are indented 0.7" and are bold, 14-point Times New Roman. Both before and after spacing is set at 12 points.

1. Application of Methodology

This evaluation of the ATF R&D Initiative was based on multiple lines of evidence, utilizing four main sources of data including key informant interviews, case studies, a literature/document review and a file review. The data collection methods consisted of the following:

- literature review (26 documents);
- comprehensive file review (four projects);
- key informant interviews (with 22 respondents);
- four case studies in hydrogen, diesel, natural gas, and ATFs generally.

Source: Evaluation of the Alternative Transportation Fuels Research and Development Initiative. URL: http://www2.nrcan.gc.ca/dmo/aeb/English/ReportDetail.asp?x=213&type=rpt. Natural Resources Canada, 2002. Reproduced with the permission of the Minister of Public Works and Government Services Canada, 2005.

FIGURE 7-1

Headings and outlines. Notice how headings are like outline items that have been inserted into the text at the points where they belong. Notice too that different formats are used to indicate the different levels of headings.

As you can see in Figure 7-1, an individual heading indicates the topic of the one or more paragraphs that follow. Headings can be a powerful tool in your writing in a number of ways:

- *Provide an overview of the document.* Headings enable readers to scan an entire document and rapidly get a sense of what it covers.
- *Indicate the logic of the document.* Headings indicate the logic and structure of a document just the way outlines do.
- *Indicate the topic of the upcoming section.* An individual heading indicates the topic of the upcoming section (one or more paragraphs), helping to focus and guide readers' attention.
- *Enable readers to read selectively, or to skip sections if they wish.* Technical, scientific, and business people rarely read documents straight through; they skip around, and they may not read certain sections at all. Headings enable them to do this type of selective reading.
- *Provide breaks and white space in dense text.* A nice side advantage of headings is that they break up text and add white space. While you shouldn't insert headings merely to create white space, functional headings do indeed increase overall readability, giving documents a less crowded, more open feel.
- *Keep readers focused.* Because headings indicate topics of upcoming sections and because readers can glance back at headings as they read, headings help keep readers oriented. Headings keep readers focused on the topic, on the sequence of topics, and on the logic of that sequence.
- *Keep the writer focused and organized.* Another side advantage of headings is that they keep you, the writer, more focused and organized as you write. Headings force you to stay on the topics you announce in those headings.

HOW DO YOU DESIGN HEADINGS?

To start using headings, you must first *design* them—that is, decide on their characteristics, such as font, face (bold, italics, underscore), size, capitalization, location on the page, and so on.

Levels of headings. Take a look at the headings used in the examples throughout this book. Notice that bold, italics, type size, alternate fonts, capitalization, and positioning on the page are all used to differentiate *levels* of headings. Although modern word processors make a variety of heading styles possible, the most traditional pattern is the alphanumeric structure. In this pattern, levels of headings correspond to levels in an outline: Roman-numeral sections are the highest level; capital-letter sections are next; Arabic-numeral sections are next. The design of headings must visually indicate these levels. You ought to be able to look at an individual heading on a page and think, "Oh yes, this is a subsection of the such-and-such section that started on the preceding page."

To create good headings, you must have some basic skills in creating outlines: you must understand how items are grouped and sequenced logically and how certain groups of items are "subordinate" to others. For a review, see **http://www.powertools.nelson.com**.

A common heading design.   Most documents have a system of three to four levels of headings. Bold, italics, type size, alternate fonts, capitalization, and positioning on the page are used so that the different levels are distinct from each other. Take a look at the design of the headings in Figure 7-1:

▪ *First-level headings.* Introduce with a capital Roman numeral. Use bold and a larger type (16-point Arial), with spacing above and below.
▪ *Second-level headings.* Introduce with a capital letter. Use bold, italics, and 14-point Arial indented 0.5", with spacing above and below.
▪ *Third-level headings.* Introduce with an Arabic numeral. Use bold, 14-point Times New Roman indented 0.7" with spacing above and below.

Common Design for Headings

Heading 1 **I.**	• Left indent = 0 • Above spacing = 12 points • Below spacing = 24 points • Line spacing = 1.5 • Font = Arial, Bold, 16 points
Heading 2 **A.**	• Left indent = 0.5" • Above spacing = 12 points • Below spacing = 12 points • Line spacing = 1.5 • Font = Arial, Bold, Italics, 14 points
Heading 3 **1.**	• Left indent = 0.7" • Above spacing = 12 points • Below spacing = 12 points • Line spacing = 1.5 • Font = Times New Roman, Bold, 14 points
Body text	• Times New Roman, 12 points, indented 1" from left margin

This heading design will work for most of your technical documents. Notice that in shorter documents, such as in the end-of-chapter examples, the first-level heading is not used at all. But, in longer reports with separate "chapters," the first-level heading is a useful tool. The headings in

Figure 7-1 use the specifications shown in the table to the left. Use these in your technical documents if you have no other preferences or requirements. However, many technical projects require a specific heading layout that the writer must follow.

Font types for headings.   The preceding design uses Arial, a sans serif font, for headings and Times New Roman, a serif font, for regular body text. Serifs are the little curlicues that guide the eyes from letter to letter in fonts like Times New Roman. Sans serif fonts don't use those curlicues. In publishing, sans serif fonts are commonly used for headings, and serif fonts for body text. Times New Roman is commonly preferred for body text, while Arial is commonly preferred for headings.

HOW DO YOU USE HEADINGS?

Once you've designed a set of headings, you can start using them. There are two issues here. One involves your word-processing software and the mechanics of getting those headings into your text; that's covered in the next section. Just as important is the issue of using those headings in a standard way. This section covers some basic guidelines you need to know to use headings effectively:

What You Should Do

- *Use a heading design consistently.* This guideline may seem obvious; but, just in case, don't vary the type styles, caps styles, font, or other characteristics you chose when you initially designed your headings. Don't create headings "on the fly."
- *Use subordinate headings.* If a section is "subordinate" to some other section—that is, at a lower level—use a lower-level heading. For example, if you have a report on fruits and vegetables, "Fruits" and "Vegetables" will be the first-level headings and things like Apples, Oranges, Bananas, Squash, and Potatoes will be second-level headings. It wouldn't make sense for both Vegetables and Potatoes to be first-level headings any more than it would for them to be I and II in an outline.
- *Make the phrasing of headings accurately and adequately descriptive.* Avoid headings like "Background" or "Technical Information." Find the right set of words to indicate the subject matter of the section and build that into the heading. Remember that readers need your headings to give them a quick thumbnail idea of what the upcoming section is about.
- *Make headings parallel in phrasing.* Use the same style of phrasing for headings at the same level within the same section. Picture a traditional outline: the Roman-numeral sections might use *how/when/where/what/why* phrasing, while the alpha items under II might use gerund phrasing (*-ing*), and the alpha items under III, simple noun phrases. Parallelism of phrasing in headings gives readers important clues as to the content of sections within a document. (See Appendix C for more on parallelism.)

- *Use task-oriented headings in instructions.* When you write procedures in which readers must perform the steps you present, use task-oriented phrasing: for example, "How to Set the Timer" (*how/when/where/what/why* phrasing) or "Setting the Timer" (gerund phrasing).
- *Use the right number of headings.* It's just as easy to use too many headings as it is to use too few. There are no ratios for the right balance of headings and text, but in a standard, single-spaced, 8.5 × 11-inch page, try for two to four headings.

What You Should Avoid

- *Avoid lone headings.* Avoid situations in which you have a single second-, third-, or fourth-level heading all by itself within a section—a problem known as a "lone heading." This problem is exactly analogous to an A without a B or a 1 without a 2 in outlines. Either delete the lone heading or find a way to create another companion heading within the same section.
- *Avoid stacked headings.* Avoid situations in which two or more headings occur without regular text between them—a problem known as "stacked headings." Ordinarily, you can insert useful introductory or overview material between headings to eliminate the problem.
- *Don't use headings as lead-ins to lists.* Avoid using headings as introductions to lists; instead use a sentence, clause, or phrase lead-in. Using headings as lead-ins to lists simply muddies the distinction between headings and regular text. (Chapter 8 on lists presents this same guideline with illustrations.)
- *Don't use headings as figure or table titles.* Figures and tables have their own title mechanism; don't confuse that with headings. Figure titles are typically located *below* figures (see Chapter 11 for details). Table titles are typically located *above* tables (see Chapter 10 for details).
- *Don't refer to headings with pronouns.* Avoid referring to headings with *this* or *it.* For example, if the heading "Lone Headings" were followed by the sentence "This problem occurs when . . ." then the phrase "This problem" would be using the pronoun "this" to refer to the heading. Because readers read and process headings differently than they do regular text, they must pause for a fraction of a second to confirm what "this" refers to. Write the text following headings as if the headings were not there at all.

HOW DO YOU CREATE HEADINGS?

Once you've designed headings, you're ready to use them in a document. When you first start using headings, you'll probably add them after you've written the draft. But as you become accustomed to using them, you'll find that you add them as you write. In fact, you may even prefer to create the headings in advance before you start writing any body text. These latter methods are preferable: they keep you organized and focused.

At whatever draft stage you create headings, you'll want to use software tools called *styles* to make your headings consistent and to make creating them easy and efficient. In the following sections, you'll see how to create and use styles in Microsoft Word.

Creating Headings: Common Word-Processing Software

In Microsoft Word, you can design headings manually by specifying font, face, size, and position each time you create a heading. Or you can use your software system of styles to speed up the process and make it easier.

Manual approach. You can certainly create headings the slow and tedious way. Here's an example of how you'd do that in Microsoft Word (and the steps are much the same in other software). See the illustrations in Figures 7-2 and 7-3 for locations of the various menu options mentioned in this next section.

1. Type the text for a heading and keep it highlighted for the next steps.
2. In the Fonts menu option, change the font to Arial (or some other distinctive font).
3. In the Type Size menu option, make the type size 14 points.
4. Bold the text by pressing Ctrl+B.
5. To define the space below this heading, choose **Format→Paragraph**. In the Indents and Spacing dialogue, change Spacing After to 18 points.

Software-supplied styles. One shortcut to the preceding approach is to use the default heading styles supplied with most software applications. See Figure 7-2 for the Styles menu option, where numerous levels of headings are available. To use these headings, follow these steps in Microsoft Word:

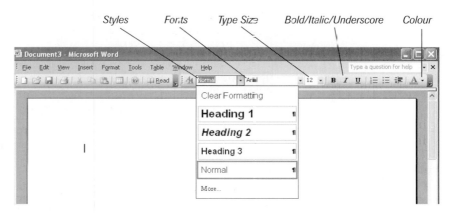

FIGURE 7-2

Menu options for typography and style options in MS Word. In Word, the Formatting toolbar contains most of the options you need to change fonts and other typographical features (choose **View→Toolbars** to access it).

1. Position your text cursor on the line that you want to change into a heading.
2. To select a software-supplied style, click the drop-down menu in the Styles box to see a list of the available styles.
3. Click on Heading 1, Heading 2, or Heading 3 to apply it to the line on which your cursor is located. The text will change to the characteristics of the heading style you selected.

Styles approach. What if you don't want to use the styles that Microsoft has decreed? You can create your own styles. (See Figure 7-3.) For advanced or professional work, styles are a great help. But for simple or brief documents, just use the styles supplied by your software, as explained in the preceding. Imagine that you want a heading style that uses a nice informal font such as Lucida Sans:

1. Move to a blank line in your document, type a few words, and highlight them.
2. Change the font to Lucida Sans (or some other distinctive font).
3. Make the type size 14 points, and make the text bold (press Ctrl+B).
4. Using the steps in "Manual approach," define the space above to be 18 points and the space below to be 9 points.
5. To record these settings as a style, choose **Format→Style**, select **New**, and give this style a distinctive name, such as my_head1.
6. To confirm that your new style is available, click on the style menu and scroll until you find it. To confirm that it does what you want, move to some new line of text in your document, and then click on your new style. The text should change accordingly in only one step instead of five!

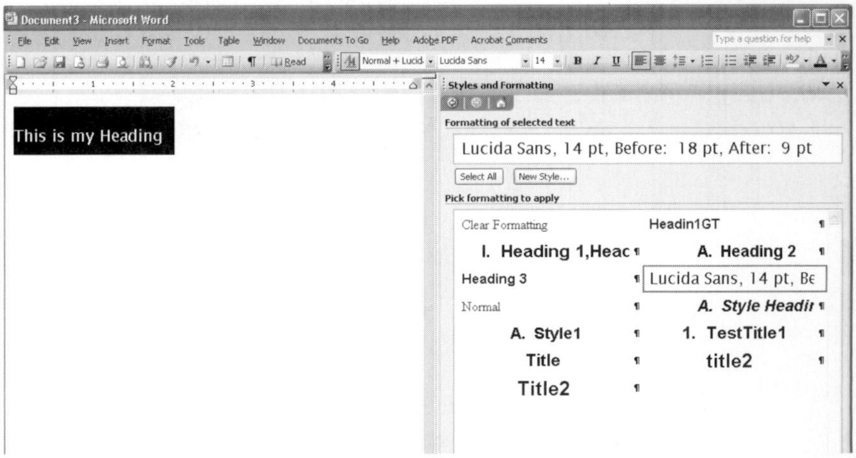

FIGURE 7-3
Using heading styles in Microsoft Word 2003.

Great, isn't it? By default, your styles may be available only to your current document. To make them available to other documents, copy them to a template of your own. Most word-processing software stores things like styles in *templates.* Procedures for adding styles to templates vary according to the software you use. Creating templates is covered in Chapter 12 on business communications.

WHAT IS HIGHLIGHTING AND EMPHASIS?

It's irresistibly fun to play with these tools, but not so much fun for readers. Overdoing it with highlighting creates a busy, uncomfortable, hyperactive-looking text that readers prefer to avoid.

This section focuses on gaining control over highlighting and emphasis, developing a logical plan for using these techniques, and avoiding the common problems associated with them. You'll also see how to add highlighting and emphasis to your text using character styles in Microsoft Word.

The terms "highlighting" and "emphasis" are almost synonymous. *Emphasis,* in this case, refers to typographical effects such as bold or italics that make text more noticeable. *Highlighting* refers to typographical effects that enable readers to anticipate the meaning of text. Used properly, highlighting and emphasis can help readers understand text more readily. For example, computer documents often use Courier for text that readers must type in verbatim. Once readers get used to this idea, they think, "Oh yes, here's that funny-looking font—I've got to type this stuff in!" In computer documents, highlighting eliminates the need for quotation marks, which readers might otherwise think they must type in as well.

However, highlighting and emphasis are easy to overuse. Typographical effects such as bold, italics, and different type sizes or fonts should *not* be used for more than a few words—at most, no more than a sentence. Beyond that, text becomes too busy, and readers are less likely to read it (see Figure 7-4). Instead of bolding or italicizing an entire paragraph, use the notice format as presented in Chapter 9. Notices provide extended emphasis in a way that remains readable.

Note: See the recommended guidelines and specifications for highlighting at the end of this chapter.

JER OPEN CALL PROCEDURES

1) The **Help Desk Technician** is to answer the phone by stating "**JER HelpDesk**" and his or her first name. The **Help Desk Technician** should immediately ask for the *customer's name, site, area code,* and *phone number,* what *credit-card company* he or she is with (American Express, MasterCard, Visa, etc....) followed by "*How may I help you?*" {**JER Help Desk. This is** [STATE YOUR NAME]**, may I please have your name, area code, and phone number? Thank you.** [STATE CALLER'S FIRST NAME]**, which credit-card company are you with?** (American Express, MasterCard, Visa, etc....) **How may I help you, please?"**}

2) Enter the station's area code and phone number on the *"Open Call Screen"* next to "**PHONE NUM** Don't worry about the ( ) or -, just type in the n and press the **<enter>** key once.

3) Make sure the flashing cursor is next to "**NUMBER:**" prompt and press the **<insert>** k (This is a macro key set for the **Find** function.) Next, ch the *"Site Search Screen"* and the flashing curso on "**KEY:**" prompt. Press the **C** key once for The flashing cursor will automatically move to prompt, just below the "**Y**" field just bel "**ACTIVE SITES ONLY:**" prompt. Type in the the *city* that the station is located in and p **<enter>** key once. Read down the list of sites for the *street number* and the *name of the stat* you are looking for. If you see "**PRESS PRE** {**PREV**}, {**NEXT**} **or** {**RETURN**} **FOR MOR** at the bottom of the screen, there are more check. Press the **<page down>** key once.

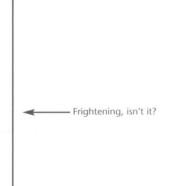
← Frightening, isn't it?

Better? ⟶

JER OPEN CALL PROCEDURES

1. As the help desk technician, answer the phone by stating that the customer has reached the JER HelpDesk and then state your first name.

2. Immediately ask for the customer's name, area code, phone number, and credit-card company.

3. Then ask how you can help this customer. For example:

> JER Help Desk. This is *YourName.* May I please have your name, area code, and phone number? Thank you, *CallerName,* what credit-card company are you with? … How may I help you, please?

4. Enter the area code and phone number on the Open Call Screen, and press Enter once.
   Note: Don't worry about the ( ) (parentheses) or - (hyphen). Just type in the numbers without spaces.

5. Make sure the cursor is next to the phone field, and press Insert once. (This starts the search process.)

6. With the cursor on the key prompt in the Site Search screen, press C once for city.

7. Type in the name of the city and press Enter once.

8. Search the list of sites for the customer's street number and the name of the station. If more sites are listed, press PageDown once.

FIGURE 7-4

Highlighting out of control. How happy would you be about reading the version on the left? Notice how much calmer and simpler the version on the right is. The bold, the italics, the curly braces, the square and angle brackets, the capital letters, the quotation marks, the thick paragraphs—the crazy mixture of all these devices—create a typographical nightmare!

WHAT CAN BE HIGHLIGHTED, AND HOW?

If you browse a selection of technical documents, you'll see some common patterns of highlighting. Here are some common uses:

- **Emphasis words.** Most commonly, words like "not," "must," "never," and "always" are emphasized. Italics has been the standard way of emphasizing such words. However, in technical text that uses lots of bold and other fonts, italics is easy to overlook. That's why you'll often see bold used for emphasis. Whichever you use—italics or bold—be consistent with it. And, *under no circumstances*, should you use all caps.
- **Words used in an unusual way.** Technical subjects often force us to use words in unusual ways. For example, the help pop-up "hovers" over the button it describes; the computer processor "fetches" an instruction; the stock market experiences a "hiccup." Until these words become generally accepted, we use quotation marks around them. If you use a word in a new or unusual way to convey a technical idea, put it in quotation marks—but on the first occurrence only!
- **Words, letters, numbers, or symbols discussed as such.** It's standard to use italics for words, letters, numbers, and symbols that you refer to as such. For example, you may have seen, "If the information is not available, enter *NA* in the blank."
- **Commands.** In computer documents involving procedures where you enter commands at a command line, such as in DOS or UNIX, the typical practice is to bold the command. For example, a computer document may say, "To delete the directory type **rmdir** followed by the name of the directory you want to delete."
- **Examples and user-entered text.** Technical documents commonly use a contrasting font such as Courier for examples. This "cues" readers that the text is an example only, not required. For example, a technical document may say, "To delete letter.doc, type `rm letter.doc`." This same technique is used for extended examples of code; in most programming books, lines of code are in another font, typically Courier.
- **Menu and menu-option names.** With menus and menu options, however, some form of highlighting is often used. For example, you click on a menu name such as **File** and then on an option such as **Open**. To reduce the number of words needed to explain such maneuverings, writers often use arrows: **File**→**Open**. This means click **File** and then click **Open**.
- **Web addresses (URLs).** Practice is mixed as to whether Web addresses should be highlighted and which style of highlighting should be used. In plenty of instances, no highlighting is used; but in plenty of others, a "monospaced" font like Courier is used: `www.powertools.nelson.com`. In monospaced fonts, each letter takes up exactly the same amount of space: the i's, l's, and j's are not "scrunched." In any case, remember to right-click and remove the hyperlink in print documents.

The preceding discussion doesn't prescribe a system of highlighting. Practice varies widely in technical documents.

HOW DO YOU PLAN A HIGHLIGHTING SCHEME?

A *highlighting scheme* is a plan for the kinds of highlighting you'll use and the situations in which you'll use them. The preceding sections presented the different tools you can use for highlighting and emphasis as well as the different textual elements you can highlight. This section puts it all together into a plan that ensures a functional and consistent usage of highlighting.

- *Functional* means that the highlighting somehow reinforces or combines with the purpose and content of the text.
- *Consistent* means that things like bold, italics, or other fonts are used the same way in the same situations throughout the document.

Remember that there is no one right way to highlight a text unless you are writing within a company, organization, industry, or profession that expressly requires a certain highlighting style. For example, if you are a technical writer for Dell, IBM, or Hewlett-Packard, you probably have a corporate style guide that tells you exactly when to use bold, italics, alternate fonts, and so on.

Once you've planned a highlighting scheme, you must create a *style guide* in which you provide a quick reference for the rules you have decided on. And, of course, another way of ensuring that you use your highlighting scheme is to have your drafts reviewed or edited by someone who knows that style guide.

Here's a simple scenario of how you might develop a highlighting scheme. Imagine that you are writing a set of instructions for one of those inexpensive toy watches featuring the latest Disney cartoon character. There is an LED display and three buttons labelled Mode, Set, and Select. The watch enables you to see the time, the date, or both, alternating back and forth every 5 seconds. (Parents, are you familiar with the item?) In terms of highlighting, you know you may want to do something to emphasize the button labels, the information displayed in the LCD, and the emphasis words (**not! never! always!**). Here are some suggestions:

Simple Highlighting Scheme

Text or element	Highlighting style
Regular body font	Times New Roman
Button names	Arial small caps (in MS Word, press Ctrl+D and select Small Caps)
LCD display	Courier (or Line Printer, System, or Terminal for a "techie" look)
Emphasis	Bold, regular body font

If you were to write the instructions for the toy watch using the high-lighting scheme in the preceding table, you might decide that the Arial font makes the text look too busy. After all, one of the standard page-design rules is not to use more than one font; we've got three: Times New Roman, Courier, and Arial. A good idea might be to use small caps on the button names and not use Arial at all. Take a look at the highlighting in the instructions for the toy watch in Figure 7-5.

Buttons: Use small-caps Arial.

Displayed material: Use a "techie" font to mimic the LED panel.

Notice: Use this format instead of bolding the entire sentence.

To change the hour:

1. Press the MODE button until the hour digit is blinking. For example, if you want to set the time to 3:05 but the Princess Warrior watch reads 2:05, press MODE until you see the following:

2: A

2. Press the SET button until the correct hour dis-plays. For example, if you want to change the hour to 3:05, stop when you see the following:

3: A

Note: To change between AM and PM, keep pressing SET until you see A or P.

3. Press the MODE button until the time is shown as normal. Do **not** leave the watch in time-change mode; otherwise, your time setting will be dis-carded.

For further information, go to the Princess Warrior website at http://www.PrincessWarrior.ca.

Regular reference: Use regular font for ordinary references to time; use the different font only when referring to what is displayed.

Emphasis: Use bold to emphasize something to do or not to do.

FIGURE 7-5

Simple highlighting scheme in action. If the Arial small-caps is too "busy" for you, consider using small caps and regular body font. Notice that "AM" and "PM" are not highlighted if they refer to actual time, whereas "A" or "P" use a "techie" font to refer to what is displayed in the LED panel of the watch.

Now consider a more complex situation. Imagine that you are writ-ing procedures for using a Web page editor. Think of all the possibilities for highlighting! But control yourself—too much highlighting will send readers diving for their barf bags. Consider the candidates for high-lighting: text you type in the editor, button and icon names, menu names, option names, screen names, file and directory names, field names, and simple emphasis. But few people would want to read text with all of those elements highlighted. The following table shows a high-lighting scheme you could use. It's typical of computer documents and, while rather heavy on highlighting, does not overdo it:

Take a look at the excerpt in Figure 7-6, which uses these guidelines.

Complex Highlighting Scheme

Text or element	Highlighting	Example
Regular body font	Times New Roman	To run Arachnophilia from the DOS command line …
Text you must type	Courier New	`c:\arach\arachno.exe\`
Simple emphasis	Italic, regular font	Do *not* edit binary files in Arachnophilia.
Terms at point of definition	Italic, regular font	A *macro* is a recorded set of keystrokes you can replay.…
Text displayed on screen (warnings, messages)	Courier New	`The file already exists. Are you sure you want to replace it?`
File and directory names	Bold, regular font	**arachnophilia.exe** **c:\arach**
Button and icon names	Bold, regular font	**OK, Help, Cancel**
Menu names	Bold, regular font	**File, Edit, Insert**
Menu-option selections	Bold, regular font	**File→Open→HTML**
Screen names	Initial cap, regular font	Arachnophilia Macro Editor
Field names	Initial cap, regular font	Name, SSN, E-mail address:
Keyboard key names	Initial cap, regular font	Ctrl, Shift, Enter
Web addresses (URLs)	Courier New	`www.powertools.nelson.com`

Definition —— A *keystroke macro* is a set of commands and text entry that you can access from the keyboard. For example, you could program a keystroke macro to

Key names —— type your full name just by pressing Ctrl+Z.

To create a keystroke macro:

Menu options —— 1. Press Ctrl+K, or select **Tools→Toolbars/Macros→Edit Keyboard Macros.**

2. Select the key you want to associate with this macro in the Press this key: ALT field.

3. Type the text or commands you want the macro to run.

Button names —— 4. Press the **Apply** button.

Notes:

User-entered text —— To include a tab in macro text, use `\t`; for a line feed, use `\n`.

System files and files —— Keyboard macros are stored in **keymacros.txt** in the directory named **arachnophilia\program\toolbars.**

Web address —— Further information is available at `www.arachnoid.com`.

Happy keyboarding!

FIGURE 7-6

A more complex highlighting scheme in action. The highlighting used in this excerpt is rather typical of what you see in computer publications.

HOW DO YOU ADD HIGHLIGHTING AND EMPHASIS?

Word-processing and desktop-publishing software makes it easy and fun to add highlighting and emphasis to technical documents—in fact, way too easy. The following sections review the basics of highlighting in Microsoft Word. If you find yourself bolding and italicizing everything in sight, go back and reread the preceding sections!

Highlighting with Common Word-Processing Software

You're probably familiar with making text bold or italic or with changing fonts or font sizes in Word. However, you may not be familiar with using character styles to achieve a well-planned and consistent highlighting scheme.

Manual highlighting.   If you've never used bold, italics, different fonts, or different type sizes before, try out the following in Microsoft Word (see Figure 7-7):

1. Open up a blank document in Word and type some text.
2. Select a word and make it italic by clicking the italics button (*I*) in the formatting toolbar or by pressing Ctrl+I.
3. Select another word and make it bold by clicking the bold button (**B**) in the formatting bar or by pressing Ctrl+B.

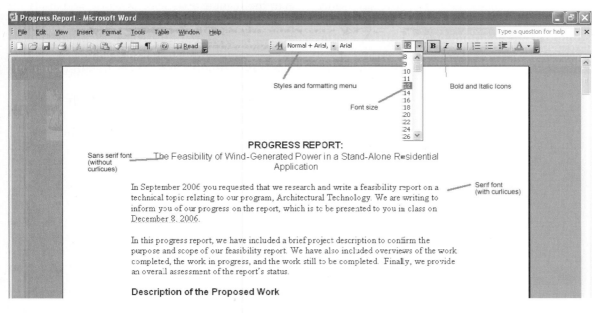

FIGURE 7-7

Basic formatting controls in Microsoft Word. Here is the formatting toolbar that provides the style, font, type size, bold, italics, and other options.

4. Select another word and change the font it uses by clicking the down-pointing arrow next to the font menu and selecting some other font, such as Arial Narrow.
5. Select another word and change its type size by clicking the arrow next to the type-size menu and selecting a number.

Highlighting with character styles. In word-processing and desktop-publishing software, character styles are advanced techniques that make highlighting more organized, more consistent, and more efficient. For example, to ensure that all device button names use Arial small caps, create a character style and call it "button names." Each time a device button name occurs, select it and apply the button-name character style. For simple or brief documents, there's no need to develop character styles. However, if you are doing a complex project, they are a great help. The following guides you through the creation of a few character styles:

1. Open up a blank document in Microsoft Word 2003 and type some text.
2. Select a word and make it italic.
3. With the italicized word still selected, create the character style by clicking **Format→Styles and Formatting→New Style**. Beside Style type, select **Character**. Beside Name, type `variable`.
4. Click **OK** or **Apply** as necessary to complete this character style.
5. Move somewhere else in the regular text, select a word, and apply the variable character style you just created.

   We named this character style "variable" because in technical documentation variables are commonly italicized. For example, if you tell your reader "delete *filename*" you're telling them to substitute their own file name for the variable *filename*.
6. Create the following additional character styles for commonly used highlighting in technical documentation. (Since 12-point Courier New looks too big in the same text with 12-point Times New Roman, 11-point Courier New is used as a highlighting tool.)

Character and Paragraph Styles

Text or element	Technique	Usage
Regular text	12-point Times New Roman	For text in which special highlighting rules do not apply
Command	Bold	For references to command names
User text	11-point Courier New	For text users must type
Screen text	11-point Courier New	For text displayed on the computer screen
Example text	11-point Courier New	For example text, such as programming code
Menu names	Arial	For references to the names of screens, windows, or menus

WORKSHOP: HEADINGS AND HIGHLIGHTING

Here are some additional ideas for practising the concepts, tools, and strategies in this chapter:

1. *Review of heading designs.* Find a sampling of technical documents (books, reports, articles, online materials) and analyze the heading designs you see in them. Use a grid like the following to record your observations:

Level	Font & size	Face	Cap style	Position	Graphic
1					
2					
3					

If you are not sure of fonts, just indicate whether the font is serif or sans serif. If you are not sure of size, just indicate whether a heading is larger or smaller in relation to others. ("Face" refers to bold, italics, and other such effects.)

2. *Simple headings for print text.* Using your preferred writing software (Word, WordPerfect, etc.), manually add the supplied headings with the specified characteristics to the text provided in the Instructor's Resource or available at **http://www.powertools.nelson.com**.

3. *Simple headings with styles for print text.* Using the same headings and text in the previous exercise, create *styles* for the different heading levels in your preferred writing software.

4. *Common heading-design problems.* In the excerpts in the Instructor's Resource or at **http://www.powertools.nelson.com**, identify the problem or problems that occur in each one (such as stacked or lone headings, lack of parallelism, and so on).

5. *Highlighting survey.* Find a technical document—preferably one that provides instructions—and make a list of the highlighting techniques that you see used there. Also, determine how the techniques are used in the document, using a table like the following:

Text or element	Highlighting style	Example

Note: See Chapter 10 for help on creating tables.

6. *Highlighting print documents.* Use the text and instructions available at **http://www.powertools.nelson.com** to get some practice creating character styles in Word, WordPerfect, or whatever word-processing or desktop-publishing software application you use.

HIGHLIGHTING: GUIDELINES AND SPECIFICATIONS

General guidelines. Here are some general guidelines to keep in mind when you design and use headings:

- Use highlighting (bold, italics, alternate fonts, or alternate colours) for emphasis or to cue readers to meaning of text (such as a button to be clicked).
- Avoid using highlighting techniques for more than a few words—and never for more than a sentence. For extended highlighting or emphasis, use notices (see Chapter 9).
- Develop a highlighting scheme for documents and use it consistently.
- When possible, use the highlighting style commonly used in your organization, field, or profession.
- Avoid redundant highlighting techniques—for example, using both bold and italics for a word or phrase.
- Never use caps or quotations as highlighting techniques. Techniques using bold, italics, and alternate fonts are developed specifically to eliminate the need for caps and quotation marks.
- Avoid over-highlighting documents. While keeping your highlighting consistent and functional, find reasons *not* to highlight certain elements—for example, keyboard key names, titles of menus, or field names.
- Have functional reasons for your highlighting techniques—for example, bold cues readers that they must press or select something; Courier New indicates that they must type something in.
- If you use colour as a highlighting technique, limit yourself to one colour in addition to black—for example, blue or teal. Readers will probably not understand the function of any additional colours.
- Avoid decorative highlighting. Avoid nonfunctional highlighting (for example, why highlight every instance of a product name?). Avoid nonfunctional use of additional colour.
- Never use a larger type size to emphasize regular text.
- Limit your fonts to three—for example, use Times New Roman for regular text, Arial for headings, and Courier New for example text.
- Never highlight more than a sentence. For extended highlighting or emphasis, use the notice format (see Chapter 9).

CHAPTER 8

Lists: Bulleted, Numbered, and Others

Topics covered in this chapter include

- Human Genome Project
- DNA Testing

HUMAN GENOME

Genetic research is a controversial topic these days. The Internet provides abundant information including research sites, forums, and blogs. You can start your research with some of the following:

Genome Canada
http://www.genomecanada.ca/home.asp?l=e

National Institutes of Health: National Human Genome Research Institute
http://www.genome.gov

Stanford Human Genome Center
http://www-shgc.stanford.edu

Geneservice
http://www.geneservice.co.uk/home

About.com. Genetics (see the link for Human Genome Projects)
http://genetics.about.com/education/scilife/genetics

DNA TESTING

Canada Online
http://canadaonline.about.com/cs/crime/a/dnadatabank.htm

Trent University
http://www.forensicdna.ca

National DNA Data Bank
http://www.nddb-bndg.org/main_e.htm

When you have completed this chapter, you will be able to

- use a variety of list formats to enhance your technical documents;
- identify appropriate spots in technical documents where lists would be beneficial;
- apply standard conventions in creating and using lists;
- create a variety of list formats using standard word-processing applications.

For almost as long as you've been reading, you've been looking at bulleted and numbered lists; but you've probably never stopped and thought about them. Lists can be a big help to your readers, enabling them to skim your text faster, see the important points, and follow sequential material more easily. They also add white space, cutting down on big, thick, dense paragraphs.

In this chapter, you learn about the different types of lists, their design and format, standard list guidelines, and some basic techniques for creating lists with your software.

WHAT ARE LISTS?

Before getting into guidelines for lists, take a moment to review the various types that you can use in your writing, all of which are illustrated in Figures 8-1 through 8-3.

- *Bulleted lists*. Use bulleted lists for situations in which you want to emphasize two or more items. The bullet says, "Hey, I'm important!" Use bullets for items that are not in any required order and that will not be referred to by number. Avoid creating bulleted lists over 7 items; but if you do, consider using bullets with introductory labels, also discussed in the following. (See Figure 8-1 for an example of a bulleted list.)
- *Numbered lists*. Use numbered lists for items that are in a required order or that must be referred to by number. The most common use for numbered lists is for instructions in which you must help readers follow a sequence of steps. The numbers say, "Hey, follow this sequence!" If a numbered list goes over 7 items, start looking for ways to consolidate shorter numbered items; if it goes way over 7 items, look for ways to break up the list, insert additional lead-ins, and renumber. (See Figure 8-1 for an example of a numbered list.)
- *In-sentence lists*. In an in-sentence list, the items are in standard paragraph format and use either numbers or lowercase letters enclosed in parentheses. In-sentence lists could be called "horizontal" lists in

Mitosis is the process of cell duplication, during which one cell produces two identical daughter cells. The process consists of four phases: prophase, metaphase, anaphase, and interphase:

1. In prophase, the genetic material thickens and coils in chromosomes, the nucleolus disappears, and a group of fibres begins to form a spindle.
2. In metaphase, the chromosomes duplicate themselves and line up along the midline of the cell. The halves are known as chromatids.
3. In anaphase, the chromatids are pulled at opposite ends of the cell by the spindle fibres. At this point, the cytoplasm of the mother cell divides to form two daughter cells, each with the number and kind of chromosomes the mother cell possessed.
4. In interphase, the daughter cells begin to function on their own, once their nucleus membranes and nuclei form.

Unprecedented progress in identifying and understanding the 50,000 to 100,000 or so genes that make up the human genome provides an opportunity for scientists to develop strategies to prevent or reduce the effects of genetic disease. Scientists have shown that straightforward inherited errors in our genes are responsible for an estimated 3,000 to 4,000 diseases, including the following:

• Huntington's disease
• Cystic fibrosis
• Neurofibromatosis
• Duchenne muscular dystrophy

More complex inheritance of multiple genetic errors also can increase an individual's risk of developing common disorders such as cancer, heart disease, and diabetes.

FIGURE 8-1

Numbered and bulleted lists. Use numbers for list items that occur in a required sequence. Use bullets for items in no necessary sequence.

contrast to the "vertical" format used in bulleted and numbered lists. (See Figure 8-2 for an example of an in-sentence list.)

■ *Labelled lists.* A nice touch you can apply to lists, particularly long or complex ones, is to add a brief identifying label, which you bold or italicize, at the beginning of each item. (See Figure 8-2 for an example of a labelled list.)

■ *Nested lists.* Occasionally, you'll create lists within lists—in other words, sublist items. For example, for a complex numbered-list item, create subitems with lowercase letters. In Figure 8-3, notice how the subitems align to the text of the higher-level items.

■ *Two-column lists.* Some lists contain paired items; for example, a technical term and its definition. You can use the labelled-list style just discussed, or you can use the two-column style. Actually, the two-column list is a table in disguise, without the grid lines showing. Use tables rather than tabs or spaces to create two-column lists. See Chapter 10 for details on tables.

■ *Simple lists.* A simple list is a vertical list in which the items are not numbered or bulleted. This type is often used for equipment or supply lists, in which the emphasis created by the bullet or number is just not needed.

Deoxyribonucleic acid (DNA) carries the genetic information that is in a cell. DNA makes up chromosomes, of which humans possess forty-six. The DNA helix resembles two snakes intertwining and is made up of bases called nucleotides. There are four of these nucleotides: (a) adenine, (b) thymidine, (c) guanine, and (d) cytosine.

Two types of genetic testing can occur in the workplace, both of which can be used unfairly to discriminate against or stigmatize individuals on the job:

- *Genetic screening.* Genetic screening examines the genetic makeup of employees or job applicants for specific inherited characteristics. It may be used to detect general heritable conditions that are not associated with workplace exposures in employees or applicants.
- *Genetic monitoring.* Genetic monitoring ascertains whether an individual's genetic material has changed over time due to workplace exposure to hazardous substances.

FIGURE 8-2

In-sentence and labelled lists. For in-sentence lists, be sure to use both parentheses.

Resources for human chromosome maps include the following:

GeneMap'98
Science/NCBI Human Transcript Map
IMAGE Consortium
NHGRI Human Chromosome 7 Mapping and
  Sequencing

Chromosome maps of other organisms include the following:

- *Arabidopsis*
  – AtDB (Stanford)
  – European Union Arabidopsis Genome Project
- *C. elegans*
  – University of Texas Southwestern Medical Center at Dallas
  – Sanger Center
- Dog Genome Project
- FlyBase
- Fungal Genome Resource (University of Georgia)
- Mouse Genome Database

FIGURE 8-3

Simple and nested lists. Use an en dash for second-level bullets. For a subnumbered list, use lowercase letters. For a bulleted list that is subordinate to a numbered list, use the regular solid-disk bullet. Similarly, for a numbered list subordinate to a bulleted list, use regular Arabic numerals.

WHAT ARE LISTS GOOD FOR?

Why bother with lists in the first place? For one thing, lists increase the readability of your text. Lists enable readers to scan your text more readily, see the important points, and follow stepwise instructions more easily. Lists also increase the "white space" in text, reducing those long deadly paragraphs and the overall density of the text.

- *Emphasis.* The primary goal in creating lists should be to add emphasis. A bulleted list of three items emphasizes those three items.
- *Readability.* Another primary goal is to increase readability. The numbered-list format used in instructional steps makes it easier to follow those steps.
- *White space.* An important side effect of lists is that they create white space, which in turn increases readability. However, don't create lists just to increase white space. Using too many lists, as well as lists with too many items, loses the advantage of the list format altogether.

The content of the text must support the list. There must be something "bullet-able" or "number-able" in the text; and even if there is, it may not automatically warrant creating lists.

WHERE SHOULD YOU USE LISTS?

If you've never used lists in any systematic way, you'll probably start by going back and searching for ways to reformat your text to incorporate lists. After a while, your sense of when to use lists will catch up with your composing practices. You'll anticipate lists and create them as you compose, or you'll reformat paragraphs into lists almost as soon as you've written them. Here are some ideas on how to recognize opportunities for working lists into your technical and business writing:

- *Sequenced items.* Whenever your text contains segments of information that are in a required order (typically, chronological order), consider using a numbered vertical list.
- *Overview list.* The individual sections of technical reports often contain overviews of the subtopics to be covered; these are good spots for in-sentence lists (using either numbers or lowercase letters).
- *Important points.* Text containing three or four key points about a topic is a good candidate for a bulleted list. If your discussion focuses on features, characteristics, elements, factors, guidelines, issues, or other such elements, that's a tip-off that you may want to reformat using bullets.
- *Paired items.* If your text contains pairs of items (for example, a term followed by its definition), try reformatting the text with a two-column list in which the terms are in the left column and their definitions are in the right column.

WHAT ARE THE GUIDELINES FOR LISTS?

Figure 8-4 summarizes key guidelines involving lists. Most importantly, use the right types of lists. In the technical world, using a numbered list for items not in a required order can cause serious confusion, as can using

GUIDELINES FOR LISTS

Follow standard guidelines for lists. Regardless of which type of list you create, you must keep some general guidelines in mind. These are standard guidelines for style and format of lists that you will see observed in most published information.

- *Use the right type of list.* Use bullets for items in no necessary order and numbers for items in some required order.
- *Include a lead-in.* Introduce all lists with a lead-in phrase, clause, or sentence, which you may punctuate with a colon. (Some styles specify that when the list items complete the sentence started by the lead-in, no colon should be used.) Don't use headings as list lead-ins.
- *Avoid using too many lists or creating lists with too many items.* Don't crowd too many lists on a page. For a standard single-spaced page, two lists is enough. If everything on a page is vertical lists, then the effect of lists is lost. Keep numbered or bulleted lists below seven items. (Researchers have found that seven is the maximum number that most people can manage cognitively.) Again, the effect of listing is lost when nearly everything is a list.
- *Avoid lists with only one item.* Avoid lists with only one bullet or only one number. Figure out how to create a second item, or don't use the list format at all.
- *Use standard punctuation and capitalization on list items.* Practice varies on how to punctuate list items. The easiest method is not to use any end punctuation except for periods on list items that are complete sentences. Practice also varies on capitalizing the first word of list items. An easy solution is always to use either upper or lowercase on the first letter of the first word of list items and not to sweat the fine distinctions.
- *Adjust spacing between list items for readability.* For short items of only a few words, use the normal spacing for body text (single-spacing). For items two lines or longer, put some space (half a line or even a full line) between the items for better readability.
- *Make the phrasing of list items parallel.* See Appendix C for details on parallelism. Parallelism is another way to increase the readability and comprehension of lists.
- *Use the lead-in to eliminate repetition, but check the grammatical connection between list items and their lead-ins.* In some lists, you can transfer repetitive words from the list items into the lead-in and cut overall word count. Each list item should read grammatically with its lead-in. This can become a problem if the list items actually complete the grammar of the lead-in—make sure each one does.
- *Avoid lead articles on list items.* Whenever possible, eliminate articles at the beginning of list items; doing so decreases verbal clutter around the item.
- *Correctly align list items and nested list items.* Carefully study how list items are aligned with nested list items.

FIGURE 8-4

Guidelines for lists. The guidelines explained in the figure are general standards used in the technical publishing industry. However, practice does vary. Take a look at the design of lists in a sampling of technical publications to study variations.

a bulleted list for items in a required order. Avoid overusing lists. Because they contrast with normal paragraphs, lists convey emphasis. If everything is a list, then that emphasis is lost. The same holds true for lists with too many items. Most of the other list guidelines you see in Figure 8-4 have to do with readability and consistency.

HOW DO YOU CREATE LISTS?

Take the time to learn how to create lists using your preferred software, such as Corel WordPerfect, Lotus Word Pro, or Microsoft Word. Merely typing the number and then spacing or tabbing to enter the text is tedious, inefficient, and unprofessional.

Creating Lists. Here's a mini tutorial on creating lists with Word 2003. (See Figures 8-5 through 8-7 for references to menu options.)

Numbered lists. To start a new numbered list or to change ordinary text to a numbered list:

1. Type several lines of text, separating each one by pressing the Enter key.
2. Highlight all lines.
3. Click on the numbered-list icon ▦ or choose **Format→Bullets and Numbering**. Click on the **Numbered** tab, and select the simple Arabic numeral format followed by a period (Figure 8-5).
4. Each time you want to create a new numbered-list item, press the Enter key.

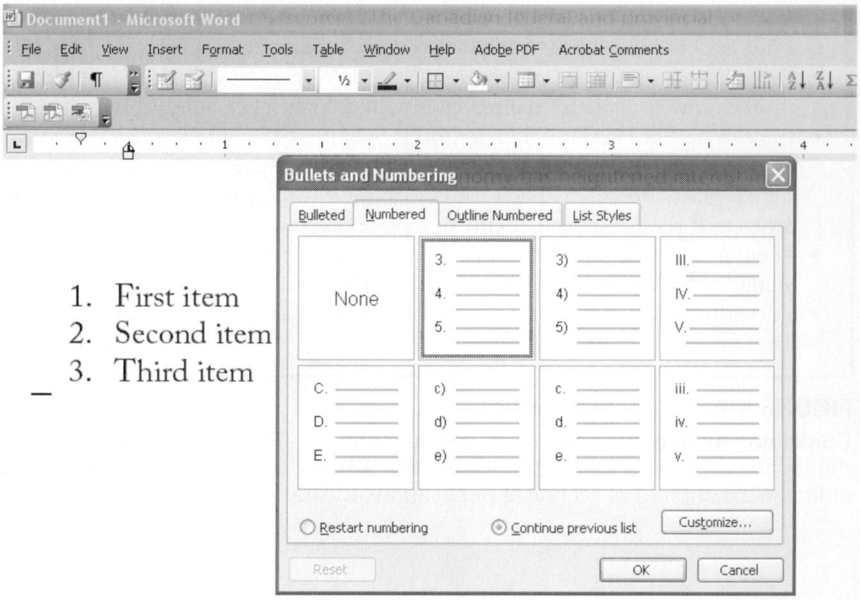

FIGURE 8-5

Creating numbered and bulleted lists in Microsoft Word. Don't create lists manually—they look tacky. Use the tools that software applications give you, such as these in Microsoft Word. Either click on the bulleted-list icon or the numbered-list icon, or use the Format menu option.

5. When you are ready to end the numbered list, press the Enter key twice, or click on the numbered-list icon.
6. If you use more than one numbered list, you must reset the numbering to 1 by choosing **Format→Bullets and Numbering**, and clicking **Restart numbering**.
7. If you want to interrupt a numbered list with a paragraph, press Enter to create the paragraph and then click on the numbered-bullet icon.

Other common word-processing programs operate similarly.

Bulleted lists. To start a new bulleted list or to change ordinary text to a bulleted list, follow these steps in Word:

1. Type several lines of text, separating each one by pressing the Enter key.
2. Highlight all lines.
3. Click on the bulleted-list icon ▦ or choose **Format→Bullets and Numbering**. Click on the **Bulleted** tab, and select the black dots.
4. Each time you are ready to create the next bulleted-list item, press the Enter key.
5. When you are ready to end the bulleted list, press the Enter key twice, or click on the bulleted-list icon.

Other common word-processing programs have similar functions.

WORKSHOP: LISTS

Here are some additional ideas for practising the concepts, tools, and strategies in this chapter:

1. *Analyzing style and format of lists.* Photocopy a half-dozen pages from various technical documents in which different types of lists are used. Compare the style and format you see used in these examples to what is presented in this chapter. In particular, look at the following:
   a. Type of list used: in-sentence, bulleted, numbered
   b. Punctuation of the lead-in to the list
   c. Capitalization and punctuation of the items
   d. Indentation of the items
   e. Apparent reasons for the list; its effectiveness

2. *Creating lists.* Convert the following text to the appropriate kinds of lists using your preferred word-processing software:
   a. To request a background report on a new employee you will need the following information: name, date of birth, social insurance number, and city and province of residence.

b. There are three main types of faults. A divergent fault occurs when two plates are moving away from each other. When two plates come together, the result is a convergent fault. A fault that occurs when two plates slide past each other is known as a transform fault.

c. When constructing a pond in your back yard, you will need to determine which size pond liner you will need. First, dig out the pond. Next, measure the length, width, and depth of your pond. Then use the following formulas to determine the pond liner size you need:

Length + twice the depth + 2 extra feet = length of pond liner needed
Width + twice the depth + 2 extra feet = width of pond liner needed

CHAPTER 9

Notices: Dangers, Warnings, and Cautions

Topics covered in this chapter include

- changing weather patterns;
- weather warnings;
- dangers of scuba diving.

CHANGING WEATHER PATTERNS
The Green Lane
http://www.ec.gc.ca/envhome.html

Natural Resources Canada
http://adaptation.nrcan.gc.ca/posters/cc_en.asp

WEATHER WARNINGS
The Weather Network
http://www.theweathernetwork.com

You can also see weather warnings at **http://www.weather.com**

DANGERS OF SCUBA DIVING
PADI
www.PADI.com (click on the Canada link)

Scuba Diving magazine
http://www.scubadiving.com

When you have completed this chapter, you will be able to

- distinguish among caution, warning, and danger notices for use in technical documents;
- use notices appropriately in your documents;
- write notices;
- design consistent caution, warning, and danger notices.

If you've ever used anything that had the remotest chance of hurting you, you've seen *notices*—specially formatted text alerting you that you could hurt yourself or others, damage property or equipment, ruin the outcome of the procedure, or just generally increase your frustration level. And if you've ever used poorly written instructions, you have probably seen monstrosities like the one shown in Figure 7-4 in Chapter 7—the very thing that notices are designed to prevent.

This chapter shows you the strategies for creating, formatting, and using these important elements of the technical-writing trade. In addition, you'll see how to create notices in word-processing software.

Note: Study this chapter when you are preparing to write instructions (Chapter 2). Notices are essential in instructions.

WHAT ARE NOTICES?

Notices are special emphasis techniques for extended text. They warn readers of the possibility of injuring themselves, damaging equipment, or ruining the outcome of a procedure. They also provide readers with tips, hints, and so on. Notices accomplish this by using special formatting; for example, the text of a caution notice may be formatted with the word **CAUTION**, with a border around it, calling attention to itself. (For individual words or brief phrases, you can use the highlighting and emphasis techniques such as bold or italics, as presented in Chapter 7.)

Each industry—and sometimes almost every organization within an industry—has its own standards for notices. For example, one corporation may use warning notices for situations involving potential damage to equipment or data while another corporation uses caution notices for the same situation. Although corporations work together to create and maintain industry standards, such as those offered by the Canadian Standards Association, individual corporations typically find these standards inadequate for their specific products.

For example, semiconductor, medical-equipment, and heavy-machinery industries must use much higher powered notices than the software industry. Fabrication (fab) workers are surrounded by extremely high voltages, toxic gases, and blinding lasers. Figure 9-1 illustrates a fairly common format for notices. It is by no means universal, but you'll see this design used often in technical publications.[1]

The types of notices are defined as follows, and are illustrated in Figure 9-1:

---

[1] Velotta, Christopher. "Safety Labels: What to Put in Them, How to Write Them, and Where to Put Them." *IEEE Transactions on Professional Communication.* 30 (1987): 121–136.

Simple note: Use this note to point out special details or exceptions.

El Niño refers to the irregular increase in sea surface temperatures from the coasts of Peru and Ecuador to the equatorial central Pacific. This phenomenon is not totally predictable but on average occurs once every four years. It usually lasts for about 18 months after it begins.

> *Note:* El Niño is Spanish for "Christ Child." Historically, the term was used by the fishermen along the coasts of Ecuador and Peru to refer to a warm, nutrient-poor ocean current that typically appears around Christmastime and lasts several months.

Recent years in which El Niño events have occurred are 1951, 1953, 1957–1958, 1965, 1969, 1972–1973, 1976, 1982–1983, 1986–1987, 1991–1992, 1994, and 1997.

Caution: Use this note to alert people to the possibility of damage or failure. This example warns you not to plan a picnic or sink all your savings into soybean futures based on weather projections.

Caution: These climate projections are intended to provide emergency managers, planners, forecasters, and the public advance notice of potential threats related to weather conditions. Although the best-known projection models are used, there is no guarantee of their accuracy.

Warning: Use warnings to alert people to possible injury—but not serious or fatal injury. Should a high-winds warning be upgraded to a danger notice?

A mostly zonal storm track with fast-moving storms and a fairly strong north to south temperature gradient should prevail across the Western seaboard from Friday, Jan. 14 through Sunday, Jan. 16, 2006. Although the overall pattern is expected to remain fairly stable, weather models are showing an amplification of the wave pattern over Canada during the week of Jan. 16, which could produce a deep enough trough over the Western provinces to bring some real winter weather into that region toward the middle of the week.

> **Warning:** High winds are expected to accompany a storm coming ashore in the British Columbia coastal region on Friday, Jan. 14.

Danger: Use this one to warn of possible serious or fatal injury. We definitely need danger notices for tornado information.

A tornado watch is issued by Environment Canada when tornadoes are possible in your area. Remain alert for approaching storms. This is the time to remind family members where the safest places within your home are located and to listen to the radio or television for further developments. A tornado warning is issued when a tornado has been sighted or indicated by weather radar.

> **DANGER!**
> Never try to outdrive a tornado in a car or truck. Tornadoes can change direction quickly and can lift a car or truck and toss it through the air.

FIGURE 9-1

Common design for notices. If you have no preferences or requirements concerning notices, use the designs illustrated here. See additional examples later in this chapter.

- *Danger:* For situations in which serious injury or even fatality could occur.
- *Warning:* For situations in which minor injury could occur.
- *Caution:* For situations in which damage to equipment or data could occur, or for problems that could cause the entire procedure to fail.
- *Note:* For situations where information needs to be emphasized, for exceptions, special points, hints, and tips—anything deserving special emphasis that does not match the criteria for danger, warning, or caution notices.

Underwater characteristics such as temperature, visibility, marine life, and other factors vary from region to region and can influence the amount and type of work that divers can carry out underwater.

The following describes the diving conditions most likely to be encountered in various regions around the United States and in other parts of the world. **WHEN DIVING IN AN UNFAMILIAR REGION, INFORMATION ABOUT LOCAL CONDITIONS SHOULD BE OBTAINED FROM DIVERS WHO ARE FAMILIAR WITH THE WATERS. A CHECKOUT DIVE SHOULD BE MADE WITH A DIVER FAMILIAR WITH THE AREA.**

Northeast
Diving in northeastern waters can be described as an exciting and chilling experience.

Who wants to read text like this that seems to be screaming at you?

In this version, the word "Note:" is bold; the text of the note uses regular font for readability.

(Notice that the passive-voice constructions in the original have been changed to active.)

Underwater characteristics such as temperature, visibility, marine life, and other factors vary from region to region and can influence the amount and type of work that divers can carry out underwater.

The following describes the diving conditions most likely to be encountered in various regions around the United States and in other parts of the world.

Note: When diving in an unfamiliar region, get information about local conditions from divers who are familiar with the waters. Make a checkout dive with a diver familiar with the area.

Northeast
Diving in northeastern waters can be described as an exciting and chilling experience.

FIGURE 9-2

Using notices to emphasize. Few readers care to read text that seems to be screaming at them. The notice format enables you to call attention to the important information without, at the same time, creating unreadable text.

Notices solve a major problem in technical writing. To emphasize a chunk of text, inexperienced writers often use motley combinations of bold, italics, all-caps, and larger type size right in the middle of the paragraph. The result is the exact opposite of what is intended: most readers avoid screaming, hyperactively busy text. Notices solve this problem by yanking the important text out of regular paragraphs and putting it in a special format. While the notice *label* (the word "warning," "caution," "danger") may use bold, italics, all-caps, or larger type, the actual text of the notice uses the regular body font. (See Figure 9-2.)

HOW DO YOU USE NOTICES?

Imagine that you've developed a terrific industrial-strength set of notices. How do you use them?

- *Search your text for situations that match the situations for which you have defined your notices.* When you first start using notices, you'll probably have to go back and study your rough drafts to find text to reformat as notices. As you become accustomed to using notices, you'll find that you add them as you write.
- *Place notices with the text to which they apply.* The standard rule is to place notices before the point at which the potential for damage, failure, or injury exists. In actual practice, however, simple notes and cautions typically follow the step to which they apply. High-severity notices are placed at the beginning of the section, chapter, or document and then repeated after the step to which they apply.
- *Present high-severity notices at the beginning of a document.* Take a look at a few operator guides. In a section at the beginning, typically entitled "Safety Notices," they repeat all the warning, caution, and danger notices occurring anywhere in the rest of the guide.
- *Align notices with the text to which they apply.* If, for example, a note refers to a numbered-list item, that note should align to the text of the numbered-list item (not the numeral). The same goes for items in bulleted lists. If the notice applies to the entire numbered or bulleted list, don't indent the notice at all.
- *Consolidate multiple notices.* If multiple warnings and cautions occur close together, combine and use a label such as "Cautions and Warnings."
- *Use notice types consistently.* Plan how you will use notices; don't use them inconsistently and thus confuse readers. Don't dilute the impact of your notice design by creating new notice types on the fly—for example, "Important!" or "Read This!"

HOW DO YOU WRITE NOTICES?

Writing the text of notices is a good challenge of your skills as a technical communicator. You must pay particular attention to the kinds of information you put in notices, the style of writing you use, and the number of words you use.

Elements of notices. When you write the actual text of notices—especially higher severity notices like warnings and dangers—consider including the following kinds of information as needed (see Figure 9-3 for a labelled example):

- *Conditions.* Describe the conditions in which readers should avoid or take the action. For example, "Before rewiring the lamp, be sure to unplug it." Place the conditional information before the action statement.
- *Actions to avoid or to take.* State clearly and firmly what readers should do or not do; for example, "Do not push the red button!" or "Be sure to unplug the lamp."
- *Consequences.* Of course, most of us want to know why we can't push the red button. Why must we avoid the action or be sure to perform the action? After stating what to do or what to avoid (and the conditions), explain what might happen if the action statement is ignored.
- *Recovery.* Of course, our best warning, caution, and danger notices will occasionally go unheeded, and people will push the red button. In some notices, you must include recovery directions—what to do in case they ignored you!

This example has all but one of these elements:

Conditions: The situation here is lack of use.

Actions: Charge, drain, and recharge up to six times if the battery has not been used recently.

Consequences: The battery will not recharge fully if it hasn't been used recently.

Recovery: This example does not involve an action to avoid; therefore, there is no recovery.

> ### Charging the Battery Pack
>
> You can charge the battery pack when the AC adapter is connected to the computer and the battery pack is installed. You need to charge the battery pack in any of the following conditions:
>
> - When you purchase a new battery pack
> - If the battery status indicator starts blinking
> - If the battery pack has not been used for a long time
>
> *Note:* If the battery pack has not been used for a long time, it cannot be fully charged with only a single charging. You will have to completely discharge it; then recharge it three to six times to maximize battery operating time.

FIGURE 9-3

Types of information included in notices. Consider including information as to actions, conditions, consequences, and recovery in the text of notices. At the same time, keep the notice as succinct as possible, but without resorting to "telegraphic writing" style.

Telegraphic style:

Danger! Never try to outdrive tornado in car or truck. Tornadoes can change direction quickly and can lift car or truck and toss in air.

Caution! Never open back of camera before film is rewound back into cassette. Doing so will expose entire roll to light thus ruining all pictures.

Revisions:

Danger! Never try to outdrive a tornado in a car or truck. Tornadoes can change direction quickly and can lift a car or truck and toss it in the air.

Caution! Never open the back of a camera before the film is rewound back into the cassette. Doing so will expose the entire roll to light, thus ruining all your pictures.

Writing style in notices. If you put all the information just described into one notice, you risk creating an overly long paragraph no one will read. Of course, not every notice needs all the material just described, and much of it can be combined. Keep notice text as succinct as possible, especially in high-severity notices. At the same time, avoid the extremes of the *telegraphic style*—omitting "understood" words like articles and verbs. Refer to the table shown above for examples of telegraphic style.

HOW DO YOU DESIGN AND CREATE NOTICES?

If your writing project requires notices, spend some time planning and designing them first. Decide which types of notices you'll use and for what situations.

Creating Notices: Common Word-Processing Software

Unfortunately, software applications like Microsoft Word do not enable you to design styles for notices easily. You can specify fonts, size, margins, and borders; but it's hard to specify the actual text for the notice label—the actual word "note," "warning," "caution," "danger," and so on. On the other hand, true desktop-publishing tools like Adobe FrameMaker and PageMaker, Quark Xpress, and Interleaf enable you to build these labels right into the style, along with graphic elements such as boxes or icons.

The following guides you through the design of notices in common word-processing programs. You don't have to use these exact designs, but these procedures will give you the tools to design your own.

Simple notices.   Here is the simplest method (Figure 9-4):

1. In Word, move to a line where you want the notice to begin.
2. Type the notice label—for example, type "Note," highlight it, and press Ctrl+I (on a PC) to make it italics.
3. Type the note text in the same font as your body text (not in italics).
4. Optionally, indent the right and left margins, by choosing **Format→Paragraph,** and under Indentation changing Left and Right to **0.5** inches.

An excess of carbon dioxide in the tissues can be caused by interference with the process of carbon-dioxide transport and elimination. In diving, carbon-dioxide excess occurs either because of an excess of the gas in the breathing medium or because of interference with eliminating the carbon dioxide produced.

Note: There is only about 0.033 percent carbon dioxide in clean fresh air.

FIGURE 9-4
Simple notice.

Caution notices.   Try the "hanging-indent" style for a caution-notice design (Figure 9-5):

1. Move the text cursor to a new line where you want the notice to begin.
2. Type the notice label; for example, type "Caution," highlight it, and press Ctrl+I to italicize it. Next, choose **Format→Font** and select **Arial** in the Font field.
3. Then type the note text in the same font as the body text.
4. Set the hanging indent by choosing **Format→Paragraph.** Under Special, select **Hanging** and set the hanging indent at **0.75** inches. Also, clear all existing tabs and set one tab at **0.75.**

Scuba regulators should be functionally tested on a regular basis; every six months is recommended.

Caution: Hoses for double-hose regulators must be washed with soap and water, and thoroughly rinsed and dried after each use to prevent rapid buildup of bacteria.

FIGURE 9-5
Caution notice.

5. Place the cursor at the beginning of the note text and press Tab.
6. If the notice doesn't look like Figure 9-5, keep changing the tab and hanging-indent values until the spacing looks right (but keep the tab and hanging-indent values the same numerical value).

Warning notices.   The warning notice needs to be more immediately noticeable and indicate a higher level of severity than the caution notice. For the warning notice, bold the label "Warning" and use the steps and format shown previously for the caution notice. The warning in Figure 9-6 alerts readers to a situation that could cause injury, but not immediate, serious, or fatal injury.

The term *hypoxia*, or oxygen shortage, is used to refer to any situation in which tissue cells fail to receive or are unable to obtain enough oxygen to maintain their normal function.

Warning: There is no natural warning that alerts the diver to
the onset of hypoxia.

FIGURE 9-6
Warning notice.

Danger notices.   The danger notice is a good spot for borders. As you can see in Figure 9-7, the border and the all-bold text make it the most visually prominent. Normally, avoid using special effects such as italics, bold, all-caps, or colour for extended text like this. Because it alerts readers to the potential for serious injury, however, the danger notice must be immediately and unavoidably noticeable. Use the following steps in Microsoft Word to create a border:

1. Type the label and text of the notice, highlight it, and then bold it.
2. With the text still highlighted, add the border by choosing **Format**→ **Borders and Shading.** Under Settings, click **Box.** To widen the distance between the borders and the text, click **Options** and then set the margins to around 18 points.

Bold, italics, alternate fonts, hanging indents, and borders enable you to create visually prominent notices that indicate increasing levels of severity. When you design your own notices, there are some design problems to avoid:

> The most widely used underwater welding process is shielded metal-arc welding. The weld is produced by creating an electric arc between a flux-covered metal electrode and the workpiece.
>
> > **DANGER**
> > Take the required precautions when using underwater cutting or welding tools. Failure to do so may cause serious injury or death.
>
> Explosives
> A variety of explosives are used for the removal of subsurface structures, stumps, or wrecks.

FIGURE 9-7
Danger notice.

- Avoid using all-bold, all-italics, all-underscore, all-caps, or other such effects for the text. People don't want to read something that is screaming at them!
- For the text of notices, use a type size no larger than the body font. The special format is enough—the larger type size is overkill.
- Use larger type sizes for notice labels, but make it no larger than the type size of the smallest heading in your document.

SOME SPECIAL NOTICES

The Workplace Hazardous Materials Information System program uses the eight symbols on page 229 to identify hazardous materials.

ESAO
The EDUCATION
SAFETY ASSOCIATION
of ONTARIO

WHMIS SYMBOLS

		Risks	Precautions
Compressed Gas		MATERIALS WHICH ARE NORMALLY GASEOUS KEPT IN A PRESSURIZED CONTAINER • Could explode due to pressure • Could explode if heated or dropped • Possible hazard from both the force of explosion and the release of contents	ENSURE CONTAINER IS ALWAYS SECURED • Store in appropriate designated areas • Do not drop or allow to fall
Flammable and Combustible		MATERIALS WHICH WILL CONTINUE TO BURN AFTER BEING EXPOSED TO A FLAME OR OTHER IGNITION SOURCE • May ignite spontaneously • May be a material which will release flammable products if allowed to degrade or when exposed to water	STORE IN PROPERLY DESIGNATED AREAS WORK IN WELL VENTILATED AREAS • Avoid heating • Avoid sources of sparks / flames • Ensure electrical sources are safe
Oxidizing Material		MATERIALS WHICH CAN CAUSE OTHER MATERIALS TO BURN OR SUPPORT COMBUSTION • Can cause skin or eye burns • Increase fire and explosion hazard • May cause combustibles to explode or react violently	STORE IN AREAS AWAY FROM COMBUSTIBLES WEAR BODY, HAND, FACE AND EYE PROTECTION • Store in proper containers which will not rust or oxidize
Toxic Immediate and Severe		POISONS / POTENTIALLY FATAL MATERIALS WHICH CAUSE IMMEDIATE AND SEVERE HARM • May be fatal if ingested or inhaled • May be absorbed through the skin • Small volumes have a toxic effect	AVOID BREATHING DUST OR VAPOURS AND AVOID CONTACT WITH SKIN OR EYES • Wear protective clothing which is effective against fumes and vapours • Wear face and eye protection • Work in well ventilated areas and wear breathing protection
Toxic Long Term Concealed		MATERIALS WHICH HAVE HARMFUL EFFECTS AFTER REPEATED EXPOSURES OR OVER LONG PERIODS OF TIME • May cause death or permanent injury • May cause birth defects or sterility • May cause cancer • May be sensitizer causing allergies	WEAR APPROPRIATE PERSONAL PROTECTION WORK IN A WELL VENTILATED AREA • Store in appropriate designated areas • Avoid direct contact • Use hand, body, face and eye protection • Ensure respiratory and body protection is appropriate for the specific hazard
Biohazardous Infectious		INFECTIOUS AGENTS OR A BIOLOGICAL TOXIN CAUSING A SERIOUS DISEASE OR DEATH • May cause anaphylactic shock • Includes Viruses, Yeasts, Moulds, Bacteria and Parasites which affect humans • Includes fluids containing toxic products • Includes cellular components	SPECIAL TRAINING REQUIRED WORK IN DESIGNATED BIOLOGICAL AREAS WITH APPROPRIATE ENGINEERING CONTROLS • Avoid forming aerosols • Avoid breathing vapours • Avoid contamination of people / area • Store only in special designated areas
Corrosive Materials		MATERIALS WHICH REACT WITH METALS AND LIVING TISSUE • Eye and skin irritation on exposure • Severe burns/tissue damage on longer exposure • Lung damage if inhaled • May cause blindness if eyes contacted • Environmental damage from fumes	WEAR BODY, FACE AND EYE PROTECTION USE BREATHING APPARATUS • Ensure protective equipment is appropriate • Work in well ventilated area • Avoid all direct body contact • Use appropriate storage containers with proper non-venting closures
Dangerously Reactive		MATERIALS WHICH MAY HAVE UNEXPECTED REACTIONS • May react with water • May be chemically unstable • May explode if exposed to shock or heat • May release toxic or flammable vapours • May vigorously polymerize • May burn unexpectedly	HANDLE WITH CARE AVOIDING VIBRATION, SHOCKS AND SUDDEN TEMPERATURE CHANGES • Store in appropriate containers • Ensure storage containers are sealed • Store and work in designated areas

People working safely in the safest
and healthiest workplaces in the world.

For More Information:

The EDUCATION SAFETY ASSOCIATION of ONTARIO 4950 Yonge Street, Suite 1505, Toronto, ON M2N 6K1 (416) 250-8005 or 1-877-732-ESAO (3726) http://www.esao.on.ca

Catalogue # BWH010102XS   Ver 2.02

Source: WHMIS (Workplace Hazardous Materials Information System) Symbols, Health Canada, 2005. http://www.hc-sc.gc.ca/ewh-semt/occip-travail/whmis-simdut/prog/whmis_symbols-sind_t_symboles_e.html#7. Reproduced with the permission of the Minister of Public Works and Government Services Canada, 2005. AND Education Safety Association of Ontario notice reprinted with permission of ESAO.

WORKSHOP: NOTICES

Here are some additional ideas for practising the concepts, tools, and strategies in this chapter.

1. *Make an inventory of notices.* Explore as many examples of instructions as you can, and catalogue the types of notices you see. For each type you find (note, warning, caution, danger, etc.), describe the situation for which it is used and the format that it uses. Photocopy one good example of each, label the types of information it includes (action, conditions, consequences, and recovery), and identify it according to type and situation.

2. *Create notices.* Using the guidelines in this chapter, write and format a notice for each of the following descriptions.
   a. Many of the operations described in this section have the potential to severely damage or permanently alter your musical instrument. Do not attempt these repairs if you have any doubt about your ability to perform a particular operation.
   b. The Overlook Cliff Trail is a wonderful place to hike and camp, but there are places and things on the trail that can be dangerous to visitors. Do not let your guard down. The trail runs through undeveloped wilderness. Please contact the forest service for the latest updates, rules, and visitor information.
   c. This script erases the partition on which it runs the test. It is used for testing purposes only. Use with great caution.

3. *Format notices in your preferred software.* Use the text in Exercise 2 to create notices in your preferred software.

4. *Anticipate notices.* Consider the following descriptions of instructions. Using the types of notices recommended in Figure 9-1, make a list of the notices that you think these instructions would need. Identify not only the type, but also make notes on the actions, conditions, consequences, and recovery.
   a. How to change a baby's diaper
   b. How to unload and load film into a camera
   c. How to open a bottle of champagne
   d. How to install a new light switch
   e. How to unstop the kitchen sink

CHAPTER 10

Tables, Graphs, and Charts

Topics covered in this chapter include

- earthquakes;
- plate tectonics.

EARTHQUAKES
Natural Resources Canada
http://www.seismo.nrcan.gc.ca/eqinfo/index_e.php

Geological Survey of Canada
http://gsc.nrcan.gc.ca/contact_e.php

University of Nevada—Reno: "About Earthquakes"
http://www.seismo.unr.edu/htdocs/abouteq.html

About.com: "Earthquakes and Plate Tectonics"
http://geography.about.com/education/geography/msub27.htm

PLATE TECTONICS
Geological Survey of Canada
http://www.pgc.nrcan.gc.ca/seismo/eqinfo/eq-westcan.htm

Canadian Geographic
http://www.canadiangeographic.ca/canadaonline/geogr12.htm

U.S. Geological Survey: "This Dynamic Earth"
http://pubs.usgs.gov/publications/text/dynamic.html

Donald L. Blanchard: "ABC's of Plate Tectonics"
http://webspinners.com/dlblanc/tectonic/ptABCs.php

Hawaii Natural History Association: "Plate Tectonics"
**http://volcano.und.nodak.edu/vwdocs/vwlessons/plate_tectonics/
introduction.html**

When you have completed this chapter, you will be able to

- use tables, graphs, and charts to enhance your technical documents;
- design tables, graphs, and charts to present information clearly and concisely;
- create tables, graphs, and charts in word-processing and spreadsheet programs.

No doubt you've seen plenty of tables, graphs, and charts, but you may not have paid much attention to their design. This chapter provides you with some strategies for when to use these communication tools and how to design them. In addition, you will learn how to use common word-processing software to design tables, graphs, and charts. You will also learn how to generate graphs and charts in Microsoft Excel and then paste them into documents.

Note: A good writing project with which to combine tables, charts, and graphs is the recommendation report (Chapter 4). This type of report compares options, the key comparative details of which can be presented with tables, graphs, and charts.

WHAT ARE THEY?

Before getting into the strategies for when to use these tools and how to design them, make sure you know what each is:

■ *Tables.* Tables are rows and columns of numbers, words, or symbols. They provide an efficient means of presenting comparative information about similar things—for example, cost, litres per 100 kilometres, horsepower, and other such details about three or four makes of automobiles. Readers can see the key comparisons more readily in tables than in paragraphs.
■ *Graphs.* A graph shows changes in data over time. For example, in a graph showing variations in high temperature over the month, you'd see a line snaking up and down accordingly. You could use multiple lines to show temperature variations in different years for the same month.
■ *Charts.* The most common types of charts are pie charts and bar charts. Others exist but you need a commercial arts degree to create them. A pie chart shows percentages of a whole; for example, who the leaders are in the market for minivan automobiles and how big each one's slice of pie is. A bar chart could show the same thing, with the length of each bar representing total sales.

WHEN TO USE WHICH?

Often, you can present the same information in a table, in a graph, or in a chart. Tables show the greatest amount of detail but require readers to study carefully to pick out the key trends or contrasts. Graphs and charts illustrate key trends or contrasts more dramatically, but sacrifice detail. To show the declining market share of Company A to the penny as opposed to the rising market share of Company B, use a table. Use a graph or chart to convey the magnitude of these declines and rises, although at the loss of the down-to-the-penny detail.

■ *Text as opposed to a table?* Writers pass up many good opportunities to use tables. Instead, information that could be presented in a table remains in a dense paragraph that some readers are reluctant to read. See the example in Figure 10-1.

It's startling how many earthquakes are located worldwide per year—between 12,000 and 14,000. However, the magnitude and intensity, as measured on the Richter scale, is such that most don't make the front page of your local newspaper. The monster earthquakes, those 8.5 and higher, occur only 0.3 times per year—but that's certainly more than enough! Earthquakes measuring 8.0 to 8.4 are slightly more frequent at 1.1 occurrences per year. Any earthquake 8.0 or over is considered a "great" earthquake. "Major" earthquakes are those between 7.0 and 7.9. In the upper half of that range, 3.1 occur per year, while 15 occur in the 7.0 to 7.4 range. The frequency is considerably higher in the 6.5 to 6.9 range: an average of 56 per year, while 210 occur in the 6.0-6.4 range per year. See www.seismo.nrcan.gc.ca/index_e.php.

Notice how much text is needed to explain how many earthquakes occur on average per year in the different magnitude ranges.

In the tables version, the writer can provide more explanation. Notice that the writer refers readers to the table and gives them a start interpreting it. Because the writer doesn't refer to this table elsewhere in the document, numbering it is unnecessary.

It's startling how many earthquakes are located worldwide per year—between 12,000 and 14,000. However, the magnitude and intensity, as measured on the Richter scale, is such that most don't make the front page of your local newspaper. As the following table shows, the monster earthquakes, those 8.5 and higher, occur only 0.3 times per year—but that's certainly more than enough! As the magnitude decreases, the average per year increases. Earthquakes 8.0 and above are referred to as "great" earthquakes; those in the 7.0–7.9 range are referred to as "major" earthquakes.

Earthquakes Worldwide per Year

Magnitude	EQ/year
8.5 – 8.9	0.3
8.0 – 8.4	1.1
7.5 – 7.9	3.1
7.0 – 7.4	15
6.5 – 6.9	56
6.0 – 6.4	210

FIGURE 10-1

Converting text to tables. Readers can see the details much faster; the writer spends less time tediously explaining statistics.

■ *Table as opposed to a chart or graph?* Just as commonly, data remains locked in dense tables when it could be more dramatically presented in graphs or charts. Figure 10-2 shows how a table can be converted to a graph.

These statistics are used for illustrative purposes only.

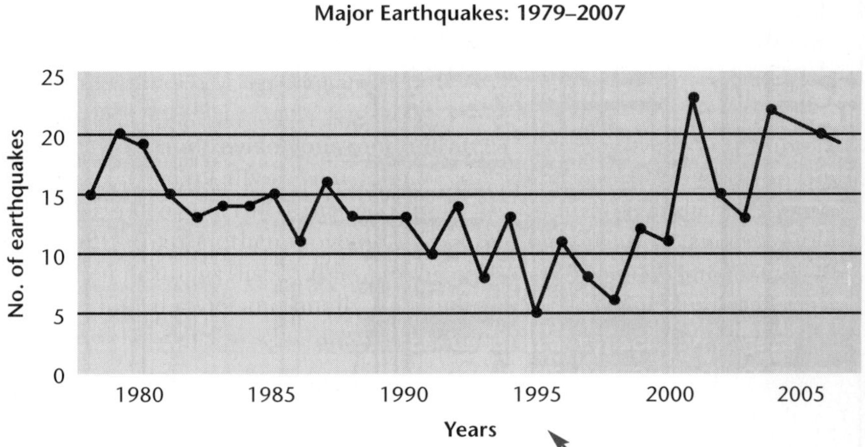

Major Earthquakes: 1979–2007

Major Earthquakes: 1979–2007

Year	EQs	Year	EQs
1979	15	1994	08
1980	20	1995	13
1981	19	1996	05
1982	15	1997	11
1983	13	1998	08
1984	14	1999	06
1985	14	2000	12
1986	15	2001	11
1987	11	2002	23
1988	16	2003	15
1989	13	2004	13
1990	13	2005	22
1991	13	2006	21
1992	10	2007	20
1993	14		

Create this line graph by copying the column for the earthquake totals into a spreadsheet program like Microsoft Excel. In Excel, select the column of cells (5 cells), click **Insert**→**Chart**, select **Line** as the chart type, then **Columns**. Fill in the title for the chart and the labels for the X- and Y-axes, and then click **Finish**. (Excel is not cooperative in modifying the numbers on the X-axis; the year intervals on the chart are a textbox overlaid on the chart. Select **Textbox** from the Drawing toolbar.)

FIGURE 10-2

Converting a table to a graph. It's easier for readers to get the exact numbers from a table, but easier to spot highs, lows, and trends in a line graph. (Note how "major" earthquake is specified in the title for the graph.)

HOW DO YOU DESIGN TABLES, GRAPHS, AND CHARTS?

If you've read the preceding sections on when to use tables, graphs, and charts, consider now how to design them. The following gives you the basic terminology to refer to the different parts of tables, graphs, and charts as well as the basic design requirements, irrespective of the tools you use to create them.

Designing Tables

Here are some of the common guidelines to keep in mind as you create and edit tables (see Figure 10-3 for definitions of the parts of a table):

■ *Double-check your text for information that could be presented as tables.* If you haven't used tables before, watch for instances where you can either convert the presentation into a table or represent the information as a table.

Table title: The title is the first row of the table, and "spans" all six columns. If you plan to use the automated "List of Figures" in Microsoft Word, then you must add the title to the figure (table) using the **Insert→Reference→ Caption** function.

Column subheadings: The column heading "Location" spans the two columns for latitude and longitude since not everyone might be familiar with those terms.

Emphasis: The main headings across the top and along the side are bolded to make finding information easier.

Cell alignment: The data in the information cells is centred in the cell so that it aligns with the adjacent cells that wrap to two lines.

Sources: You must acknowledge the source of any data, figures, or tables. Usually, but not always, the citation will be at the bottom of the figure.

Some Significant Earthquakes in Canada 1600–1900					
Year	**Date**	**Location**		**Estimated Magnitude**	**Comments**
		Lat (°N)	**Lon (°W)**		
1663	5 February	47.6	70.1	7.0	Charlevoix–Kamouraska Region
1700	26 January	Offshore	B.C.	9.0	Cascadia Subduction Zone
1732	16 September	45.5	73.6	5.8	Western Quebec Seismic Zone, Montreal Region
1791	6 December	47.4	70.5	6.0	Charlevoix–Kamouraska Region
1860	17 October	47.5	70.1	6.0	Charlevoix–Kamouraska Region
1870	20 October	47.4	70.5	6.5	Charlevoix–Kamouraska Region
1872	15 December	48.6	121.4	7.4	Washington–B.C. Border
1899	4 September	60.0	140.0	8.0	Yukon–Alaska Border

Source: Significant Earthquakes in Canada 1600–1900, taken from Earthquakes Canada website (seismo.nrcan.gc.ca/historic_eq/canhisseis). Reproduced with the permission of the Minister of Public Works and Government Services Canada, 2005 and Courtesy of Natural Resources Canada, Geological Survey of Canada.

FIGURE 10-3

Components of a table. This complex table shows you almost all of the components—title, column and row headings, column and row subheadings, and of course the actual columns and rows of data.

- *Include titles for tables.* For all but the simplest tables, create a title. Centre the title either in the first row of the table or just above the first row. Cite the source of any information you borrow to create the table.
- *Use bold or italics for the title, column headings, and row headings.* Highlighting for table titles, column headings, and row headings varies widely. In a small table, using bold for all three elements is too much. Instead, try bold for the table title and italics for the column and row headings.
- *Design for horizontal comparison.* Imagine that you have three products to compare in three categories (cost, reliability, and ease of use). Standard table-design wisdom says to make the products the row headings and the categories of comparison the column headings. That way, to compare costs of the three products, readers look down rather than across.
- *Align columns according to the material in the cells.* Left-align columns containing text material; right-align columns containing numerical materials; left-align cells containing a mix of textual and numerical material.
- *Left-align or centre columns with column headings.* Centre column headings within their cells. If the column heading is roughly the length of the material in the column, left-align the column heading with the column. If the column heading is significantly longer than the items in the column, centre the items in the column in relation to the column heading.
- *Specify measurements in the column or row headings.* Instead of specifying a measurement (inches, pounds, millimetres) in each cell, put the measurement or its abbreviation in the column heading. (Figure 10-3 puts Lat (°N) and Lon (°W) in the column headings rather than in each data cell.)
- *Explain key points of the table in Figure 10-3.* Refer to tables in nearby text and give readers some idea as to their significance. For example, say something like, "As you can see in Table 4, Product A is less expensive but is also less reliable."
- *Create sub-columns and sub-rows as needed.* If Company A has Models 1, 2, and 3 and Company B has Models X, Y, and Z, create two main rows for the companies and sub-rows for their respective products. Similarly, for a main category called Performance and two subcategories called City and Highway, create columns and sub-columns. See Figure 10-3 for illustrations of the format of sub-columns and sub-rows.

Designing Graphs and Charts

Here are some of the common guidelines to keep in mind as you create and edit graphs and charts:

- *Double-check text and tables for possibilities to represent them as graphs.* Check the tables you include in your technical documents:

would the dramatic effect of a graph or chart be better than the detail of a table?

- *Include titles for graphs.* Create a descriptive title for your graph or chart, and position it just below the graph or chart. Remember to cite the source of the information you borrow for graphs and charts.
- *Label the axes of graphs.* For the typical graph, the left edge is one axis and the bottom edge is the other axis. For a graph of sales over a five-year period, you'd label the vertical axis something like "Total Sales (millions Canadian dollars)." For the horizontal axis, you'd mark off each of the years and label each mark with the appropriate year. No need to label for this axis—the year numbers make that obvious.
- *Label the graph lines or provide a legend.* For the sales graph, you could label the individual graph lines, or you could include a legend. In a graph, a *legend* is a key telling readers what the different colour, textures, or shadings represent.
- *Discuss the key points in the graph.* Refer to graphs and charts in text just preceding them, and comment on the key points in those graphs.

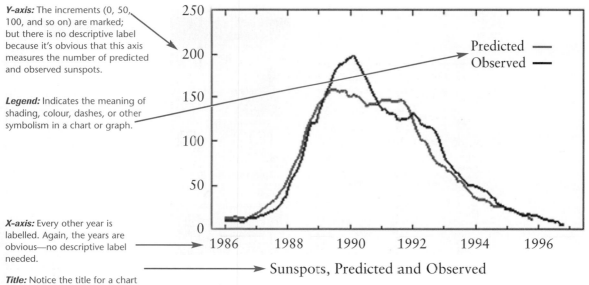

Y-axis: The increments (0, 50, 100, and so on) are marked; but there is no descriptive label because it's obvious that this axis measures the number of predicted and observed sunspots.

Legend: Indicates the meaning of shading, colour, dashes, or other symbolism in a chart or graph.

X-axis: Every other year is labelled. Again, the years are obvious—no descriptive label needed.

Title: Notice the title for a chart or graph occurs beneath the item.

FIGURE 10-4

Components of a graph or chart. In this example, you see the X-axis label, Y-axis label, legend, and title. If the meanings of the two axes were not obvious, descriptive labels would be included (for example, "No. of sunspots" and "Year").

Source: National Oceanic and Atmospheric "Geosynchronous Operational Environmental Satellites (GOES) Stuff to Look For." <spidr.ngdc.noaa.gov:8080/production/html/GOES/goeslook.html>.

HOW DO YOU CREATE TABLES, GRAPHS, AND CHARTS?

The following shows you some techniques for creating tables, graphs, and charts in common word-processing and spreadsheet software.

Creating Tables

Here's a quick introduction to creating tables in Microsoft Word.

Creating Tables: Common Word-Processing Software.   To create a table, follow these steps:

1. To start a table in Microsoft Word, choose **Table→Insert Table**.
2. Specify the number of rows and columns you need, and then press Enter or **OK**. (No need to be exact; you can modify later.)
3. Enter your information into the cells of the table, using the suggestions discussed previously. In particular, consider using bold or italics for the column and row headings.
4. Most tables require some fine-tuning; here are some of the most common revisions:
   - *Resizing columns or the entire table.* To change the size of certain columns or the entire table, move the mouse pointer over one of the

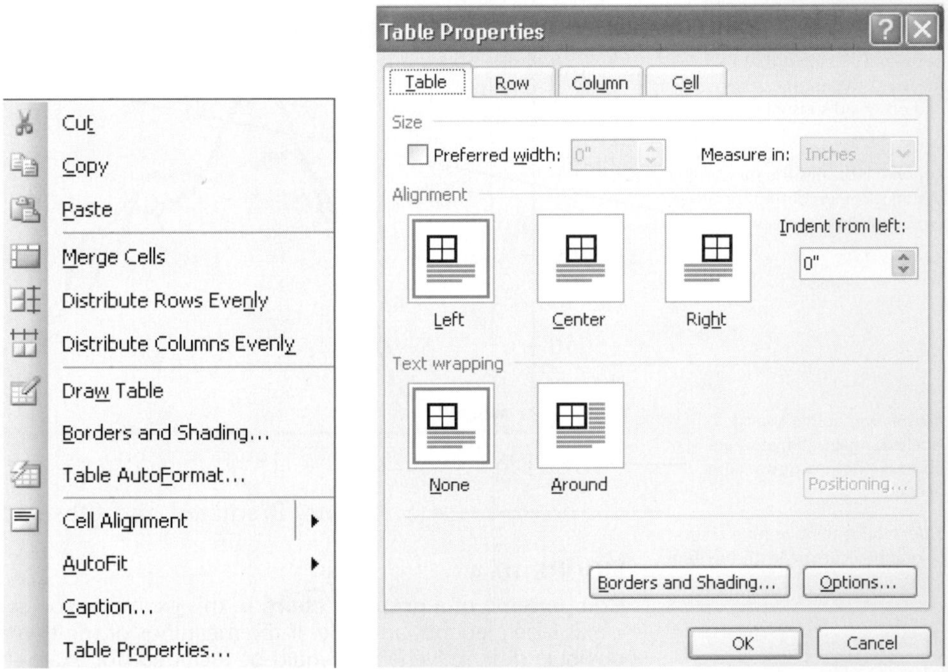

FIGURE 10-5

Table tools in Microsoft Word. To access the Tools dialogue box, start a table, right-click, and select the property that you want to change.

vertical grid lines of the column you want to change, and then drag it to the position you want.

- *Changing the alignment of the table with nearby text.* To align the table to a preceding paragraph, choose **Table→Table Properties**, select the Row tab, and change Indent from left.
  - *Aligning columns.* By default, text is usually jammed to the left edge of cells. Remember that *text* columns should be left-aligned, and *numerical* columns should be right-aligned. To right-align items in a column:
    — Move the mouse pointer into the column, choose **Table→ Select Column**, choose **Format→Paragraph**, and then change Indentation to **Right**. To move items in a column more to the middle of the column, select the column, select **Format→ Paragraph**, and then change the left or right margin (for example, to 0.25 inches).
    — Alternatively, right click in the table, select Cell Alignment, and choose the diagram that represents the alignment that you want.
  - *Adding rows and columns.* If you must insert a row or column, in Microsoft Word (see Figure 10-6), click **Table→Insert Row** to insert a blank row *above* your cursor location. To add a row at

Table	Window	Documents To
Draw Table		
Insert		▶
Delete		▶
Select		▶
Merge Cells		
Split Cells...		
Split Table		
Table AutoFormat...		
AutoFit		▶
Heading Rows Repeat		
Convert		▶
Sort...		
Formula...		
Hide Gridlines		
Table Properties...		

FIGURE 10-6

Table control tools in Microsoft Word. These options become available when the cursor is located in a table.

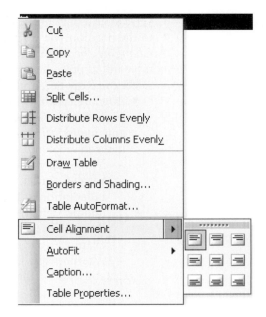

FIGURE 10-7
Table options in Word 2003.

the bottom, move the cursor to the last cell and press the Tab key. To add a column, select the column at which you want the new column to occur and then click **Table→Split Cells**.

■ *Joining and splitting cells.* To create a title for a table, use one row that spans all the columns. To create such a row, you combine all the cells of that row by selecting the entire row, and clicking **Table→Merge Cells**. To split one or more cells, select each cell to split and click **Table→Split Cells**.

■ *Formatting text within cells.* You can change font, type size, bold, italics, and other such features within cells just as you would any other text. For example, to change the type size to 9, select the entire table, click **Font Size** in Microsoft Word, and select **9**.

Creating Tables: Spreadsheet Software. While some word-processing software like WordPerfect, Word Pro, and Word enable you to perform calculations within tables, spreadsheet software like Microsoft Excel is much better suited. Enter data, calculate, and then copy or link the table into a document:

1. Open Excel, and enter the data shown in Figure 10-8. (See the Help functions in Excel for how to calculate the column and row totals.) Select it all by holding down the Shift key and using the arrow keys.

	Microsoft Excel

E5 ▼ *fx* =SUM(E3:E4)

	A	B	C	D	E	F
1						
2		Region	2004	2005	2006	
3		Southwest	5000	16500	14300	
4		Northeast	20000	21500	21350	
5		**TOTALS**	25000	38000	35650	
6						

FIGURE 10-8
Data for spreadsheet.

2. Copy the range by pressing Ctrl+Insert (or select **Edit→Copy**; or press the right mouse button and click **Copy**).
3. Move to the line in the document into which you want to insert the data, and press **Edit→Paste**. If you are inserting the cells from Excel into Word, you will probably have a table whose grid lines are hidden.

Creating Graphs and Charts

The following shows how to create graphs and charts in Microsoft Excel and how to copy them into print documents.

Creating Graphs and Charts: Common Spreadsheet Software. Graphs provide a more visually dramatic view of changes in data over time. If you want to show how Company B is taking a nosedive compared to Company A, a graph will show that comparison far more dramatically.

1. Open Microsoft Excel and enter the data shown in Figure 10-9. Entering data into a spreadsheet is fairly easy: use arrow keys, the Tab key, or the mouse to move to the cell and enter data.
2. When you've entered this data, select it and then click **Insert→Chart**. The application provides an "assistant" or "wizard" to guide you (see Figure 10-10). Take a look at all the types you have to choose from. Select **Column** and the chart sub-type as shown in Figure 10-10, and then click **Next**.
3. In Excel, the wizard prompts you for the title and labels.

	Region	March	April	May		June	July	
	South	15000	16500	14300		15600	17000	
	West	3000	4500	7000		8800	11300	
	East	22000	21500	21350		19150	16500	
	North	17000	16900	17100		17060	17110	

FIGURE 10–9
Entering data in Microsoft Excel for a graph or chart.

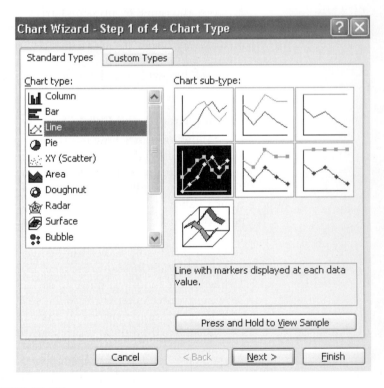

FIGURE 10–10
Microsoft Excel Chart Wizard.

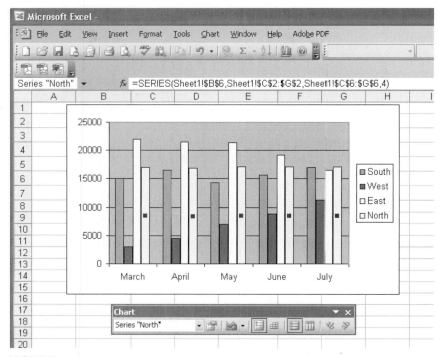

FIGURE 10-11
Bar graph in Microsoft Excel.

4. To copy this chart into a document, make sure the chart is selected, and then choose **Edit→Select** (or click the right mouse button and click **Copy**).
5. Move to the document into which you want to place the chart, position the cursor at the point in the text where you want the chart, and choose **Edit→Paste**.

With this introduction, you'll be able to figure out how to create other charts. But just to be sure, use the same data to create these charts:

■ *Line graph* (Figure 10-12): In Excel, click **Insert→Chart** and select **Line**. From this point, the process is the same as when you created the column chart.
■ *Pie charts* (Figure 10-13): In pie charts, percentages of a whole are expressed in wedges of a circle. In Excel, click **Insert→Chart** and select **Pie**.

Although you may need plenty of refinements and special features, this introduction should get you started.

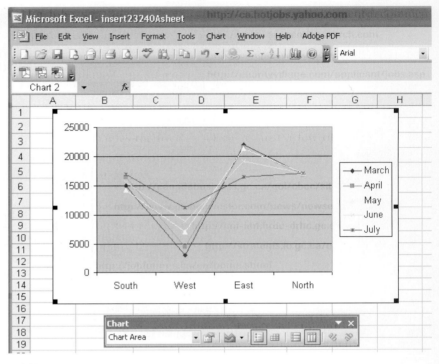

FIGURE 10-12
Line graph.

WORKSHOP: TABLES, GRAPHS, AND CHARTS

Here are some additional ideas for practising the concepts, tools, and strategies in this chapter:

1. *Simple table.* Using your preferred software, create a simple, informal table (with table title, source, and column headings) from the following data:

   Column headings should be year, month, day, time (GMT), latitude (north), longitude (west), magnitude, location. 1995, 2, 19, 403, 40 37.00, 125 54.00, 6.6, W. of Eureka; 1995, 9, 20, 2327, 35 46.00, 117 38.00, 5.5, Ridgecrest; 1996, 7, 24, 2016, 41 47.04, 125 54.66, 5.7, W. of Eureka; 1997, 1, 22, 717, 40 16.32, 124 23.64, 5.7, Punta Gorda; 1999, 8, 1, 1606, 37 23.40, 117 4.80, 5.7, Scotty's Junction, Nevada; 1999, 10, 16, 947, 34 35.64, 116 16.26, 7.1, Hector Mine; 2000, 3, 16, 1520, 40 23.16, 125 16.74, 5.9, Mendocino Fracture

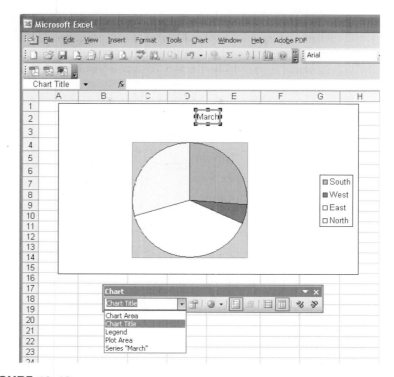

FIGURE 10-13

Pie chart. Double-click the chart in Excel to get the toolbar to make changes to the graphic, title, etc.

Zone. (Title "California Earthquake History 1769-Present." URL: http://pasadena.wr.usgs.gov; last updated 05/04/00; visited 05/31/00; source: Ellsworth, William L., "Earthquake History, 1769-1989" in USGS Professional Paper 1515, Robert E. Wallace, ed.,1990; William Ellsworth, personal communication; and USGS earthquake catalogues; maintained by Lisa Wald.)

2. *Text to table.* Study the following text and convert the comparative data to a table; use other text as introduction to the table. Include table title and column headings, as well as a source citation:

Magnitude measures the energy released at the source of the earthquake. Magnitude is determined from measurements on seismographs. The following table gives intensities that are typically observed at locations near the epicentre of earthquakes of different magnitudes. Earthquakes with a magnitude ranging from 1.0-3.0 are

generally not felt except by a very few under especially favourable conditions. Earthquakes with a magnitude ranging from 3.0-3.9 are felt only by a few
persons at rest, in a few cases quite noticeably, especially on upper floors of buildings. Many people do not
recognize it as an earthquake. Standing motor cars may
rock slightly. Vibrations are similar to those of passing a truck. Earthquakes with a magnitude ranging from
4.0-4.9 are felt indoors by many, outdoors by only a
few during the day. At night, some are awakened.
Dishes, windows, and doors are disturbed; walls make
cracking sounds. Standing motor cars rock noticeably.
Closer to 4.9, earthquakes are felt by nearly everyone;
many are awakened; some dishes and windows are broken;
unstable objects are overturned. Earthquakes with a
magnitude ranging from 5.0-5.9 are felt by all; many
are frightened. Some heavy furniture is moved, but damage is slight. Closer to 5.9, damage is negligible in
buildings of good design and construction; slight to
moderate in well-built ordinary structures; considerable in poorly built or badly designed structures.
Earthquakes with a magnitude ranging from 6.0-6.9
result in slight damage to specially designed structures; considerable damage in ordinary substantial
buildings with partial collapse; and great damage in
poorly built structures. Chimneys, factory stacks, columns, monuments, and walls collapse. Heavy furniture
overturned. Closer to 6.9, damage is considerable even
in specially designed structures; well-designed frame
structures thrown out of plumb. Damage great in substantial buildings, with partial collapse and buildings
shifted off foundations. In earthquakes with a magnitude of 7.0 and higher, even well-built wooden structures are destroyed; most masonry and frame structures
are destroyed with foundations; few if any structures
remain standing. Bridges are destroyed; rails bent
greatly. Damage is total; objects thrown into the air.
("Magnitude/Intensity Comparison." URL: http://www.neic.
cr.usgs.gov. Last updated: May 12, 2000; visited: May
31, 2000. Maintained by M. Zirbes.)

3. *Graphs.* Using your preferred software, create a line graph from the following data and paste it into a document (such as a report):

Major earthquakes (7.0-7.9 on the Richter scale) by year:
1969 – 15; 1970 – 20; 1971 – 19; 1972 – 15; 1973 – 13;
1974 – 14; 1975 – 14; 1976 – 15; 1977 – 11; 1978 – 16;
1979 – 13; 1980 – 13; 1981 – 13; 1982 – 10; 1983 – 14;
1984 – 08; 1985 – 13; 1986 – 05; 1987 – 11; 1988 – 08;
1989 – 06; 1990 – 12; 1991 – 11; 1992 – 23; 1993 – 15;
1994 – 13; 1995 – 22; 1996 – 21; 1997 – 20. (Title:
"Are Earthquakes Really on the Increase?" URL: http://
www.neic.cr.usgs.gov/neis/general/handouts/increase_in
_earthquakes.html; visited May 31, 2000; last updated
May 12, 2000. Maintained by M. Zirbes.)

4. *Bar charts*. Using your preferred software, create a bar chart from the
   following data and paste it into a document (such as a report):

   Estimated deaths per year worldwide from earthquakes
   6.0 to 9.9 (Richter scale): 1980 – 8620; 1981 – 5223;
   1982 – 3328; 1983 – 2372; 1984 – 174; 1985 – 9846; 1986
   – 1068; 1987 – 1080; 1988 – 26552; 1989 – 617. Try
   including the total number of 6.0-9.9 earthquakes for
   the same 1980 to 1989 period, respectively: 119, 103,
   95, 140, 99, 124, 94, 123, 101, 86. (Title: "Earthquake
   Facts and Statistics." URL: http://www.neic.cr.usgs.
   gov/neis/eqlists/graphs.html; updated May 12, 2000;
   visited May 31, 2000. Maintained by M. Zirbes.)

5. *Pie charts*. Using your preferred software, create pie charts from the
   following data and paste it into a document (such as a report).

   This series of three pie charts will show distribution
   of water on our planet Earth: 97% is in the oceans,
   while 3% is classified as "other." Of that 3% described
   as "other," 22% is ground water, 77% is in glaciers,
   icecaps, and inland seas, while 1% is classified as
   "other." Of that 1%, 61% is in lakes, 39% in atmospheric and soil moisture, while 0.4% is in rivers.
   Title of this pie chart is "Distribution of Water on
   Earth." (Title: "Earth's Water Distribution." URL:
   http://ga.water.usgs.gov. Last updated: February 3,
   2000. Visited May 31, 2000.)

CHAPTER 11

Illustrative Graphics

Topics covered in this chapter include

- fractals;
- Web graphics;
- copyright issues.

FRACTALS
The Spanky Fractal Database
http://spanky.triumf.ca

You can also search for a U.S. site named The Geometry Junkyard.

WEB GRAPHICS
The most common place to find graphics for a report is online. However, you need to be careful when you take graphics. To find available graphics, search for "public domain" images. For some places to start, go to **http://www.fiftyup.net**, a site developed by one of this textbook's authors.

COPYRIGHT ISSUES
faircopyright.ca (Laura J. Murray)
http://www.faircopyright.ca

Canadian Heritage
http://www.pch.gc.ca/progs/ac-ca/progs/pda-cpb/index_e.cfm

When you have completed this chapter, you will be able to

- use graphics to enhance your instructions, background reports, and other technical documents;
- find or create illustrations using a variety of methods;
- format, size, and label illustrations appropriately for your documents;
- add titles and cross-references to your illustrations;
- incorporate functional and attractive graphics into your documents.

This chapter shows you some techniques for finding or creating illustrative graphics and getting them into your technical documents. *Illustrative graphics* include things like drawings, photos, diagrams, schematics, flow charts, and so on.

Note: Tables, bar and pie charts, and line graphs, which illustrate concepts and data rather than objects, are discussed in Chapter 10.

WHAT SHOULD BE ILLUSTRATED?

Before getting into details about creating and using graphics, stop a moment to think about what can be illustrated in technical documents:

- *Instructions:* Imagine providing instructions on grafting a fruit tree, performing CPR, setting up a VCR, or installing a ceiling fan. Illustrations are needed for the various components of the objects involved, the tools used to work on those objects, and the orientations between the objects and tools in the procedure. Locations of certain features on the objects—for example, the MIDI plug on the VCR—must be shown. Actions must also be illustrated; for example, VCR instructions may include an illustration of someone pushing a videocassette into the VCR.
- *Technical background reports:* Imagine the illustrative graphics for reports on the Sable Island Offshore Energy Project, the causes and effects of El Niño, or new developments in solar automobiles. Maps combined with diagrams and drawings could show the possible environmental effects of an oil spill or the formation of El Niño. Photographs of oil-spill effects on shorelines or photographs of several solar cars could be used. Drawings and diagrams could be used to illustrate the design of solar cars. Conceptual drawings combining maps, illustrative details such as clouds, rain, and sunshine, and indications of movement and cycle could be used to illustrate the process involved in El Niño or La Niña.

Certain key elements in technical documents need to be illustrated:

■ *Objects, parts and features of objects:* Obviously, objects (mechanisms, places, areas, things, stuff!) central to the discussion must be illustrated. In instructions for grafting, readers need to see the graft and the root stock. To make readers fully aware of the horror of an oil spill, include some photographs of the Valdez spill. (The same company is developing the Sable Island project.) To refer to the components of the VCR, include an illustration with each of those components labelled.

■ *Orientations, relationships:* Some illustrations, particularly for instructions, must show the position of things or people in relation to each other. In CPR instructions, show how to position your body in relation to the victim's body, where to apply pressure on the victim's chest, and so on.

■ *Actions, movements:* Some illustrations must also convey a sense of movement and direction. For example, an arrow indicating the direction that pressure needs to be applied or an arrow indicating the direction one object needs to be in to be inserted into another may be part of your illustration.

■ *Concepts, ideas:* Graphics can also be used to illustrate concepts. For example, a company's organizational chart doesn't depict anything in the physical world; instead, it shows interrelationships of individuals and groups within the organization. The same is true of flow charts, which can be used for a manufacturing process, for example. When you explain a complex idea, look for ways to illustrate that idea conceptually or symbolically.

As you plan, write, and revise technical documents, look for opportunities to illustrate important objects, parts or features of objects, orientations and relationships, actions and movements, and concepts and ideas.

WHAT ARE THE TYPES OF ILLUSTRATIONS?

To keep it simple, let's define four types of illustrations (illustrated in Figures 11-1 through 11-4) based on the amount and kind of detail they contain:

■ *Photographs (Figure 11-1):* Photographs contain the most illustrative detail, although for some technical contexts they have too much detail. For an oil-spill report, photographs of wildlife victims along the shoreline are painfully dramatic. However, if you want to orient readers to the components of a solar energy system (shown in Figure 11-1), photographs provide too much detail, and the detail is often obscured by lack of contrast. Still, the photograph in Figure 11-1 gives readers a nice visual sense of what a system would look like installed at their homes as well as a schematic of the system.

Source: From www.canren.gc.ca/tech_appl/indez.asp?CaId=5&PgId=302#heat_outdoor_pools. Reproduced with the permission of the Minister of Public Works and Government Services Canada, 2005.

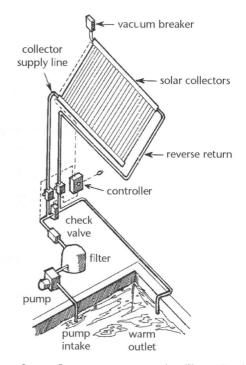

Source: From www.canren.gc.ca/app/filerepository/64306F7730774536853C48ECA6088161.pdf Pg. 8. Reproduced with the permission of the Minister of Public Works and Government Services Canada, 2005.

FIGURE 11-1

Photographs. Homeowners considering "going solar" will want to know what those photovoltaic panels will look like on their roofs.

■ *Drawings (Figure 11-2):* For many technical contexts, drawings are the ideal type of illustration. Drawings suppress unnecessary detail and allow readers to focus on the important objects, tools, and actions. Drawings illustrate relationships and concepts that photographs simply cannot. You've probably seen exploded and cutaway illustrations. You can also use drawings to show, for example, a cross-sectional view of a volcano or the movement of an oil spill.

■ *Flow charts and other conceptual drawings (Figure 11-3):* Consider the classic organization chart: it illustrates relationships between people and subgroups within the organization; it also depicts the flow of information within the organization. Consider conceptual drawings: the classic illustration of hypertext shows squares ("nodes") with arrows connecting them in a spiderweb-like manner, introducing us to the concept of hypertext.

■ *Diagrams and schematics (Figure 11-4):* This final type of illustration removes so much detail that the object being illustrated is no longer recognizable. The classic example is the wiring schematic for an electronic appliance. Is that really your microwave oven?

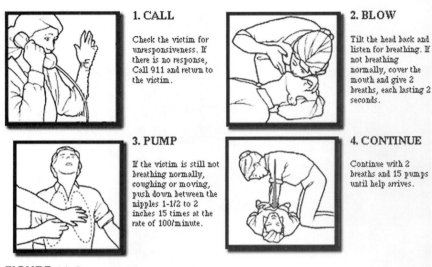

FIGURE 11-2

Examples of drawings. Simplified drawings in this case are better than fully detailed photographs. They clarify the critical actions, positions, and orientations. *Source:* Learn CPR: http://www.learncpr.org.

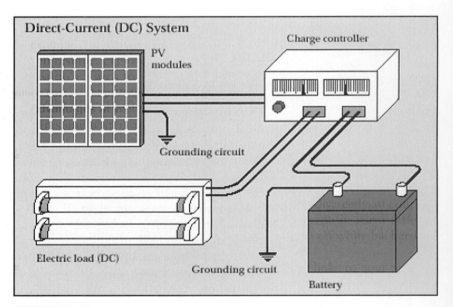

FIGURE 11-3

Example of a flow chart. This flow chart depicts the flow of solar energy and electricity through a photovoltaic system. The PV modules are typically located on a roof to gather solar energy. *Source:* U.S. Department of Energy. *Photovoltaics: Basic Design and Components*, DOE/GO-10097-377.

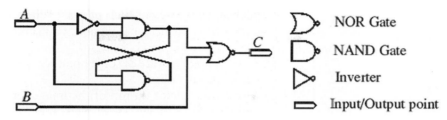

FIGURE 11-4

Example of a diagram. Notice how the graphic artist provides a "legend" here to define the meanings of the symbols used in the diagram.

HOW DO YOU FIND OR CREATE ILLUSTRATIONS?

You've seen some nice, professionally done illustrations in this chapter so far. But you are right to wonder: "How can I get such illustrations without hiring a commercial artist?" One solution is to request permission to use electronic copies of the illustrations you want. You can embed them electronically right into your documents rather than manually taping them into printouts. However, the old-fashioned cut-and-paste method is an option. This method is presented later in this chapter.

Finding illustrations. Search for your topic, just as you would search for textual information on that topic. (See Chapter 18 for strategies for information searching.)

Practical Ethics: Manipulating Photos

Photos always present an accurate picture of reality, right? Well, no. With a home computer, digital imaging software, and a few clicks, a photo can be manipulated to show what we want it to. Slim models become even slimmer; political enemies are removed from snapshots of historic meetings; people are added to a crowd, turning a few protesters into a mob. In the past it was possible to compare a photograph with the original negative to determine if it had been altered. Digital cameras make this impossible.

Publications now have difficulty keeping readers' trust. Retaining trust involves more than saying no to digital manipulation. A conscious effort has to be made to size and crop photos so the essential content is left intact, eliminating only irrelevant clutter that would confuse readers.

Let's say you're writing a detailed promotional report for an air conditioning system. Your boss is concerned that the size of the unit will discourage consumers from considering it, especially because it is larger than that of the competition. You are given a picture of the system to use, which includes a man, and the system comes up to his chest. If he weren't in the picture, there would be nothing to visually establish the size of the unit. What would you do?

Would you use the entire photo or would you crop the man out? Would you state the dimensions in the caption below the photo or anywhere else in the report? What if your boss told you specifically to crop the photo and not mention the dimensions? How would you justify your answers? Remember to consider the basic principles of the AUTHOR ethical guidelines in the Introduction of this text.

Copying images from Web pages. When you find graphics on Web pages, with the owner's permission, you can copy them. Try this out:

1. To get a great picture of some potatoes, go to this Web page: **http://www.powertools.nelson.com**.
2. Move your cursor on top of the image, press the right mouse button, and click **Save Image As** (in Netscape) or **Save Picture As** (in Internet Explorer).
3. In the dialogue box, rename the graphics file however you wish, and store it in a folder with a name you'll remember.
4. Make a note of the full Web address (URL), title, date on the Web page, author name (either individual or corporate), and date you copied the image. You'll need this for the source citation.

Skip to the section on formatting to see how to bring illustrations into a document.

Making screen captures. Another way to get illustrations into documents electronically is to make screen captures directly from your computer screen. Try this example:

1. Select a software application you often use, and open it to an area that might require some illustration—for example, the dialogue box for a macro editor.
2. When you have the screen set up just the way you want it, you can do one of two things using the standard personal computer keyboard:
   ■ Press the Print Screen key on your keyboard. This captures what's displaying on the entire computer screen.
   ■ Press and hold the Alt key and press the Print Screen key. This captures the "active" window (the window in which your application is running).
3. You can now paste this captured image into a document or into a graphic application such as Microsoft's Paint (available through **Start** →**Programs**→**Accessories**→**Paint**).

You will probably want to crop (select a portion of) or size (reduce or enlarge) the image. These techniques are explained later in this chapter.

Using clip art. The Internet contains a wealth of clip art resources. Here are a few addresses of the many websites available:

■ *Clipart.com.* Categorized site for links to clip art, fonts, photos, and Web graphics: **http://www.clipart.com**.
■ *Web Developer's Virtual Library. VL-WWW: Images_and_Icons:* **http://wdvl.com/icons** and **http://wdvl.com/images**.
■ *Clip Art Sources.* Go to **http://auillac.inria.fr/~lang/hotlist/clipart** for links to dozens of clip art and icon resources, including tools to create or edit graphics.

These will get you started and will lead to many more. When you borrow clip art from the Internet, be sure to cite the source properly. You must cite the source of *any* borrowed information, including graphics.

Drawing your own illustrations. Although you may not be ready to draw complex images such as people, animals, vegetation, or machinery, you can indeed draw some things right now. Notice the hand-drawn illustration of the flashlight in the example at the end of Chapter 1.

HOW DO YOU FORMAT ILLUSTRATIONS?

Once you have an electronic copy of the illustration you want, the next steps involve editing and inserting it into a document and adding cross-references, titles, and source citations.

Cropping illustrations. When you *crop* an image, you select just a portion of it to show in your document. There are several ways to crop images. Follow these steps using Microsoft Word or a similar application:

1. Paste the image you want at the point in the text where you want it.
2. With the image selected, click the right mouse button over the image, select **Show Picture Toolbar.** Select the cropping tool (shown in Figure 11-5), position the mouse pointer over any of the sizing handles on the image to drag the edges inward as necessary.

FIGURE 11-5

Cropping and sizing tools. Click on the cropping tool and then move the mouse pointer to one of the handles and crop.

Sizing illustrations. Sometimes, you may also need to size illustrations. *Sizing* an image means reducing or enlarging it. Select an image and then drag the sizing handles (see Figure 11-5) to get the image the size you want it.

Labelling illustrations.   As with cropping images, you can either add labels to images within your word-processing software or add the labels separately in a graphics application. To add labels to a graphic in Microsoft Word, follow these steps:

1. Scroll to the area in which you've displayed the graphic you want to label and then display the Drawing toolbar by selecting **View→ Toolbars→Drawing**. Click the text box icon, and then create a text box by dragging the mouse with the left mouse button held down. (See Figure 11-6 for locations of the icons and tools.)

FIGURE 11-6
Drawing toolbar in Microsoft Word. When you are formatting and labelling graphics, display this toolbar to make your work easier.

2. Type some words in the text box. For labels, try a type size 1 or 2 points smaller than regular body text (but *never* larger than body text). A nice design is to make labels the same font you use for headings. For example, if you use Arial for headings and 12-point Times New Roman for regular text, try 9- or 10-point Arial for labels.
3. To hide the border of the text box, select the text box, click the right mouse button, and then select **Format Text Box**. For Fill and Line, select **No Fill** and **No Line**, respectively.
4. To resize the text box, select it and then move the cursor over the sizing handles. Hold down the left mouse button and drag the text box until it is the size you want.
5. To move the text box into a position where you want it, select the text box and drag it to the correct location.
6. If you want to add a line or arrow pointing from the label to a specific area in the image, click on the line tool in the Drawing toolbar. (Use the arrow-style tool to specify which end of the line is used for the arrow-head.)
7. Once you've created all the labels and arrows you want and have positioned them where you want, you must *group* them. That way, all the parts of the graphic move as one piece. To group the graphic, labels, and arrows, select the objects by holding the **Shift** key and left-clicking each object. On the Drawing toolbar, click **Draw**, and then click **Group**. Objects must be either all floating or all on a canvas for you to select them. If you have trouble selecting your picture and a text box, click the picture and then **Insert→Text Box**. Reverse the procedure to ungroup objects.

Adding figure titles and indicating sources. Place figure titles below graphics, and make them descriptive. Readers who skim through your text will appreciate these identifiers. Use a figure number if you cross-reference graphics from other pages. To format figure titles, use the same font that you use for headings but one or two point sizes smaller than regular body text. For example, if you use Arial for headings and 12-point Times New Roman for regular text, try 10-point Arial for figure titles. Identify the source of your borrowed graphics.

Cross-referencing illustrations. Don't just toss graphics into documents without alerting readers to them and helping them to understand those graphics. Cross-reference each graphic before it appears in the text. For example, this chapter refers to tools for creating graphics, and cross-references have alerted you to illustrations of those tools; otherwise, you might have been unaware of them. In cross-references, include as many of the following elements as you think readers will need:

- *Title.* You can refer to the graphic merely as "Figure 3," or go a bit further and refer to it as "Figure 3, Drawing Toolbar." Citing the exact title of the figure helps indicate its subject matter.
- *Page number.* If your graphics are numbered, if the cross-referenced graphic is nearby, and if the document is not overly long, readers can find the graphic *without* a page reference. Keep it simple!
- *Subject matter and relevance.* Briefly indicate the subject matter of the graphic—this helps readers decide whether to go look at it. Explain how the graphic is related to your discussion; otherwise, readers may not bother.
- *Description or interpretation.* Provide brief explanations of your graphics; don't force readers to interpret them on their own.

You'll find all these elements in Figure 11-7.

From 1995 through 1996, the Hubble Space Telescope (HST) was able to resolve Cepheid variable stars in galaxies in the Virgo cluster (which includes the M100 galaxy as shown in Figure 5). This ensured a much better calibration of distance measures. This has allowed more accurate estimates to be made of Hubble's constant H. Early galaxies and quasars have also been observed by the HST, raising serious doubts about current structure formation models.

Cross-reference

Illustration

Figure title

Figure 5. M100, one of the spiral nebulae in the nearby Virgo cluster of galaxies [11].

Figure source

FIGURE 11-7

Key elements of a graphic in text. Make sure to cross-reference each graphic from nearby text, include a descriptive figure title, and indicate the source (if you borrowed it).

HOW DO YOU INCORPORATE GRAPHICS INTO DOCUMENTS?

Let's imagine that you have a nice graphic out there just waiting to be added into your technical document. How do you get it into your file where you want it?

Inserting and positioning illustrations. Once you've copied a graphic from another application such as MS Paint or have made a screen capture, you can paste it into a document:

1. Move to the spot in the document where you want to insert the graphic. Press Enter to create a blank line, and move your cursor to that blank line. Then in Microsoft Word, choose **Edit→Paste** (in some instances, it may be **Edit→Paste Special**).
2. To force text out from under the graphic and to force text to appear above and below the graphic only, select the graphic and then with the cursor in the shape of a four-pointed arrow icon, click the right mouse button. Select **Format Picture→Layout→Advanced→Text Wrapping→ Top and bottom**.

3. To "lock" the graphic into place between the text elements above and below it, click **Format Picture→Layout→Advanced→Picture Position**, and then check the boxes **Move object with text** and **Lock anchor**.
4. To set a standard distance between preceding text and the graphic as well as between the graphic and following text, select the graphic, right-click the mouse, and then select **Format Picture→Layout→ Advanced→Text Wrapping**. For starters, try 0.2 (inches) for both top and bottom under Distance from text.
5. To fine-adjust the location of the graphic, select it and then use the arrow keys to move it in small increments.

HOW ABOUT THE OLD-FASHIONED WAY?

If you simply refuse to use computers to incorporate graphics into your technical documents, you can do it the old-fashioned way—with real scissors, real tape, and photocopy machines (as shown in Figure 11-8).

1. Collect the illustrations you need from books, magazines, reports, the Internet, and other such sources. See the preceding pages of this chapter for strategies. (If you're using these materials for documents that will be published, to avoid copyright infringement, you should request permission to use them.)
2. When you have the illustrations you need and a draft of the text you want them in, photocopy the illustrations or print them out. Reduce or enlarge them so that they fit neatly within the normal margins of your document.

FIGURE 11-8

Taping illustrations into technical documents. The old-fashioned way still works! Follow the suggestions in this section to make the results look neat and professional.

3. Just after those points where you mention the illustrations, add space so that the illustrations fit, with about a half-inch white space above and below. If space is lacking, push the graphic to the top of the next page, and fill the remaining open space with text.

4. In the open space you've created for the illustration, type the figure title, including source information if you borrowed the graphic. Don't forget to add a cross-reference to your graphic in nearby text.

5. Tape in your illustrations carefully, making sure they are right in the middle of that open space both horizontally and vertically.

6. If your illustrations need labels, print them separately and tape them in (unless you have very neat handwriting). Don't draw or colour directly on final pages.

7. When you have done all this, get a sharp photocopy of the entire report, bind it, and hand it off to your instructor or client. Test a few of your pages with taped-in illustrations first. If the edges of the taped-in material show, see if making the copy lighter will make them go away.

WORKSHOP: GRAPHICS

Here are some additional ideas for practising the concepts, tools, and strategies in this chapter:

1. *Making screen captures.* Imagine that you are writing instructions that will enable people to perform some task on your computer and that you need screen captures:
   a. Set up your computer screen so that it displays the application for which you are providing instructions, and make the screen capture.
   b. Bring the screen capture into a graphics program and crop it to an appropriate portion.
   c. Use any of the methods suggested in this chapter to add labels to the graphic. When you are done, group all the labels and the graphic into one unified graphic.
   d. Import the graphic into a text file, and add a figure title just beneath, including information on its source.

2. *Cropping, sizing, and changing file format.* Using the screen capture you made in the preceding exercise, trim away the unnecessary parts of the image (cropping), adjust the overall height and width of the image (sizing), and convert it to a GIF image (changing file format). For these tasks, use your preferred word-processing software or graphics application such Adobe Photoshop, Jasc Paint Shop Pro, or Microsoft Paint.

3. *Adding labels and figure titles with source.* Add at least three labels to the screen capture you made in the preceding exercise. Make sure that the text box for each label is transparent and that the lines do not

show. Draw arrows from each text box to the related part of the image. Create a figure title as a text box and attach it to the bottom edge of the image. In it, Use the label "Figure," followed by a number and period, followed by a descriptive title, followed by the label "Source:" in italics, followed by the manufacturer, name, and version number of the software. Group all of these image elements together.

4. *Adding images to documents.* Use the instructions, text, and graphics available at **http://www.powertools.nelson.com** (go to the Chapter 11 link) to create a document in your preferred word-processing software and add graphics with labels and figure titles to it.

5. *Creating old-fashioned graphics.* Paste in a graphic the old-fashioned way, using the directions provided in this chapter:
   a. Go to the Chapter 11 link at **http://www.powertools.nelson.com** for the text and the graphic.
   b. Print out the graphic, and then copy the text into a word-processing document with software such as Word or WordPerfect, leaving enough room for the graphic.
   c. Just below the open space, use the notes available with the text to create a figure title.
   d. Print out this document, trim the graphic you printed, and then tape it into the open space in the text.
   e. Finally, photocopy this page and see how good it looks!

PART III

Document-Delivery Tools

CHAPTER 12

Business Communications: Letters, Memos, and E-Mail

Topics covered in this chapter include

- wind energy;
- international business.

WIND ENERGY

Alternative energy sources are in the limelight, especially with the rising cost of traditional energy sources. The Canadian federal and provincial governments have produced great amounts of material on the development of wind energy. Search any provincial or federal website for materials.

INTERNATIONAL BUSINESS

Again, the trend toward the global economy has heightened interest in international business and an awareness of the customs and traditions in other countries.

"A one-stop shop to a world of knowledge on Canadian foreign policy and international relations"
http://www.dfait-maeci.gc.ca/canada-magazine/hyperlinks-en.asp

The Canadian Corporate Leadership Council for the UN
http://www.unac.org/en/projects/peace/background.asp
http://www.unac.org/en/get_involved/cclcun/index.asp

The Communication Initiative, Victoria, B.C.
http://www.comminit.com/universities/uc/sld-2499.html

When you have completed this chapter, you will be able to

- use a standard structure for writing effective letters, memos, and e-mails;
- format business letters in generally accepted styles;
- format memos in accepted styles;
- create memo and letter templates for future use;
- decide on appropriate situations for e-mail communication;
- write effective complaint, adjustment, and inquiry communications.

Business communications—letters, memos, and e-mail—often must convey technical information just like other sorts of documents. In fact, business letters and memos are often the "wrapper" for brief technical reports. This chapter provides tips on writing effective business communications, no matter what the medium; how to format letters and memos; and finally, how to write effective e-mail. Also included in this chapter is a step-by-step explanation of how to create a template. Of course, you can use templates for any document that has a standard format and layout, not just a letter or memo.

Note: For additional examples of the documents discussed in this chapter, see **http://www.powertools.nelson.com**.

HOW DO YOU WRITE EFFECTIVE LETTERS, MEMOS, AND E-MAIL?

This chapter covers format and style for types of business communications. However, more important are the strategies you need to write *effective* letters, memos, and e-mail.

Tone. Think of tone as the personality, attitude, or mood of a document. You can define tone in terms of a range. For example, business letters can range from formal to informal, impersonal to personal, and so on. In an e-mail inquiry to an expert, you want the tone to be respectful, friendly, but somewhat formal. In a complaint letter concerning a faulty product, you want the tone to be firm, formal, demanding, but not threatening.

Brief, state-your-purpose introduction. The first lines of any business communication—letter, memo, or e-mail—should clarify topic and purpose. Keep it brief—no more than four or five lines. Our tendency is to dive into details, leaving readers to figure out the point of the communication for themselves.

Review the context. If your communication is in response to some other communication, repeat the details of the context. For example, to reply to a customer's complaint letter, the first paragraph can say something like "in reference to your June 15 letter concerning the problem you had with …" Context is particularly important in e-mail. If you write and read lots of e-mail every day, it's hard to remember what you are discussing with whom.

Good-news-first, bad-news-last strategy.   A common strategy in business correspondence is to state good news—or at least neutral news—first and then bad news. For example, if you have lots of good qualifications for a job, except for one detail, state the positive first. Save the not-so-good for later, or don't even mention it at all! In a response to a complaint letter, don't state the rejection of the customer's request until after you've explained the reasons for rejecting it.

Reader-first strategy.   Business communications are typically efforts to achieve a transaction with the recipient. For example, you want to get information, a job interview, or compensation for a faulty product. In such transactions, both parties need to feel as though they have gained something. In an employment situation, the employer gets someone to handle important tasks and you get a salary! In a customer-complaint situation, the customer gets her money back and the company retains that customer's business and goodwill. Thus, business correspondence must focus on the needs and interests of the recipient.

Organization-based paragraphing.   Make the paragraphs of your business communications indicate the logic and topics of your message. Always reserve the first paragraph for the introduction, in which you indicate the topic, purpose, and context of the communication (and provide an overview of what follows if your communication is longer than a page). Make sure that each paragraph has an obvious purpose and topic. For example, after the introduction in a complaint letter, use a paragraph to narrate and describe the problem; use the next paragraph to state the compensation you are requesting; then use still another paragraph to explain why your request is justified. Don't let these three basic functions overlap paragraphs.

Short-paragraphs strategy.   Keep the paragraphs of business communications short—for example, fewer than eight lines. People can read and scan short paragraphs faster. They are less likely to read long, dense paragraphs. To achieve such scannability, you may also need to reduce line length and use a type size of 12 points. (While you can't control these variables in e-mail, you can certainly keep the paragraphs short.) Even so, don't break paragraphs just anywhere. Break paragraphs at those points where you shift from one topic to another.

Headings, lists, tables.   Just because it is a business letter, memo, or e-mail doesn't mean you can't use headings, lists, tables, and other page-design tools such as those covered in Part II of this book. In fact, look at the memo report on the Almonte Heritage house renovation study at the end of Chapter 1. Except for short communications under a page or two, use headings to mark off main sections, use bulleted lists for key points, use numbered lists for sequential items, and use tables to enable comparison of information.

Action conclusion.   Because most business communications attempt to transact something, the final paragraph should make clear what you expect the recipient to do. Avoid limp-noodle endings such as "Hoping to hear from you soon" or "Let me know if you have any questions." In a job-application letter, end by telling the potential employer that you hope to hear from him in the next two weeks and will call if you have not. Gently and politely force the reader to do something: take control of the situation.

HOW DO YOU FORMAT A BUSINESS LETTER?

The following shows you formatting details such as margins, indentation, and type style for different types of business letters. For details on using business letters or memos for technical reports, see Chapter 14.

Types of business letters.   Traditionally, these are the common business-letter formats, which are illustrated in Figure 12-1.

- *Block letter.* The block format is nearly the only style used in business letters. It's certainly the easiest, requiring no indentation of any of its parts. The date, heading, inside address, salutation, body paragraphs, and signature block (containing the complimentary close, signature, typed name, initials, and enclosures all start on the standard left margin.
- *Modified block letter.* In this format, the date, complimentary close, signature, and typed name are indented as far to the right as possible. These elements are not right-aligned; they are just indented such that the longest element still fits on the same line.
- *Simplified letter.* The simplified format omits the salutation, and thus the problem of deciding whether to write "Dear Sir" or "To Whom It May Concern." Be careful about using this format. In letters in which personal relations are important, use the block or modified block style—for example, in a job application letter.

Format of business letters.   Whichever type of business letter you write, follow these guidelines:

- *Salutation.* Punctuate the salutation with a colon, not a comma. The comma is for personal letters. (It's easy to forget this detail; Microsoft Word's letter template insists on a comma.) In the salutation, use the name of the person to whom you are sending the communication. If you don't know the name, use the title of the position or the department name. Avoid "Dear Sir" (sexist), "Dear Sir/Madam" (clumsy), "Dear People" (stupid), and "To Whom It May Concern" (trite).
- *Complimentary close.* Phrases like "Sincerely" and "Regards" are common for the complimentary close. Punctuate the complimentary close with a comma and capitalize only the first word, as in "Best wishes."

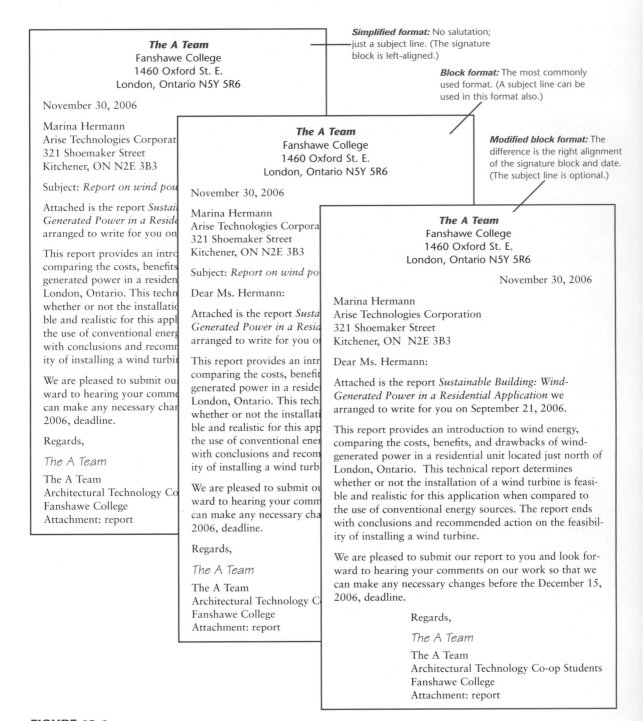

FIGURE 12-1
Business letter format. The simplified, the block, and the modified block letter formats.

- *Signature block.* Skip four lines between the complimentary close and your typed name. Single-space the lines for your typed name, the initials (yours and the typist's), and the enclosure.
- *Continuation pages.* If your letter goes over one page, use one of the formats shown in Figure 12-2 for the header on all following pages.
- *Margins.* Left, right, top, and bottom margins for business letters are variable. Notice that some software has a default left margin of 1.25 inches and default margins of 1.0 inch for the others. You can "fudge" these margins up to a half-inch to make the contents of a business letter fit the page better.
- *Alignment, justification.* Keep everything left-aligned in your business letters, unless you use the modified block format. Don't use full justification (where the right margin is also aligned). "Ragged" right margins actually help readers get through your letter faster.
- *Paragraph indentation.* The first line of paragraphs in business letters is typically not indented.
- *Line spacing.* Single-space *within* the paragraphs of business letters; skip a line *between* paragraphs of business letters. (Use the default line spacing of 13.95 for 12-point type as commonly offered by word-processing software.)
- *Type style.* Use a standard type style such as Times New Roman, Arial, Garamond, or Century Gothic. Unusual fonts may be fun for you, but they are not fun for your readers. Don't use all bold, all caps, all italic, or other such special effects for any extended segment of your letter. (See Chapter 12 on highlighting.)
- *Type size.* Standard 12-point type size works for most type styles, such as Times New Roman. You can vary type size to fit the contents of a letter to a page. However, don't go smaller than 9 points or larger than 14 points. Also, notice how much smaller or larger some type styles look in the same type size. For example, take a look at the difference between 12-point Times New Roman and 12-point Arial.

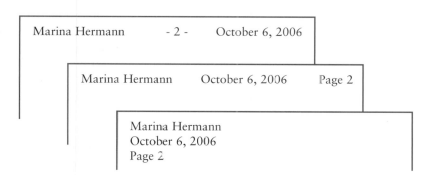

FIGURE 12-2

Continuation headers for letters and memos. Use any of these three formats at the top of secondary pages of your letters or memos.

> ***The A Team***
> Fanshawe College
> 1460 Oxford St. E.
> London, Ontario N5Y 5R6
>
> November 30, 2006
>
> Marina Hermann
> Arise Technologies Corporation
> 321 Shoemaker Street
> Kitchener, ON N2E 3B3
>
> Subject: Report on wind power in residential application
>
> Dear Ms. Hermann:
>
> Attached is the report *Sustainable Building: Wind-Generated Power in a Residential Application* we arranged to write for you on September 21, 2006.
>
> This report provides an introduction to wind energy, comparing the costs, benefits, and drawbacks of wind-generated power in a residential unit located just north of London, Ontario. This technical report determines whether or not the installation of a wind turbine is feasible and realistic for this application when

FIGURE 12-3

Letterhead business letters. You can create nice, attractive letterheads for your business letters, such as in this example. It uses Arial italics. In Word 2003, create the separator line by selecting **Format**→**Borders and Shading** and selecting the lower border icon:

- *Paper.* Use standard white 8.5 × 11 paper. Odd shapes or sizes of paper, colours, and other such departures are not a good idea in most business contexts. Metric-sized paper is also commonly used. In Word 2003, choose **Tools**→**Options**→**Print** and check **Allow A4 letter paper resizing.**
- *Letterhead.* Use letterhead stationery for the first page only. For following pages, use the same quality of paper as is used for the letterhead page. If you are writing as an individual, unassociated with an organization, consider making up your own letterhead. See the example in Figure 12-3. And while you're at it, create a template with your letterhead in it, as explained later in this chapter. That way, it's ready whenever you need it.

HOW DO YOU FORMAT A MEMO?

Memos are business communications that stay "in house"—within an organization. However, they are not necessarily less formal than business letters. Imagine a department manager sending a memo to tell everyone to stop surfing the World Wide Web for entertainment and get back to work.

Just about any purpose or content in a business letter has its equivalent in the memo: job applications, complaints, refunds, inquiries, bad news, and good news of practically any kind. Also, plenty of reports are also formatted as memos. For details, see Chapter 14.

- *Memo header.* Standard format for a memo includes DATE:, TO:, FROM:, and SUBJECT: at the top. These labels are typically bold. A nice touch is to set margins about a quarter-inch past the longest label (in this case, SUBJECT:) so that all the text items following these labels left-align. (See Figure 12-4 for an illustration.)
- *Margins.* Left, right, top, and bottom margins for memos are variable. Some software has a default left margin of 1.25 inches and default margins of 1.0 inch for the others. You can "fudge" these margins up to a half-inch to make the contents of a memo fit the page better. To change the measurements to metric, Choose **Tools**→**Options**→**General**, and in the Measurement units checkbox, click **Centimetres**.
- *Alignment, justification.* Keep everything left-aligned in your memos. Don't use full justification (where the right margin is aligned also). "Ragged" right margins actually help readers get through your memo faster.
- *Paragraph indentation.* The first line of paragraphs in memos is typically not indented.

Howitt Home Improvements
Specializing in the One-Tonne Challenge
357 Elmira Road North
Guelph. Ontario N1K 1S5

Memo

TO:	John Howitt, Manager Howitt Energy Consultants
FROM:	Michael Carrier, HVAC Specialist
CC:	Almonte Heritage Foundation
DATE:	May 6, 2006
SUBJECT:	Report on my preliminary investigation of meeting the one-tonne challenge in a heritage house

I have just returned from my inspection trip to the heritage house project in Almonte, Ontario. On March 25, 2006, our team met with the Almonte Heritage Foundation that is renovating the building. I interviewed the main historical and architectural team.

FIGURE 12-4

Header alignment in memos. Set tabs so that text left-aligns after DATE:, TO:, and the other memo header elements.

- *Line spacing.* Single-space *within* the paragraphs of memos; skip a line *between* paragraphs of memos. (Use the default line spacing of 13.95 for 12-point type as commonly offered by word-processing software.)
- *Type style.* Use a standard type style such as Times New Roman, Arial, Garamond, or Century Gothic. Unusual fonts may be fun for you, but they are not fun for your readers. Don't use all bold, all caps, all italic or other such special effects for any extended segment of your memo. (See Chapter 7 on highlighting.)
- *Type size.* Standard 12-point type size works for most type styles, such as Times New Roman. You can vary type size to fit the contents of a memo to a page. However, don't go smaller than 9 points or larger than 14 points. Also, notice how much smaller or larger some type styles look in the same type size. For example, take a look at the difference between 12-point Times New Roman and 12-point Arial.
- *Paper.* Use standard white 8.5 × 11 paper. Odd shapes or sizes of paper, colours, and other such departures are not a good idea in most business contexts.
- *Continuation pages.* If your memo goes over one page, use any of the same formats for business letters shown in Figure 12-2.

HOW DO YOU CREATE A LETTER OR MEMO TEMPLATE?

Templates are handy tools to make your professional writing more efficient and consistent. You can use the templates supplied by your software, or you can create your own. And you can create templates for any type of document you use often, not just letters and memos. Here's how to create and use a template in Microsoft Word 2003:

1. To start a template file, click **File→New** in the menu bar. In the pane on the right-hand side of your screen, select **On my computer** under the **Templates** heading (see Figure 12-5).

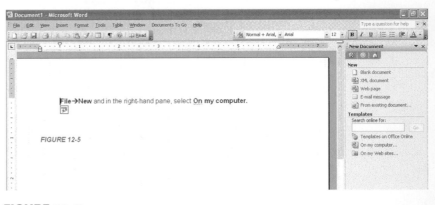

FIGURE 12-5
Create your own templates in Word 2003.

In the dialogue box that appears, check the **Template** radio button and double-click **Blank Document** (see Figure 12-6).

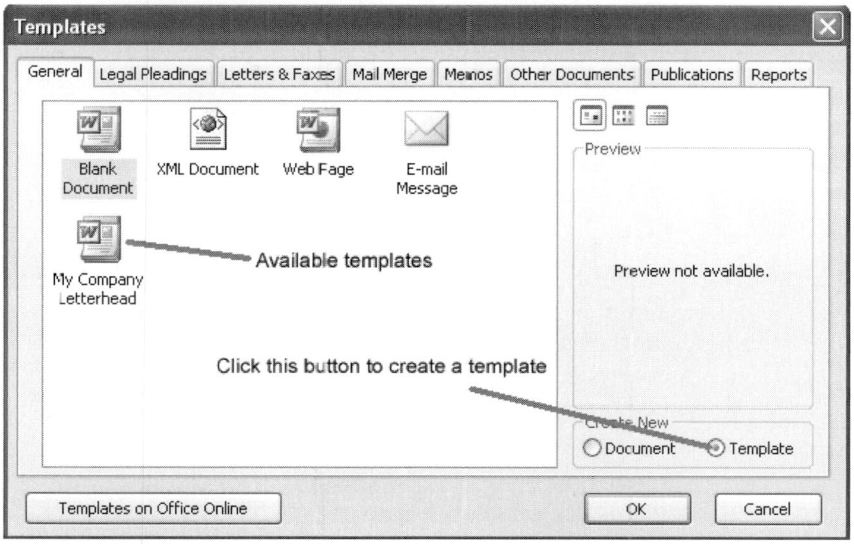

FIGURE 12-6

Templates in Word 2003. From this same dialogue box you can create a new template or select an existing template.

2. Change all margins to 1.5 inches by pressing **File→Page Setup**. Under the Margins tab, change Top, Bottom, Right, and Left to **1.5**.
3. To create a logo in the header portion of this template, click **View→Header and Footer**. In the header box, type your name and address in italic 10-point Arial and centre it.
4. To save this template, click **File→Save** and give your template some distinctive name. Notice that MS Word gives your template the **.dot** extension and stores it in a templates directory.
5. To use the template you just created, click **File→New** again. Once more, in the right-hand pane, click **On my computer**. Check the Document radio button and then double-click your template file (for example, mine is My Company Letterhead in Figure 12-6). If you have already started a document, you can import your template: click **Tools→Templates and Add-Ins**, then click the **Attach** button, and select your template (see Figure 12-7 for where my template My Computer Letterhead.dot is).

FIGURE 12-7

Importing a template in MS Word. To use a template you've created, you must "import" it into the document on which you are working.

WHAT ABOUT E-MAIL?

In scarcely more than five years, e-mail has become an essential business-communication tool. It's faster and easier than print communications and has more permanence than a telephone call. Still, e-mail has distinct limitations—not to mention some distinct risks. Because of its convenience, e-mail often replaces telephone conversations, notes, memos, and even in some cases, letters. As a result, it is especially important to understand the nature of the communication that you are sending with e-mail, before clicking the **Send** button.

E-mail lacks the reputation for permanence that printed letters and memos have. It's easy to delete or misplace e-mail. E-mail also lacks the formality of printed letters and memos. Would you send a job application to a potential employer by e-mail? Would you announce your resignation by e-mail? If you would hesitate, you understand the limitations of e-mail. Here are some guidelines for e-mail:

- Decide whether e-mail is the best method for the communication. Maybe your message would be more appropriate as a letter or memo?
- Compose an adequately descriptive subject line. E-mail in-boxes give you only about 8 to 10 words. To ensure that the recipient doesn't ignore your e-mail, make those words indicate your subject or purpose.

- Keep a copy of all e-mail you send; make sure your e-mail software does so. (For example, Outlook Express keeps all sent e-mail in the "Sent Items" box.) Use folders to keep your e-mail organized by subject matter or recipient.
- If you are responding to e-mail, be sure to indicate the context at the very beginning. If you handle lots of e-mail, you may forget what you are discussing with whom. If someone writes you, "I don't agree with you on that," without explaining the context, you're lost! If you are replying to someone else's e-mail, attach the original at the bottom. (Most e-mail software prompts for this.)
- Keep the paragraphs of e-mail messages short—even shorter than in business letters and memos. Avoid going over 5 lines.
- If your message is long and detailed, make it a separate document in your word-processing software and attach it to the e-mail. That way, the recipient can download and print it for easier reading.
- Be careful about sending e-mail abruptly. Ensure that it's addressed to the correct recipient and reread your message. Typos are rather common in e-mail—clean them up. Look for missing words such as *no* or *not!* If you are angry, don't send the e-mail right away. Reread it an hour or two later.
- Make sure you know who will be receiving your e-mail. Double-check that e-mail address to make sure other recipients will not mistakenly receive your e-mail.

HOW DO YOU WRITE PROBLEM COMMUNICATIONS?

In business and professional life, you face all kinds of problems, many of which require written documents. The three kinds discussed here are the following:

- *Complaint communications:* For complaints about a bad product or service and requests for appropriate compensation.
- *Adjustment communications:* For responses to complaint communications, granting or denying the requested compensation.
- *Inquiry communications:* For requests for information and other sorts of help.

These are "communications": they can be sent not only as conventional printed business letters or memos, but also as e-mail.

Complaint Communications

If you experience a problem with a product or service, sometimes you can't resolve it over the phone. Instead, you must put your complaint in writing, along with your request for compensation. The complaint communication describes the problem, requests compensation, and justifies the request. It's an interesting exercise in persuasion. See Chapter 6 for a review of persuasive strategies.

1. **Find a problem with a product or service you've experienced.** That's probably not so hard for most of us. Ideally, find a problem that has a technical aspect to it. Give your technical-writing skills a workout.

   Imagine that your class has recently selected you to be photographer for a class trip to the National Gallery as part of your History of Canadian Art class. In preparation, you purchased a new digital camera from Business Station so that your class would be able to record the highlights of the gallery for its semester-long research project. Although you tested the camera before leaving, once at the gallery, you had several difficulties. The camera would not cycle through the resolution settings, and displayed the warning message, "Memory card problems." Periodically, the digital display was "pixilated" and impossible to read. You found that you were unable to delete pictures from the camera, and although the lithium battery displayed a full charge, the battery went dead after only a few minutes. (Your photography career is coming to a quick end.)

2. **Describe and/or narrate the problem.** Write a detailed narration and description of the problem you experienced. Supply specifics such as times, dates, individual or company names, addresses, and brand and model names. If you find yourself gleefully blowing off steam, get over it. Then rewrite the account of the problem neutrally. This information supports your logical appeal (but it brings in the emotional appeal through the back door).

   In one or more paragraphs, narrate and describe the camera problems. Cite the exact name and model number of the camera, the date of purchase, and the name and address of the store where you bought it. Provide exact dates on which you tested the camera, how you initially charged the battery, the operating system of your computer, and any other information you think important, such as the RAM on your machine. Explain in as much detail as you are able to how the situation changed once you were on the field trip, and give as much detail as possible of the symptoms of the camera's operation. Make this discussion as objective as you can. You'll get to blow off steam in the next paragraph.

3. **Describe the compensation you are requesting and the reasons why that request is justified.** Keep your complaint neatly compartmentalized. In one (or more) paragraphs, tell the story and describe the problem. Save the request for compensation and its justification for the next paragraph.

   Now comes the fun part—but the challenging part as well. What do you want to request as compensation? Your class probably worked hard for the money

Practical Ethics: Murky Waters

Some ethical dilemmas don't really feel like dilemmas. Should you blow the whistle on a company that is knowingly polluting a river? The answer seems to be a resounding "Yes!" Yet, as with many ethical dilemmas, the deeper you dig, the murkier the water and the harder it is to figure out what to do.

Imagine you are the public relations representative for a paper mill that is polluting a river. What should you do? Mike Markel says in his book *Technical Communication* that you have three obligations: to your employer, to the public, and to the environment.[1] A fourth obligation is to yourself.

Like most people in America, you are environmentally conscious. It is disturbing that a river is being polluted. Pollution affects fish, birds, and any other animals that use the river as a source of food or water. You suspect the pollution is making its way into the soil where it will affect plants and may damage entire ecosystems. If this is true, your obligation to the environment says the pollution must stop, whatever the cost.

On the other hand, your obligation to your employer tells you that news of the pollution could have an adverse effect on the company image and sales. Large fees could be imposed and cleanup would be costly. The possibility exists that the company would be forced to go under.

Your obligation to the public says that you need to inform them of safety risks. In this case, they would need to know if their health is being compromised. However, the paper mill is the largest employer in the county and if it went out of business, thousands of people would be out of work without much possibility of finding employment. Large-scale unemployment would have a detrimental effect on the economy. Which is worse? Living with pollution or being unemployed? It's a difficult question (and who are you to decide this for thousands of other people?).

You also have obligations to yourself. Even though it is your job to keep the public informed, letting this information out could bring you under fire from your supervisors. People have been fired for less. Is losing your job a price you're willing to pay? Your conscience says yes, but the financial and emotional strain it would put your family under says no.

In the process of considering all these angles, you have come up with competing answers to a dilemma that once didn't seem so complicated. In your mind, which obligations hold the most weight? Why? What would you do in this situation?

What if you talked to your supervisors and were told that they knew of the pollution and "had it under control." A little investigating on your part revealed that Environment Canada also knew of the problem and assessed your company a yearly fine of a few hundred dollars, but hadn't demanded the pollution stop or be cleaned up. What would you do then?

[1] Markel, Mike. *Technical Communication: Situations and Strategies,* 4th edition. St. Martin's Press: New York, 1996, 24–28.

to purchase the camera for the trip. Also, the work of an entire semester is made more difficult by not having photographs of the pictures that you were counting on for your project. You no doubt want a working camera, but in addition, perhaps the company could supply you with an extra battery pack or another memory card. More importantly, you'd like the manufacturer to know about the problem to prevent others from experiencing it. Thus, you may be asking for both monetary or product compensation and reassurance, not to mention some abject apologies.

4. **Write a firm but civil conclusion.** You'll get nowhere by threatening or name-calling in a complaint. In the conclusion, say that you are confident that the recipient will grant your request and that you can continue doing business together. Obviously, that's a veiled threat, but it's civil and controlled. Keeping the lid on throughout this complaint creates a personal appeal: it establishes you as a calm, levelheaded, fair-minded person.

> In the final paragraph, you can express confidence that the manufacturer of the camera will grant your requested compensation and investigate the problem. You might also express the hope that your class can continue to use the product and not have to warn other classes and students of the difficulties you experienced with the camera.

5. **Write the introduction.** To counteract the tendency to start blasting away from the very start, it's wise to write the introduction last. Indicate the purpose of this communication and provide an overview of what it contains. As with any persuasive effort, you don't necessarily state your main argumentative point in the introduction: some readers might just stop reading. Instead, you can say that you are writing about a problem you've had with the recipient's product or service. And don't forget to keep paragraphs of business communications short, especially the introduction!

> Start this way: say that you are writing about a serious problem you had with the camera—that indicates the topic and purpose of the letter. For the overview, you can state that you want to explain what happened and request that something be done about the problem. Having said this in 4 or 5 lines, you have avoided diving headlong into the gory details. Obviously, anybody can read between the lines, but you stand a better chance of having the entire letter read.

6. **Review and revise your rough draft.** Use the strategies in Chapter 16 to systematically review and revise your communication. Use the top-down approach described there: start by reviewing for audience, purpose, and situation; then move on to content, organization, and transitions; then headings, lists, tables, and graphics; then on to sentence style and technical style; and finally, grammar, usage, spelling, and punctuation problems.

Adjustment Communications

An adjustment letter, memo, or e-mail is a reply to a complaint. Its job is either to grant or to deny the requested compensation, explain why, find some way to placate the customer and thus keep that customer's business, and defend the company's concern for quality and for its customers. Whether denying or granting a request, the adjustment communication is a challenging exercise in persuasion.

1. **Find a situation involving a problem with a product or service.** The ideal situation is a problem occurring in your own workplace. If you can't find such, think of a problem you experienced, and put yourself in the position of the poor customer-relations employee who must answer your complaint.

   Imagine that you work for the admissions and records department of your college. Today, you were given a student complaint letter to answer. A student has received an F for a course in which she actually made an A. She has made several prior requests for the grade change, but somehow her requests have been lost in your office. While this grade remained unchanged and her grade point unrealistically low, she missed an opportunity to get a scholarship. She is requesting not merely the grade change, but monetary compensation equalling the amount of the scholarship she lost.

2. **Decide whether you can grant the requested compensation or some portion of it.** If you write a reply to your very own complaint letter, don't get greedy. Perhaps you can write *two* adjustment communications—one granting the request and one denying it. Also consider the idea of some partial compensation or some goodwill gesture—for example, a discount on future purchases.

   Certainly the grade can be changed, but the college cannot reimburse the full scholarship amount. Even though the student's request s unrealistic, there is the concern that she might bring a lawsuit against the college. What to do? Knowing that you cannot grant her monetary request, what can you do to placate this individual?

3. **Define the reasons for your decision.** If the request is totally outrageous, you may have to invent diplomatic reasons for the denial. The problem may have occurred because of the customer's clumsiness. Or the customer may be acting unscrupulously. You still must find diplomatic ways to state your reasons for denial. Doing so establishes your personal appeal as a calm, levelheaded, fair-minded, and caring person.

   What are your reasons for denying the student's request? First, it isn't certain that the student would have won the scholarship anyway. Second, the student cannot expect such a large compensation for an honest mistake. Can you think of others?

4. **If you deny the request, find a way to placate the customer.** What can you do to soften the blow of the denial? Some companies offer coupons, discounts, and other things. Perhaps you can offer partial compensation. In some cases, the best option may be to express your regrets and your hopes that business relations can continue and just be done with it.

There are various possibilities: you could offer the student a discount on her next registration or reimburse her expenses for the course in question. If these seem like blatant attempts to buy her off, then let's just say we are truly sorry and sign off.

5. **If you grant the request (or even deny it), find a way to defend your organization.** In an adjustment letter, your job is to defend the reputation of your organization. If your organization made a mistake, acknowledge it but insist that it doesn't reflect on your organization's concern for quality.

   Privately, you are all too aware that your department is understaffed. You stay too busy to overhaul your process. Everybody certainly tries hard and cares about students. In defence of your department, you might want to mention these things—but no whining!

6. **Write the introduction.** Now, at long last, you are ready to write an introduction. Start by indicating that your letter is in response to the complaint—that's the topic and purpose. Explain that your letter reviews the problem and addresses the writer's concerns—that's the overview. But don't blurt out the denial. Doing so might upset readers and prevent them from reading the rest of what you have to say.

   Begin by expressing your thanks that the student took the time to write. Express concern over the problem, and indicate that you'll address that problem as well as her request. This indicates topic and purpose, provides an overview of what the rest of the letter contains, but does not blurt out your outright refusal of her request.

7. **Review and revise your rough draft.** Use the strategies in Chapter 16 to systematically review and revise this letter. Use the top-down approach described there: start by reviewing for audience, purpose, and situation; then move on to content, organization, and transitions; then headings, lists, tables, and graphics; then on to sentence style and technical style; and finally, grammar, usage, spelling, and punctuation problems.

Inquiry Communications

In an inquiry communication, you ask someone for information. If you address an organization that advertises its products or services, it's a "solicited" inquiry. If you address the inquiry to a researcher who is quietly working away in her field and has done nothing to invite your inquiry, it's "unsolicited." In unsolicited inquiries, you must use some quiet persuasion to convince the recipient to help you. Here are some steps for writing this kind of communication.

For an inquiry communication, imagine you are working on the project discussed in Chapter 6. Your job is to contact cities and ask specific questions about their recycling programs. For this communication, e-mail might be the best approach.

1. **Make a list of exactly what information you want.** If it's a series of questions, make those questions precise. Throw out general questions that would require writing a textbook to answer. Whenever possible, seek local experience. For example, if you inquire about a new insulin system for diabetics, ask about the experience of patients at the recipient's clinic.

   Imagine that you want statistics on participation in recycling programs. If there have been increases, you want to know why they happened. You also want to know about the volumes of recycled materials handled, variations in prices, and problems experienced with suppliers and vendors. Avoid asking general questions such as "What problems have you experienced" or "How's it going?"

2. **Ensure that the information you are requesting is not easily available elsewhere.** What could be more aggravating than to be asked for information easily found in general textbooks and encyclopedias?

   You've checked to see if any municipal reports are available for the city's recycling project—none are. The information is safely tucked away in electronic databases in various computers in municipal offices. This is legitimate information to request.

3. **Explain why you need the information and how you've tried to get it elsewhere.** In an unsolicited inquiry, your inquiree will be more cooperative if you explain why you need the information. People are receptive to students working on technical reports. To reassure them that you're not lazy, explain the efforts you made to get this information by other means.

   You are working on this project for your city. Thus, you can hope for some comradeship with the recipient of your inquiry. Mention that you've made several phone calls and e-mail inquiries trying to find out if any reports exist.

4. **Find ways to make replying easier.** In the actual request, try to ease the recipient's job of replying. For example, number the questions; create a form to fill out; include self-addressed stamped envelopes; offer to visit to copy materials; or ask for information sources, websites, or contacts.

   You're asking mostly for numbers. Therefore, you might be able to set up a fill-in-the-blank questionnaire. Or the recipient of this inquiry might be able to send you electronic files containing the data you need.

5. **Write a closing paragraph indicating how the recipient of this inquiry might benefit.** Try to find some way to return the favour—some gesture of gratitude and goodwill. Offer to send your completed project, with the recipient's contributions gratefully acknowledged.

   > In this inquiry, express sincere appreciation for the recipient's efforts in helping you. As a gesture of gratitude, perhaps you can promise to send a copy of the report or pass along cost-saving techniques if you stumble across any. Otherwise, you can appeal to the recipient's general sense of comradeship regarding recycling programs.

6. **Review and revise your rough draft.** Use the strategies in Chapter 16 to systematically review and revise your letter. Use the top-down approach described there: start by reviewing for audience, purpose, and situation; then move on to content, organization, and transitions; then headings, lists, tables, and graphics; then on to sentence style and technical style; and finally, grammar, usage, spelling, and punctuation problems.

WORKSHOP: BUSINESS LETTERS, MEMOS, E-MAIL

Here are some additional ideas for practising the concepts, tools, and strategies in this chapter:

1. *Choose a type of communication.* Consider the following situations. Which forms of communication discussed in this chapter (in-person conversation, phone, e-mail, memo, letter, or other) would be the best to use, the worst to use, and why?
   a. You want to request from your instructor an extension of the due date on your report project.
   b. You want to complain about the rudeness and lack of responsiveness of the human resources department in handling your questions concerning your health benefits.
   c. You want to ask your manager for a raise.
   d. You want to see if a certain business might be interested in your services (courier, computer maintenance, janitorial service, etc.)
   e. You want to request that your fellow employees format their monthly status reports a certain way before they give them to you (you integrate them into one comprehensive department report).
   f. You want to make sure your client understands that the technical staff of that client has not provided you with any reviews or other input on the project you are doing for that client.
   g. You want to wish your manager a happy birthday.

2. *Get the tone right.* Consider the following situations. Describe the tone that you would try for in each and explain why.
   a. You signed up for a cruise and put down a deposit. Now you read on an Internet travel discussion list that the company is no longer using the ship you signed up to travel on—it is using a smaller, older ship. Customers are returning from their cruises complaining about safety, service, and quality of food on the cruise. There's a rumour the company is going into bankruptcy. You write a letter cancelling your trip and requesting a refund of your deposit.
   b. Your child's high school always has a prayer at its commencement. You don't mind the prayer, but because a large minority of the students belong to other religions, you write the administrators requesting that any prayer be nonsectarian.
   c. You've been the principal of a small private school for 12 years and every year you have to nag the parents to follow the designated traffic pattern when they pick up or drop off their children. Some of the parents ignore the rules, and yesterday one of the teachers was almost run over. If parents don't cooperate, you feel that you must hire officers to direct traffic every day, and this cost will have to be passed on in the cost of tuition. Write a letter to all the parents.

3. *Survey international communication styles.* Select any of the example letters, memos, or e-mail messages in this book and do a survey on how people from other cultures would respond to them. Find out not only whether the language is understandable but also whether the style strikes your international readers as blunt, rude, impersonal, or impolite.

4. *Create personalized templates for your letters and memos.* Use the steps discussed in this chapter to design your own templates for business letters and memos. For the letter template, put your name, address, phone number, and e-mail address in the header. Try putting a solid ruled line at the bottom of the header area, and another such line at the top of the footer area. Also, try changing the margins. Do the same with the memo, but be sure to include the DATE:, TO:, FROM:, and SUBJECT: lines. See if you can automate the date in both the letter and memo templates. And, if you're really adventurous, try including a graphic logo in the header of either or both templates.

COMPLAINT LETTER

Letter format: This complaint letter uses the block format, in which all letter components start at the left margin.

Heading and inside address: When you use the traditional business-letter format, put your address and the date at the top, followed by the full name and address of the recipient of the letter.

Salutation: Notice this writer's solution to the problem of what to put after "Dear." This works for a complaint letter but not other types of communication, such as the application letter.

Introduction: Notice how short this first paragraph is, how it announces the purpose of the letter, and how it does not get into the details of the problem.

Problem description: Notice that the writer calmly and objectively describes the details of the purchase and then the details of the problem, providing dollar amounts, dates, and other such specifics.

Justification: In this fourth paragraph, the writer explains why he believes he should be reimbursed. Notice the diplomatic assumption that this was a "temporary" problem that can "easily" be fixed.

Compensation request: Notice that this writer chooses to state his request for compensation in the very first paragraph rather than toward the end of the letter. Not one to beat around the bush, he probably assumes that his situation is so obvious no rhetorical finesse is needed.

1313 Horse Trail Rd.
Buda, Texas 78610

6 June 2006

Customer Relations/Claims Department
John Duke Manufacturing Company
1104 Sutton Drive, Suite #112
Cairo, MI 45006

Dear Representative:

I am writing in regards to a digital multimeter (DMM) that I recently purchased by mail-order from your company. Because the DMM only functions partially, I am requesting repairs, another DMM with comparable features, or a refund of the purchase price plus C.O.D. charges, and shipping and handling.

I purchased the meter for $250.00 by calling the 1-800 number listed in an advertisement. My phone order occurred on August 20. The meter was delivered on August 23 via UPX C.O.D. The total purchase price was $282.50. The following items were included with the DMM: one set of meter leads, one power supply cord, and one black nylon-fiber carrying case.

The DMM (Duke Model 8012A) will not register an accurate voltage or current reading. The other features function as intended, and the fuse that protects the AC circuitry is in good operating condition. However, when a regulated AC voltage or current is applied to the meter leads, the only reading displayed is a low negative value. This is true whether the function switch is set to measure either AC voltage or current.

When I received the DMM, I inspected the packaging in which the meter was shipped, and there was no evidence of damage. Styrofoam inserts were used to protect the meter from any shock during the shipping process. Because I saw no loose components when inspecting the primary fuse, I am led to believe the problem somehow occurred during manufacture. No doubt, there is a temporary malfunction that can easily be fixed.

Your prompt attention and response would be greatly appreciated as I intend to use the meter in conjunction with my job.

Sincerely,

Terry Ward

Terry Ward

Enclosures: This writer is sending everything back, including a copy of the receipt. This will act as evidence supporting his request.

Enclosed: 1 Duke 8012A DMM, Lot #3308-WIC4,
1 set of meter leads, 1 power supply cord,
1 black nylon-fiber carrying case,
copy of purchase receipt

Many thanks to Robert Hutchison, Austin Community College technical writing student, for this complaint letter and permission to adapt it here.

Letter format: This adjustment letter uses the standard block format, in which all letter components start at the left margin.

ADJUSTMENT LETTER

Canamera Electronics
1203 Conestoga Road
Waterloo, ON N5M 1T6
519-487-7560

Heading and inside address: This letter, coming from a company, uses a simple header as the inside address. The recipient's full name and address are left aligned. Notice that the postal code is on the same line as the city and province.

December 13, 2006

Ms. Ericka Desjardins
890 London Road
Sarnia, Ontario M7Y 3H5

Salutation: Since the letter responds to one from the recipient, the recipient's name is used in the salutation.

Dear Ms. Desjardins:

Introduction: This short, direct introduction places the letter in context, expresses appreciation, and foreshadows the contents.

Thank you for your letter of November 14, 2006, outlining the difficulties you have experienced with your model 466XL digital camera. We have reviewed your claim and reached the conclusion outlined below.

Body detail: In the detail section, the writer reviews the circumstances of the original complaint, explains the process, and provides the solution to the problem with the camera.

Using the information that you provided, our technicians resolved the problem. We understand that you experienced difficulties with the digital display, memory, resolution, and the battery. Our technologists analyzed the information you sent and concluded that the likely cause of the malfunctions was a battery fault. Because you gave us such detailed information, we were able to ask the supplier of the lithium battery about a specific batch of the product. They surveyed their other customers, and found that there were apparently quality control problems with that specific run. Consequently, they are supplying the distributors of the cameras with replacement units. These batteries will be installed by the retailers. If you take your 466XL to the original retailer, their employees will be happy to replace the battery on your camera.

Compensation: The writer politely denies, with justification, the requested compensation, but provides an alternative.

In your letter, you suggested that we might help compensate for your disappointment by sending you an extra memory card. Unfortunately the memory cards are supplied by another company, so we cannot give you a card. However, we are sending you a handsome carrying case for your 466XL that will help protect the camera from any unfortunate bumps and scrapes for years to come.

Closing: The letter urges continued customer loyalty and is signed personally by the service representative.

Our company strives to provide the best products and services to our customers, and we always welcome any feedback from customers about our products. Thank you again, and we trust that you will experience many happy years of picture-taking with your 466XL.

Sincerely,

Felicia Jones

Felicia Jones
Customer Service Representative
Canamera Electronics

Enclosure: The alternative compensation is included with the letter.

Enclosed: one black nylon carrying case for a model 466XL Canamera camera

INQUIRY LETTER

Letter format: This letter uses the standard block format in which all components are on the left margin. Other letter formats are shown earlier in this chapter.

Dugan Land Surveyors
118 Centrepointe Drive
Nepean, Ontario M6G 8Y8
705-555-0000

Heading and inside address: In the traditional business-letter format, the writer's address and the date go at the top, followed by the full name and address of the recipient of the letter.

November 14, 2006

Research in Motion
295 Phillip Street
Waterloo, Ontario
Canada N2L 3W8

Salutation: Notice this writer's solution to the problem of what to put after "Dear." Addressing the letter to a department—any responsible individual within it—works fine.

Dear Sales Representative:

Introduction: Notice how the writer takes an ingratiating tone, paying the recipient a compliment just after the initial statement of the purpose of the letter.

I am writing to ask you some technical and sales questions about the features and pricing of your Blackberry™ communicators. I have been reading reviews and asking questions of many pleased users of your units. I am quite impressed both with the reviews in the technical journals and the firsthand testimonials of your customers. Our company is seriously considering equipping our survey crews with Blackberry devices, but before deciding, we must be sure that the units will provide our crews with the best possible communication system.

Inquiry: Notice that this writer asks specific questions and explains that he has already sought but not found answers in the company's literature. Also notice how the questions are numbered for ease of reference and readability.

I have three questions for which I have been unable to find answers in your product literature or on your website (blackberry.com). I really need to have the answers to the three following questions before making a final decision:

1. Does your company provide a coverage map of the areas serviced by the devices? Since our crews operate in remote regions, it is important for them to know whether the device will establish communication or not.

2. Do you plan in the near future to make the Blackberry GPS enabled? Again, this feature would have great benefit for us.

3. Does your company have a corporate pricing policy covering bulk purchases?

Rationale and benefit: This writer explains why he needs this information. This writer also suggests why it is in the interests of the recipient to help him—he's a potential customer!

I know that the Blackberry communicators enjoy a well-deserved reputation worldwide. Before providing the devices to our employees, however, I must be certain that the units will provide the coverage that we need, that the current versions contain the features that we require, and, of course, that our company is getting the best possible value in this fine product.

For your convenience, you can respond to me by e-mail at Dugan@DuganLS.ca. If you prefer to respond by telephone, you can contact me at (519) 555-0000. I appreciate any assistance that you can provide me.

Sincerely,

Kimberley Dugan

Kimberley Dugan
Dugan Land Surveyors

CHAPTER 13

Employment-Search Tools: Application Letters and Résumés

Topics covered in this chapter include

- gearing up for a job search;
- employability skills.

GEARING UP FOR A JOB SEARCH
You will need to think about your job possibilities well before you finish college. To find out if you are developing the necessary skills to work full time, look at these sites:

Conference Board of Canada: Employability Skills
http://www.conferenceboard.ca/education/learning-tools/ employability-skills.htm

HRSDC: Essential Skills
http://www.hrsdc.gc.ca/en/hip/hrp/essential_skills/essential_skills_ index.shtml

EMPLOYABILITY SKILLS
Services Canada (Test your employability skills!)
http://www.jobsetc.ca/toolbox/checklists/employability.jsp?lang=e

Human Resources and Skills Development Canada
http://www.hrsdc.gc.ca

Monster (for students)
http://launch.monster.ca

Hot Jobs
http://ca.hotjobs.yahoo.com

Apprentice Search
http://www.apprenticesearch.com

Workopolis Campus
http://campus.workopolis.com

Charity Village Career Centre
http://charityvillage.com/applicant/jobs.asp

When you have completed this chapter, you will be able to

- plan a job search;
- write a focused, well-organized résumé with covering letter;
- prepare for a variety of interview styles.

This chapter focuses on two important job-getting tools—application letters and résumés. Although other aspects of the job hunt, such as finding jobs, researching companies, developing a portfolio, interviewing, and negotiating are not covered in detail here, you will find links to websites and references to printed resources that will help.

Résumés and especially application letters are essentially efforts to persuade people to interview you for a job or to hire you. Thus, persuasion is the key infrastructure of these two employment-search tools. If you understand the concepts and strategies associated with persuasion as they are discussed in Chapter 6, you've got a fighting chance to write more effective application letters and résumés.

This chapter focuses briefly on things you can do to gear up for a job search, then discusses planning and designing résumés and application letters. The résumé section provides suggestions on designing scannable and online résumés.

Note: For additional examples of application letters and résumés, as well as the documents discussed in this chapter, see **www.powertools.nelson.com.**

HOW DO YOU GET STARTED ON A JOB SEARCH?

Here are some things you can do to begin a job search:

- **Find jobs you are interested in.** In addition to bulletin boards at school or work and the classified sections of newspapers, look at job announcements in professional journals. Watch for "job fairs" and "career days" held locally. Check the local chapters of professional organizations in your field: they often maintain "job banks." Don't forget the World Wide Web, where you can search nationally and internationally. Job-search websites are easy to find; consider these for starters:

Human Resources and Skills
  Development Canada   **http://www.hrsdc.gc.ca**
Monster (for students)   **http://launch.monster.ca**

Hot Jobs	**http://ca.hotjobs.yahoo.com**
Apprentice Search	**http://www.apprenticesearch.com**
Workopolis Campus	**http://campus.workopolis.com**
Charity Village Career Centre	**http://charityvillage.com/applicant/jobs.asp**

- **Research the company, organization, or industry.** When you've found a job or two, research the industry those companies operate within and the companies themselves. Here are just a few of the resources on the Web:

  Canada Business: **http://canadabusiness.gc.ca/gol/cbec/site.nsf/en/index.html**

  Globe Investor: **http://www.globeinvestor.com/news/newsearch.html**

  Labour Market Information: **http://lmi-imt.hrdc-drhc.gc.ca**

  Strategis Company Directories: **http://strategis.ic.gc.ca/engdoc/main.html**

  Job Futures: **http://jobfutures.ca/en/home.shtml**

- **Conduct information interviews.** In an information interview, you gather information about the company, its products or services, and possible employment opportunities. Don't ask for information that is readily available in a library or on the Internet. Information interviews give you contacts, get your name "out there," and enable you to know what's going on in your field. However, don't expect to walk in unannounced for an information interview. Make a formal appointment, and prepare your questions ahead of time.
- **Start a job-search database, log, and timeline.** In the thick of a job hunt, it's easy to get confused and forget. Start a database in which you list every contact you've had with a potential employer, including dates, names (especially the names of administrative assistants), addresses, phone numbers, and so on. Also, start a combination log, timeline, and to-do list. After sending an application letter, make a note of that on a timeline. Make another note about two weeks to the right on that timeline as a reminder to send a follow-up letter if you've not heard from the potential employer.
- **Check with placement agencies.** Since the 1990s, employers have increasingly relied on placement agencies for temporary workers. Employers sometimes use a "try-and-buy" approach: if they like a particular contract worker, they hire that individual full time. Find one or two placement agencies that handle your kind of work, schedule an information interview, and bring along your résumé. Have a placement specialist assess your qualifications and tell you what you'll need to do to become more employable.
- **Visit with local professional organizations.** One of the best ways to get started is to join or attend the meetings of a professional society related to your career. One of their important functions is to enable people to

network. Often these groups have job banks (listings of open jobs) and résumé-posting services. Go to these meetings, get to know a few people, and get some advice.

■ **Rehearse for interviews.** It's not a bad idea to practise answering some of the common interview questions such as the following:

Can you tell us about your previous work experience in relation to this job?

How has your education gotten you ready for this job?

Do you like working on your own or as part of a team?

What do you know about our corporation? Why do you want to work here?

Explain how your background has prepared you for this position.

Tell us about a difficult situation you faced and how you dealt with it.

Do you have any questions for us about this job or our corporation?

Quite a few of the employment websites have tips on interviewing, proper attire for interviews, and much more. As of the year 2005, for example, you could visit the following websites:

WetFeet.com: **http://www.wetfeet.com/asp/home.asp**

JobSmart: Advice on résumés, sample cover letters, electronic résumés: **http://www.jobsmart.org/tools/resume**

Monster Interview Centre: **http://interview.monster.ca**

Help for the job hunt, including tips and samples for letters and résumés: **http://www.rileyguide.com**

Yahoo Canada hotjobs: **http://ca.hotjobs.yahoo.com/interview**

As many businesses now use the behavioural interview, make sure you read up on this type of interview on the Monster resource site above. Prepare stories that show how you have dealt with particular situations.

HOW DO YOU WRITE A RÉSUMÉ?

A résumé is a summary of your work experience, education, training, and anything else that supports your efforts to get employment.

Plan a Résumé

To get a sense of the planning process for a résumé, follow these planning steps for the job announcement shown in Figure 13-1:

Company: DigiCam1
Job Title: Web Developer
Status: Full-Time Employee
Relevant Work Experience: 2 to 5 years
Education Level: College Diploma
Location: CA-ON-Toronto/GTA
Job Category: Computers, Software
Career Level: Experiences (Non-Manager)
Salary: $35,000+

In business since 1999, DigiCam1 is Canada's newest online retailer of digital cameras. We offer a range of products, which include digital cameras and lenses, 35mm, video cameras, scanners, lighting, filters, and exclusive lines of professional studio gear. Our client base is mostly high-end consumers and professional photographers. Our storefront on Queen Street East is one of the busiest photography stores in Toronto.

Our Web department produces an attractive, easy-to-navigate, e-commerce site (www.digicam1.ca) and there are big plans for the coming year. Digicam1 currently has an opening for a Web Developer with a minimum of two years' experience, who enjoys a fast-paced, multitasking environment.

With a thorough understanding of Web development and programming (Perl, C++, HTML, JavaScript, Photoshop, ASP Classic, CGI, Flash, and experience with SQL), you bring a keen eye for detail and an appreciation of the integration of expert programming and creative design with e-commerce functionality.

With excellent communication and programming skills, you bring up-to-date experience in the development of e-commerce sites, including shopping carts. You have a solid and sophisticated understanding of what it means to sell products on the Web. An adaptable, creative thinker, you have an excellent eye for design, a strong esthetic appreciation, and are self-motivated and deadline oriented. Working in a small office, you are comfortable dealing with management and with customers who demand a high level of service and expertise.

In order to be considered for an interview, you must submit your portfolio as well as your résumé.

Apply by July 25, 2006, to employment@digicam1.com.

FIGURE 13-1
Example job announcement.

1. **Find a job to apply for.** Use the suggestions in the preceding sections to find a job.

   Imagine that you are interested in getting an entry-level job as a "webmaster"—Web designer, programmer, manager, and other such. In the local newspaper, you find six local webmaster or Internet-technician jobs under Employment–Internet. When you call some placement agencies, you find out that they also have jobs for webmasters, Web technicians, and similar positions.

At yahoo.com, your search on "webmaster jobs" delivers 60,000 hits. You see rates ranging from $15.00 to $135.00 per hour and salaries ranging from $20,000 to $85,000 per year. You see a wide variety of requirements and a dizzying array of abbreviations: HTML, DHTML, XML, Perl, CGI, ASP, Java, IIS, TCP/IP, UNIX, NT, PHP, and more.

2. **Analyze the job announcement carefully for the stated job requirements and any underlying assumptions.** Make sure you understand exactly what the potential employer is looking for.

   While these jobs look rather intimidating, you find several that you may be able to talk your way into. After all, job requirements are sometimes more like wish lists. The job announcement shown in Figure 13-1 requires creating and editing Web pages (HTML), programming in ASP, C++, CGI, and JavaScript, and using your eye for design to create attractive websites. Since only two years of experience are required, you believe you might have a chance.

3. **Find out what you can about the company, its operations, and the job.** See the preceding suggestions on researching companies and industries.

   You try some of the company-research tools listed in the preceding, but to no avail. This company is not listed anywhere. You go to the company's current website and get a sense of its business—selling digital cameras—but not much else. You get a friend to check out the company in person: the people at the store are very casual, very young.

4. **Make a list of your work experience.** For each of your work-experience items, take notes on the beginning and ending dates, the full name and address of the organization you worked for, your primary duties, the names of projects you worked on, the departments or areas you worked in, the names of the equipment you used, awards you received, and any other quantifiable information such as employees supervised, throughputs (such as calls answered, problems resolved, product manufactured), savings you were able to accomplish for your employers, and so on.

   As a graduating college student, you have little work experience. You've created basic websites for your hockey league and for a family reunion, and worked in the college bookstore and a nearby coffee shop. You take notes on the two website jobs: the dates you did the work; names and addresses of contacts; URLs for the websites you designed; descriptions of those websites; and details on the JavaScript and ASP scripts you used to create guest books, chat rooms, and popup information. For the other jobs, you list names, addresses, supervisors, beginning and ending dates, your hours, and your primary responsibilities. Knowing that the potential employer is involved in retail, you plan to emphasize the bookkeeping work you did using various software applications.

5. **Make a list of your education.** For each education item, take notes on beginning and ending dates, degrees or certificates received, important courses and projects, grade point average, major topics covered, instructor names, awards or scholarships, organizations you belonged to, and so on.

> You write down as many potentially helpful details as you can think of relating to your education: your applied-business degree, the dates started and completed, important courses (including the course on e-commerce and marketing on the Web), your GPA, instructors' names that may be recognized in the community, and your research project about the potential impact of the Web on telecommuting. You also list the special seminars you attended on creating Web pages with HTML and that Introduction to CGI and ASP workshop you took (offered free by the college). To connect with the "esthetic" requirement, mention that History of Art course you took. Unfortunately, you never received any awards or scholarships. Also, you decide to become a member of a national professional webmaster society—and quick!

6. **Make a list of your unpaid work.** Take the same kind of notes for your volunteer and internship or co-op work. Merge work you have done as an intern into your education section, and your volunteer work into your work section, or present this information in a separate section on your résumé, depending on how relevant the experience is.

> Unfortunately, you don't have any volunteer experience other than selling chocolate bars for your hockey team. However, one of the courses you took while at college included a project you did for a local business. You designed a feedback form for the website of a local RV manufacturer, and the company actually still uses the form. List the work under your work experience as a "special project."

7. **List other related activities and experience.** You can include in a résumé hobbies, organizations you belong to, and other skills you possess. They "round you out" as a real person and can help you fill up the rest of a résumé page if you are at the beginning of a career.

> What makes you a real person, not a work-obsessed robot? You might be a great lover of jazz or classical music, an avid back-yard gardener, an amateur gourmet chef, or a connoisseur of the detective fiction of certain choice authors. Maybe you like hanging out in all-night coffee shops with friends—oops, better leave that one out. At the beginning of a career, details like these can help fill résumés and prevent them from looking skimpy.

8. **Develop an organizational strategy for the résumé contents.** Résumé writers typically use one of three strategies to organize and present

information about their work experience, education, training, military experience, and other such qualifications:

- *Reverse-chronological strategy.* Divide your background into areas such as work experience, training, military experience, and education, and then list related items for each in reverse-chronological order.
- *Functional strategy.* Find the "themes" or "functions" in your career (such as computer networks, bookkeeping, supervision, recruitment, project management, programming, intensive-care nursing, and so on). For each, list work experience, training, education, or anything else that relates.
- *Combined strategy.* Some employers dislike the functional strategy because it does not show the chronology of a career. Others dislike the reverse-chronological strategy because it does not adequately show your qualifications in each area. You can combine the two strategies to get the best of both. Present the functional sections first, then present your career chronology under a heading like "Work History" toward the bottom.

Which to use? Standard wisdom says to use the reverse-chronological strategy if you are at the beginning of your career. But experiment with both.

You consider the functional approach. You could have headings such as Web Page Design, Web Programming, Business Experience, and so on. Under each of these headings, list your jobs, course work, seminars, and any related self-teaching you've done. But that may look skimpy. Instead, you decide on the reverse-chronological approach: a straight listing of your education and training with *lots* of detail about each item, and a following section listing your work experience—again, with *lots* of detail.

9. **Plan to include lots of detail.** Pump in as much detail as you can for each experience, education, training, or service item. Cite specific product names, specific industry-standard names, and specific statistical detail (number of employees, average calls handled per month). Details like these with capital letters and numbers force potential employers to slow down and read carefully—which is exactly what you want them to do. Don't say "Familiar with many software applications"; list the ones you know. Don't say that you work in a "fast-paced, high-throughput office." Put some actual numbers with those statements: "fast-paced" in terms of what and how many? What was being "through-put" and how much? Where was the office? What do they do there?

In this résumé, you want to emphasize that you entered HTML directly into plain-text files using MS Notepad and Paul Lutus's Arachnophilia. You want to mention that your Web pages made extensive use of tables and frames. Also mention that you used Photoshop to create or edit graphics and add text labels to them. Describe the ASP, C++, and JavaScript applications—guest books, bulletin boards, questionnaires, quizzes, and so on. You don't have a lot to put in your résumé, so push details like these extra hard—they help fill a résumé with legitimate "stuff."

10. **Plan the résumé heading section.** Think about what to include at the very top of your résumé: name, addresses, phone numbers, mailing addresses, e-mail addresses, your home Web page, professional or occupational title, key certifications, name and reference number of the job you are seeking, and so on.

   In the résumé heading, you decide to include your name (using the same style you use in your major headings). Beneath that will be your apartment and parents' addresses. Associated with these will be phone numbers. The heading will include your e-mail address and the URL of your personal home page. Anything else?

11. **Consider an objectives section.** An objectives section states your career goals or objectives in two or three lines. However, some believe that such a section limits your opportunities. For example, you may have done design, training, and supervision in your field. If your objective mentions only design, you may not make the cut for training and supervision jobs. Also, these sections are sometimes embarrassingly general and self-congratulatory. Still, an objectives section can define your professional focus sharply.

   An objectives section may help—it will certainly help fill out the résumé page, which is something you're worried about. You want to spotlight your applied-business education, your experience with website development, and your interest in business possibilities on the Web. Find a statement general enough not to lock you into one area or to exclude you from others. Still, it must be specific enough so that potential employers understand what you are about.

12. **Consider a highlights section.** Many résumés include a highlights section. Typically, it is a bulleted list just below the résumé heading. Listing a half-dozen or so of your best qualifications, it provides a quick-reference to the rest of your résumé, a kind of résumé-at-a-glance to draw employers in.

   You could create a highlights section, although it would be a stretch considering your lack of experience. The bullets might include the following: direct, manual work in HTML, with thorough knowledge of HTML tags; programming in ASP and Perl to create guest books, chat rooms, and online questionnaires; skills with SQL systems and Internet connectivity; basic JavaScript abilities for creating banners, quizzes and popups; or knowledge of business software such as spreadsheets and databases. Seeing that a key part of the job is to work on the e-commerce side of the website, you emphasize the fact that your degree focuses on e-commerce. You haven't actually built an online shopping cart, but you are sure you will be able to learn how to do so very quickly. In fact, you purchase some books that show you how to do it. You feel comfortable claiming "some knowledge" of shopping carts to go with your in-depth understanding of e-commerce.

Okay! You've developed a rather detailed idea of the contents, organization, and even the format for a résumé. Now start thinking about putting this material into different delivery media—specifically, the conventional printed résumé, the scannable résumé, and the Web-based résumé.

Design a Standard Print Résumé

For the print version of a résumé, decide on margins, type style (font), type size, heading styles, body text styles, use of bold and italics (highlighting), special indentation, bulleted and numbered lists, multicolumn text or tables, and so on.

For the print version of your résumé, you decide to try these specifications (the results of which are shown in the résumé at the end of this chapter):

- *Margins:* 1.5-inch margins to ensure that the résumé fills the page; "hanging-head" style (body text indented a half or full inch in relation to headings).
- *Body type:* 12-point Arial for body text, including address, phone, and Internet information; the objective statement; the bulleted items in the summary section; the text in the work-experience and education sections; and the text under the personal-details section.
- *Headings:* 14-point bold Arial for your name and for the major headings (Objective, Summary, Education, Employment, and Personal Interests and Activities).
- *Other format:* Bulleted lists to itemize the details of your education, training, work experience, projects, technical skills, and personal information (which will also help extend the résumé farther down the page). Bold the names of the educational institutions you've attended and organizations you've worked for.

Design a Scannable Résumé

In the 1990s, organizations began scanning résumés into databases so that they could do electronic searches. For example, a company looking for medical-technical professionals experienced with certain MRI equipment could search an applicant database for a specific manufacturer, or a specific MRI model name, as well as "MRI" and "magnetic resonance imaging." The recruiters would then review only those résumés retrieved from the search.

Considering this scenario, you can see why it is of the utmost importance to include specific manufacturer names, model names and numbers, version and release numbers, and other such specifics in any résumé, especially scannable ones.

However, you must avoid fancy formatting such as that discussed in preceding chapters. Instead, use a common type style and size (for example, 12-point Times New Roman) throughout the scannable résumé, including headings. Avoid using bold, italics, different type sizes or fonts, or indented text. Instead of bullets, use asterisks. Separate the asterisk and the text following it with a single space, and let following lines of bulleted items wrap back to the left margin.

Obviously, this feels like a retreat into the dark ages! However, software applications and scanning equipment are likely to evolve to the point that your beautifully formatted print résumé will scan nicely and will convert to HTML at the touch of a button—someday.

Design a Web Résumé

Now that the World Wide Web has moved onto centre stage of professional life, you need a résumé in every conceivable format: standard print format, scannable, and online. Posting your résumé on the Web gives you a number of opportunities to provide more detail, make it more rapidly accessible, and of course more easily updatable and more readily available. You can cite the URL (Web address) of your Web résumé on your business card or in your letters and e-mail and link to it from your home page.

Examples of Web résumés. To get an idea of what's possible with a Web résumé, explore the résumés at some of these résumé-posting sites, or just do a search for "résumés" at **http://www.monster.ca**, **http://www.careers. yahoo.com**, or **http://www.jobsmart.org/tools/résumé**.

Advantages of Web résumés. Notice some of the techniques that these Web-résumé writers use:

■ *Centralized menu of links and use of colour.* Place links to all the main sections of your résumé at the top of the page. That way, readers can go directly to highlights, work experience, education, or technical skills as they wish. Web pages make it easy to use colour—discreetly, of course— to brighten up the overall appearance. Don't overdo it: use a different colour only for headings, and stick with black text on white background for the body of the résumé.

■ *Links to home pages of other employers.* Adding links to your previous employers enables the prospective employer to find out where you previously worked and what sort of organization it is. Obviously, this capability is special to the Web résumé.

■ *More extensive detail, if desired.* As you gain experience, you run into problems keeping everything on a single résumé page. Using links, you can provide as much detail as you want: readers can link to it if they want, but the main page of your résumé stays neat and concise.

- *Links to projects and other examples of work.* A Web résumé also enables you to link to examples of your work. You can show off documents you developed by converting them to Web pages or portable document files (PDFs). If you've developed websites, set links to them. If you've done construction work—decks, pools, landscaping, renovations, restorations, or artwork—you can set links to pictures of this work.
- *Different versions of the résumé.* As you know from earlier in this chapter, you can arrange résumé details several ways—namely, the functional, the reverse-chronological, and combinations of the two. Instead of fretting over which to use, you can provide both, and readers can link to the one they prefer.
- *Links to printable and scannable versions.* To enable potential employers to print out or scan your résumé, provide links from your Web résumé to these versions of your résumé, as well.

Problems to avoid. Web résumés enable you to provide much more information about your qualifications, experience, and education than conventional print media normally could. However, it's easy to overdo it:

- *Don't include personal details unrelated to employment.* Don't include pictures of yourself, your family, your pets, or other unrelated items in an online résumé any more than you would in a conventional print résumé.
- *Avoid garish multicolour, multifont combinations.* Keep the use of colour under control. Avoid hard-to-read colour combinations; for example, blue letters on a red background. Conventional black text on white background is okay.
- *Avoid creating a jumbled, cramped-looking résumé.* Design your Web résumé so that it feels neat, clean, simple, roomy, and well-organized.

HOW DO YOU WRITE AN APPLICATION LETTER?

Addressed to a specific employer, an *application letter* highlights your best qualifications for a specific position. Sometimes, the application letter is called a "cover letter." Strictly speaking, a cover letter just identifies the job and introduces the résumé. A real application letter has a lot more work to do.

Think of the application letter as an intermediary between the job announcement and your résumé. The letter helps employers see the match between your qualifications and the job requirements. In a résumé, employers have to dig for these details; they are showcased in an application letter. The letter is not a qualifications summary. It is a careful selection of details that show you're right for the job, along with careful, low-keyed self-promotion (not the shameless kind).

Strategies for Application Letters

Think carefully about the contents and organization of an application letter, particularly the introduction, as well as the tone.

Organizational strategies.   To achieve this selective showcasing of your qualifications for a particular job, consider using one of the following organizational strategies:

- *Education–experience approach.* Particularly for people just beginning a career, a common strategy is to have an education section followed by a work-experience section. You're not limited to these two. For example, you could have separate sections for your military experience, volunteer work, or special projects you've done.
- *Functional approach.* If you're further along in your career, another approach is to create sections for each area of your qualifications to match the job requirements. For example, for a job as a Web designer, the requirements might include graphic design using specific software tools, HTML work, and experience with adapting audio and video to Web pages. Three of the main paragraphs of your application letter could focus on those three areas. Each paragraph would summarize work experience, training, or education related to that job requirement.

Strategies for the introduction.   The first paragraph of the application letter is critical—it must use just a few lines to do the following:

- *Indicate the purpose of the letter.* You don't have to make it sleep-inducing (for example, "The purpose of the following letter is to apply for …"), but *indicate* that the purpose of the letter is to apply for a job.
- *Identify the job you're applying for.* Cite the specific job title, job number, and your source for finding out about the job.
- *Draw readers in and make them read further.* Classic strategies include naming your best qualification or mentioning the name of someone with whom you've worked that readers will recognize. If none of these strategies work, try sounding enthusiastic about the job or the company.

Content strategies.   Regardless of the organizational approach you use, keep the following in mind as you write and revise the application letter:

- *Address readers' needs rather than your own.* Explain how you can help the potential employer and how your background enables you to do the work. It won't help to rave about how much the job fits into your career plans, how convenient the location is, or how much you like the dental plan.
- *Provide specifics, details, and examples.* Include the full names of companies, departments, product names and numbers, years and dates, people's names and titles, dollar amounts, and other directly relevant numerical

information. Your letter should contain lots of capital letters and numbers, which slows readers down and makes them read more carefully. Take a look at the contrasting examples in Figure 13-2 to see the effect that specifics have.

■ *Avoid self-congratulatory statements.* Saying that you are a "quick learner," that you "work well under pressure," or that you are "people oriented" just doesn't help. In fact, some readers may mutter, "Oh yeah, sez who?" Let the details, the specifics, and the examples in your application letter *show* that you are these things. Let readers make these judgments for themselves.

As for my work experience, I have been employed with organizations that have drawn on my computer-programming skills. At one organization, I was involved in setting up new software, training personnel, and managing networked users. In the other organization, I basically did various aspects of programming. I work well under pressure and am team oriented.

I will soon graduate with a computer degree. In my degree program, I have studied numerous programming languages and have developed an excellent grasp of them.

How can anyone get interested in this blah individual? Can you find a single specific detail? There's not much here to support this individual's claims.

As for my work experience, over the past three years I have been employed with two organizations that have drawn on my computer-programming skills. In my eighteen months with CMB*LIC Mortgage Corporation, I was involved in setting up new accounting and management software, training groups of ten employees on a monthly basis, and managing users of AutoCAD on a 10-user LAN. In my ten months with Hydronic Corporation as an assistant programmer, I did much of the same design, code, and test work as the regular programmer/analysts.

In June, I will graduate with a Bachelor of Applied Information Sciences from Humber College. My overall grade point average is 3.125. In my degree program, I have studied and developed a portfolio of applications in the following programming languages: Pascal, Assembler, COBOL, RPG, and C++.

Notice how many specifics this version has: specific organization names, months there, employees trained, network size, university name, degree name, expected graduation date, GPA, and specific programming languages.

FIGURE 13-2

Power of details in application letters. Don't just summarize your résumé; highlight key details that make you right for the job. Notice how the revised version drops the annoying self-praise ("work well under pressure" and "team oriented"), but the details create a stronger sense that this individual really does have these qualities.

■ *Sound interested.* Ideally, your application letter should have some energy and sparkle to it, without sounding phony. An application letter should be direct, energetic, and positive while remaining an expression of your essential personality. If you are excited about this line of work, if you admire the company, if you like its products—say so!

■ *Avoid negatives such as salary requirements or complaints about former employers.* Imagine how complaints about other employers sound to a potential employer. By including complaints, you may label yourself as a malcontent and a whiner. Similarly, don't mention salary requirements unless directed to do so by the job announcement.

Plan an Application Letter

To get an idea of how to develop an application letter, follow the process through these common stages. Use the job announcement shown in Figure 13-1.

1. **Analyze the job announcement.** Look carefully for the stated job requirements and try to uncover any underlying assumptions. Ordinarily, it's best to develop the application letter after the résumé. The résumé is like an inventory of your professional background and skills. Select from that inventory to write the application letter.

   Study that job listing in Figure 13-1. The ad asks for a thorough understanding of Web development and programming, which you think you can show with the courses you have taken at college. It also expects you to be able to integrate your expert programming experience with e-commerce functionality. For someone with two years' experience, that's quite a lot to ask. Perhaps this is just the employer's wish list. Don't be deterred by a list of skills and cut yourself off from a job because you don't quite match up. Keep in mind that the company is offering a salary of only $35,000 a year. A developer of an e-commerce site could expect a much higher salary. This company will expect to do some training.

2. **Find out what you can about the company.** Research the company (or its local site), its operations, and this particular industry or area of work.

   You've visited the company's website and read everything there. You make note of unfamiliar terms and look them up. You get a friend to visit the company in person to pick up brochures, look around, and check out the staff and store. You check the local Better Business Bureau to see if anyone has complained about this company. You ask around—*network*—to see if you can find businesspeople who might know this company or its principals.

3. **Make a list of your strongest qualifications.** List what makes you right for this position, as well as areas where you lack qualifications.

What will get you employed at this place? The websites you did for your hockey league and your family reunion were fun, but added up to less than a year's experience, even though the hockey site has taken up a lot of your spare time, as it needs constant updating. You can honestly claim to know HTML rather than relying on Web-page editors. You are good with graphics and are an experienced photographer. In fact, the family reunion site was all about photographs. Your strengths are in C++ and JavaScript. You are still learning ASP, but you can modify and adapt existing code for most of the basic interactive facilities: chat rooms, bulletin boards, forms, questionnaires, quizzes, and simple databases. As for your sense of design and your esthetic appreciation, the websites you designed for your hockey league made fairly extensive use of Flash, so they are impressive, and they were more than the company asked for as far as appearance. You also designed advertisements and menus for the college bookstore and Java Shop coffee shop using Photoshop. You took art courses all through high school and still visit art galleries frequently.

4. **Plan the strategy for the main paragraphs of your application letter.** Decide whether you want to use a functional or an education–experience approach (as discussed earlier).

   You have two choices in terms of organization and content for this letter:
   - *Education–experience approach.* You can have separate paragraphs about your work experience and about your education. In the experience paragraph (or paragraphs), discuss that website you did for your hockey league, making sure to say "HTML," "ASP," "CGI," "C++," and "JavaScript" often. In the education paragraph, mention your Bachelor of Applied Business degree and your special project involving e-commerce. Say something about that art history course and your museum habit. As for your work at the bookstore and the coffee shop, you developed skills with business software like Quicken, Excel, and Lotus 1-2-3, and you exercised your design skills by designing advertisements and menus. Mention the business-graphics software you know—the potential employers will want to show graphics, charts, and tables "dynamically" on their Web pages, even if they don't realize it yet.
   - *Functional approach.* Instead of the education–experience approach, you can include a paragraph about your Web page work using HTML, a paragraph about your ASP, CGI, C++, and JavaScript programming work, a paragraph about your applied business studies with references to business software tools you learned, and perhaps a final paragraph about your "creative thinking."
   In general, you want this letter to have a youthful, energetic, perky, good-natured feel to it—just like you in person. You want the potential employer to get the sense that you'd be fun to work with, a dependable and reliable worker, a flexible and adaptable person, and a quick learner.

5. **Select the details for each of the main sections.** When you write the actual draft of these sections, remember to use specific details—specific company names, dates, product names, dollar amounts, and so on. (See Figure 13-2 for an example.)

This is easy. You'll cite the names of the people you worked with on the hockey website. You'll mention that you used HTML 3.2 and Arachnophilia as your design tools. You used Photoshop for graphics work and Netscape as the browser, although you tested your pages in MS Internet Explorer as well. You've used Intuit Quicken version 6.3, Lotus 1-2-3 version 7, Harvard Graphics 3.07 and CorelDRAW 9. Your advertisements for the University Bookstore at Humber College appeared throughout the spring 2003 semester in Humber *Et Cetera*. The menus you designed for the Java Shop in 2004 are still being used, although a few items and some prices have changed. You'll mention that research paper you wrote in the spring semester of 2003, "E-commerce Potential for Small Rural Businesses." You can cite *by full name* those e-commerce and Web marketing courses you took. This is the kind of detail you want in the letter (although the swarm of software version or release numbers might be overwhelming).

6. **Plan the introduction to this application letter.** Remember that, while it must be brief, the introduction must indicate that a résumé follows, provide some reference to the job you are applying for, capture readers' attention, and make them want to continue reading.

   Remembering that the introduction paragraph must be brief but compelling, you decide to begin with a simple statement saying that this is an application for the company's webmaster position, which you found on the monster.ca website. Also, you'll state that you have a good combination of Web-development skills, business background, and design sense that will enable you to do a great job. You hope these statements will get these employers curious enough to read the rest of the letter to find out just what that "combination" is and how you acquired it.

7. **Plan the conclusion to this application letter.** The main jobs of the conclusion are to press readers for an interview and to facilitate readers getting in touch with you.

   You decide to finish off this letter quickly, mentioning your phone number, e-mail address, and times when you'll be available to interview. To ensure that this process moves forward, you state that you'll call in 10 days if you've not heard from him or her.

8. **Plan the delivery mode.** In this new world of fax machines, e-mail, and the World Wide Web, how should you send a job application or make it available? Study the job advertisement; do what it says. If you are uncertain, contact the employer and find out what's preferred.

   The job ad (in Figure 13-1) gives an e-mail address and asks that you send a portfolio of your work. You decide to write a smaller version of your application letter and use it in your e-mail. You also decide to send your portfolio attached to your e-mail. To do this, you create a folder and put all your documents—résumé, covering letter, an HTML page of links to your Web development work,

Most of us at some time or other have had a gap in employment or an unexplained job loss. Teachers will tell us that the résumé is a "sales tool" rather than record of employment, and that we should put our best foot forward in order to get an interview. Sometimes that means tweaking the résumé a little, or making much out of what is perhaps a very small bit of experience.

At what point does the "tweaking" become outright lying?

Jana Ritter, in an article published online in *The Galt Review*, takes a matter-of-fact view, pointing out that honesty is often more important to an employer than education. And, she notes, "employment and education are the most common résumé distortions and, therefore, the most likely to be checked and cross-checked." Industry statistics indicate that "About 30 percent of people exaggerate on their résumés, and one in 10 makes false claims about their education...." It's become so rampant that background checking is now a standard part of the hiring process in Canada.

Sometimes, the tweaking may just be an exaggeration of a personal trait or something as difficult to prove as the amount of work someone has done as part of a team. Were you a member of a team, or did you actually coordinate the team's projects? If it's the former and you are hired to manage a team, your lack of skills will soon become evident to your new employer. If you claim to be a go-getter who can win new customers, but in fact are more of a quiet behind-the-scenes type of person, that will also soon become apparent. A résumé is a tool to get you an interview, but for the sake of your future career, it is always best to tell the truth about yourself up front.

Source: Jana Ritter, "The Lying Game: A Matter of Fact Approach to Résumé Fraud." *The Galt Global Review.* December 2, 2002. Accessed July 22, 2005. http://www.galtglobalreview.com/careers/lying_game3.html.

a report you wrote for an e-commerce course, some design work you've scanned to files—inside the folder. You also create a main page or index in HTML and use it to explain what is in each document. On that page, you link each file in the folder. You then zip the folder and attach it to your e-mail. You explain in your e-mail that the folder needs to be unzipped, and that the index page links to all the other documents in the folder.

Design and Format the Application Letter

Chapter 12 covers the essentials for formatting business letters. Here are some reminders:

- Remember that you can adjust page margins so that the letter fits nicely on the page. You don't want just a few lines falling over to a second page, nor do you want the letter huddled at the top of one page, making it look skimpy.
- Use a standard font and type size—avoid the unusual or strange (unless that's just you). Text using 12-point Times New Roman and Arial works fine.
- Use a "block" format as shown in the example at the end of this chapter. Left-align all the elements of the application letter. (Don't forget to sign your name between the complimentary close and your typed name.)

- A nice professional touch is to design your own letterhead like the ones shown in the examples. Doing so also gets your name at the top of the letter.

WORKSHOP: APPLICATION LETTERS AND RÉSUMÉS

Here are some additional ideas for practising the concepts, tools, and strategies in this chapter:

1. *Search for jobs.* Using any of the tools mentioned earlier for finding jobs, list a half-dozen jobs that fit your current qualifications (or those you will have upon graduation).

2. *Define job qualifications.* For several of the jobs you found, make a list of the qualifications you'd need to be seriously considered. Don't just repeat the qualifications stated in the job—include the unstated ones as well.

3. *Research a company.* For one of the jobs you found in the preceding, use the tools discussed earlier in this chapter to find pertinent information about the company. Don't just grasp at any information—find information that you could actually use in an interview in some way. For each item of information, jot some notes as to how you would use that item.

4. *Design a "perfect" résumé.* Imagine that you are a perfect fit for one of the jobs you found. Sketch the corresponding résumé, making up the appropriate details.

5. *Design a "first-job" résumé.* Imagine that you want to apply for one of the jobs, but are just out of college with no formal work experience in the field. Sketch a résumé in which you include every conceivably related bit of experience (internships, volunteer work, semester projects, and so on).

6. *Anticipate interview questions.* For one of the jobs you found, write a script, complete with the questions the interviewers would ask you and your answers. For ideas, see some of the employment sites on the World Wide Web such as **www.wetfeet.com/asp/home.asp**.

7. *Prepare stories.* Think of some tough work situations you have encountered and practise describing them in a positive way. Focus on how well you handled the situations.

APPLICATION LETTER

Application letter: In this letter, the writer seeks a position as a system-support specialist. Although he presents an enormous amount of detail in the experience section, it's based on only a few years of work experience.

Letter format: This letter uses the standard block format as discussed in Chapter 12. All elements of the letter are left-aligned. Notice that this writer uses the subject line as a way of avoiding the "Dear Sir:" dilemma.

Introduction: This introduction does the basics: identifies the purpose of the letter, the position title, and his source of information about the job. He makes good use of that source: it happens to be someone within the company who can vouch for his abilities.

Experience section: Notice the amount of detail this writer packs into this paragraph. It bristles with specifics! Even without reading it, you sense this person is indeed well qualified. Even so, these details are based on 10 months of experience. More importantly, he knows how to push the details of his experience for all they are worth!

In an application letter, don't summarize your résumé. Instead, select details that directly relate to the job you are applying for. The more proper nouns (words with capital letters), product and company names, and numbers, the more you force readers to slow down and pay attention.

Education section: This paragraph contains a nice touch: the writer mentions a special project he did in his course work that relates directly to the job he is seeking.

3010 Norwood Hills
Bayport, ON N0M 1T0

June 3, 2006

Sulzer Orthopedics Inc.
90 Dundalk Drive
Kitchener, ON N6M 4C6

Subject: Application for full-time position as System Support Specialist

Please consider me for the full-time position of System Support Specialist. I found out about this position from Adrian Dupre, who currently works for Sulzer Orthopedics in the IS Department as the Help Desk Supervisor. My work in the IS Department as a part-time temporary employee for the last 10 months will enable me to begin contributing immediately with little or no transition time.

I have extensive experience in configuring, installing, and troubleshooting PCs, laptops, servers, and Palm Pilots. I have personally set up over 50 desktop PCs including hardware, operating system, and application installation. I have also provided technical support to the Help Desk in troubleshooting hardware and application failures in the DOS, Windows 2003, Novell, and UNIX environments. Typical hardware support included troubleshooting motherboards, CD-ROMs, hard drives, floppy drives, video cards, modems, and network cards. Typical application support included Microsoft Word, Excel, PowerPoint, Access, Internet Explorer, Outlook, Netscape Navigator, and Oracle. In the IS department, I have also done customer-service work, for which I have received several recognition awards.

While pursuing my Diploma in Electronics, I have also taken numerous programming classes, which gave me some proficiency in Pascal, C++, and assembly language. One of my projects involved creating a front-end prototype in C++ for a system-support database, which enables rapid documenting, searching, and tracking of customer problems.

I look forward to meeting with you at your convenience. I can be reached at any time at (519) 926-6266 or at msalinas@rogers.com.

Sincerely,

Michael Salinas

Michael Salinas
Encl: résumé

PRINT RÉSUMÉ

Using standard page margins and type sizes, this résumé would fit on one page. For presentation in this book with annotation, it runs over to two pages.

Contact information: The address area uses a two-column table so that the applicant's current and parents' address information aligns nicely.

Highlighting: Notice how this résumé writer attempts to highlight her Web-design experience, her experience with the worlds of business and investment, and her graphic design experience.

Organization: This writer uses the "reverse-chronological" strategy, presenting education first, then work experience.

Style: The entire résumé is done in Arial font. The heading uses bold 11-point Arial; the address area uses 9.5-point Arial; the main headings (Objective, Summary, etc.) use 9.5-point bold Arial; and the main text uses 9-point Arial.

Consistency: Notice that this résumé writer bolds the name of the organization and italicizes her job title, major, or degree name. Doing so provides a consistent overall design across the education and employment sections.

Kaharen Ennderson

kennderson@webnet.com

1300 Oak Path
Newmarket, ON
(905) 555-1234

100 Amherst Crescent
Toronto, ON
(416) 555-5678

Objective

To obtain an entry-level position with a company needing my abilities in World Wide Web development and business administration.

Summary

- Proficient at developing, maintaining, and using direct HTML coding with graphics, tables, frames, and forms.
- Experienced in customizing and maintaining guest books, listservs, questionnaire databases, and other interactive facilities, using Perl/CGI and JavaScript.
- Proficient with Web graphics using tools such as Photoshop.
- Proficient with business-related software such as Microsoft Excel, Lotus 1-2-3, and Intuit Quicken.
- Completed Degree in Applied Business with special courses in finance, marketing, and e-commerce

Education

Humber College, Toronto, ON
Bachelor of Applied Business: e-Commerce (2002–2006)
- Member of Association of Information Technology Professionals and World Organization of Webmasters.
- Computer skills include HTML, Perl/CGI, JavaScript, Visual Basic, COBOL, SQL, Windows, MS Access and Excel, Intuit Quicken, Lotus 1-2-3.
- Related course work includes e-commerce, Web marketing, finance, accounting, systems analysis, COBOL, Visual Basic, database design, management information systems, data communications, Web databases, client/server applications, art history.
- Continuing education credits in Perl/CGI, HTML, JavaScript.

Algonquin College, Ottawa, ON
Webmaster Certification Program (2004–2005)
- Earned ACC Webmaster Certificate with specialization in System/Application Programming.
- Took courses in JavaScript, Java, Perl, CGI, Web database applications, ASP, TCP/IP, UNIX, and Windows applications.
- Completed June 2005

Notice how this writer gives herself a job title even though she probably did not have an official title in these rather informal jobs.

Buzzwords: Notice how she accentuates Perl, CGI, HTML, Web page, and JavaScript every chance she gets—these are the buzzwords the potential employer is looking for.

Notice how this writer "plays up" her graphic design experience by emphasizing her design work on advertisements and on websites. At the time, this work might have seemed no more glamorous than sweeping the floor, but now it counts!

Additional details: She uses this final section to "round" herself out as a human being with her own personality and interests. But notice that even in a section like this, she has an agenda: professional interests and activities involving computers and the World Wide Web, team activities and leadership, and esthetics (cuisine, jazz, and art museums).

Employment

Southern Ontario Junior Hockey League (www.sojhl.com)
Web designer (2002–present)
- Developed and currently maintain league website
- Developed Web pages in direct HTML coding, with tables, frames, graphics, and forms
- Developed interactive forms using Perl/CGI and JavaScript

Java Shop, 1703 Queen St. W., Toronto, ON
Store assistant manager (2002–present)
- Designed menus and ads for local newspapers
- Kept books in Intuit Quicken
- Interviewed and trained new employees
- Managed store during weekends
- Waited tables

College Bookstore, 1200 University Blvd., Toronto, ON
Clerk (2002–2003)
- Designed advertisements for student newspaper
- Stocked shelves, did inventory, ran cash register

Personal Interest and Activities
- Active member of the World Organization of Webmasters and Association of Information Technology Professionals.
- Computer-game design hobbyist using Java and Visual Basic.
- Jazz piano enthusiast, particularly the work of Red Garland, Thelonious Monk, Kenny Barron.
- Humber Sport Cycling Team (past vice-president)
- Toronto Eagles Cycling Team (co-founder, secretary)
- Frequent visitor to the fine arts museums in Ottawa, Toronto, Kleinberg, and Quebec City.

Formal Reports: Design, Format, Abstracts

Topics covered in this chapter include

■ wind energy.

WIND ENERGY

Alternative energy sources are in the limelight, especially with the rising cost of traditional energy sources. The Canadian federal and provincial governments have produced great amounts of material on the development of wind energy. Search any Canadian provincial or federal website for materials. Here are a few examples of useful sites:

Canadian Wind Energy Atlas
http://www.windatlas.ca/en/index.php

Natural Resources Canada
http://www.canren.gc.ca/tech_appl/index.asp?Cald=6&Pgld=232

Information about Wind Energy
http://www.on.ec.gc.ca/pollution/fpd/technologies/t-1000-e.html

Organizations also are concerned about energy conservation:

Greenpeace Canada
http://www.greenpeace.ca/e/campaign/climate_energy/index.php

When you have completed this chapter, you will be able to

■ distinguish among various design and delivery options for reports;
■ design and create the several different elements of a typical formal report following required guidelines;
■ write appropriate research abstracts, descriptive abstracts, and executive summaries.

This chapter focuses on design and format for various types of technical documents. You'll see common designs for the following:

- *Business-letter reports*. Used for relatively short documents sent to a client or customer (external to your organization).
- *Memo reports*. Used for relatively short documents that stay "in house"—within your organization.
- *Formal reports*. Used for longer documents (more than 4 pages, for example). Use a cover letter or cover memo, depending on whether the document is external or internal to your organization.

This chapter also covers strategies for writing executive summaries (also called abstracts), an important component of longer technical reports.

Note: For additional examples of the documents discussed in this chapter, see **http://www.powertools.nelson.com**.

DESIGNING TECHNICAL DOCUMENTS

You have a number of possibilities for the design and delivery of a technical document, depending on how formal the situation is, whether the document is for external or internal readers, how long the document is, and how it will be used (see table on next page).

Regardless of which design and delivery method you choose (except for oral presentations), use headings, lists, tables, and graphics just as you would in any other technical document.

FORMAL REPORTS AND OTHER TECHNICAL DOCUMENTS

Formal reports are "formal" because they have special covers, are bound, and contain front- and back-matter elements such as title pages, tables of contents, lists of figures, abstracts, and so on. Formal reports are used

Technical Documents: Design and Delivery Options

Self-contained business letter	Put a short document (for example, under 4 pages) that goes to an external audience in a business letter. Still use headings, lists, tables, and graphics.
Self-contained memo	Use the memo format (TO, FROM, SUBJ) if the document stays in house. Take a look at the sample informal memo report at the end of Chapter 1.
Self-contained e-mail	Brief reports can be sent through e-mail. The entire document occurs within the body of the e-mail, which limits how much fancy formatting you can do.
Formal document with transmittal letter	Put longer documents (for example, over 4 pages) in their own separate bindings with formal elements such as identifying cover labels, title pages, and tables of contents. Paper-clip the transmittal letter (cover letter) to the front of the bound document. This design is discussed later in this chapter; see the example at the end of this chapter as well as the progress report at the end of Chapter 6.
Formal document with transmittal memo	Instead of a transmittal letter, attach a transmittal memo if the document stays in house.
Formal document as attachment to e-mail	If you ship a document attached to e-mail, your e-mail can serve as the transmittal. However, because your e-mail may not stay with the printed document, create a transmittal letter or memo as the first page of the document.
Oral presentation	You can also deliver a report orally. See Chapter 15 for strategies on delivering oral presentations.

more like books: people read and reread them, pass them around, and store them on shelves. They are not necessarily for readers external to the organization. Plenty of formal reports stay in house in organizations like Research in Motion, IBM, Hewlett-Packard, and Dell.

General Layout

Although the Canadian government officially adopted metric-sized paper and measurements, the practical issues involved (expense) in the conversion led to their being dropped as a standard. If you, for some reason, need to print on A4 (metric) paper, in Word 2003, click **Tools→Options**, and on the **Print** tab, check "Allow A4/Letter paper resizing."

For most formal documents, consider using the following specifications unless you have special requirements:

- Use standard 8.5 × 11 paper, and use only one side of the paper.
- Use 1, 1.25, or 1.5 inches for the top, bottom, left, and right margins. In some documents, the left margin is a half-inch larger than the right in order to accommodate the binding.

- Use a standard serif font such as Times New Roman, Garamond, or Century for the body text. Use 9-, 10-, 11-, or 12-point type size for body text. Again, make sure to check for special document requirements.
- Use a sans serif font such as Arial or Helvetica for headings. Type size, of course, varies according to the level of the heading but ranges from 24 points down to the same point size as the body text.
- Choose a line spacing according to local requirements or your preferences. In the days of the typewriter, body text was double-spaced. With word-processing and desktop-publishing software, double-spacing is unnecessary. For readability, however, use a line-spacing value that equals 1.5 to 2.0 points plus the point size of the font. Notice in Figure 14-1, for example, that Microsoft Word defaults to 13.95 points for 12-point text.
- Keep lines from becoming too long: for example, 6.5-inch lines of 10-point type is no fun to read! Try increasing the type size to 12 and adjusting margins to 1.0 inches.

Indentation: This paragraph is indented 1 inch.

Paragraph spacing: This paragraph has 12 points of space below it.

Line spacing: The text for this paragraph is 12-point Times New Roman. The line spacing is nearly 2 points greater (creating roomier, more readable lines).

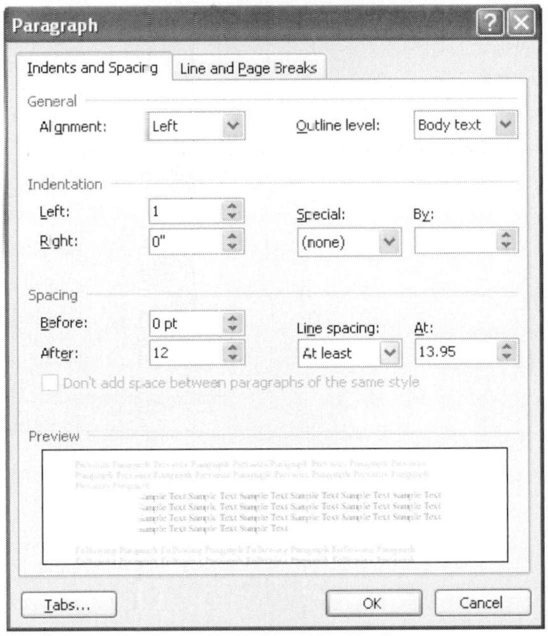

FIGURE 14-1

Controls for paragraph format. In Microsoft Word, access this dialogue box by clicking **Format→Paragraph**.

Covers, Labels, and Binding

A formal report needs sturdy covers, a label, and binding because it gets read, reread, and passed around. For report covers, pick a simple card stock (a thicker paper). For the binding, pick something that will enable the report to lie flat when open. (Simple brad-type folders prevent pages from lying flat and force readers to hold pages down.) Avoid the clear-plastic covers with the plastic sleeves.

Use ring binders if the actual use of the report necessitates doing so. Ring binders are particularly useful if readers will need to add or substitute pages periodically.

Often, the best bindings for reports are the plastic-spiral, wire-spiral, or "perfect-bound" styles (see Figure 14-2). Spiral bindings enable the report to lie flat without forcing the reader to pry it open or struggle to keep the pages down. The perfect-bound style looks like thick tape has been

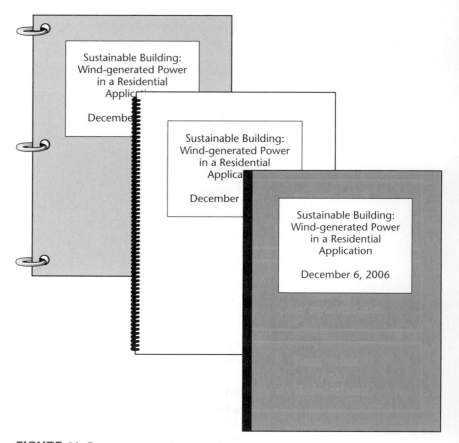

FIGURE 14-2

Different possibilities for report bindings. Avoid the clear-plastic covers with the plastic sleeve! Spiral or perfect bindings are the best.

applied to the inner half-inch edge of the report. It also enables a report to lie flat easily when open.

Transmittal Letter or Memo

The transmittal letter or memo is essentially a "cover" letter or memo. It tells the reader, "Here it is!" Although quite brief, its contents include the following:

- Reference to some initial agreement between the recipient and you as to the production of the report and its due date.
- Brief review of the report's purpose and overview of its contents.
- A closing that urges the recipient to review the report and to get in touch with questions or concerns.

Don't forget: if your document is for an external audience (an individual or organization external to you or your organization), use a business-letter format such as in the sample report at the end of this chapter and the progress report and proposal at the end of Chapter 6. If the report stays in house, use a cover memo. Unless you have local requirements, paper-clip the transmittal letter or memo to the front of the document. See Figure 14-4A at the end of the chapter for an example of a transmittal letter.

Title Page

Although the contents of the title page can vary, the following are the minimum requirements:

- Full title of the report
- Name, title, and organization for whom the report was prepared
- Name, title, and organization of the preparer of the report
- Date of the report
- Descriptive abstract (quick overview of the report's purpose and contents)

If you browse a sampling of formal reports, you'll find other elements, such as report tracking numbers (for in-house storage), contract numbers, and logos, as well as copyright and trademark symbols. If you are preparing a report in house for an organization, be sure to find out the preferred format and use it.

Notice these details about the design of the title page in Figure 14-4B at the end of this chapter:

- All of the material on the title page, except for the descriptive abstract, is centred.
- The same font type and size is used for the title of the report as for the main headings within the body of the report. Specifically, a 16-point, bold, sans serif font is used for the title.

- The identifying labels, names, titles, and organizations of the preparer of the report and its recipient use a smaller, nonbold type style, but that is sans serif as well. Notice that italics are used to provide contrast.
- Regular body text font (specifically, 12-point Times New Roman) is used for the descriptive abstract.

Table of Contents

The table of contents (TOC) is typically the next component after the title page. In the sample TOC shown in Figure 14-4C at the end of this chapter, notice the following details:

- The title, "Table of Contents," is centred and uses a sans serif font, bold, and all caps.
- All first-level items are on the left margin, using the sans serif font, but without bold, and all caps.
- Second-level items are indented to the *text* of the first-level items, and use the same but smaller sans serif font. Headline-style caps are used for these items.
- Third-level items are indented to the *text* of the second-level items. They use the same font and type size as the second-level items, but sentence-style caps instead.
- "Leader dots" guide the eye to the page number corresponding to each item. The page numbers indicate the page on which the section *starts* and are right-aligned (for example, the number 9 aligns to the 0 in the number 10).
- The list of figures and the executive summary are listed at the top of the TOC. The heading "Appendixes" followed by an indented list of the individual appendixes would be at the bottom of the TOC.
- Vertical spacing in a TOC can vary as long as it is consistent. If you have relatively few items in a TOC, you can double-space everything. If you have many items, you can single-space between lower-level items.

Some documents may have so many headings and so many levels of headings that you can use only two of those levels. An overly long, overly detailed TOC is unusable.

List of Figures and Tables

For documents containing graphics, tables, or both that are numbered and labelled, include a figure list just after the TOC. Remember that, except for tables, everything is a figure—illustrations, photographs, drawings, diagrams, charts, and graphs. If you have six or fewer figures and tables total, put them on the same page. Notice the following details about the figure list in Figure 14-4D at the end of this chapter:

- The title, "List of Figures," uses the same style and format as the TOC.
- Two column headings are used, one over the figure and table numbers and one over the page numbers. Notice that these column headings use the same style as the second-level headings in the TOC.
- The figure and table titles use the same style and size as the body-text font (a serif font) and they use sentence-style caps. (If you look at the figure title as it occurs in the actual text, notice the title is considerably longer than it is in the figure list. In the figure list, you can trim it to something brief but meaningful.)
- Leader dots guide the eye to the page number on which the figure or table occurs; the page numbers are right-aligned just as they are in the TOC.
- Spacing between the column headings and the figure- or table-list items and between the figure- or table-list items themselves is variable. In Figure 14-4D, the vertical distance between the title and the column headings is the same as it is between the title and the first TOC item in the table of contents. The vertical distance between the figure- and table-list items resembles double-spacing.

Executive Summary (Informative Abstract)

See "Summaries and Abstracts" in the following for details on these parts of technical reports.

Body

At long last, we get to the actual text! The body text uses all the standard characteristics discussed throughout this book, such as headings, lists, notices, tables, figures, and highlighting. The body uses the same margins, type style, and vertical spacing as in the title page, table of contents, executive summary, and so on.

Keeping margins, fonts, vertical spacing, and other such details consistent throughout will give your document a clean, simple, inviting look. Readers won't notice your careful attention to fonts, type sizes, type faces, margins, and vertical spacing, but they will be put off by variation in these elements. Such variation creates a busy, complicated, uninviting text that readers would prefer not to read. See Figures 14-4G through 14-4J at the end of the chapter.

Appendixes

Appendixes are good places to stash material that just doesn't fit in the regular text. Full-page maps, multipage tables, detailed specifications, forms used for questionnaires, and names and addresses of companies or individuals just get in the way in the regular body text:

- The appendix title uses the same style and format as first-level headings in the body of the report.

- Each appendix title begins with "Appendix," followed by a letter, ending with a descriptive title.
- Otherwise, all other style and format details are the same as in the body of the report—headings, lists, tables, figures, highlighting, font types, margins, vertical spacing, and so on.

Information Sources

For some technical documents, the only appendix you may have is the list of the information sources. Here are essential details of the information-sources list:

- Lists all books, articles, encyclopedias, reference works, government documents, online resources, and experts used to research and write the report (see Figure 14-4J at the end of the chapter).
- If there are no other appendixes, omit "Appendix A" from the title of the information-sources section and just centre the title ("References" or "Works Cited") at the top.
- There are numerous styles for indicating the sources from which you borrowed information. Use your local requirements (those of your instructor or organization) or the style used by your field or profession.

Practical Ethics: Anecdotal Evidence

 Anecdotes, or stories of personal experience, are powerful things. They are used in almost every form of communication to sell items ("I took this diet pill and lost two hundred pounds"), to illustrate a point, to persuade ("This is my experience and will be yours, too"), or to simply pique people's interest so they will listen or keep reading.

Using anecdotes in communication is perfectly legitimate, but they have limitations. Certainly, using anecdotes to create interest or make a topic more personal is often a good idea. Wouldn't you rather listen to a speaker who uses lively stories or interesting anecdotes rather than one who simply recites dry statistics? Most people would. However, when you are trying to inform or convince an audience of something important, hard evidence and statistics are far more credible than personal experience.

Let's say you tried a new brand of soap and your face broke out. There seems to be a definite cause-and-effect relationship between the soap and your allergic reaction, and it makes sense that you would warn friends or family away from the soap based on your personal experience. But it is also possible that the allergic reaction was influenced by something you aren't aware of, like a change in your diet, a drug interaction, or the poison oak you inadvertently brushed up against. So to conclude that *no one* should be allowed to use or manufacture this soap is not a fair use of anecdotal evidence, and unless your personal experience is corroborated by outside sources, you probably won't get very far in lobbying for the soap's removal from the market.

When used correctly, either in personal situations or combined with scientific research, anecdotes are powerful tools of communication. If you are making recommendations or conclusions in a technical report, make sure you back up your anecdotes with solid research.

Page Numbering

If you have a choice, use sequential page numbering from beginning to end of your report; centre page numbers at the bottom of pages; don't display page numbers on the title page and the appendix divider page. Otherwise, follow your local requirements (those of your instructor or organization).

Positioning. Formal reports use various styles for page numbering:

- *Alternating bottom left and right corners.* Standard book styles use "alternating-page" format: typically, the odd-page page number appears on the outer right edge of the odd page (usually the right-hand page); the even-page page number, on the outer left edge of the even page (usually the left-hand page).
- *Alternating top left and right corners.* This style is similar to the previous except that the page numbers appear on the outer *top* corners of the pages. These are even more complicated than the previous style because you must keep page numbers from showing on the first page of any major section.
- *Bottom centre.* By far, the easiest solution is to show page numbers at the bottom centre of each page.

Numbering styles. You have just a few choices on page-numbering styles:

- *Sequential page numbering.* You can number each page sequentially from beginning to end of the report. (If you use the sequential style without front-matter page numbering, the first piece of paper within the report covers would be page 1—although the number is not actually displayed.)
- *By-section numbering.* You can restart page numbering at each section or chapter: for example, page numbers for Chapter 2 would be 2–1, 2–2, and so on; for Chapter 3, 3–1, 3–2, and so on.
- *Numbering for front-matter pages.* You may be expected to use lower-case Roman numerals: i, ii, iii, iv, and so on. These page numbers would be positioned the same way they are in the body of the format. In this style, the first piece of paper after the front cover is page i, even though the number is not actually displayed.
- *Numbering for back-matter pages.* If you use by-section page numbering for the body of your report, use the same style in the back matter of your report as well. For example, page numbering for Appendix A would be A–1, A–2, and so on; for Appendix B, B–1, B–2, and so on.

Displayed page numbers. Regardless of which page-numbering style you use, page numbers are *not* displayed on certain pages, such as the title page or the appendix divider page. If you can't figure out how to suppress the display of page numbers on certain pages, make those pages separate files.

In Microsoft Word, to create page numbers, choose **Insert→Page Numbers** and select the position and alignment you want. In the same dialogue box, click **Format** to change the starting number or the number style (lowercase Roman numerals, for example). To change the number style within the document, you must insert a section break: **Insert→Break→ Section**.

SUMMARIES AND ABSTRACTS

Different types of abstracts, also called summaries, accompany most formal reports. They summarize the key ideas and facts, the important findings and conclusions, main contents, or some combination. Abstracts and summaries enable readers to get a quick overview of the full report, as if someone had highlighted the key material in the report for them. Abstracts and summaries help readers decide if they should read the full report.

■ *Abstract*. Illustrated in Figure 14-3, the traditional research abstract (also called an informative abstract) summarizes the background, the research methods, the findings, and the discussion of those findings. For a background report, this type of abstract summarizes key points in each of the main sections of that report, including the introduction and conclusion.
■ *Descriptive abstract*. Also called a descriptive summary, this type is short—three to four sentences at most, regardless of the length of the full report. It states the purpose of the report and provides an overview of the report's contents. It does not reveal any of the actual information presented in the body of the report; it just tells readers what topics the report covers. You can see an example of a descriptive summary in Figure 14-4B at the end of this chapter.
■ *Executive summary*. The executive summary is a hybrid of the descriptive and informative summaries. Written for "executives" whose focus is business decisions and whose background is not necessarily technical, it focuses on conclusions and recommendations but provides little background, theory, results, or other such detail. It doesn't summarize research theory or method; it makes descriptive-summary statements like, "theory of heat gain, loss, and storage is also discussed." You can see an example of an executive summary in Figure 14-4E at the end of this chapter.

Introduction and background: This first part of the abstract summarizes key material from the introduction, including background on the research.

Methods: The next segment summarizes the methods used in the research.

Results: This segment discusses the results of these observations.

Discussion: The final segment of this abstract discusses and interprets the findings.

Abstract—Recent technological advances have made wind power a viable source of alternative energy production, and the number of windplant facilities has increased in the United States. Construction was completed on a 73-turbine, 25-megawatt windplant on Buffalo Ridge near Lake Benton, Minnesota, in spring 1994. The number of birds killed at existing windplants in California caused concern about the potential impacts of the Buffalo Ridge facility on the avian community.

From April 1994 through Dec. 1995 we searched the Buffalo Ridge windplant site for dead birds. Additionally, we evaluated search efficiency, predator scavenging rates, and rate of carcass decomposition.

During 20 mo of monitoring, we found 12 dead birds. Collisions with wind turbines were suspected for 8 of the 12 birds. During observer efficiency trials, searchers found 78.8% of carcasses. Scavengers removed 39.5% of carcasses during scavenging trials. All carcasses remained recognizable during 7 d decomposition trials. After correction for biases, we estimated that approximately 36 ± 12 birds (<1 dead bird per turbine) were killed at the Buffalo Ridge windplant in 1 y.

Although windplants do not appear to be more detrimental to birds than other man-made structures, proper facility siting is an important first consideration in order to avoid unnecessary fatalities.

Source: Osborn, Robert G. et al. "Bird Mortality Associated with Wind Turbines at the Buffalo Ridge Wind Resource Area, Minnesota." *American Midland Naturalist* 143: (2000): 41–52.

FIGURE 14-3

Abstract from a research journal. This type of abstract appears just after the title of the article and before the main text. It summarizes key concepts and facts from each of the main sections: introduction (which includes background on the study), methods, results, and discussion.

To get a sense of how to develop an executive summary or informative abstract, use the process shown in the following examples. It is based on the recommendation report shown at the end of Chapter 4 and the primary research report show at the end of Chapter 3.

1. Review the text carefully, referring to its table of contents, if available. Identify the type of readers who would be reading the document and the type of abstract required.
   - *Recommendation report.* The recommendation report at the end of Chapter 4 is clearly to help executives make decisions about purchasing and implementing voice-recognition software. This report needs an executive summary.
   - *Research report.* The research report at the end of Chapter 3 is clearly for bat researchers who are interested in acquiring and advancing their knowledge about their favorite *Chiroptera*. This report needs an informative abstract.
2. Identify the major sections of the report. You must decide which of these sections to summarize and how much.
   - *Recommendation report.* The recommendation report at the end of Chapter 4 contains background on voice-recognition software, how it works, and what its memory requirements are. It moves on to a point-by-point comparison of four software packages, followed by a summary of conclusions, ending with a recommendation. For an executive summary, summarize the conclusions and recommendations and leave out the technical background.
   - *Research report.* The research report at the end of Chapter 3 contains the standard sections for the research question and background, research methods, findings, and discussion. For an informative abstract, summarize key details out of *each* of these sections.
3. When you write these abstracts and summaries, use good English; don't write telegraphically, but pack as much detail as you can in sentences to keep the abstract or summary as short as possible. You don't need to define key terms or cite sources: that's done in the body of the report.

WORKSHOP: DOCUMENT DESIGN AND FORMAT

Here are some additional ideas for practising the concepts, tools, and strategies in this chapter:

1. *Report-formatting review.* Find a sampling of technical reports—produced either by governmental or corporate organizations—and compare their design and format to what you've read in this chapter. Make notes on any differences you find in the sequence of components (such as title pages, tables of contents, and abstracts), different components, or different contents or format of those components.

2. *Business-letter report formatting.* Use the instructions and unformatted text at **http://www.powertools.nelson.com** to create a short business-letter report.

3. *Memo-report formatting.* Use the instructions and unformatted text available at **http://www.powertools.nelson.com** to create a short memo report.

4. *Formal-report formatting.* Use the instructions and unformatted text available at **http://www.powertools.nelson.com** to create a formal report.

Transmittal letter: The transmittal letter identifies the report—what it is for, for whom it is written, what situation it addresses, and so on. The transmittal letter is typically paper-clipped to the front cover of the report. Imagine a report landing on your desk with no such identifying information!

Notice the letterhead: In your report, try creating your own letterhead design. Make up your own company name and address.

Introduction: Notice the short introductory paragraph: it identifies the purpose of the letter and the attached report (notice that the report title is in italics, like a book title).

Body: The middle paragraph of the letter reviews the purpose and contents of the report.

Conclusion: The concluding paragraph has an "action" focus: it encourages the recipients to review the report and to be ready for a follow-up review.

The A Team
Fanshawe College
1460 Oxford St. E.
London, Ontario N5Y 5R6

November 30, 2006

Marina Hermann
Arise Technologies Corporation
321 Shoemaker Street
Kitchener, ON N2E 3B3
Canada

Dear Ms. Hermann:

Attached is the report *Sustainable Building: Wind-Generated Power in a Residential Application* we arranged to write for you on September 21, 2006.

This report provides an introduction to wind energy, comparing the costs, benefits, and drawbacks of wind-generated power in a residential unit located just north of London, Ontario. This technical report determines whether or not the installation of a wind turbine is feasible and realistic for this application when compared to the use of conventional energy sources. The report ends with conclusions and recommended action on the feasibility of installing a wind turbine.

We are pleased to submit our report to you and look forward to hearing your comments on our work early in January 2007.

Sincerely,

Katie Mulder   *Lee Pearsons*   *Kristen Schwartzentruber*

The A Team
Architectural Technology Students
Fanshawe College

Attachment: Report

FIGURE 14-4A

Sample report pages—transmittal letter. Don't forget to use the memo format if the report stays "in house." (This letter is typically clipped to the report front cover.)

Title page elements: The title page can be designed many different ways and contain a wide variety of information. This one has the standard minimal elements: title, recipients, authors, date, and descriptive abstract.

The writer of this report has created a realistic situation and audience for her report: Arise Technologies has contacted the co-op students to prepare a report on wind power in a residential application.

Descriptive summary: Notice that it is very similar to the middle paragraph of the transmittal letter. That's because you cannot expect the transmittal letter to remain attached to this report and because, in any case, you want readers to have multiple opportunities to understand the purpose and contents of the report.

Sustainable Building: Wind-Generated Power in a Residential Application

For
Arise Technology

Prepared by
The A Team:
Katie Mulder
Lee Pearsons
Kristen Swartzentruber,
Co-op Students

November 26, 2006

This report compares the costs, benefits, and drawbacks of wind-generated power for a rural residence. The feasibility of installation costs and long-term costs of a wind turbine when compared to the costs and use of conventional energy sources will be determined along with conclusions and recommended action for this application.

FIGURE 14-4B

Sample report pages—title page with descriptive summary. The first page inside the report, or the first piece of paper you see when you open the report.

Notice the items included in this table of contents (TOC): the title page is excluded, as is the TOC itself. The list of figures, which occurs directly after the TOC, is the first item. In that it is the third page (third actual piece of paper) within the report covers, the list of figures is page iii. The traditional lowercase Roman numerals are used for all pages before the first page of the introduction.

Headings: Notice that all top-level items in this TOC are uppercase. The next-level items use headline-style caps (initial caps on the main words).

If including third-level headings would make the page too crowded, do not show them in the TOC.

The page number for the TOC is traditionally not displayed, even though it is page ii.

TABLE OF CONTENTS

Page

LIST OF FIGURES iii
LIST OF TABLES iii
EXECUTIVE SUMMARY iv

    I. INTRODUCTION 1
      A. Purpose and Scope 1
      B. History and Background of Wind Energy 1
      C. Wind as an Alternate Energy Source 1

    II. ENVIRONMENTAL IMPACT 2
      A. Noise Pollution 2

   III. SITE PARAMETERS 4

   IV. WIND TURBINE SELECTION 6
      A. Components of a Wind Turbine 6
      B. Tower Selection 6
      C. Turbine Selection 7

    V. ENERGY CONSUMPTION AND PRODUCTION 9
      A. Energy Consumed by the Proposed Building 9
      B. Energy Produced by the Turbine 9
      C. Production and Consumption Relationship 10
      D. Management of the Power Supply 10
        1. Storage of energy in batteries 10
        2. Direct feed to local hydro grid 10

   VI. COSTS 11
      A. Product and Installation 11
      B. Maintenance 11
      C. Money Savings 12

  VII. CONCLUSION 13

 VIII. RECOMMENDED ACTION 14

REFERENCES 15

FIGURE 14-4C
Sample report pages—table of contents.

The list of figures and tables shows readers the titles of figures and tables and the page number on which they occur in the report. You don't have to include the complete figure or table title, just the first few words that convey a full, grammatically complete idea of the figure or table contents.

Numbering Figures: You may be used to textbooks and reports numbering figures and tables according to chapter or section numbers. For example, figures in Chapter 3 would be numbered 3-1, 3-2, and so on. For a report under 30 to 40 pages, that's not necessary.

Page Number: Notice that this page is numbered iii. This is a traditional report (and book) design. In traditional report design, all pages before page 1 of the introduction are numbered with lowercase Roman numerals. You may have noticed that no page number appeared on either the title page or the table of contents page, even though they are i and ii, respectively. Again, that's traditional.

LIST OF FIGURES

Figure   Page

1: Energy sector growth rates from 1990 to 1999 2

2: Noise level comparisons 3

3: Average wind speeds for Southwestern Ontario 4

4: Wind turbine photo 5

5: Site photo 5

6: Turbine components 6

7: Tower height vs. wind power percentage 7

LIST OF TABLES

Table   Page

1: Turbine noise measurements 3

2: Energy output 9

3: Cash flow model 12

iii

FIGURE 14-4D
Sample report pages—lists of figures and tables.

The executive summary provides a summary of the important facts, conclusions, and recommendations contained in the body of the report. It is a summary written specifically for executive readers, focusing on their typical needs and interests. (See Chapter 19 for more on executive audiences.)

Summarize: Not only does the executive summary condense this essential information in as few words as possible, it also selects the kinds of information an executive reader wants to see. In this example, the executive would be a planner who needs to know what works, what doesn't work, what the installation and operating costs are, and what the best systems are.

Format: Notice the format of this executive summary: it may use headings, subheadings, and bulleted lists to make the information more scannable. If executive readers want to go directly to particular information, they don't have to struggle; they can find the related heading and go straight to it.

EXECUTIVE SUMMARY

This feasibility study analyzes the cost implications of a wind-generated energy system used to supply a rural home with supplementary power.

Site Parameters

The most common site concerns when installing wind turbines are wind power, lot space, and visual impact. Before purchasing a wind turbine, a minimum of 1 year's worth of data should be recorded on site before installation. This information determines whether or not there will be enough wind to power the turbine. Local weather networks are helpful but commonly take measurements at only 10 m off the ground, so wind ratings tend to be lower than at the height of the actual turbine. It is important to note that wind speed is required to be a minimum of roughly 5 m/s or 18 km/h. The turbine should be spaced roughly 250 to 300 m from neighbouring properties in order to ensure they have a fair amount of privacy.

Wind Turbine Selection

Several important factors must be considered to make the proper selection of a turbine. First, a required output of energy must be determined and a turbine capable of supplying it must be found. Next, the issues of location, turbine costs, maintenance, and lifespan must be considered. For this feasibility study, a 10 kW turbine system from WestTech Energy, Inc. was best suited because of its 25 year minimum lifespan, ease of maintenance, low initial cost, and sufficient energy output.

Energy Production and Consumption

The consumption of energy for the home in question averages out to about 1,800 kW per month. The turbine selected from WestTech was able to generate close to 75% of that amount, which leaves only 25% of the power used to be billed for.

Costs

Initially, the wind turbine system costs $20,000.00. This amount includes everything required to connect the system to a household and begin saving on energy costs. Biannual services, however, are required, along with a blade replacement every 12 years. Proper maintenance of the turbine does add up, but it will pay itself back through efficiency and greater output. The average first year savings equals over $1,600.00, with greater savings in subsequent years. Over the lifespan of 30 years, the turbine system will generate $61,990.00 in total energy savings and after subtracting the initial cost, it will generate a net savings of $41,990.00.

iv

FIGURE 14-4E
Sample report pages—executive summary.

Notice the format of this introduction. It repeats the full title of the report at the top of the page. Below that is the section number and section title.

Introduction: Remember that the primary responsibilities of an introduction are to get readers ready to read the report—to indicate the topic, purpose, situation, and appropriate audience—and to provide an overview of the contents of the report.

Providing background on the topic of the report is only a secondary responsibility for an introduction. For a report and introduction of these lengths, only a few sentences of background (history, conceptions, definitions) are necessary. If you have more background than that, put it in a section of its own following the introduction.

List: Notice the use of the bulleted list for the overview of contents. This format makes this material much more readable. (See Chapter 8 for more on lists.)

Notice that no page number is displayed here, even though it is Arabic number 1. (Again, this is traditional report and book design.) Even though this section does not fill the page, the next section begins on a new page.

Sustainable Building: Wind-Generated Power in a Residential Application

I. INTRODUCTION

The following technical report is a feasibility study analyzing the cost implications of wind-generated energy. Using a modern home in rural Middlesex County, Ontario, and a stand-alone wind turbine system, we addressed several aspects regarding the benefits, drawbacks, costs, and savings. This feasibility study provides the recommended action once the following factors have been examined:

- Environmental Impact
- Site Parameters
- Wind Turbine Selection
- Energy Production and Consumption
- Costs

A. Purpose and Scope

This feasibility study is prepared for Arise Technologies. We target the report to public consumers interested in the use of alternate energy sources to save on energy costs, reduce pollution, and conserve nonrenewable resources. For this study, a 2,500 sq. ft. home on a large lot will be used in tandem with a stand-alone 10 kW Horizontal Axis Wind Turbine (HAWT) energy system made by WestTech Energy, Inc (WestTech, 2004). An explanation of this selection can be found later within this report. An average monthly hydro power consumption of 1,800 kWh will be used, and this turbine will supply the home with the majority of the hydro power required.

B. History and Background of Wind Energy

Dutch-style windmills were first used in the 12th century and by the 1700s had become a major source of power in Europe. The first Canadian windmill was built near the St. Lawrence River in the 1620s and roughly 100 years ago farmers began to use windmills to pump water. Wind energy has been a reliable power source for hundreds of years and recently has become competitive with conventional energy sources.

C. Wind as an Alternate Energy Source

The Canadian Wind Energy Association (CanWEA) believes that wind energy could potentially supply up to 20% of Canada's electricity requirements (CanWEA, 2004). Small wind turbines, the type that we analyze in this report, are most often used by farms, homes, and small businesses for a source of backup electricity or to reduce the total use of utility power and electricity costs. Wind energy is a constant, inexhaustible way not only to conserve nonrenewable resources but, more importantly, to save money.

FIGURE 14-4F
Sample report pages—introduction.

First-level headings: Here's a typical page from the body of a formal report. Notice that the first-level heading ("IV. Wind Turbine Selection") always begins on a new page, no matter where the previous section ended on the preceding page.

Second-level headings: A typical report section is made up of multiple second-level headings such as the one shown here ("Components of a Wind Turbine"). (For more on headings, see Chapter 7.)

Illustrations: When your report contains illustrations, attempt to place them on the pages where they are referenced, as is done here. Don't just stuff them at the end of the section or report. Be sure to use a descriptive figure title—not just "Figure 6." (For more on illustrations, see Chapter 11.)

IV. WIND TURBINE SELECTION

There are many variables that can affect the choice of turbine. Required output, location, rotor size, tower height, and wind speeds all must be considered in order to make an appropriate selection.

A. Components of a Wind Turbine

The basic components of a wind turbine are as shown in Figure 6:

- Rotor consisting of three blades with aerodynamic surfaces. Blades are typically made of fibreglass since it is strong, flexible, and will not interfere with television signals.
- Generator or alternator in the turbine converts wind energy into electricity when the wind blows over the blades and turns the rotor.
- Gearbox matches the rotor speed to the speed of the generator/alternator (usually not required for a 10 kW turbine).
- Enclosure protects the gearbox and generator from rain and snow and other elements.
- Tailvane aligns the turbine with the wind.
- Tower to mount the rotor to can come in three types.

B. Tower Selection

Tower height greatly affects the energy production of a wind turbine. The taller the tower is, the greater the wind speeds are; therefore, a higher output of energy is achieved.

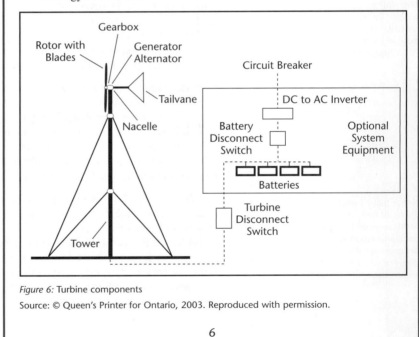

Figure 6: Turbine components

Source: © Queen's Printer for Ontario, 2003. Reproduced with permission.

6

FIGURE 14-4G

Sample report pages—body pages from the body of a formal report.

Another page from the body of this report; in this case, a page that does not begin with a first-level heading.

An acre is generally suggested as ample space to fit a tower, but not required. Three types of towers are available and each occupies a different amount of land:

- Guyed lattice towers are the least expensive and are held upright by wires, therefore requiring the most room.
- Guyed tilt-up towers are similar to lattice towers but the support wires are not permanent, which allows for adjustment of the tower height.
- Self-supporting towers are the most expensive, but take up little space due to the lack of guyed wires.

For the site in study, the ideal support for the turbine is a guyed lattice tower, given that there is enough space on site. This type of tower will also reduce the cost of the overall project.

C. Turbine Selection

There are several aspects to consider when choosing which stand-alone wind turbine to purchase. The 10 kW HAWT system from WestTech was chosen for the following reasons:

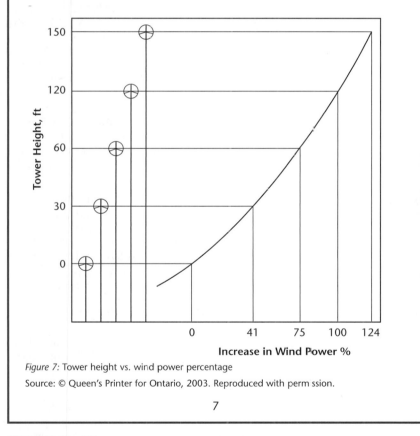

Figure 7: Tower height vs. wind power percentage

Source: © Queen's Printer for Ontario, 2003. Reproduced with permission.

7

FIGURE 14-4H
Sample report pages—body page of a formal report.

Another second-level heading, which is shown in the table of contents.

C. Money Savings

According to the Ontario Ministry of Electricity, the average cost of hydro power is 10.1 cents/kWh. Included in this fee is 5.5 cents/kWh for the electricity commodity and an estimated 4.0 cents/kWh plus GST of regulated costs. When applied to our production and consumption relationship, the turbine will generate a rough savings of just over $1,600.00 in the first year. This reduces the hydro bill by 74%, leaving only $573.00 left to be paid. Hypothetically, the cost of hydro is expected to increase approximately 2% on an annual basis. This will generate even larger savings as time goes on (see Table 3). Total amount of money saved on hydro in 30 years is a significant $61,990.00. Table 3 takes into account the initial cost of $20,000.00 for the purchase and installation of the turbine, which results in a net savings of $41,990.00.

Table 3: Cash flow model

WestTech 10kW HAWT System Cash Flow			
Assumptions (Inputs)		*Results*	
Total Installed Cost ($):	$20,000	**Avg. Monthly Savings on Bill**	
Annual Energy Output (kWh):	15,952	Year 1 ($):	$134
Electricity Cost ($/kWh):	$0.1010	Year 10 ($):	$164
Electricity Inflation Rate (%):	2	Year 20 ($):	$200
O & M Cost ($/kWh):	$0.005	Year 30 ($):	$243
O & M Inflation Rate (%):	3		

Annual Cash Flow Model				
Year	*Net Energy*	*O&M Costs*	*Annual Cash Flow*	*Total Cash Flow*
0			($20,000)	($20,000)
5	$1,744	$0	$1,744	($11,616)
10	$1,925	($104)	$1,821	($2,849)
15	$2,126	($121)	$2,005	$6,802
20	$2,347	($140)	$2,207	$17,427
25	$2,591	($162)	$2,429	$29,121
30	$2,861	($188)	$2,673	$41,990

Conservative assumption of no scrap value after 30 years. Cash flow analysis is pre-tax.

Table design: Notice the design of this table: the title is the first row; the numerical material is centred beneath the column headings and right-aligned; the table title uses bold; the column headings use italics. For more on table design, see Chapter 10.

Source note: Notice the APA-style citation of information that this author has borrowed. See the References page at the end of the report for details on Bergey.

Source: Adapted from Bergey, 2004.

Note that this figure takes into account the initial cost of material and installation, inflation rate on the cost of electricity, and operating and maintenance costs.

12

FIGURE 14-4I
Sample report pages—body pages with a table.

References

APA-style list of references, occurring at the end of a report.

Bergey Wind Power Co. (2004). *Small wind turbines for homes, businesses, and off-grid.* Retrieved October 13, 2004, from http://www.bergey.com

Bisio, Attilio. (1997). *Wind Power. The Wiley encyclopedia of energy and the environment* (Vol. 2, pp. 1523-1534). New York: Wiley Publishers.

Canadian Wind Energy Association. (2004). *Stand-alone wind energy systems: A buyer's guide.* Retrieved Sept. 30, 2004, from http://www.canwea.ca

Gipe, Paul. (1993). *Wind power for home and business: Renewable energy for the 1990s and beyond.* White River Junction, Vermont: Chelsea Green Publishing Company.

McIntyre, Tobi. (2004). *Energy facts and figures. Canadian Geographic.* Retrieved October 13, 2004, from http://www.canadiangeographic.ca/ Magazine/MJ01/solar_facts.asp

Ontario: Ministry of Agriculture and Food. (September 2003). *Electricity generation using small wind turbines at your home or farm.* Retrieved October 13, 2004, from http://www.omafra.gov.on.ca/english/ engineer/facts/03-047.htm

Potts, Michael. (1993). *The independent home: Living well with power from the sun, wind, and water.* Post Mills, Vermont: Chelsea Green Publishing Company.

WestTech Energy, Inc. (2004). *WestTech Energy.* Retrieved October 13, 2004, from http://westtechenergy.ca

15

Notice the inverted-indentation format of items in this list. It enables you to see the author (individual or corporate) and the year of publication more readily.

FIGURE 14-4J

Sample report pages—references list. This lists the information sources from which the author borrowed directly to write this report.

CHAPTER 15

Oral Presentations: Preparation, Visuals, and Delivery

Topics covered in this chapter include

- oral presentations;
- emergency preparedness.

ORAL PRESENTATIONS

For many students, oral presentations represent their worst nightmare. The best antidote to this nightmare is preparation. For some great tips, see these sites:

Corrections Canada
http://www.csc-scc.gc.ca/text/pblct/guideorateur/sec1_e.shtml

The Sideroad
http://www.sideroad.com/Public_Speaking/index.html

EMERGENCY PREPAREDNESS

September 11 made us all aware of the need to be prepared for the worst, and the Asian tsunami of 2005 reminded us that disasters aren't always man-made. See how well Canada is prepared:

Public Safety and Emergency Preparedness Canada
http://www.ocipep.gc.ca

The Canadian Centre for Preparedness
www.ccep.ca

When you have completed this chapter, you will be able to

- plan the parts of an oral presentation;
- organize an oral presentation according to generally accepted guidelines;
- present to small or large groups using appropriate technology.

If you have ever spent any time in the corporate or governmental worlds, you have probably experienced painfully disorganized, time-wasting oral presentations. Just as the working world needs good technical-writing skills, it needs good oral-presentation skills. That's why many technical-writing courses include oral presentations. The classroom becomes the conference room, and the other students in the class become your work colleagues.

This chapter shows you some strategies for getting ready for and delivering oral presentations, for developing visuals, and for using Microsoft PowerPoint.

HOW DO YOU PLAN AN ORAL PRESENTATION?

In corporations and governmental agencies, groups of employees—departments, areas, sections—often get together once a week for announcements, status reports, and other sorts of presentations. These presentations must be pertinent, focused, organized, and succinct.

1. **Find a situation requiring an oral presentation.** Try to find a real or realistic situation in which a specific group of listeners wants to hear your presentation. For example, imagine you have to give a talk to your manufacturing company about emergency preparedness.

   If you can't find a situation, try these ideas:

   - *Start with a report type.* Practically any of the types of technical documents in Part I can be developed for oral presentation, only in a shorter, less detail-dense form. For example, a progress report can work well as an in-person presentation. In fact, status reports, a near-cousin of the progress report, are often presented orally rather than in writing.
   - *Use an existing report.* You can rework a technical document you've already written. If you had written a technical background report on

the use of wind energy in residential areas, you could present the highlights of that report orally.

▪ *Do some brainstorming.* And, of course, you can use the project-finding ideas presented at **http://www.powertools/nelson.com**. Find a topic that is of interest to you, and then work "backward" to a real or realistic workplace situation.

For a sample oral-report project, assume we start with a topic: in this case, emergency preparedness. Since the September 11, 2001, attack on New York, the London and Madrid attacks, not to mention the various natural disasters that have occurred worldwide, being prepared to pick up after a disaster has become a priority for many companies.

2. **Define an audience and a purpose.** In a technical-writing course, the audience is obviously your instructor and the people in your class. If possible, invent a realistic audience and situation. At the beginning of your oral presentation, describe that audience and that situation to the class, and ask people to pretend that they are those listeners in that situation. For more about audiences, see Chapter 17.

For this oral presentation, you will have the immediate attention of the class, who will have a broad understanding of the problems a company might encounter, but no idea of the breadth of the problems. According to one document, "up to 86% of small-/medium-sized businesses fail within 3 years of a major incident" if they don't have a tested plan in place. You could scare the class with some possible scenarios, and then tell them what kinds of things they would have to do to be prepared for a major incident.

3. **Define a purpose.** Technical presentations in any medium have informative, instructional, recommendational, evaluative, or persuasive purposes. Are you going to show people how to perform a procedure, persuade them to approve a project, explain the status of an ongoing project, recommend one product over others, discuss a new technology, or argue for the feasibility and necessity of a plan or program?

For this sample oral presentation, imagine that you want to focus on one particular type of incident—a natural disaster. What kinds of things could happen in your area? If you live on the West coast, possibly a tidal wave or an earthquake. In central Canada, a tornado or flooding is more likely. Many parts of Canada have had ice storms that bring down hydro wires and stop traffic movements. Imagine that you work for a medium-sized recreational vehicle manufacturer that gets its parts from the United States on a just-in-time basis. All your accounting and other records are on your computer system on site at the plant, except for those that the accountant takes home with him every night on a backup tape. The plant is next to a train line and would be vulnerable in the event of a derailment caused by weather or any other reason. Looking at all these possibilities, you outline a plan for the company.

4. **Research the topic.** Of course, it would be easy to come up with all kinds of fun things a company could do. You've seen disaster movies. However, now is the time to get serious and do some research. Why do companies fail? What do they need to do? How are you going to find out?

> Fortunately for you, a conference on emergency preparedness recently took place locally and you are able to find the name of the company that ran it. The Canadian Centre for Emergency Preparedness (**www.ccep.ca**) has a full page of links to sites on how small businesses should prepare for a natural or other kind of disaster. You'll also want to find the most attention-grabbing information (as well as accompanying pictures) on recent natural disasters. The more your audience can identify with a disaster, the more interested they will be. However, they will expect you to deliver suggestions for readiness, and your research in this area should be thorough and focused.

5. **Find the infrastructure.** Despite the differences between oral and written presentations, the infrastructure, or organizational pattern, should be the same. For example, to show listeners how to perform a

Infrastructure	Description
Description	Part-by-part or characteristic-by-characteristic discussion of objects, mechanisms, places, organisms, even people. (See Chapter 1.)
Process	Step-by-step, event-by-event discussion of natural, mechanical, or human events, including historical events. (See Chapter 2.)
Causes and effects (problem–solution)	Cause-by-cause or effect-by-effect discussion of a situation, existing or potential. (See Chapter 3.)
Comparison	Point-by-point comparison of two or more products, plans, programs, places, even people, with a goal of recommending one. (See Chapter 4.)
Definition	Selection of infrastructures best amplifying a potentially unfamiliar term. (See Chapter 5.)
Classification	Category-by-category discussion of a topic, using definition to discuss each category. Also, the attempt to place a topic into one of several categories (to categorize the topic)—an effort that relies on comparison. (See Chapter 5.)
Persuasion	An effort to persuade readers to adopt a certain point of view or to take a certain action. Relies on logical arguments, sometimes personal and emotional appeals, as well as rebuttals and concessions. (See Chapter 6.)

procedure, use the step-by-step process pattern. To present recommendations, use the point-by-point comparative pattern. The following table reviews the infrastructures presented in Part I.

In this presentation, start with examples of several possible disasters. Use problems that have occurred within a radius of 250 kilometres or so to bring home the reality of your topic. The presentation will be primarily informative, with secondary persuasive and instructional purposes. On the one hand, you will agree with your audience that the chances of a tornado throwing a train onto the plant are unlikely; on the other hand, you will want them to think about what they stand to lose if something does happen. Could they operate for more than a day without the information on their computers?

6. **Plan and develop the main content.** With the infrastructure identified, it's easier to define the content of the main sections. For example, to demonstrate a procedure, your main sections will be explanations of procedural steps. However, listeners may need more than just the steps. They may need background—for example, a definition of the procedure, its importance, skills needed, equipment needed, or conceptual background. That's how you work "backward" to the introduction, identifying additional main content that listeners may need to be able to understand the main sections.

In this oral presentation you will probably have the following sections: (1) an introduction; (2) a main section on likely disaster scenarios; (3) a main section on possible problems that will arise from a disaster; (4) a main section on what a company can do to prepare for a disaster; and (5) a conclusion.

7. **Plan and prepare the visuals.** Whenever possible, use graphics in your oral presentations. Ideally, you can display graphics on an overhead projector, but you can also show physical objects, use flipcharts, or provide handouts. If you want to get fancy, prepare a series of "slides" using presentation software such as Microsoft PowerPoint. Strategies for visuals in oral presentations are discussed later in this chapter.

Some visuals are obvious for this presentation: shots of the Quebec ice storm, floods in Manitoba, and the aftermath of a tornado. These kinds of images will stir the emotions of your audience. Of course, you will want to show the images as part of a PowerPoint presentation, keeping in mind that the best presentations are graphic-based rather than text-based. If, for example, you are talking about how to prepare in case of theft of all your office computers, a background image of thieves removing the computers (use your friends to pose for a digital photo!) will drive home the points you make in the text about the importance of backing up your files and having loss-of-business insurance.

8. **Plan the introduction.** The introduction to an oral presentation is almost as important as the rest of the presentation put together. Your listeners need to know the following (but not necessarily in this order):

   - who you are, whom you represent;
   - what the purpose of your presentation is (avoid clumsy mechanical openers like "The topic of my speech is …");
   - what you are going to cover;
   - some brief, essential background to enable people to get interested and to understand the rest of your presentation (you may want to give the background in the form of a scenario).

   In the introduction, start by explaining who you are—establish your credibility. Think of yourself as an expert brought in to advise a company on changes it needs to make and describe yourself that way. Don't assume that everyone knows who you are when you introduce yourself. Once you have made the introduction, state the purpose of the presentation clearly. You will cover possible disaster scenarios, results of those disasters, and inform your audience what to do to prepare for a major disaster.

9. **Plan the conclusion.** The wrap-up section can summarize, conclude, provide some final thought, or do some combination of these. Avoid mechanical summaries; phrases like "In this presentation, we have seen that …" can be deadly.

   - *Summary:* For complex oral presentations, a summary can be useful: it refocuses listeners on the main points you've covered.
   - *Conclusion:* A conclusion is a logical thing: if you presented lots of conflicting interpretations, a conclusion states the right interpretation.
   - *Final thoughts:* Another way of wrapping up is to consider one final topic, but in a general way, not obligating yourself to go into details.
   - You can also combine these methods of concluding an oral presentation.

   The conclusion for this presentation will be a summary of what needs to be done. What needs to be covered in a disaster preparedness plan? Backup procedures put in place; lists of contacts, including customers and insurance agents, prepared; essential operations and functions identified; vital records stored safely; and, of course, more immediate needs such as lists of nearby hospitals and evacuation procedures arranged.

10. **Rehearse!** Unless you have lots of oral-presentation experience, do some rehearsal. Don't assume you'll know what to say when you are standing in front of everybody. Here are some ideas for rehearsing your presentation:

    - *Write a script.* One of the best ways to get ready for an oral presentation is to draft a script. It forces you to make sure of your facts and get the words and timing right. As you practise reading, look for areas to cut, problems to fix, discussion to make clearer, and topics to expand on. During your presentation, keep the script handy, but don't read from it verbatim. Instead, deliver your presentation so that it feels like an organized conversation to your listeners.

■ *Create an outline.* Outlines are another method some presenters use to stay organized during an oral presentation. Outlines are useful if you've rehearsed your script so much you don't need the script any longer.

■ *Cue cards.* Cue cards are one other familiar method. They are particularly useful if you have specific details that you might forget—for example, statistical information that you just can't memorize. Don't overuse cue cards, however. Someone shuffling and reading through a pile of cue cards can appear nervous and unprepared.

In any case, don't assume the words will just come to you, smoothly and effortlessly, when you get in front of the group. We see so many glib, smooth performers on TV that it's easy to fall under the notion that we can be just like them. Oral-presentation day is a tough way to find out that's not the case!

HOW DO YOU PREPARE VISUALS FOR AN ORAL PRESENTATION?

Plan to use visuals in your oral presentation, unless it's a very brief, very informal one. Visuals give listeners another way of absorbing information. Some listeners may process detailed information better visually than aurally (by ear).

Media for Oral-Report Visuals

You have a lot of choices for visuals, but some, such as the following, take a lot of work to prepare and rely on specialized equipment:

■ **Presentation software.** Presentation software is the generic name for applications like Microsoft PowerPoint and Lotus Freelance Graphics. If you've watched a speaker fumble with a pile of transparencies, you know all too well what's great about using presentation software. PowerPoint is discussed later.

■ **Flip charts.** If an overhead projector is not available, consider drawing your visuals on flip-chart pages. Use good wide-tip markers and a straight edge to make your flip-chart pages look neat and professional.

■ **Objects.** Some oral presentations necessitate having actual objects on hand. Do you dare demonstrate how to do an oil change in the classroom? If so, bring a can of oil, an oil filter, and an oil wrench. Do you dare demonstrate how to fillet a fish? If so, bring the fish, a pan, fillet knives, and some paper towels! Or else act out the tasks involving these objects with props or imaginary objects—and leave your fish at home.

■ **Handouts.** Some presenters hand out brochures, illustrations, and other such materials for listeners to look at during the presentation. However,

Practical Ethics: Biased or Slanted Graphics

Several years ago a new manager was hired to turn around the poor performance of a satellite branch of the company you work for. You have been asked to do a financial analysis to help your boss determine whether the branch manager has adequately increased sales. Your analysis shows a series of ups and downs, but overall, a significant increase. As you're writing your report, you decide to use graphs to show the growth in sales.

Look at the line graphs in Figure 15-1. Which would you use, graph A or B? Why? Is one more accurate than the other? Alternately, you could use a three-dimensional bar graph. Which would you choose in Figure 15-1, C or D? What's the difference between the two?

A key to creating graphs is finding a balance between too much detail and not enough. The problem with graph B is that it doesn't present an accurate picture of the overall climb in sales. Quarterly figures, especially in the short term, would appear to contradict graph B because the actual numbers would show a series of downturns that the graph leaves out.

Graph D is inaccurate because the 2000 column is doubled in width as well as height. To the eye, this implies that the sales were higher than they actually were, especially because all of the other columns have a smaller width. You may want to emphasize the amazing growth, but you shouldn't overemphasize it by playing with a graph's visual scale.

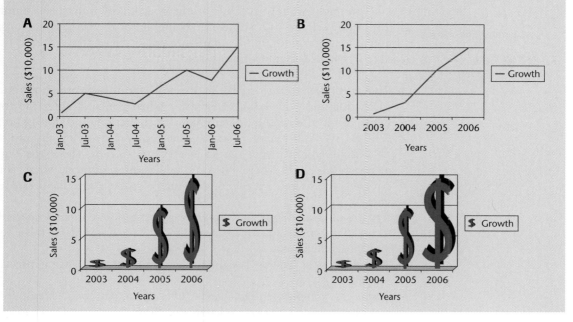

FIGURE 15-1

Graphs. Which graph(s) accurately depicts growth in sales?

handouts take away listeners' focus from you. Still, an occasional handout can be a nice change of pace. As with any visual, be sure to discuss your handouts, explain them, and walk your listeners through their most important details.

- **Video clips.** If your presentation requires portrayal of action and movement, you may need video clips. Arrange for the equipment, and make sure that it is working and that you know how to operate it. Don't let the video take over your presentation though. Listeners should spend more time listening to you than viewing the video. Play a portion of the video, pause it, discuss that portion, introduce the next portion, and so on. That way, you are clearly in charge—not the video machine. If you are comfortable with the technology, consider embedding video clips in a PowerPoint presentation.

Content for Oral-Report Visuals

To plan for graphics in an oral presentation, be sure of what's available in the room where you'll present your report. Ideally, your classroom will have a vdp (video data projector), allowing you to project images from a computer monitor to a screen. Don't plan to write your display material on a blackboard—at least, not the main parts of it. For whatever you think you might want to scribble on the board, type it up, print it out, or put it in PowerPoint. If a vdp is not available for the classroom, consider drawing your graphics on flip-chart–size paper. Here are some additional ideas for visuals for your oral presentations:

- *Title page.* Prepare a title page with details about your presentation such as its title and your name. Display it when you first enter the room, while you are setting up, during your introduction, and during breaks.
- *Outline.* Give listeners a strong sense of an overview by showing an outline. As you move from section to section, show the outline again, reinforcing where you are in the presentation, what you've covered, and what's left. An outline may also save you, the presenter, if you get lost.
- *Key terms and definitions.* If your presentation contains specialized terms that you spend some time defining, have a visual for those terms and their definitions.
- *Actual physical objects.* See the discussion of this idea in the preceding section.
- *Drawings, diagrams, flow charts, photos, animations, videos.* If you can't bring in the objects you refer to, show diagrams. Don't forget to create and show flow charts relating to your presentation.
- *Tables: statistical detail, summaries.* Listeners can't absorb as much statistical detail through oral presentation as through print. For even simple statistics, display tables during your presentation. Put verbal summaries in tables as well: just list the key words and phrases associated with each topic.
- *Main conclusions.* A good way to summarize certain types of oral presentations is to review the main conclusions. For example, if you've compared several products, display a list of the main conclusions concerning which products were best in which categories.

■ *Information sources*. In a "real" situation, your listeners would have attended your presentation out of a real need for your information or curiosity about your topic, so provide a listing of other sources of information about your topic, particularly those you used to prepare your presentation.

HOW DO YOU USE PRESENTATION SOFTWARE?

With the rise of presentation software like Microsoft PowerPoint, oral presenters have a powerful tool. You show a series of computer screens called *slides* that display words and graphics related to your presentation. Also, presentation software enables you to integrate photographic slides, video clips, and audio into one delivery medium. You don't have to roll in a fleet of overhead projectors, video players, and slide projectors and hope that they all work that particular day. And using design templates, creating electronic presentations is surprisingly easy.

1. To begin developing a PowerPoint presentation, click the icon on your desktop, or select **Start→All Programs→Microsoft Office→PowerPoint**.
2. Click on the first slide in the left-hand panel.
3. Hit the Enter key several times to create new slides.

You now have everything you need to create a PowerPoint presentation on your screen (see Figure 15-2). Sort the slides by clicking on any slide in the left panel and dragging and dropping. Select a different layout for any one slide using the slide layout panel on the right (this panel is known as the Task Pane). Use the centre panel to add text and graphics to your slides (the slide showing in the centre panel corresponds with the slide selected—outlined in blue—in the left panel).

4. To add a design template, click the arrow next to the words "Slide Layout" and select **Slide Design** from the drop-down list. The design templates will then be available in the right panel. Click on one of the designs to change all your slides.
5. When you have completed the slide show, hit F5 to run it.

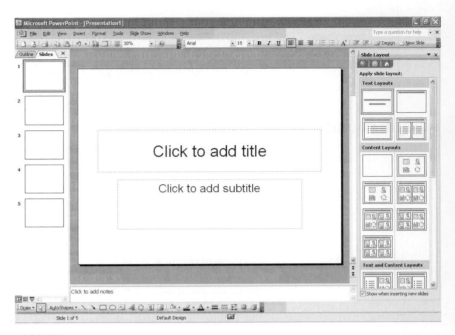

FIGURE 15-2
Editing View. This view lets you do almost anything you want in PowerPoint.

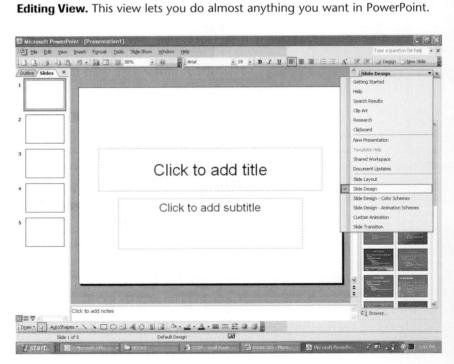

FIGURE 15-3
Task Pane. The task pane on the right is now showing the Slide Design choices.

HOW DO YOU DELIVER AN ORAL PRESENTATION?

The best way to deliver an oral presentation is to be well prepared. If you know your material and have rehearsed it, you'll do well no matter how nervous you are. Your first concerns should be meeting the needs of your audience and accomplishing your purpose. Unless you are working for the wrong organization, substance ought to come first—way before showmanship. Here are some suggestions, though, for improving your delivery:

■ *Control those nervous verbal mannerisms such as "uh," "you know," and "okay?"* If you practise from a script, develop an awareness of which of these annoying mannerisms you use and how often you use them. Practise just saying nothing instead.

■ *Get in control of body language, eye contact, and gestures.* Although situations vary, normally you'll want to maintain a relaxed, confident, open demeanour during an oral presentation. Use gestures, move around, and perhaps even interject humour. But don't be so relaxed that you slouch over the lectern. Avoid the extremes of frenetic movement, on the one hand, and stonelike immobility, on the other. If your hands move everywhere when you speak, keep that under control, but don't get out the handcuffs. Occasional gestures are good; your listeners shouldn't think you are a statue.

■ *Speak slowly.* It's just not as easy to hear an oral presentation as it is a face-to-face conversation. Also, because oral presentations don't permit the same give-and-take that conversation does, give listeners more time to get the gist of what you are saying. And finally, speak more slowly to counteract our natural tendency to speak more rapidly when we get excited or nervous.

■ *Speak up.* Whether listeners will be able to hear you depends a great deal on the room in which you give your oral presentation. In some rooms, the acoustics are so good that you can practically whisper and still be understood. But don't count on it. To find out, start your presentation with the familiar "Can everybody hear me all right?" Be ready to speak up.

■ *Don't be reluctant to summarize or repeat.* Effective oral presentations rely on more repetition than do written ones. You just can't expect to have your listeners' complete attention at every moment. You can't expect listeners to pop up and say, "Hey, will you repeat that?" The best kind of repetition in an oral presentation is not exact word-for-word repetition, but summaries that use slightly different words and connect to the preceding or upcoming topic. This kind of summarizing and linking creates a cumulative effect that will give listeners a sense of increasing understanding.

■ *Use plenty of verbal headings.* This book emphasizes how important headings are to written technical documents. Oral presentations need something analogous to headings—some indication to listeners that you're finishing up one topic and moving on to another. See examples of verbal headings in the oral report at the end of this chapter.

- *Begin with a strong introduction.* As mentioned earlier in this chapter, a strong introduction is essential for a good oral presentation.
- *Hammer home your main points.* A common guideline for oral presentations is that the typical 7- to 15-minute presentation can't support more than three or four main points. That can mean three or four main subtopics, three or four main conclusions leading to a general conclusion, or three or four main sections (between the introduction and conclusion).
- *Emphasize the transitions.* As discussed in the section on transitions at **http://www.powertools.nelson.com**, transitions show people how segments of information are connected. We use weak transitions without thinking, but strong transitions take some thought and practice. Look at the transitions in the example at the end of this chapter. While readers can go back and reread a document, they can't go back and "re-hear" your presentation. That's why strong transitions are extremely important in oral presentations.
- *Walk listeners through your visuals.* Take time to show listeners the important details of your visuals. Don't just throw visuals out there, and never refer to them; introduce them, and explain their main points. And position yourself next to the screen so that people can see you—don't hide in the dark!
- *Only glance at a script—avoid reading it word for word.* Avoid monotone, head-down, line-by-line reading from a script. (When you look up, no one will be listening—some may even be asleep.) Instead, practise reading your script until you can look away from it without getting lost. During your presentation, know your script so well that you need only glance at it occasionally.
- *Don't get locked in to your script, outline, or plan.* Whichever method you use, be prepared to slow down when people don't seem to be getting it, speed up when they are looking bored, digress or add detail when they seem particularly interested, and be prepared to scrap segments of your presentation if people are clearly not interested or if you are running out of time.
- *Have a backup plan.* If you are using PowerPoint slides or accessing the Web, make sure you have an idea of what to do in the case of a catastrophe. Have handouts of your slides, for example. Don't wait too long to go to plan B.

HOW DO YOU EVALUATE ORAL PRESENTATIONS?

You can learn almost as much by listening to and evaluating oral presentations as you can by preparing and delivering them. If you deliver your presentation to the rest of your technical-writing class, your instructor may ask everyone to evaluate each presentation using a standard form, like the one shown in Figure 15-4.

ORAL PRESENTATION EVALUATION

Using a 1 to 5 scale (with 5 being the highest), evaluate the presenter in two ways: yes/no and a numeric rating. For example, if the presenter used verbal headings, answer yes; but if they were not particularly effective, rate the verbal headings 1 or 2.

Date:			
Start time:	**End time:**		**Total:**
Presenter's name:			
Presenter's topic:			

Evaluative category	Yes/No	Rating
Began with an explanation of audience, situation, topic (before starting the actual presentation)?		
Began the actual presentation with an introduction?		
Introduction indicated topic?		
Introduction indicated purpose?		
Introduction gave overview?		
Introduction attempted to motivate, interest?		
Used one or more visuals?		
Visuals were effective?		
Referred to, explained visuals?		
Used verbal headings?		
Presentation was organized?		
Explained technical information clearly?		
Speaking style/delivery was effective?		
Held my attention?		
Ended with a real conclusion?		
Presentation was the expected length?		
Presentation was adequate (overall rating)?		

Comments:

FIGURE 15-4

Oral-presentation evaluation form. This form enables you to answer yes or no, rate the category, or both.

WORKSHOP: ORAL PRESENTATIONS

Here are some additional ideas for practising the concepts, tools, and strategies in this chapter:

1. *Evaluate a live oral report.* Try to find city-council, school-board, or regulatory-commission meetings on television, and evaluate one of the presentations, which are usually brief. Use the evaluation form shown in Figure 15-4.

2. *Prepare an oral presentation of a written report.* Select a report you have written or one of the reports in this book, and plan how you'd rework it for oral presentation. Identify the audience and situation in which this oral presentation of the written report would realistically take place. Take notes on why you couldn't just read it verbatim to a group of listeners.

3. For the next three workshop items, choose from this list of oral-report projects (or use your own!):

Presentation to city council requesting more softball parks

Presentation to PTA concerning children's safety at school

Presentation to senior citizens concerning municipal recycling

Presentation to city gardening club concerning advantages of organic pest control methods

Presentation to parents concerning an initiative for all students to have notebook computers at school

Presentation to management requesting that employees be allowed to use the World Wide Web

   a. *Audiences and situations for oral reports.* Take a look at the preceding list of oral-report projects, pick one, and write descriptions of one or more audiences and situations for that project.
   b. *Infrastructures for oral reports.* Return to the list of oral-report projects, pick one, and identify the infrastructure you'd use for that report.
   c. *Visuals for oral reports.* Return to the list of oral-report projects, and make a list of the visuals you might use in it.

PART IV

Tools for Project Development

CHAPTER 16

Reviewing and Revising

Topics covered in this chapter include

■ vehicle maintenance.

VEHICLE MAINTENANCE
Diesel Truck Resource
http://www.dieseltruckresource.com/dev/index.php

The Diesel Stop
http://www.thedieselstop.com/

General Motors Light-Truck Diesel Engines
http://www.62-65-dieselpage.com/

Dodge Diesels
http://www.dieselram.com

GM-Diesel.com
http://www.gm-diesel.com

Turbo Direct Injection Diesel Engines
www.tdiclub.com

When you have completed this chapter, you will be able to

■ review and revise your documents for audience, purpose, and content;
■ review and revise your documents for design and format;
■ review and revise your documents for style, grammar, and mechanics.

Once you've written a rough draft, it's time to do some reviewing and revising. When you "review" a document, you study it to see if it meets its requirements—whether it works for the intended audience and purpose. When you "revise" a document, you make improvements that will enable it to meet those requirements, making it work for its intended audience and purpose.

Revising includes much more than fixing spelling errors and grammar mistakes. Most important is making sure the document meets the needs of its intended readers. Among other things, that includes checking content, organization, transitions, format, and other "high-level" issues.

This chapter brings together the various concepts, strategies, and tools discussed throughout this book. It puts them into a unified overall strategy you can use when you are reviewing other people's written work as well as when you are reviewing and revising your own.

To make this process less complex, divide your reviewing and revising into three stages: (1) address the high-level issues such as audience, purpose, content, organization, and transitions; (2) address format issues such as headings, lists, notices, highlighting, tables, and graphics; and (3) edit for technical style, sentence style, grammar, usage, and punctuation.

FIRST PASS: AUDIENCE, PURPOSE, CONTENT

Read through your rough draft, looking for problems involving audience, purpose, situation, content, organization, and transitions.

1. **Review your draft from the point of view of its intended readers, their situations, and their purposes.** See Chapter 17 for strategies for audience review.

    If readers are reading this document for a specific purpose, will they be satisfied?

    In what ways might readers be frustrated by this document?

    How might this document not meet their needs?

    Does this document meet the needs of the situation in which it is required?

2. **Review your rough draft in terms of its content.** Check to see if you've provided too little information, too much information, information at the wrong level, or useless information. Use the brainstorming strategies provided in the section on content at **http://www.powertools. nelson.com** to help you identify additional content that might be needed. As you read a rough draft in this first pass, ask yourself questions like the following:

Do my readers really need this information?

Will readers understand this material? Is it way over their heads?

Is this material above, below, or just right for their level of understanding?

Is there anything left out—any important information vital to readers' understanding?

Are the sources of borrowed information indicated properly?

3. **Review your rough draft in terms of organization.** Consider the organization of the content of your draft—specifically, the sequencing of the major sections, the subsections, the paragraphs, and even sentences within individual paragraphs. See the section on organization at **http://www.powertools.nelson.com** for strategies for checking organization. As you review, ask yourself questions like the following:

Does the sequence of the main sections make sense?

Does the sequencing of segments within each main section make sense?

Are any paragraphs out of sequence within subsections?

Can you find any individual sentences out of sequence within paragraphs?

4. **Review your rough draft for transitions.** Do the same kind of phased review of transitions in your draft. Check transitions between major sections, between subsections, between paragraphs, and even within major portions of paragraphs. See **http://www.powertools.nelson.com** for strategies to use in checking transitions. As you review, ask yourself questions like the following:

Are there transition techniques at the beginning of each major section that indicate how it is related to the preceding?

Are transition sentences, complete with review and preview words as well as transition signals, used to link major sections and subsections?

Do transitions link one paragraph to the next, or groups of paragraphs to the next?

Are strong transitions—review words and preview words—used to link groups of related sentences to the following?

Years after Shakespeare first penned his plays, people are still producing and going to see his dramas and comedies. Classics by Austen and Tolstoy are still being read. Shakespeare's bawdy humour still makes us laugh and we still fall in love and make tragic decisions. These are universal themes that can be found in the oldest and the most modern narratives.

While you might not write about such universal themes as love in technical projects, you can still increase your effectiveness by writing universally. This means being careful not to alienate readers by using language that makes them, in all their diversity, feel excluded.

In the past, "man" and "mankind" were frequently used to mean "all humans." The pronoun "he" was used similarly—not necessarily to mean a male person, but just a person in general. Today, however, it has been recognized that the use of these words has the potential to exclude and offend a percentage of your audience; in fact, careless use of these words is considered sexist. Communication is difficult enough without using words that turn off your listeners or readers.

The solutions are relatively easy. Just replace these nouns and pronouns with more universal ones. For instance:

1. **Problematic:** Man first encountered gorillas …
This excludes women. Don't give any of your readers reason to tune you out!
    Solution: Humans first encountered gorillas …

2. **Problematic:** When a surgeon washes his hands before surgery …
This implies that all doctors are male, which simply isn't true. Be careful not to stereotype any profession by gender.
    Solution A: When a surgeon washes his or her hands before surgery …
Constantly using "he or she" can be awkward. When appropriate, use plural nouns to eliminate the problem altogether:
    Solution B: When surgeons wash their hands before surgery …
    Solution C: When individual surgeons wash their hands …

3. **Problematic:** Chairman, deliveryman, postman, etc.
Once again, these words are not universal. Find ways around this.
    Solution: Chairperson, delivery person, postal service worker, etc.

You may not feel like Tolstoy when you're working on a report or memo, but you can at least help your readers feel universally included.

SECOND PASS: DESIGN AND FORMAT

After reviewing high-level issues, consider design and format.

1. **Review the rough draft in terms of the document type and use.** Chapter 14 on format and the chapters of Part I provide strategies for deciding whether to use a formal report, business letter, or memo design.

   Are you using the right type of document in terms of content and purpose—background report, instructions, recommendation report, proposal, research report, or progress report?

   Are the right components included in the document according to its type?

Are you using the right document format—memo report, business letter report, or formal report (with cover memo or letter)?

Have you used the right binding on this report—paper clip, spiral, or ring binder?

2. **Review the headings in your rough draft.** A good way to review the high-level organization of a rough draft is to review the headings in that draft. Chapter 7 provides strategies for designing and formatting headings. As you review, ask yourself questions like the following:

Are these headings explanatory and descriptive enough of the sections they introduce?

Are the headings designed to indicate levels?

Are there too few headings? Too many?

Are there lone headings or stacked headings?

Are certain headings not parallel in phrasing?

Are headings used incorrectly as figure or table titles or as lead-ins to lists?

3. **Review your rough draft for its use of lists.** Chapter 8 presents strategies for designing various types of lists, which can increase the readability of a draft. As you review your rough draft for lists, ask yourself these questions:

Is there text you can reformat as in-sentence, bulleted, or numbered lists?

Are numbered lists used for list items in a required order?

For in-sentence lists, are list numbers or letters enclosed by both parentheses?

Are all lists introduced by a lead-in and punctuated correctly?

Are list items parallel in phrasing?

Do you capitalize and punctuate list items consistently and according to some standard, such as those presented in this book?

4. **Review your rough draft for its use of tables, graphs, and charts.** Chapter 10 presents guidelines and strategies for tables, graphs, and charts. As you review your rough draft, consider these related questions:

Can you find text that can be presented more effectively as tables?

Are your tables designed for vertical comparison?

Are table titles centred at the top of tables?

Are measurement types (in., mm, $) kept in row or column headings when possible?

Are text columns left aligned with their headings?

Are "skinny" columns centred and numeric columns right or decimal aligned?

Is the source of information borrowed to create tables cited properly?

Are tables placed just after the point in the text where they are relevant?

Are there cross-references to tables, which discuss their main significance?

Could text or tables be presented more effectively as graphs or charts?

Do you include appropriate titles, axis labels, and legends in your graphs and charts?

5. **Review your rough draft for its use of graphics.** Technical documents typically include illustrations, drawings, diagrams, flow charts, and so on. Review Chapter 11 for guidelines and strategies for the creation and use of graphics. When you review a rough draft, ask yourself these questions:

Are there areas where graphics are needed but not supplied?

Are the graphics in the draft right for the needs and level of the audience?

Are graphics placed near the point in the text where they are relevant?

Do cross-references briefly explain the important aspects of the graphics?

Are numbered, explanatory titles used for graphics as necessary?

Are the sources of any borrowed graphics indicated?

6. **Review your rough draft for its use of highlighting.** Chapter 7 covers guidelines and strategies for bold, italics, alternate fonts and colour, and different type sizes. As you review your draft, ask questions like the following:

Is your use of bold and italics consistent and in keeping with a standard?

Do you avoid using capital letters and quotation marks for emphasis?

Do you limit the document to one alternate font (for example, Arial for headings, Times New Roman for body text, and Courier New for the alternate font)?

Except for headings, do you keep type size no larger than that for body text?

THIRD PASS: STYLE, GRAMMAR, MECHANICS

Once you've revised a rough draft for high-level issues and for design and format, you're ready to check for style, grammar, mechanics, and spelling problems.

1. **Review your rough draft for sentence problems.** Look for classic wordiness problems such as bad passive voice, weak *be* verbs, and redundant phrasing as covered at **http://www.powertools.nelson.com**. Don't forget—as a technical writer, you are not being paid by the pound! Specifically, ask yourself questions like these:

Can you find passive-voice sentences that would be clearer, more direct, and more succinct using active voice?

Can you find complicated noun stacks that could be "unstacked," making your document more immediately understandable?

Can you find unnecessary use of expletives (any variation of *there is* or *it is*)?

Can you find redundant phrasing that could be cut?

2. **Review your rough draft for technical-style problems.** Technical documents typically contain vexing problems involving abbreviations, acronyms, numbers, hyphens, symbols, and the like. Use Appendix A to resolve them. As you review, ask yourself questions like these:

Do you use digits for numbers as opposed to words for numbers consistently and according to a standard?

Do you use symbols in your document consistently and according to a standard, defining the potentially unfamiliar ones on first use?

Do you establish the meaning of acronyms and unfamiliar abbreviations on first use?

3. **Review your draft for grammar, usage, punctuation, and spelling problems.** Don't forget to review for the old favourites—fragments, run-ons, comma splices, agreement errors, parallelism problems, sexist language, and the like. Use Appendix C for help in these areas.

Can you find any comma splices or fragments in your rough draft?

Can you find verbs or pronouns not in agreement with their counterparts?

Can you find series items (in headings, lists, or sentences) that are not parallel in phrasing?

Can you find introductory elements, compound sentences, or series "and" elements not punctuated with a comma?

Do you use hyphens for potentially confusing compound modifiers?

Do you avoid using quotation marks for emphasis?

Do you avoid Latin abbreviations such as *e.g., i.e.,* and *etc.*?

Have you run a spell-check on your document?

Can you spot any problems with similar-sounding words, such as *affect/effect, principle/principal, to/too/two,* or *its/it's*?

4. **Check the readability statistics on your document.** Most word-processing software includes readability statistics. Readability formulas use syllables per word, words per sentence, and vocabulary ratings to calculate grade level. Although there is much skepticism about these formulas, some organizations use them, requiring a seventh- or eighth-grade reading level. In Microsoft Word, to see readability statistics on your draft, open it, choose **Tools→Options→Spelling & Grammar**. Check **Check grammar with spelling** and **Show readability statistics**, click **OK**, and choose **Tools→Spelling and Grammar**.

WORKSHOP: REVIEWING AND REVISING

Here are some exercises to give you some practice reviewing and revising. For additional practice, see **http://www.powertools.nelson.com**.

1. *First-pass reviewing.* Use the strategies discussed in this chapter to review for audience, purpose, content, organization, and transitions in the excerpt at the end of this section.

2. *Second-pass reviewing.* Use the strategies discussed in this chapter to review for design and format in the same excerpt.

3. *Third-pass reviewing.* Use the strategies discussed in this chapter to review for style, grammar, and mechanics in the same excerpt at the end of this section.

4. *Revision.* Now, use your review notes to revise the excerpt.

AN INSTRUCTION TO REVIEW AND REVISE

Student Matthew Shaw created this instruction, and kindly allowed us to introduce the errors

In reviewing this document, use the three passes outlined in Chapter 16.

HOW TO CHANGE THE OIL ON A CUMMINS DIESEL

The Cummins Diesel is a motor like no other. It is one of the most powerful diesel motors available for your truck. Like other motors, it requires regular maintenance to keep it performing at its best. Dodge recommends that you change your oil every 5000 km. or every 3 months. This is a simple task, and if you have an hour or two you can save a trip to the garage. You can complete this by following these three simple steps: (1) setting up your vehicle, (2) draining the oil and changing the filter, (3) adding fresh oil.

Equipment and Supplies

To get started changing your oil you will need the following:

- 8L of Dodge approved 20w40 diesel grade motor oil
- Cummins compatible premium oil filter
- Oil filter strap wrench
- Socket set
- degreasing agent
- A few rags
- A plastic bag
- floor jack and axle stands (optional)
- Waist pail

What you will need

Caution: WHEN SELECTING MOTOR OIL AND OIL FILTERS MAKE SURE YOU CONSULT YOUR TRUCKS MANUAL TO BE SURE YOU SELECT THE PROPER GRADE OF MOTOR OIL. THIS WILL ENSURE THAT YOU DO NOT VOID YOUR VEHICLES WARRANTY.

Setting Up Your Vehicle

Before you begin changing your oil you should park you vehicle in a cool dry place on a level surface. If your vehicle has a high enough ground clearance you do not need a jack and axle stands. This is the time where you would change into work clothes, you will get dirty. Place a piece of cardboard under the motor to prevent spilt oil from destroying your driveway or garage floor. Follow these next steps: (1) open the hood (2) disconnect your battery.

Open the Hood

1. Locate the hood release latch inside the cab. It is usually located to the left of the brake pedal.
2. Standing facing your truck, notice that the hood is now popped up. Locate the release latch and raise the hood.
3. The hood will stay in its place because of the springs on the firewall.

Disconnect the Battery

1. Locate the battery in the engine compartment.
2. With the appropriate size wrench remove the negative lead from the battery post.

Draining the Oil and Changing the Filter

Now that the vehicle is ready you can now begin to drain the oil and change the filter. Follow these easy steps to achieve this: (1) remove the drain plug and collect the waist oil (2 remove the old filter (3) install the new filter and re-install the drain plug.

Warning: Give the vehicle time to cool off before attempting the following steps. Changing hot oil could result in sever burns.

Remove the Drain Plug

1. With your ¾" ratchet and 1½" extension locate the drain plug on the oil pan.
2. Slowly back the drain plug off.
3. Have your waste pail ready.

On the first pass, check for audience, purpose, and content.

Next, in the second pass, review the document for design and format.

4. When the drain plug is loose, put the ratchet aside and finish by hand.

5. Let the drain plug fall into the pail and adjust the pail to receive the stream of oil.

Removing the Drain Plug

Remove the Old Filter

1. When the oil has finished draining from the oil pan place the pail under the oil filter.

2. Using the oil filter strap wrench, crack the filter loose and put the wrench aside.

3. Slowly back the oil filter off until oil begins pouring over the side.

Oil Filter in the Bag

4. When the oil has stop coming out remove the filter completely.

5. Place it in the plastic bag.

Install the New Filter and Re-installing the Drain Plug

1. With a rag, clean the oil filter mating surface on the motor.

2. Take the new filter out of the package.

3. Dip your finger in the waste oil and spread it over the rubber seal covering it completely.

4. Begin to thread the filter onto the motor.

Oil the Rubber Seal

Caution: Do not over tighten the oil filter. Just simply snug it up.

5. Retrieve the drain plug from the waste pail.

6. With a rag clean the drain plug and the mating surface on the oil pan.

7. Thread the drain plug in by hand and snug it up with the ratchet.

Adding Fresh Oil

You are now finished under the vehicle. Only a few steps remain to have completed your oil change. These are: (1) adding fresh oil (2) re-connecting your battery (3) starting your vehicle and checking the level.

Open the Oil

Adding Fresh Oil

1. Remove the oil cap located on the valve cover.
2. Pour slowly, 7 of the 8 Liters of oil into the vehicle.
3. Re-install the oil cap.

Re-connecting Your Battery

Caution: Bring the negative cable quickly to the negative terminal of the battery. Excessive fiddling around could cause sparks, causing the battery to explode or damage your vehicles computer.

1. With the appropriate wrench re-connect the negative lead to the negative post on the battery.

Starting Your Vehicle and Checking the Level

1. Now start your vehicle and get out. Check for leaks under the vehicle. Wait roughly 45 seconds for oil pressure to build up and turn off your vehicle. With a rag in hand pull out the dipstick and clean it off.
2. Re-insert the dipstick all the way and remove again.
3. Examine the markings on the dipstick.
4. Add more oil if required until and ideal level has been reached.

Your oil change is now complete. Please be sure to have the oil and the filter disposed of properly in accordance with environmental laws in your area.

Finally, check the document for style, grammar, and mechanics.

Photographs courtesy of Larry Ellis.

Brief Checklist for Reviewing

First Pass	**Audience:** Does it suit the readers?
	Content: Is the content complete, and is there no extra material?
	Organization: Is it logical?
	Transitions: Is there clear movement between sections? Are there cues for the reader?
Second Pass	**Document type:** Is the document the correct type for the purpose?
	Headings: Are the headings logical and consistent?
	Lists: Does the document use a variety of lists appropriately?
	Tables, graphs, and charts: Is information presented suitably in labelled figures?
	Graphics: Are graphics clear and properly placed?
	Highlighting: Is a clear and consistent highlighting scheme used?
Third Pass	**Sentence problems:** Is there wordiness, redundancy, complicated constructions?
	Technical-style problems: Are numbers, abbreviations, acronyms used correctly?
	Grammar, usage, and all that stuff: Check with Appendix C. Use the spell and grammar checkers!
	Readability: Use the readability scale on your grammar checker.

CHAPTER 17

Audience and Task Analysis

Topics covered in this chapter include

- genetic engineering.

GENETIC ENGINEERING
These days, few topics in Canada are more hotly debated than genetic engineering, especially of genetically modified foods.

Here are some controversial Canadian sites:

Canadian General Standards Board: Food Label and Advertising
http://www.pwgsc.gc.ca/cgsb/032_025/standard-e.html

Genetic Modification—The Facts
http://www.soilassociation.org/web/sa/saweb.nsf/GetInvolved/geneng.html

What Is Biotechnology? Dispelling the Myths
http://www.biotech.ca/EN/myths.html

An Alternative to Genetic Engineering in Agriculture
http://www.ota.com/organic/benefits/generic.html

Provincial Health Ethics Network, Alberta
http://www.phen.ab.ca/materials/intouch/vol3/intouch3-04.html

Genetic Engineering, Factory Farming & Organics
http://www.inmotionmagazine.com/geff.html

Greenpeace Canada
http://www.greenpeace.ca/e/campaign/gmo/index.php

When you have completed this chapter, you will be able to

- identify typical audiences for instructional and noninstructional technical documents;
- perform task analyses for instructional documents;
- perform task analyses for noninstructional documents;
- write instructional and noninstructional documents for particular audiences;
- review and revise documents for audience and purpose.

Technical documents often fail because their writers lose sight of their readers' needs, interests, and knowledge—or they never understood their readers to begin with. One of the great paradoxes of technical writing—in fact, of all writing—is that the simplest, most fundamental of concepts is the most overlooked: What could be more obvious than not talking rocket science to your kindergartner? Closely related to audience analysis is task analysis—the business of determining the tasks about which readers want information.

This chapter explores just who the readers of technical documents are, how to identify characteristics affecting their ability to understand, what tasks they typically need explained in technical documents, and then how to plan, write, and revise with readers fully in mind.

Note: Audience and task analysis is the starting point for any study of technical communication as well as any technical-writing project. If you are not familiar with the organization of this book, see the Preface.

WHO READS TECHNICAL DOCUMENTS?

To begin with, readers of technical documents are not all rocket scientists. More commonly, readers of technical brochures, instructions, handbooks, and manuals are nonspecialists—entry-level people just breaking into the field, or just plain consumers.

One of the long-standing definitions of audiences for technical documents is the four-audience definition developed by Kenneth Houp and Thomas Pearsall. It defines technical audiences this way:

- *Laymen.* Nonspecialist readers who lack background (knowledge or experience) in the subject matter of the technical document.
- *Technicians.* Readers who have or need the sort of background required to assemble, operate, maintain, or repair equipment, or to run complex processes.
- *Executives.* Readers who may not have much technical background but who use technical information to make decisions: to purchase, sell, implement, regulate, and so on.
- *Experts.* Readers who know everything about the technology—its design, construction, uses, operation, as well as the theory behind it.

If you've read Chapter 5 on classification, you'll recognize that *two* bases of classification are used here: how much technical knowledge the audience possesses and how the audience will use the technical information. This definition works because it matches what we often find in the real world.

What people do with technology is possibly the best approach to defining audience categories. Consider the uses of the technology—the way people associate themselves with it—and define the different types of readers accordingly. The computer industry is an interesting example.

You'll typically find some combination of the following types of audiences for computer information:

■ *System administrators.* Install, configure, customize, and manage computer hardware and software.
■ *Programmers.* Develop new applications to be used on the computer, fix "bugs" in the existing applications, or both. Also known as "software engineers" or "developers."
■ *Engineers.* Develop the computer hardware, the chips, the buses, the drives, the cases, and so on. Also known as "hardware engineers" or "developers."
■ *Support technicians.* Provide help to customers who have problems with their computers.
■ *Site planner/purchasers.* Plan the purchasing and implementation of computer installations. Although this role was much more important in the days of the big mainframes, people still play this role, which is largely an executive one.
■ *End users.* Actually use computers to get work done—write documents, print them, create graphics, update spreadsheets, generate graphs, use the Internet, and so on.

Once you've defined the audience's relationship to the technology, you can then define that audience's background—knowledge, experience, even attitude—in relation to that technology. Background is typically defined this way:

■ *Entry-level, novice users; nonspecialist, layman readers.* They know next to nothing; they need lots of hand-holding, tutorials, and reinforcement.
■ *Intermediate, occasional users.* They've done this before but have forgotten some details. They don't want tutorials—just reminders or memory-joggers. These users present a special challenge for technical writers: their needs are right between those of the beginning and experienced user.
■ *Expert, advanced, heavy users or readers.* They know the subject matter very well; they need to know the new stuff, the theory, and the latest research.

WHY DO THEY READ? WHAT ARE THEIR TASKS?

Readers of technical documents read to solve practical problems, accomplish important tasks, and gather information. While audience analysis focuses on the characteristics of your readers—their knowledge, experience, and skills—*task analysis* focuses on what kinds of information they need, which tasks they seek to accomplish, and which types of information they need to make decisions.

Instructional Task Analysis

To get a sense of one common form of task analysis, consider that microwave oven in your house, apartment, or residence room. What are the tasks you do with it?

Task analysis for instructions is straightforward, as the microwave example shows. Define the common uses of the device and then write accordingly. If you don't have much experience with the equipment, go observe typical users—and even interview them as to the tasks they typically perform with that equipment.

Task Analysis—Instructions: Microwave Oven

Unpacking and setting up	You may need information on how to set up the microwave, or how to break it in.
Safety considerations	Although safety considerations are not really tasks, they are certainly important. Don't leave that metal spoon in your coffee cup when you reheat!
Simple cooking	You need quick information on how to heat up a cup of coffee or those leftovers!
Occasional cleaning	Your parents are paying a visit; you've got to get the place cleaned up, especially the microwave.
Cooking with different power levels	You also need to know how to use the power levels if you are trying to cook something fancy to impress your date.
Setting the time	When the power goes out, you need to reset the time on the microwave, along with dozens of other electronic devices.
Using the timer	You need to use the timer: it's finals week, and you're making brownies and don't want them to burn.
Packing and moving the microwave	When the semester is over and you're moving back home, you may need some tips on packing the microwave to keep from damaging it during transit.

Noninstructional Task Analysis

However, consider a noninstructional project in terms of task analysis. It could be called a "topic analysis"—readers reading a background report are looking for certain topics to meet their needs. Consider a global warming report for coastal real-estate developers.

This task analysis addresses the readers' need to understand the theory, understand its worst implications, see the other side of the argument, see your balanced view of the matter, and get a better perspective from your report with which to make their own decisions. Using this report, they can make their own decisions on whether to hold on to their coastal real-estate investments.

Task Analysis—Noninstructional Information: Global Warming Report

Global warming causes	Explain the standard model used by proponents of the global warming theory; explain how radiation is trapped in the atmosphere. Discuss the sources of this trapping effect. Perhaps discuss the theory of "natural" warming and cooling trends in relation to the theory of a human-induced warming trend.
Global warming effects	Discuss predictions made by proponents of the theory, from the most dire to the most conservative. Discuss any scientific support that research has uncovered to support the predictions.
Arguments against the theory	Review the arguments against the global warming theory.
Balanced view	Compare the arguments of the proponents of the theory against those of the critics, and state your own view.
Current research	Briefly survey the research being done on the theory; provide some ideas on how to stay current with developments relating to the global warming theory.
Current efforts to combat global warming	Review what governments and other organizations are doing in relation to global warming and their chances for success.

HOW DO YOU IDENTIFY TASKS?

In a technical-writing course, your audience is almost always your instructor. However, technical documents are written for real workplace situations. Find out how your technical-writing instructor wants to handle this problem.

■ *Real projects—real audiences—real feedback*. In some technical-writing courses, you must find real projects with real audiences. They will give you real feedback as to how well your technical document meets their needs. For example, a guide might be needed for the printers in the computer lab: the actual users of your guide (as well as your instructor) will let you know how successful you are in meeting their needs and solving their problems.
■ *Invented, "hypothetical" projects and audiences*. In other courses, you are invited to use your imagination and define a hypothetical audience. For the topic of global warming, you might invent an audience of coastal real-estate investors. Rising sea levels and increased storm activity would have a major impact on their investments.

With this background on audience, let's walk through an audience definition and analysis. We'll use two scenarios—one involving a printer guide for the school's computer lab, and the other a global warming report.

Instructional Walk-Through—Printer Guide for the Computer Lab

For this first scenario, imagine that you want to do a "real" project, one that will be used by real people to meet their needs, answer their questions, and help them solve technical problems.

1. **First of all, you need a project, which includes a topic and purpose.**

   Imagine you are writing a printer guide for one of the school's computer labs. The faculty sponsor has requested that you write this guide as a part of your work there.

2. **Make a list of the people who will be using your technical document. Identify them by roles.**

   The people who will use the printer guide will be both students and lab technicians. Students are "end users," as defined above. Lab technicians are "system administrators" or "technicians," as discussed above.

3. **Make a list of the tasks these readers must perform—not just the most common ones, but also those infrequent but critical tasks.**

   Students come to the lab to print their papers. Because the lab is busy and typically understaffed, they may have to fix a paper jam, add paper, turn on the printer, or determine on which machine their papers will be printed. Lab technicians, on the other hand, have standard system administrative and maintenance jobs: changing the destination of a printout, reestablishing network connection to a printer, and most likely adding paper and clearing paper jams (rather than students doing this). As the technical writer, you need to determine who can or should do what.

4. **Identify the amount of experience, knowledge, and skills these readers typically have in relation to the technology you are documenting.**

In the typical school computer lab, some students have very little experience while others have enough to act as lab technicians. As the technical writer, you must decide "just how low you can go." Lab technicians can range from relatively experienced end users without system-administrative background to experienced lab technicians who don't need the printer guide at all. As a technical communicator, you realize that the printer guide will take the load off the experienced lab technicians and enable the entry-level lab technicians to find answers to their own questions—especially when there is no one to provide help.

5. **Observe your audience and identify the tasks for which they may need information. Interview them to ensure you get a complete list of tasks.**

Go to the computer lab and watch the students—see how they print out documents; see what problems or questions they have. Watch the lab technicians and make a list of the tasks they perform. Interview several lab technicians (both experienced and brand-new ones). Add to your list of tasks. And finally, interview the head administrator of the computer lab. Find out if you've missed any tasks; find out how that individual wants the printer guide to be used in the lab.

6. **Make a list of the concepts and terminology your readers must know.**

Students using the lab may need help with unfamiliar terms; for example, "print queue" or "network printer." If students can designate a different networked printer, you may want to explain the concept of computer networks. The lab technicians, on the other hand, will need discussions of networks, permissions, queues, and much more.

7. **Create an audience description in which you briefly describe the audience (or audiences), their uses for the information, and their background.**

The project will be a printer guide for use by students and lab technicians in the school computer lab. To enable students to print their documents, check printer queues for the status of their print jobs, and to determine to which printer their documents will print, the guide will provide step-by-step instructions and explain concepts and terms that must be used. To enable lab technicians to clear queues, restart printers, check networks, fix paper jams, and add paper, the guide will also offer step-by-step instructions as well as explanations of key terms and concepts. The guide will assume that students have general familiarity with the operating system and the applications but, in terms of printing, nothing more than the location of the print option in their application. The guide will assume that entry-level lab technicians have at least a student's level of understanding and the ability and intention to learn the rest.

The following is an example audience description like the type that your technical-writing instructor or your lead writer may ask you to prepare:

> *Audience description:* For a printer guide to be used in the computer lab in NRG 4209 by both lab assistants and students using the lab. The guide will be aimed at two audiences: lab assistants who have just started working in the lab who are not much more than well-experienced end users; and students who need to do certain tasks when a lab assistant is not available. The guide will be divided into two sections: one for lab assistants; the other for students using the lab. The guide will take the load off experienced lab assistants and help new assistants when they are on their own. It will also help students who are using the lab to accomplish simple tasks when a lab assistant is not available.

Noninstructional Walk-Through—Global Warming Report for Real-Estate Investors

For this second scenario, imagine that you "invent" an audience with a direct, vital interest in a report on a technical topic (which just happens to be of great interest to you, the technical-writing student).

1. First of all, you need a project, which includes a topic and purpose.

For this noninstructional scenario, imagine you are writing a technical background report on global warming for real-estate investors.

2. Get exact information on the individual who is requesting the report.

For this report, imagine that the requester is the head of an association of real-estate investors, or some deputized agent of it. This report is being commissioned and paid for by the association; any member who requests a copy will get one. Imagine that the hypothetical requester is Mr. John Smith, President, New Brunswick Coastal Real Estate Association. His hypothetical address is 745 Main St., Moncton, NB E1C 2E6.

3. Identify the readers' interests in or needs for the report. How are they going to use the report?

Having heard gloom-and-doom predictions of a ten-foot rise in sea level and dramatic increases in tropical-storm activity, these real-estate investors want balanced, objective information on the global warming issue. They are not requesting a recommendation, just detailed information they can use to make their own decisions. They want to understand the basic theory and some essential terminology presented in nonspecialist terms—not in-depth scientific detail.

4. Identify the concepts and terminology your readers can be expected to know and those that your readers can't be expected to know.

Your readers are investors, businesspeople, and experts in real estate. As such, their backgrounds are business, marketing, real estate, and finance—not science. If you could interview them, they might prove to be political conservatives and thus skeptical of "environmentalists" (which they pronounce with a certain hissing noise).

5. Determine which topics you should discuss and which you should leave out of the report. Determine the level of detail and technical specifics you should discuss in the topics you do cover.

You know that you must discuss the basic cause-and-effect mechanism of the global warming theory and present some statistical and theoretical support—in other words, why some people take the theory seriously. You must survey the dire predictions regarding the theory: this will enable your real-estate-investment audience to consider "worst-case" scenarios. You'll want to summarize the viewpoints of opponents of this theory. You can also discuss what governments are doing or proposing to do about the problem. You might even discuss current research and how to stay abreast of the issue. And finally and most importantly, your readers expect you (the expert whose professional services they are paying for) to provide your balanced, objective perspective on the matter.

6. Create an audience description in which you briefly describe the audience (or audiences), their uses for the information, and their background.

This report is being commissioned by Mr. John Smith, President, New Brunswick Coastal Real Estate Association. You will address the report to his address: 745 Main St., Moncton, NB E1C 2E6. Mr. Smith and his associates have business, real estate, marketing, and finance backgrounds and know little about environmental science. Using your report, they hope to gain a basic understanding of the theory of human-induced global warming, its causes and effects, the full range of predictions associated with the theory, arguments by critics of the theory, and your balanced or objective perspective. You will discuss only those scientific concepts necessary for these readers to meet their needs and will use specialized terminology only when absolutely necessary. Your readers are not looking for investment recommendations but, rather, information they can use to make their own decisions.

> *Audience description:* For Mr. John Smith, President, New Brunswick Coastal Real Estate Association (745 Main St., Moncton, New Brunswick); a technical-background report on global warming for the coastal real-estate association of which he is president. The report will summarize current scientific thinking on the possibilities of the worst predictions based on the theory of global warming, designed for nonscientific, executive readers. The client wants a balanced, objective summary of this issue, which his membership will use to make long-range investment plans. Association members can get copies of the report by sending a request to the association's main office.

HOW DO YOU WRITE FOR AN AUDIENCE?

If you have carefully analyzed your audience, you should be able to write for that audience, right? Not exactly. It's one thing to know your readers and quite another to write with them fully in mind at all times. Writing with an audience firmly in mind is not a step-by-step process like audience and task analysis. It's a frame of mind, a mental perspective, an attitude.

A model: in-person communication. Think about how live, in-person communication works: the speaker and listener engage in a give-and-take process. The listener may look puzzled, exasperated, bored, and may even interrupt to ask questions; the speaker reacts accordingly, restating, clarifying, answering the listener's questions, or moving on to more interesting topics. When you write, the reader is not there to react and help you with clarity or interest level. Nor are you, the writer, likely to be there when the reader reads your document.

Contemporary rhetoricians have theorized that as writers we construct an imaginary audience with whom we engage in a mental give-and-take right inside our own brains. We mentally re-create the live, in-person situation. Although this may sound like a short path to therapy, the logical implications of this idea are as follows:

- Successful writers possess more detailed, more clearly defined understanding of their audiences.
- Those imaginary audiences somehow match more closely their real flesh-and-blood counterparts—actual readers.
- As they write and as they review and revise, successful writers carry on a much more active, more detailed dialogue with those imaginary readers.

If you look at written documents in the right light, you'll see traces of this internal dialogue with imaginary readers. The wisecrack in the preceding about a "short path to therapy" is an example. It directly addresses you, the reader, and attempts to provoke a little humour. If it had been face-to-face communication, you might have been glazing over or becoming impatient with this heavy philosophical digression. It also acknowledges what might be highly skeptical reactions on the part of some readers. Weird stuff, huh?

New metaphors for written communication. How can you develop this ability to dialogue internally with your imaginary readers? Obviously, new metaphors are needed. The story of Pinocchio might work as an analogy. Jiminy Cricket is Pinocchio's imaginary audience ("always let your readers be your guide"). When he stops listening to that pesky cricket, his nose grows (he has strayed from his audience) Find something to hang over your computer—a toy cricket, a fake Halloween skull, a spider, a Barbie doll, or a GI Joe doll. Regardless of which trick you use to stay "ever mindful" of your reader, that imaginary reader should occasionally scold you and pester you with annoying questions like those in Figure 17-1.

Can you stand hearing voices like those in Figure 17-1 in your head? Do they resemble those of your eventual flesh-and-blood readers? If so, your writing stands a better chance of connecting with its readers (but that's another metaphor).

FIGURE 17-1

Questions from your "inner audience." Know your audience so well and write with those readers' needs and interests so fully in your mind that questions like these pop up as you write or as you review.

HOW DO YOU REVISE FOR AN AUDIENCE?

No matter how detailed your image of your audience is, no matter how closely that image resembles your real audience, no matter how active your dialogue with your imaginary audience is—you still lose them at times. That's why the review and revision phase is so important. Just as you listen to that internal voice as you write, you need it again as you review. (See Figure 17-2 and Chapter 16 for reviewing strategies.) In fact, try to undergo a complete (though temporary) personality change and *become* your intended reader as you review your draft. (Just be able to snap out of it!)

If the internal-voice metaphor just does not work for you, you might try something a bit more mainstream. See Chapter 16 for a multi-phase method of reviewing: you start with high-level issues such as content, audience, and organization and work all the way down to grammar, usage, and punctuation.

FIGURE 17-2

Reader-based questions and comments in the review process. The excerpt shown was obviously written for geneticists, but imagine the questions non-geneticists would have. When you review, pretend you are your intended readers and see what questions, frustrations, comments, and even wisecracks they are likely to have as they read.

Source: Collins, Francis and David Galas, "A New Five-Year Plan for the U.S. Human Genome Program." <www.genome.gov/10001476>. 14 Sept. 2005.

WORKSHOP: AUDIENCES AND TASKS

Here are some additional ideas for practising the concepts, tools, and strategies in this chapter:

1. *Defining audiences' needs and interests.* Take a look at the following pairs of technical topics and audiences. Make a list of the audiences' likely interests and needs in relation to those topics:

   Child abuse—New caseworker

   Internet privacy issues—New Internet user

   Internet privacy issues—E-commerce website developer

   Bioengineering—Student considering a career

   Lyme disease—Camping enthusiast

   Lyme disease—Family practice physician

   Wildlife rehabilitation—Veterinarian

   Food-borne pathogens—Restaurant worker

2. *Inventing audiences.* Consider the following technical-document projects, or topics, and invent audiences for them. Make sure your audiences are realistic and have a very definite need for the technical information.

Food-borne diseases	Accident prevention
Biodiversity	Big Bang Theory
Pesticides	Human Genome Project
Acoustics	Computer viruses
Math anxiety	Video game violence
Artificial intelligence	Fire ants

3. *Deciding what to include and what to leave out.* Choose one of the pair of technical topics and audiences in Exercise 1, and think of a writing project for it. Then, for the writing project, make a list of topics, concepts, and terminology you would include and those you would leave out.

4. *Listing tasks.* Consider the writing project in the following. Identify the tasks that the readers would expect information on.

Writing Project	Audience
Guide for above-ground pool maintenance	Ordinary homeowners without chemistry background
Cable modems: installation and use	Purchasers for home installation and use
Report on super-string theory	College physics instructors

5. *Listening to your "inner audience."* Take a look at the excerpt from a technical-writing project in the following table. Based on the audience described, what questions would pop up in your mind if you were reading from their point of view?

Audience & Purpose:	Information included in a CPR handbook for nonmedical people learning CPR.
Excerpt:	Cells in our bodies need energy to perform certain processes, such as contracting or producing chemicals such as insulin and adrenaline. They obtain this energy through *cellular respiration*—the conversion of nutrients and oxygen into carbon dioxide, water, and energy: $$nutrients + oxygen \rightarrow carbon\ dioxide + water + energy$$ The nutrients used are typically sugars stored in the cell—for example, glucose: $$C_6H_{12}O_6\ (glucose) + 6\ O_2 \rightarrow 6\ CO_2 + 6\ H_2O + energy$$ Therefore, for each oxygen molecule used, a molecule of carbon dioxide is produced as waste. This CO_2 molecule passes out of the cell, through the capillary wall and into a red blood cell. The transfer of gases between cells and the bloodstream is a two-way process—as oxygen is taken out of the red blood cells in the oxygenated blood, it is replaced with carbon dioxide to produce *deoxygenated blood*. As you exhale, air in the lungs is forced out of the body. This air contains about 15% oxygen, with about 4% carbon dioxide and an appreciable quantity of water vapour. The overall change in composition between air breathed in and out is summarized below:

Continued

Percentage compositions: air breathed in and out

	Air In	Air Out
Nitrogen	78	78
Oxygen	21	15
Carbon dioxide	0.03	4
Water vapour	<1	2
Others	**<1**	**<1**

As you would expect, there is a net input of oxygen into the body and a net output of carbon dioxide. The proportions of each in the air we exhale varies—when doing vigorous exercise, for instance, cells in our muscles would be working much harder and therefore using more energy. As a result, these cells convert oxygen to carbon dioxide much more quickly than when at rest, and therefore there is less oxygen and more carbon dioxide found in exhaled breath when exercising than when resting.

CHAPTER 18

Finding Information: Print, Internet, Informal Sources

Topics covered in this chapter include

- reusable launch vehicles (RLVs);
- the Ansari X Prize Cup;
- space tourism.

REUSABLE LAUNCH VEHICLES
Although there are few books on this subject, there are many websites. For a good overview of the background, go to Wikipedia.com and search for "reusable launch system."

The Canadian Space Agency
http://www.space.gc.ca

THE ANSARI X PRIZE CUP
The X Prize Cup
http://www.xpcup.com

The DaVinci Project, the "world's biggest reusable balloon," a Canadian contender for the cup
http://www.davinciproject.com/beta

The Canadian Arrow, a "3-man reusable, sub-orbital spacecraft"
http://www.canadianarrow.com

SPACE TOURISM
For an overview, start at How Stuff Works (**http://www.howstuffworks.com**) and search for "how space tourism works." Also try:

Richard Branson's Virgin Galactic
http://www.virgingalactic.com

Space Adventures
http://www.spaceadventures.com

You might also want to search Google for information on 'N Sync's Lance Bass, a space tourist wannabe.

When you have completed this chapter, you will be able to

- plan a focused information search;
- understand how to search online and evaluate what you find;
- use a wide variety of sources, including government documents and personal interviews.

This chapter provides strategies for finding information on the Internet, in libraries, and from other resources, such as informal, unpublished sources. You'll also see how to evaluate the information you find.[†] For full details on how to cite a wide range of borrowed information, see Chapter 19.

HOW DO YOU SEARCH FOR INFORMATION?

Before you go racing off to the library or spend all night surfing the Web, think about the kinds of information you need and where they might be located.

Find a Librarian

Experienced librarians know where to start looking, how to choose keywords to make a search more precise, how to choose another strategy if the first one doesn't work, and how to help you narrow and focus a topic so you can complete your project within a specified period of time. Explain your project to a librarian and you'll get valuable guidance as to which resources are likely to be the most useful. If an experienced librarian is not available, try asking yourself these questions about your project:

- *What am I really looking for?* Write your topic as one or more questions. Examine those questions to determine what kind of information you need: descriptions, technical information, history, analysis. What's your "take" on your topic? Which aspect of the topic do you want to focus on? If your topic is reusable launch vehicles (RLVs), for example, you might want to focus on the Ansari X Prize Cup. The first award, for $10 million, was given to Burt Rutan and Microsoft billionaire Paul Allen, developers of SpaceShipOne, but the awarding of the cup is now an annual event. Or you might prefer to focus on a Canadian entry for

---

[†]Many thanks to Teresa Ashley, MLS, Austin Community College Librarian, for her work on this chapter.

the prize, the Canadian Arrow. Perhaps you are more interested in the potential of space tourism, a topic with many possible angles.

■ *What are the key terms for my topic?* List *keywords* before you start searching; add to them as you find new ones. For example, you might start with "global warming" but then realize that "greenhouse effect" and "global climate change" are also useful.

■ *Do I need recent information, or is there a period of time when this topic was really "hot"?* As of the year 2006, a topic like the development of RLVs is current, whereas Halley's comet, which was in the news in 1986, is not.

Find a Guide

Although an experienced librarian is the best guide you could ask for, certain websites and reference books act as "guides" to specific fields of knowledge and practice. See the examples of print and website guides in the following discussions.

Choose Your Resources

An experienced librarian can help you avoid wasting time searching information in the wrong resources. For example, a topic like the Ansari X

WEBSITES WITH SUBJECT OVERVIEWS AND LINKS

To find a site that will give you an overview as well as links to the best sites on your topic, try the following examples:

About.com: A commercial enterprise that employs "guides"—human beings who are experts on their topics—who select and present Web resources. **http://www.about.com**

Wikipedia: The online "encyclopedia" is under constant development by volunteers. Information is available as it occurs—the Air France plane crash at Pearson International Airport on August 2, 2005, was covered within a day, for example. Errors are corrected by the millions who keep constant watch on the site, and if you see an error yourself, you can correct it. You'd better have your facts straight, however. **http://www.wikipedia.com**

How Stuff Works: This site is one of the best places online for an overview and links. **http://www.howstuffworks.com**

RefDesk.com: Bob Drudge's wonderful collection of everything imaginable for a complete reference desk. **http://www.refdesk.com**

Columbia University Libraries: Selected Subject Guides and Resources. **http://www.columbia.edu/cu/lweb/eguides**

Internet Public Library: Take a look at the links under Subject Collections on the main page. For example, click on Science and Technology/Environmental Sciences and Ecology. This page links to the appropriate pages on sites from About to Yahoo. **http://www.ipl.org**

The Brain at Mohawk College: Click on Web Links or Quick Reference. **http://brain.mohawkcollege.ca**

Prize Cup is so new that newspaper and magazine articles may be the best, or only, resources, rather than books. Here are strategies for choosing information resources. See also the list on page 382 for some suggestions for guidebooks and guide websites for information searching:

- *Internet.* The World Wide Web is a great starting point. However, information on the Web can change overnight. While most news sites constantly update their coverage of news topics, they do not archive them. Nor are you likely to find Internet versions of material that is expensive to produce or that dates from the 1980s or earlier. Often, you have to pay for the best information. After all, information is a commodity. Even if you find plenty of information on the Web, don't stop there. Get out of the apartment and go to the library.
- *Books.* Books usually represent stable, well-established knowledge. Because of the time and expense it takes to produce books, the information in them is not as up-to-date or "last-minute" as the information in newspapers, magazines, and journals or on the Web. Although you may not find a reliable book on a new scientific discovery reported on the ten o'clock news, you will find books providing background to help you understand that discovery.
- *Encyclopedias and other reference books.* Reference books (encyclopedias, handbooks, and dictionaries) are even more settled, well-established resources. Information in these works has been accepted by many and is not likely to be challenged. These resources give you the "lay of the land" on a topic—basic theory, formulas, definitions, overviews, diagrams, history, and so on. For an unfamiliar topic, encyclopedia articles are good places to start; in particular, subject-specific encyclopedia articles written by experts.
- *Magazines and journals.* Use magazine and journal articles to "zoom in" on specific parts of a topic. Although magazines and journals contain information that is more up-to-date than books, you typically cannot expect the same depth of information that you can from a book. An article in a scholarly journal may be so specific that it's the only published material on a particular aspect of a topic.
- *Newspapers.* Articles published in newspapers often contain the most up-to-date information on a topic. If you had been researching advances in computer memory when Hewlett-Packard announced its nanotechnology-based computer-switching devices, news articles would have been the only place to find any information on that topic.
- *Government documents and reports.* The U.S. government commissions book-length reports as well as pamphlets that are so specialized that they are not commercially viable. Certain large university and public libraries act as "depository libraries" to store these publications. Government publications are increasingly available on the Internet. To find government documents, see "What about Government Documents?" later in this chapter.

■ *Product literature.* Information published by makers of products can be very useful—so long as you keep in mind its natural tendency for bias. Not only might a manufacturer send you product specifications, you might also receive white papers and other general literature about the technology.

■ *Informal, unpublished resources.* Don't forget, you can also interview local experts, send e-mail inquiries to knowledgeable individuals, investigate local facilities as well as conduct surveys or send out questionnaires. (See the suggestions at the end of this chapter.)

Know How to Search Online

Whether you search the Internet, an online periodical index, a Web-based encyclopedia, or a library's computer catalogue, you are doing online searches. Common to all of these resources is the electronic database, which provides some combination of the following search tools:

■ *Boolean searches.* Boolean operators ("and," "or," and "not") define logical relationships between search terms. Different search engines perform searches differently. Read the "search hints" to see how your search engine works. For explanations of the Boolean operators, see:

   ■ Finding Information on the Web on the University of British Columbia library website at **http://www.library.ubc.ca/websearch/quick.html**.

   ■ InfoPeople Project's "Search Engines Quick Guide" at **http://infopeople.org/search/guide.html**.

■ *Proximity searches.* Proximity operators ("near," "with," "adjacent," and others) specify how close to each other your search terms should appear. For example, "global n2 warming" means that the word "global" should appear near "warming" with no more than two words between the two terms.

■ *Phrase searches.* Phrase searching (two or more words commonly found together) is another way to limit your search results. In a search on global warming, you'd want to exclude global warfare, global travel, warming up leftovers, and so on. Different search engines perform phrase searching differently. In Excite, you type in global AND warming. In other search engines, you might type "global warming" (with the quotation marks) or "global+warming."

■ *Searches using truncation.* Use truncation to search on a portion of a word to retrieve alternate forms: "politi*" may retrieve "political," "politics," "politician," and "politicians"—which is like doing four separate searches!

Start Collecting Keywords

When you start your information search you need a good set of keywords:

- For a report on RLVs, keywords like "space transportation," "space travel," or even "space tourism" might be useful.
- For global warming, you might use "global warming," "greenhouse effect," "global climate change," and even something as broad as "environment."

No one magical reference book contains all known keywords. Last updated in 2005 (28th Edition), *Library of Congress Subject Heading* may help, but not for current technology topics. Instead, do some brainstorming, think of synonyms, use keywords you know, look in encyclopedias and other introductory resources, and keep a running list of additional synonyms you find.

WHAT ABOUT THE INTERNET?

The Internet has become quite the resource for technical-writing projects. Whatever you find on the Web you must evaluate carefully. Anyone can publish on the Web—Nobel prize winners, well-intentioned amateurs, and any fringe group. Imagine what you'd find on the Web about UFOs!

Searching for Information on the Internet

To start investigating Internet resources for a writing project, first learn something about how search engines work and what's "out there." The following lists some tutorials and information on searching the Web.

**TUTORIALS AND INFORMATION ON SEARCHING
THE WORLD WIDE WEB**

University of South Carolina. Bare Bones 101—A Basic Tutorial on Searching the Web: **http://www.sc.edu/beaufort/library/pages/bones/bones.shtml**

Cal Poly State University. Information Competency: **http://www.lib.calpoly.edu/infocomp/modules**

The Brain at Mohawk College. The Brain Research Survival Guide: **http://www.mohawkcollege.ca/dept/library/brain/researchsurvguide1.htm**

InfoPeople Project. Best Search Tools: **http://infopeople.org/search/tools.html**

Queen's University. Research Strategy Guide: **http://library.queensu.ca/inforef/strategy.htm**

The American Library Association. Using Primary Sources on the Web: **http://www.lib.washington.edu/subject/History/RUSA**

Guide sites. A "guide" site contains links carefully selected and organized by real people—often by librarians, professors, and subject experts. To find subject-specific guide sites, try Google at **http://www.google.ca**. Because Google ranks a page by how many other pages link to it, guide sites come to the top. They are valuable starting points in Internet searching.

General search engines. General search engines claim to search the entire Web. Actually, they search only that part of the Web that they have collected into a database. These search agents use "spiders" or "crawlers" that continuously search for websites to add to their databases. Most general search engines provide for a basic search or quick search as well as for an advanced or power search. After you have run a basic search, read the search hints and make use of the advanced features for greater precision. General search engines include Google at **http://www.google.ca**, MSN at **http://www.msn.ca**, Yahoo at **http://www.yahoo.com**, Altavista at **http://www. altavista.com**, Excite at **http://www.excite.com**, and Lycos at **http://www.lycos.com**.

Meta-search engines. Meta-search engines let you run a search on several general search engines simultaneously, enabling you to scan what is available quickly. However, none of the special search features of general search engines are available. Meta-search engines are great for "quick and dirty" searches. Meta-search engines include Dogpile at **http://www.dogpile.com**, MetaCrawler at **http://www.metacrawler.com**, HotBot at **http://www.hotbot. com**, and Savvy Search at **http://www.savvysearch.com**.

Specialized search engines. Specialized search engines focus on a particular type of site or query (for example, people, businesses, or Usenet newsgroups). **http://www.groups.google.com** provides different search methods— "Quick Search," "Power Search," and "Browse"—to get to newsgroups, forums, and threads on the Internet, plus keyword searching for specific subjects. Reference.com at **http://www.reference.com** is very similar to the Google Groups site, except that you can search mailing lists as well as newsgroup postings.

Another specialized search tool is Northern Light at **http://www. northernlight.com**. It can search more than one database simultaneously; it searches its own database along with a database of about 2,000 journal articles and other publications. Northern Light is expensive for a student, but you can sign up for a 30-day free trial. **http://www.SearchEdu.com** searches educational sites only, which is helpful when you are looking for reliable sites. Similarly, **http://www.SearchGov.com** enables you to search for specific subjects in just about every area of U.S. federal and state governments. Google now also has Google Scholar at **http://scholar.google.com**, which allows you to search scholarly publications.

Another source of information on the Web is that buried in databases and not accessible through normal search methods. These areas are called the "deep" or "invisible" Web. Access buried information using The Invisible Web at **http://www.invisible-web.net** or The Deep Web at **http:// aip.completeplanet.com**.

Evaluating Internet Information

Be careful about websites you use to support a research project. Anyone can put Web pages out there for the whole world to read and believe. On the Internet, anyone can copy a website and pass it off as the original. **http://www.whitehouse.net** satirizes the official White House website, which is at **http://www.whitehouse.gov**. How can you determine whether the information at a website is reliable, credible, and legitimate? Although there are no sure-fire answers, the following list provides some suggestions:

- *Look for bias in the title*. Titles often indicate a friendly or hostile attitude toward the topic. The phrase "rising CO_2 content in the atmosphere" quietly indicates an acceptance of the theory. View pages like these with a certain amount of skepticism.
- *Look for bias in self-described balanced, neutral "resource" sites*. You'd expect oil companies to oppose the global warming theory and Greenpeace to embrace it. Even so, organizations like these provide "resource sites," which implies a wide range of links reflecting different opinions. Instead, they may have carefully filtered out the opposition.
- *Look at the information itself*. How much careful research is evident in the website? If links point to other well-established sites, if the information tries to present both sides, if the author cites sources, or if the information is detailed and provides plenty of support for its assertions, these are all good signs. However, if the information is old, if you can't find the date for it, or if it is weak on facts and full of generalizations and emotional rhetoric—watch out!

**EVALUATING INFORMATION FROM
THE WORLD WIDE WEB**

University of South Carolina. Bare Bones 101—A Basic Tutorial on Searching the Web: **http://www.sc.edu/beaufort/library/pages/bones/bones.shtml**

Cal Poly State University. Information Competency: **http://www.lib.calpoly.edu/infocomp/modules**

Grassian, Esther. UCLA College Library. Thinking Critically about World Wide Web Resources: **http://www.library.ucla.edu/libraries/college/help/critical/index.htm**

Rice University, Fondren Library. Internet Searching Strategies—Evaluating Internet Resources: **http://www.rice.edu/fondren/netguides/strategies.html#evaluate**

University of Alberta. Critical Evaluation of Resources on the Internet: **http://www.library.ualberta.ca/guides/criticalevaluation**

Queens University Library. CARS Evaluation Checklist: **http://library.queensu.ca/inforef/guides/evalchart.htm**

- *Find out about the website.* If the website is owned by an educational institution, government agency, or professional organization, you can view its information with some confidence.
- *Find out about the author.* Look for information that authors of websites provide about themselves, particularly their affiliations with organizations. If they provide no information about themselves, that's a problem. Use a meta-search engine like Dogpile at **http://www.dogpile.com** or one of the many "people finder" search sites like WhoWhere? People Finder at **http://www.whowhere.lycos.com**, or try e-mailing the author directly. You can also find the name of the owner of a website using a "whois" search. Go to **http://www.accesswhois.com**.

WHAT ABOUT ENCYCLOPEDIAS AND OTHER REFERENCE BOOKS?

Good encyclopedia entries give you a sense of the "landscape" of a topic—key terms, main issues, major categories, historical names and events, and so on. Background reading in encyclopedias also helps to narrow and focus a topic.

1. *General encyclopedias.* Start with a current "general" encyclopedia such as the *Encyclopaedia Britannica*, *World Book,* or *Americana*. For "global warming," the index of the 1995 *World Book Encyclopedia* lists Greenhouse effect G:383; the 1998 *Encyclopaedia Britannica* lists seven different articles. Skim the main and cross-referenced articles; make a note of books, articles, or other sources cited. Don't expect to find information on new, "hot" topics, however.
2. *Yearbook supplements to encyclopedias.* Also take a look at any of the "yearbook" supplements available with some encyclopedias, particularly multivolume ones. Look for your topic in the index. If you find it, you'll find some excellent updated information.
3. *Specialized encyclopedias and reference works.* For a technical-writing project, don't stop with general encyclopedias. Look at subject-specific encyclopedias, handbooks, and dictionaries. To locate these encyclopedias, find out the call number range for your topic, and then browse the reference stacks in that range. Most library reference areas have handouts or charts on the Library of Congress classification system. For example, music will be in the M's, art in the N's, and psychology in the BF's. Librarians can direct you to specialized encyclopedias, but try a keyword search on your library's online catalogue. For example, the keywords "engineering" and "encyclopedia" should retrieve a list of the library's encyclopedias related to that field. Here are some examples of what you might find:

Encyclopedia of Crime and Justice

Encyclopedia of Educational Research

Encyclopedia of Religion

Encyclopedia of World Art

Labour Law in Canada

International Encyclopedia of Sociology

McGraw-Hill Encyclopedia of Electronics and Computers

McGraw-Hill Encyclopedia of Physics

McGraw-Hill Encyclopedia of Environmental Science & Engineering

McGraw-Hill Encyclopedia of Quality Terms and Concepts

McGraw-Hill Encyclopedia of the Geological Sciences

McGraw-Hill Encyclopedia of Engineering

McGraw-Hill Encyclopedia of Science and Technology

McGraw-Hill Encyclopedia of Astronomy

McGraw-Hill Encyclopedia of Environmental Science

An Encyclopaedia of Metallurgy and Materials

Note that you should try searching both spellings of encyclopedia (encyclopaedia).

4. Increasingly, encyclopedias are appearing in full on the Internet; for example, *Encyclopaedia Britannica* at **http://www.britannica.com**. Here are some ways to find others:

   ■ Internet Public Library. Provides a good list of online encyclopedias: **http://www.ipl.org/ref/RR/static/ref32.00.00.html**

   ■ Refdesk.com, Encyclopedias. Also provides links to online encyclopedias: **http://www.refdesk.com/factency.html**

   ■ Michigan Electronic Library (MEL). Provides an extensive list of links to free online encyclopedias, dictionaries, and almanacs: **http://mel.org**

These free online sources are useful more for quick reference than in-depth research. That's because they are older, abridged, or concise versions of the print editions and their fee-based electronic counterparts. Go to your library for the more recent and most complete versions.

WHAT ABOUT BOOKS?

Before starting a search for books, make sure that books are what you need. If your topic is new, no books may be available yet. Instead, articles, reports, or other kinds of publications may be what you need. Books treat a topic in-depth and can take a year to research and write and another year to publish. The information in books is not so much outdated as it is conservative in its approach.

Searching for books will become increasingly easier. These days all but the smallest and most under-funded libraries have their entire collections searchable on the World Wide Web. That means you can sit at home and search your local library for books on a topic (and see whether they are checked out). Here are some suggestions for finding books:

1. *Start with local libraries.* Your local library is the best "first stop." Obviously, you can use the World Wide Web to find books, but they may be sitting in a library in London, England, while you are down home in London, Ontario. When you get search results on your topic, print them out, and go take a look at those books. Skim through them, checking the footnotes and bibliographies for additional titles that might be useful.

2. *Check online library resource pages.* These provide specialized library resources as well as links to online libraries all over the world:
   - Try the worldwide directory of library home pages, web-based catalogues, and library e-commerce links at LibDex, found at **http://www.libdex.com**.
   - Visit Library and Archives Canada's Canadian Library Gateway at **http://www.collectionsCanada.ca/gateway/s22-200-e.html**.
   - Take a look at Library Information Services from Refdesk.com at **http://www.refdesk.com/factlib.html** for links to libraries all over the world.

3. *Check the Library of Congress.* Check a major library for books on your topic, such as the Library of Congress at **http://catalog.loc.gov**. Click on Basic Search and select "keyword" from the drop-down menu. Enter a keyword or phrase such as "reusable launch vehicles" in the search box, and click the search button (see Figure 18-1).

4. *Search commercial books.* Take a look at what is available commercially on your topic. See what you can find at one of the well-known online bookstores: as of August 2005, Chapters.ca produced one direct hit on reusable launch vehicles and three or four on space tourism.

5. *Use Interlibrary Loan, if necessary.* How do you get books that are far away? When you find such books through an online catalogue, print out the information you'll need to acquire it. Your local library may be able to borrow it for you through Interlibrary Loan (ILL). In the ILL process, your librarian acts as your agent, requesting a book from another library for you.

WHAT ABOUT MAGAZINE, JOURNAL, AND NEWSPAPER ARTICLES?

If your focus is a "hot" topic, your best or only information may come from magazine, journal, and newspaper articles. Even if your topic has "cooled," see what magazines, journals, and newspapers have to offer.

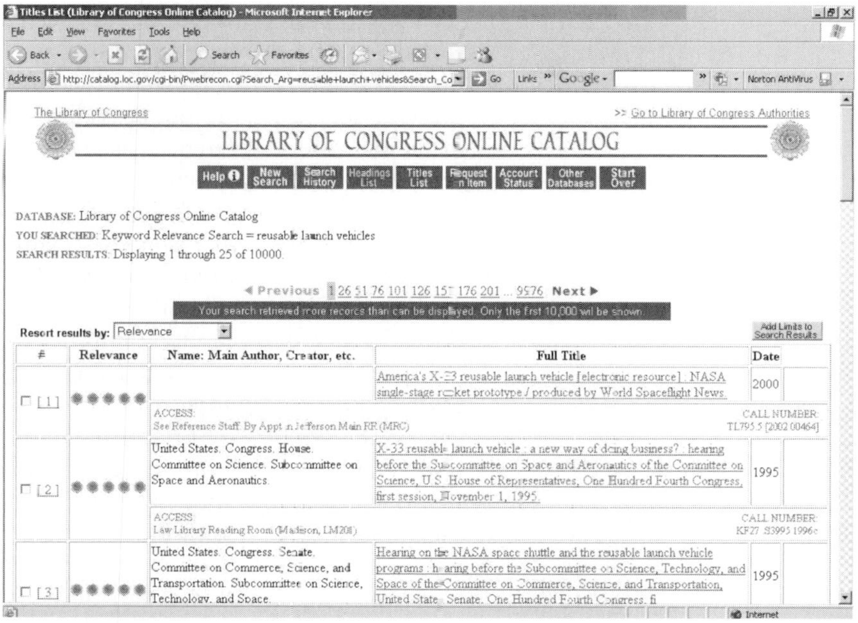

FIGURE 18-1

Search results from a Library of Congress Query. See what's available from the biggest library in the world.

Magazines and journals. Periodical indexes are the keys to finding articles. An index like *Reader's Guide to Periodical Literature* covers a broad range of subjects, whereas other indexes are devoted to a single discipline or field (for example, *Engineering Index*). Indexes called "abstracts" provide summaries of the articles listed (for example, *Chemical Abstracts* and *Psychological Abstracts*).

Although not very long ago indexes were available only in printed form, most libraries now have at least one index available in an electronic format—either on CD-ROM or on the Web. *Readers' Guide to Periodical Literature*, for example, is available in both electronic formats. Do the following to use a periodical index:

1. *Make sure you have a good set of keywords.* If you were looking for articles on Internet 2, use search terms like "Internet2" and "Internet II" also. Perhaps try "Internet" just in case good materials are hidden under a phrase like the "new Internet." For a search on global warming, try "greenhouse effect" and "global climate change" as well.

2. *Start with a general periodical index.* General indexes help you find articles for general audiences: these are good starting points. Most electronic indexes let you mark citations so that you can look more closely at them and start choosing the best ones. If your library subscribes to

two or three online periodical indexes, try them all. Here are some examples:

- *MasterFILE Premier*, an online general periodical index, provided full-text for nearly 1,960 periodicals covering nearly all subjects, including general reference, business, health, and much more as of 1999. A search for "e-commerce and security" results in 138 hits, many full-text and in such journals as *American Banker, Information Systems Security, Management Accounting: Magazine for Chartered Management Accountants*, and *Security Management*.
- *Periodical Abstracts*, another online general periodical index, produces 71 hits for a search on Internet 2 OR Internet2 OR Internet II. The publications cited range from the general and popular (*Rolling Stone, Smart Computing, US News & World Report*) to the technical (*IEEE Network, IEEE Software*) to the special audience publication (*Training & Development, Journal of Academic Librarianship*).

3. *Search the most active time frame for the topic.* If your topic has a specific time frame, start with index entries in that period. For example, you'd find more articles on the most recent visit of Halley's Comet or the nuclear-reactor disaster at Chernobyl in months just following those events. Online periodical indexes cover articles published from the late 1980s or 1990 forward. For material published in the early 1980s or earlier, use a print index.

4. *Examine the actual articles.* Take a look at the articles you find, especially the references to other articles or to reports and books. If the full text of your article is available online, you may be able to e-mail it to yourself or copy it to disk (but libraries typically charge for printing articles).

   If your library doesn't subscribe to the periodicals you need or if the articles aren't available online, read the abstracts of those articles to see if they are worth acquiring. For the articles you really need, try ILL.

5. *Check specialized indexes.* If you haven't found the right articles or enough articles, or if you are curious as to the content of the more specialized articles, take a look at one or more specialized indexes related to your topic, such as the following (the numbers in parentheses are the total periodicals indexed):

Applied Science & Technology Index (485)

Art Index (377)

Biological & Agricultural Index (292)

Business Periodicals Index (528)

Education Index (478)

Essay and General Literature Index

General Science Index (190)

Humanities Index (451)

Library Literature & Information Science (292)

Social Sciences Index (520)

Readers' Guide to Periodical Literature (270)

Biology Digest

6. *Check field-specific indexes.* Finally, take a look at the articles for your project in indexes that cover specific fields. Find these field-specific indexes by consulting a reference librarian or by searching the library's online catalogue (for example, type something like "chemistry indexes" in the word search field).

7. *Search online magazines and journals.* Another possibility is to check "e-journals," which have no counterpart in either print or full-text online indexes. Internet Public Library has an extensive listing of periodicals at **http://www.ipl.org/reading/serials**; click on Computers & Internet, then on Internet.

Newspapers online. Many newspapers provide the complete text of their current issue online, although most charge for back issues. See the Internet Public Library for an extensive list of online newspapers by country, state, and city. (For the online edition of the *New York Times*, click on New York State, then on New York City.) Online newspapers offer some features you don't get in print: searchable archives and links to background information that never made it into the print edition. Here are some links to online newspapers:

■ Internet Public Library provides a list of online newspapers by continent, country, state or province, and city: **http://www.ipl.org/reading/news**
■ Refdesk.com offers a good selection of newspapers in its Newspapers section: **http://www.refdesk.com**. If you searched *The New York Times* for "Canadian Arrow" (a Canadian contender for the X Prize), you would find three articles. You have to pay to see the entire article, but you can read the abstracts before you decide to buy.
■ AJR Newslink from *American Journalism Review* links to both print and broadcast sources and provides search capability: **http://www. newslink.org**.
■ TotalNews is searchable: **http://www.totalnews.com**. To find Canadian news, click on "World." Click on "C" to find Canada.
■ Newspapers Online has a broad range, including specialized news sources such as ethnic, minority, and religious publications: **http://www. newspapers.com**.
■ Of course, you can also find many news articles using Google News: **http://www.news.google.ca**.

In addition to newspapers online, visit the websites of television broadcast news and network news sites. These are online equivalents to TV news broadcasts:

■ CBC, the Canadian Broadcasting Corporation, at **http://www.cbc.ca**, and BBC, the British Broadcasting Corporation, at **http://news.bbc.co.uk**, provide international coverage.

- ABC News has headlines and in-depth stories in such categories as travel, world, entertainment, and sports. Link to **http://www.abcnews.com**, and click Contents for a listing of recent stories or Search for a particular story.
- City TV has national, international and local news at: **http://www.pulse24.com**.
- NBC News has headlines, quick news, and stories in clickable categories as well as local news that you can select from a region on a map: **http://www.nbc.com**.
- CNN has top news stories by category, with in-depth coverage of individual issues: **http://www.cnn.com**.
- C-SPAN mirrors its television counterpart with in-depth coverage of topics and source material on events currently in the news: **http://www.c-span.org**.
- ZDNet, at **http://www.zdnet.com**, is a hybrid news/magazine site, providing Ziff-Davis magazine online equivalents as well as news articles and product reviews.

For finding archived news that is specifically Canadian, or at least published in Canadian newspapers, go to Julian Sher's Journalism.net site at **http://www.journalismnet.com/archives/canada.htm**. As well as archived news, this site has links to many people-finding sites. A website called News-Directory allows you to narrow your search down to individual provinces and find links to every newspaper in that province. Under Ontario, for example, you can find links to *Strathroy's Age Dispatch*, the *Timmins Times*, and the *Parry Sound North Star*.

WHAT ABOUT GOVERNMENT DOCUMENTS?

The depth and variety of information collected by government agencies or published as government-funded research is astonishing. The Canadian government has a large depository of documents available to the public. Search for documents on the Depository Services Program website at **http://dsp-psd.pwgsc.gc.ca**. The U.S. government publishes more information than any other entity. Luckily for the trees, though, the federal governments—and state and provincial governments—are publishing this material on the World Wide Web.

Certain large university research libraries and large public libraries serve as "depositories" for U.S. government publications. They are often placed in special areas, forming a "government document" collection. Government documents are often shelved by Superintendent of Documents (SuDoc) numbers, which groups documents by the agency that issues them.

Government documents were difficult to search and access just a decade or two ago. The process has improved but still has a way to go. Try these suggestions:

1. Think about which agencies of the Canadian or U.S. government would likely have the best material on your topic. For Canadian documents, start at the Depository Services Program site mentioned above.
2. The gateway to Canadian government sites is at **http://Canada.gc.ca/ depts/major/depind_e.html**. FedWorld, at **http://www.fedworld.gov**, is the gateway to U.S. government publications, regulations, and statistics. Click on the category link, and use the first search box to search the entire FedWorld network and then narrow your search to the most appropriate agency.
3. Also search for your topic in the National Technical Information Service, at **www.ntis.gov**. This collection of nearly three million titles is the U.S. federal government's central sales point for scientific, technical, engineering, and related business information produced by or for the U.S. government. For interesting items, go to a nearby depository or library, or order them for a fee.
4. Try Thomas Legislative Information on the Internet at **http://thomas. loc.gov**. For example, you can search committee reports for "global warming," click report titles in the result list, and then "Best Sections" to access the prepared statements of expert witnesses and others who have testified before Congress on the subject.
5. Once you've found potentially useful government documents, try to get a look at them. Some government documents may be fully online and therefore downloadable. Others may be available in government-depository libraries (indicated in the government catalogues and indexes). If you don't know where the nearest such library is, ask a librarian. For all other government documents, you have to order and pay for them.

WHAT ABOUT BROCHURES AND OTHER PRODUCT LITERATURE?

Some projects may require product literature. For example, imagine you were working on a comparison of wind turbines used to generate electricity from the wind. To survey this equipment, you'd want manufacturers to send you their brochures and related literature. Here are several ways to do that:

1. Try using the *Thomas Register of American Manufacturers*, available both in most libraries and at **http://www.thomasregister.com**. Canadian companies are also available through the Thomas Register. A search for "wind turbines" would produce results similar to those in Figure 18-2.
2. For listings of Canadian companies, try Industry Canada's Strategis site: **http://www.strategis.ic.gc.ca/sc_coinf/ccc/engdoc/homepage.html**.

FIGURE 18-2

Thomas Register of American Manufacturers. This tool can be used for looking up manufacturers in Canada or the U.S. by province or state. Use the Register to find information about products and the technologies used in those products.

Source: Screenshot used with permission from Thomas Industrial Network.

WHAT ABOUT INFORMAL, UNPUBLISHED SOURCES?

If you get information from a salesperson, an expert, or someone generally in the know about your topic, treat these sources the same as you would a published book or journal article. In fact, citing phone interviews, in-person conversations, e-mail, or responses to inquiries shows what careful, thorough, professional research you have done. Readers are far more likely to be impressed with the research you've done and confident about your information and your conclusions. (See Chapter 19 for style and format in citations of these informal, unpublished sources.)

Interviews and Inquiries

Interviews and inquiry letters or e-mail can be good sources of information for a technical-writing project.

Interviews. Consider interviewing local experts or otherwise knowledgeable people on your topic—but *only after* you've reviewed your published information sources. It's not a good idea to go asking questions of a busy expert when you could have found the answers in any general encyclopedia or introductory textbook on the subject. To get ready for an interview:

1. Get in touch with the interviewee by phone and set up a date and time. Don't expect to be able to walk in any time you choose and hold the interview.
2. Make sure you've done your homework before going to the interview; don't ask questions whose answers you could have easily found elsewhere.
3. Prepare your questions in advance and bring them with you. Make sure they are both specific enough to get the information you need and general enough to get the interviewee talking about the topic.
4. Bring some money for photocopying costs in case the interviewee has some potentially useful materials that you can't take away with you. Bring a memory stick in case the information is in electronic files.
5. At the beginning of the interview, explain who you are and what you are working on. If you have a digital recorder, ask the interviewee if you can tape the interview.
6. Encourage the interviewee to tell you about any other resources, such as other experts, printed documents, or associations, that might be useful.
7. Don't allow the interview to run on longer than you had initially requested. At the end of the interview, offer to send a copy of your writing project to the interviewee.

Postal-mail or e-mail inquiries.   Another good informal source of information is the inquiry letter or e-mail:

1. Find knowledgeable individuals to whom you want to direct inquiries; for example, authors of books, articles, or reports related to your project.
2. If necessary, search for these individuals' e-mail addresses on any of the search tools available on the World Wide Web such as Google, Yahoo, Excite, AltaVista, or HotBot.
3. See Chapter 12 for ideas on content, organization, and strategies for writing inquiries.

WHAT ABOUT SURVEYS AND QUESTIONNAIRES?

Some technical-writing projects lend themselves to direct information gathering—not from published sources but straight from the "real world." In ordinary language, there's not much difference between the terms "survey" and "questionnaire." For this discussion, however, the following will apply:

- *Survey.* A type of direct information gathering in which you directly observe and record. For example, the city might assign you the task of counting traffic at an intersection to determine whether a stoplight is needed there.
- *Questionnaire.* The kind of direct information gathering in which you gather people's opinions, preferences, or demographic data through in-person, print, or electronic means. For example, if you were a member of a recycling action group, you might send out questionnaires to ascertain your fellow citizens' opinions about curbside recycling.

When you develop forms for surveys or questionnaires, include them in the appendix of the document that includes the data you gathered with those tools.

WORKSHOP: INFORMATION SEARCH

Here are some additional ideas for practising the concepts and strategies in this chapter:

1. *Determining keywords.* Pick one of the following topics and list as many synonyms for it as you can think of. (These might come in handy as additional keywords to use in an information search on this topic.)

Media violence	Old growth forests
Workplace discrimination	Renewable energy sources
Childhood diseases	Big Bang Theory
Narcotic addiction	Aging
Space travel	Aerospace medicine

2. *Choose your resources.* Consider the following topics, and make a list of the order in which you would search the different types of information resources (books, articles, encyclopedias, government documents and reports, product literature, informal resources):

Media violence	I LOVE YOU virus
Remote sensing	Privacy legislation
Renewable energy sources	Aerospace medicine
Human Genome Project	Toxic waste sites
Family planning	The X Prize

3. *Find books.* Choose one of the topics in the preceding exercises, think of as many keywords as you can, and then find up to six books on that topic. Use one of the online libraries discussed in this chapter.

4. *Find articles.* Choose one of the topics in the preceding exercises, think of as many keywords as you can, and then find up to 12 articles on that topic. Use one of the online periodical indexes discussed in this chapter.

5. *Find online articles.* Choose one of the topics in the preceding exercises, and find six online newspaper articles related to that topic. Use the suggestions in this chapter for finding online newspaper articles.

6. *Find encyclopedia articles.* Choose one of the topics in the preceding exercises, think of as many keywords as you can, and then find up to six articles on that topic in one encyclopedia. Try using one of the online encyclopedias discussed in this chapter, but also use an encyclopedia, such as the *Britannica* or *McGraw-Hill Encyclopedia of Science and Technology*, in your library.

7. *Find websites.* Choose one of the topics in the preceding exercises, and find six websites related to that topic in some way. Use the strategies discussed in this chapter to find these websites. In particular, try to find at least one "guide" site. Use suggestions in this chapter to evaluate each of the websites you find: rate them on a scale of 1 to 5, with 5 being highly reliable and 1 being highly unreliable.

8. *Find government documents.* Choose one of the topics in the preceding exercises, and find six government documents related to that topic, using the strategies discussed in this chapter.

9. *Find companies.* Choose one of the topics in the preceding exercises, and try to find three manufacturers or companies associated with that topic, using *Thomas Register* or some similar resource as discussed in this chapter.

10. *List other possible resources.* Choose one of the topics in the preceding exercises, and make a list of the unpublished, nonprint information resources you might need to research that topic. Consider experts, technicians, executives, product users, site visits, questionnaires, surveys, experiments, and so on as sources.

CHAPTER 19

Citing Sources
of Borrowed Information

Topics covered in this chapter include

■ extraterrestrial intelligence.

EXTRATERRESTRIAL INTELLIGENCE
About.com: UFOs/Aliens
http://ufos.about.com/culture/ufos/mbody.htm

Beginner's Guide to UFOs & Aliens:
http://ufos.about.com/culture/ufos/library/bldata/blguidea.htm

The Active Mind: SETI
http://www.activemind.com/Mysterious/Topics/SETI/index.html

Journal of Scientific Exploration (research-style articles on "fringe science")
http://www.jse.com

When you have completed this chapter, you will be able to

■ identify situations that require you to cite borrowed information;
■ use the MLA system to prepare in-text citations;
■ use the MLA system to prepare works-cited pages;
■ use the APA system to prepare in-text citations;
■ use the APA system to prepare reference pages.

This chapter shows you how to acknowledge information sources you've used to write your technical documents. Not acknowledging those sources, as you probably know, is called *plagiarism*. You may have already encountered the MLA system or the APA system, in which you indicate the sources of borrowed information in parentheses. This chapter reviews those. In addition to these common systems, several others are widely used in the technical and scientific fields. Also, some corporations may have their own requirements. It is important to follow whichever system is required for the document.

To provide a frame of reference for this process of acknowledging the sources of borrowed information, we'll review the idea of *intellectual property*. The individual's intellectual property includes the ideas of an individual and the words or images that the individual uses to express those ideas. Intellectual property may not have the same concrete reality that a house or an automobile has, but it can be just as valuable, if not more so.

When you indicate whom you have borrowed information from, put quotation marks around the exact words of someone else, ask for permission to use a direct quotation from an author, affix trademark symbols to product names, you're honouring, protecting, and respecting the intellectual property of others, as well as your own.

Note: Some examples of books, articles, and other information sources in this chapter are fictitious.

INTELLECTUAL PROPERTY AND PLAGIARISM

Before getting into the details of citing borrowed information sources, take a moment to understand the concept of *intellectual property*. When you cite the source of borrowed information, you are honouring the creator or originator of that information. You are also preventing people from thinking you were the creator or originator of that information. What are some of the forms of intellectual property that can be borrowed?

- Someone's exact words, or a similar rendition of them
- Someone's carefully researched data
- Someone's graphic (photo, drawing, chart) or an exact, or almost exact, replica of someone's graphic
- Someone's musical composition, or a similar rendition
- Someone's design; for example, a building, a software interface, or a website

It's hard to think of someone's words, data, images, and sounds as property the same way we think of land, automobiles, and other physical things as property. But they are—and every bit as valuable.

For more information on intellectual property rights, trademarks, and Canadian copyright issues, see these resources:

- Law professor Michael Geist's blog at **http://www.michaelgeist.ca/index.php**
- Professor Laura J. Murray's website at **http://www.faircopyright.ca**
- Lesley Ellen Harris's website at **http://copyrightlaws.com/index2.html**
- Copyright Policy Branch of Canadian Heritage at **http://www.pch.gc.ca/progs/ac-ca/progs/pda-cpb/index_e.cfm**
- Trademarks Canada at **http://www.trademarkscanada.ca**

When you are taking a technical-writing course and are using information from others, what does intellectual property mean to you? What's the difference between copyright violation and plagiarism? Both are violations of the intellectual property rights of others. You can be sued for plagiarism, but plagiarism is more of an ethical offence. Copyright violation is both an ethical and legal offence, often involving a direct intention to use someone else's copyrighted material for monetary gain. While you are more likely to be sued for violating copyright, plagiarism—although it's free—will merely cause you to be haunted by shame and other such moral anguish for the rest of your life. For example, in the 1980s, a U.S. presidential candidate was discovered to have plagiarized some of his law school work. He suffered shame and embarrassment and dropped out of the campaign, but was never sued.

NAME–YEAR SYSTEM (APA)

The *Publication Manual*, 5th ed. (2001) of the American Psychological Association (APA) has long been used as the documentation style by a wide range of disciplines, such as medicine, nursing, and sociology. In APA style, you put the name of the author whose information you are borrowing and the year that borrowed information was published in parentheses at the point in your text where you borrow that information. Because its focus is author name and publication date, the APA style is often called the "name–year" style:

Practical Ethics: Plagiarism

In 1994, singer Michael Bolton was found guilty of plagiarizing a song by the Isley Brothers and was ordered to pay them $5.4 million.[1] When an instructor at a Vermont college asked her students to write about John F. Kennedy's inaugural address, two out of sixteen students unwittingly handed in the same papers. They had both copied an article from *The New York Times* and turned it in as their own work. Both were given Fs for the class (although one student contested this grade).[2]

Simply stated, plagiarism is using someone else's words and passing them off as your own. Perhaps it's competition that leads us to steal phrases, paragraphs, or entire documents and claim ourselves to be the original authors. Then again, maybe it's just laziness or panic—writing is hard work, especially under deadline.

Plagiarism obviously poses some serious risks. However, avoiding it shouldn't be simply a matter of avoiding the consequences. It should be a matter of respect. Acting with integrity as a student in college or a professional in the workplace means giving others credit for their work; you should expect no less from them. If you want to take a totally selfish point of view, citing your sources (avoiding plagiarism) actually makes your work appear more professional and authoritative. Citing sources indicates you've done your homework, know your stuff, and take a professional attitude toward your work.

Respect others' intellectual property, and take some simple precautions. Cite your sources clearly and accurately. Ask permission to use copyrighted material. When in doubt, ask for a second opinion; an instructor supervisor, colleague, or lawyer would be happy to help.

[1] Farhi, Paul. *Washington Post:* 22 February 2000, p. C01.

[2] Lieberman, Trudy. "Plagiarize, Plagiarize, Plagiarize ..." *Columbia Journalism Review* July/August 1995 <www.cjr.org/year/95/4/plagiarize.asp>.

Because this study is the only unclassified investigation of the UFO phenomenon carried out by an established scientific organization under contract to a U.S. federal agency, the report based on this study (Condon & Gillmor, 1968) constitutes a landmark in the study of the UFO phenomenon, to which all later work must be referred.

You can also show the page number:

Condon argues that a civilization from a planet attached to a nearby star would not set out on a journey to Earth until that civilization knew that an advanced technology had been established here. Thus, he estimates that there is no possibility of such a civilization visiting earth in the next 10,000 years (Condon & Gillmor, 1968, p. 28).

If you've already cited the name or the year, or both, in the text, you can omit those elements in the parenthetical citation:

The history of the UFO phenomenon in the United States is long and complex. Jacobs (1975) has given a comprehensive account of this history up to 1973 in his book *UFO Controversy in America*.

You can indicate that you are borrowing from a combination of sources:

```
Soon after its publication, the Condon Report was
widely reviewed (Jacobs, 1975; McDonald, 1969; Chiu,
1969; Hynek, 1972).
```

Full details about the information sources should be provided in "References" at the end of the document, as illustrated in Figure 19-1. Notice the following details that are displayed in Figure 19-1.

■ Items in the list are arranged alphabetically but not numbered. Notice the "hanging indent" format: following lines are indented, not the first line.

References

Celestron International. (1999). *Ultima 2000-8 Schmidt-Cassegrain Telescope*. [Product brochure.]

Chiu, H. Y. (1969). The Condon report: scientific study of unidentified flying objects (book review). *Icarus*, 11, 447–450.

Condon, E. U. (Proj. Dir.), & Gillmor, D. S. (Ed.). (1968). Scientific study of unidentified flying objects. New York: Bantam.

Easterbrook, G. (1988). Are we alone? *Atlantic Monthly*. Retrieved December 1999, from http://www.the atlantic.com/issues/88aug/easterbr.htm.

Hannesonne, L. <remlynn@eathlinx.net> (1999, July 7). No UFOs here. [Personal e-mail]. (1999, July 8).

Hynek, J. A. (1972). *The UFO experience*. Chicago: Henry Regnery.

Jacobs, D. M. (1975). *The UFO controversy in America*. Bloomington: Indiana University Press.

McDonald, J. E. (1969). The Condon report: scientific study of unidentified flying objects (book review). *Icarus*, 11, 443–447.

Petit, J. P. (1986, September). Shockwave cancellation in gas by Lorentz force action. Proc. 9th Meeting on Magnetohydrodynamic Electrical Power Generation, Tokyo.

Sturrock, P. A. (1977). *Report on a survey of the American Astronomical Society concerning the UFO phenomenon*. Stanford University Report SUIPR 681R.

Sturrock, P. A. (1994a). Report on a survey of the membership of the American Astronomical Society concerning the UFO phenomenon: Part 1. *Journal of Scientific Exploration*, 8, 1.

Sturrock, P. A. (1994b). Report on a survey of the membership of the American Astronomical Society concerning the UFO phenomenon: Part 2. *Journal of Scientific Exploration*, 8, 153.

FIGURE 19-1

APA-style references page. The items in this sample references page show you the most common types of bibliographic entries using the APA style.

- Last name comes first, followed by initials (not full names).
- Following the name is the year of publication in parentheses, which is followed by a period.
- The title of the book comes next—italicized. Notice that only the first word of the title and any proper nouns in it are capitalized. The title of an article is not italicized.
- For books, notice that the city of publication comes first, followed by a colon, followed by the name of the publisher.
- For articles, notice that in the title of the article only the first word is capitalized and it is *not* enclosed in quotation marks. The name of the magazine or journal is italicized, and all important words are capitalized. Depending on the type of periodical, volume and issue numbers, page numbers, and date are handled in one of the following ways:
  - McMurrey, J. (1999). Photographic techniques and UFOs. *Journal of UFO Research 51*(2), 113–117.
  - McMurrey, P. (1999, July). UFO personalities. *UFO Monthly*, pp. 51–52.
- When more than one source was published in the same year by the same author, differentiate them with lowercase letters attached, as shown in Figure 19-1. In text, you would cite one of the Sturrock sources like this: (1994b).

NAME–PAGE SYSTEM (MLA)

As a college student, you may have learned the documentation style of the Modern Language Association (MLA). See *MLA Handbook for Writers of Research Papers*, 6th ed. (2003). In MLA, parentheses are used for the name of the author whose information you are borrowing and the page number where that information occurs at the point in your text where you borrow it. For example, notice the style of the following:

```
Most scientists who study UFOs, however, adopt a more
restricted definition that rules out reports that are
readily explainable (Hynek 3-4).
```

If you've already cited the name in the text, omit it in the parenthetical citation:

```
Hynek, however, adopts a more restricted definition that
rules out reports that are readily explainable (3-4).
```

If you don't cite a specific page, MLA doesn't expect you to create a citation at all (but you would still list the source in works cited):

```
The history of the UFO phenomenon in the United States
is long and complex. Jacobs has given a comprehensive
account of this history up to 1973 in his book UFO
Controversy in America.
```

If no author's name is available, use the first meaningful words of the title:

```
The past fifty years have seen several distinct periods
of heightened interest in UFOs ("'Tis the Season" 3).
```

For multiple authors, use the following format:

```
Because this study is the only unclassified investiga-
tion of UFOs carried out by an established scientific
organization under contract to a U.S. federal agency,
the report of this study (Condon and Gillmor 28) con-
stitutes a landmark in the study of the UFO phenomenon,
to which all later work must be referred.
```

Provide full details about your information sources in "Works Cited" at the end of the document, as illustrated in Figure 19-2.

Works Cited

Celestron International. "Ultima 2000-8 Schmidt-Cassegrain Telescope. Product brochure, 1999.

Chiu, Hi Y. Rev. of *Scientific Study of Unidentified Flying Objects* by Edward U. Condon and Daniel S. Gillmor. *Icarus* 11 (1969): 447-450.

Condon, Edward U., and Daniel S. Gillmor, ed. *Scientific Study of Unidentified Flying Objects*. New York: Bantam, 1968.

Easterbrook, Gregg. "Are We Alone?" *Atlantic Monthly*. August 1988. 19 Dec. 1999 <http://www.theatlantic.com/issues/88aug/easterbr.htm>.

Hannesonne, Lynn. "No UFOs Here." Personal e-mail. 8 July 1999.

Hynek, J. Allen. *The UFO Experience*. Chicago: Henry Regnery, 1972.

Jacobs, David Michael. *The UFO Controversy in America*. Bloomington: Indiana University Press, 1975.

McDonald, J. E. Rev. of *Scientific Study of Unidentified Flying Objects* by Edward U. Condon and Daniel S. Gillmor. *Icarus* 11 (1969): 443-447.

Petit, Jean-Pierre. "Shockwave Cancellation in Gas by Lorentz Force Action." Proceedings of the 9th meeting on Magnetohydrodynamic Electrical Power Generation. Tokyo, 1986.

Sturrock, Peter A. "Report on a Survey of the American Astronomical Society Concerning the UFO Phenomenon. *Journal of Scientific Exploration*. Stanford, CA: Stanford UP, 1994.

"'Tis the Season for UFOs." *UFO Times* 19 July 1990: 3–5.

FIGURE 19-2

MLA-style references page. The items in this sample page show you the most common types of bibliographic entries using the MLA style.

Notice the following details, illustrated in Figure 19-2.

- Items in the list are arranged alphabetically and are not numbered. Notice the "hanging indent" format: following lines are indented, but not the first line.
- Last name comes first, then first name and middle initials.
- After the name comes the title of the book (in italics) or article (in quotation marks). Notice that headline capitalization style is used (all main words).
- For books, after the title comes the city of publication (and province or state unless it is a large, well-known city such as Toronto or New York), followed by a colon, the name of the publisher, a comma, and the year of publication.
- For articles, the name of the magazine or journal is italicized. Depending on the type of periodical, volume and issue numbers, page numbers, and date are handled in one of the following ways:
  - McMurrey, Jane. "Photographic Techniques and UFOs." *Journal of UFO Research* 51.2 (1999): 113–117.
  - McMurrey, Patrick. "UFO Personalities." *UFO Monthly*. July 1999: 51–52.

FOR ADDITIONAL INFORMATION

The scope of this chapter can cover only the most common types of information sources. For additional information on the APA, MLA, CBE, and IEEE styles of documentation—in particular for unusual or complex sources—see the following resources:

- Gibaldi, Joseph. Modern Language Association of America. *MLA Handbook for Writers of Research Papers*, 6th ed., New York: 2003.
- American Psychological Association. *Publication Manual of the American Psychological Association*, 5th ed., New York: 2001.
- Institute of Electrical and Electronics Engineers. IEEE Transactions, Journals, and Letters. 1996.
- Perelman, Leslie C., James Paradis, Edward Barrett. *Mayfield Handbook of Technical and Scientific Writing*. Mountain View, CA: Mayfield, 1998.
- Harnack, Andrew, and Eugene Kleppinger. *Online! A Reference Guide to Using Internet Sources*. New York: St. Martin, 1998.

WORKSHOP: SOURCE DOCUMENTATION

The following exercises give you some practice with the concepts, tools, and strategies presented in this chapter:

1. *Create a reference or works-cited list.* Format the bibliographic information available at **http://www.powertools.nelson.com** using the name–year (APA) or name–page system (MLA).

2. *Add references in text.* Using the text at **http://www.powertools.nelson.com**, revise the citations according to the documentation style you picked in the preceding exercise.

CHAPTER 20

Managing Team Projects

Topics covered in this chapter include

- working in teams;
- groupthink;
- group editing.

WORKING IN TEAMS
Canada, with its wonderful outdoor adventure facilities, is a popular place for executive and team-building retreats.

Corporate Quest
http://www.corporatequest.org/blog.html

Find many team-building websites through Google
http://www.google.com/Top/Business/Education_and_Training/Team_Building

GROUPTHINK
Groupthink was a term coined by Irving Janus, who believed that groups often made bad decisions because of the pressure each member felt from the group as a whole.

Wikipedia.com, the online user-edited encyclopedia
http://en.wikipedia.org/wiki/groupthink

You can combat groupthink by using the 1965 Bruce Tuckman model, "Forming, Storming, Norming, and Performing."

Mount Royal College
http://www.mtroyal.ab.ca/studentlife/study_groups.shtml

GROUP EDITING
To learn how to use Track Changes, the function that allows several people to work collaboratively on one document, visit the Microsoft Office website at **http://office.microsoft.com/en-us/assistance/HP051888551033.aspx**.

When you have completed this chapter, you will be able to

- work as part of a writing team;
- plan a writing schedule and a document design prototype;
- review the work of other team members using a style guide.

As the workplace has become less formal and as hierarchies have become less defined, people are increasingly working in "teams"—shifting groups that are re-formed at practically each new project (or crisis). In fact, "teams," "teamwork," and even "teaming" became quite the buzzwords in the 1980s and 1990s. In a team, hierarchy is ill-defined. No one is officially the boss of anyone else; you don't do your work because the boss told you to, but because you feel loyalty to the team.

The modern workplace wants "team players" (another buzzword): people who know how to work effectively within teams. Teamwork is essential in completing large-scale projects, including technical documents. Some computer software products require several thousand pages of documentation. To get that amount of material out on time, writers must work in teams, which also consist of editors, graphic artists, testers, technical reviewers, product specialists, document designers, managers, and production and distribution specialists.

In response to the emergence of teams in the workplace, colleges and universities have increased the amount of team projects students do. To reflect the workplace movement, this chapter reviews the roles typically played in the production of technical documents and then explores how you can develop writing teams in your technical-writing courses.

HOW DO INDUSTRY WRITING TEAMS WORK?

Before developing your own writing team, spend some time getting to know how writing teams function in the workplace and what their roles and tasks are.

Teams in Industry

Technical documentation is handled in many different ways in industry. The following list reviews the organization of a typical well-staffed and well-organized writing team such as you might find at IBM, Dell, RIM, Adobe, or Microsoft. See Figure 20-1 for an organizational chart of a well-staffed documentation group. The point of this discussion is not to get you ready to work in a technical-writing department but to demonstrate the roles and tasks required in the production of a technical document—whatever the organization.

- *Managers.* Needed to make decisions, settle disputes, and ensure that the organization runs smoothly (despite what Dilbert thinks).
- *Planners.* Handle overall technical responsibilities for documentation projects, such as scheduling, library design, contents, and delivery media. Planners are also referred to as "lead writers" and "information architects." (In small "shops," the manager and planner may be the same person.)

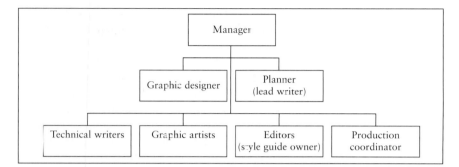

FIGURE 20-1

Typical organization for a documentation group. Remember that in smaller, or "downsized" organizations, some of these roles are combined into an individual team member's role.

- *Document designers.* Make decisions as to a documentation project's colour, graphics, page design, type style, headings, media, and so on. (These people often handle graphic-artist responsibilities as well.)
- *Writers.* Create, revise, and maintain the documents for a product, often specializing in certain kinds of documentation, such as Web pages, online helps, or print, or in certain technical areas, such as electronics, graphics, or networking. (In downsized organizations, a writer often must handle design, editing, and graphics as well.)
- *Technical reviewers.* Plan, develop, and test the actual product as well as write "specifications" that describe product functions. They review writers' documentation to ensure that it is technically correct and complete.
- *Graphic artists.* Develop and maintain "artwork" for a documentation project: illustrations of the products and other such graphics.
- *Editors.* Copy edit and proofread drafts of the documentation, assess whether it meets the needs of the intended readers, maintain the style guide, and ensure documents meet internal requirements (such as for legal notices).
- *Information testers.* Supervise individuals typical of the target audience who try using the documentation to perform product tasks. Testers summarize this feedback, which writers can use to improve their documents.
- *Production specialists.* Coordinate the scheduling, delivery, and inspection of completed documentation projects. They put it "into production."
- *Distribution specialists.* Handle the logistics of how the product and its documentation are distributed to customers. They coordinate how the product and all of its pieces, including the documentation, are packaged, or "kitted."

In most smaller documentation teams, many of these roles and tasks are combined and handled by one individual.

Teams in the Technical-Writing Classroom

In your technical-writing course, you won't have such a complex writing team as just described. Even in an introductory technical-writing course, you still must think about the functional roles performed by your team members. See Figure 20-2 for an idea of how you can structure your own technical-writing team. The project on wind energy used in chapters 6 and 14 was done by a team. Note their comments in the progress report.

■ *Writing.* Everybody on your writing team gets to do some writing for the project. Divide the writing tasks evenly among the members of your team—after all, it is a *writing* course!
■ *Reviewing.* Likewise, everybody on your team should get some experience reviewing—an important skill often lacking in the professional world. Review each other's drafts to enable your team to produce a better document; to help your team reach consensus on content, organization, and style issues; and just generally to help you think as one about the project. In this context, reviewing means looking at documents in

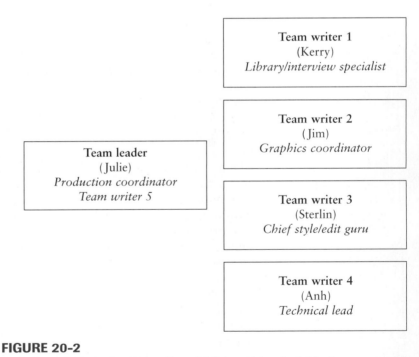

FIGURE 20-2

Team for a technical-writing class. Make sure that individual team members get their fair share of the writing, but find out if anybody on your team has special skills as editors, proofreaders, or graphic artists.

terms of technical accuracy, completeness, comprehension (understand-ability), organization, and usability.

- *Editing*. Editing is a specialized skill. Try finding that one team member who has a sharp eye for typos and grammar, usage, punctuation, and style problems. Reduce this individual's other project responsibilities accordingly. In this context, editing means looking at documents for spelling, grammar, usage, and punctuation errors, as well as other mechanical and style problems. In industry, many teams use functions such as Track Changes in Microsoft Word (**Tools→Track Changes**). Learn to use this function yourself.

- *Revising*. When your team members revise, individual team members use the feedback they get from other team members and do their own revising. To produce a consistent document that does not read like a patch-work written by four very different individuals, assign the final revision to one individual (and reduce that individual's workload accordingly).

- *Developing graphics*. As mentioned in Chapter 11, your technical-writing course is a *writing* course—not a graphics course. You can use various techniques to produce effective, professional-looking graphics without being a professional graphic artist. If one team member does have graphics talent, have other team members draw rough sketches of the

Practical Ethics: Groupthink

Being assigned to a group project is not only a reality in the classroom, but in many workplaces as well. When groups of people get together, conflict is almost inevitable. For many people, conflict is a negative thing to be avoided at all costs and, to them, a group without conflict is a successful one.

The author of *The Art and Science of Leadership* points out that a lack of conflict can actually indicate that members of a team are reluctant to disagree with the person in charge. "In some cases, the subordinates follow the leader because of personal commitment ... or they may truly respect their leader's expertise and personal integrity. In other cases, the compliance is simply due to fear of retribution."[1] When people are afraid to voice their opinions, "groupthink" can result—a situation in which team members keep their concerns to themselves, alternative ideas are frowned on, and bad or even unethical decisions are made.

The Team Handbook teaches that consensus decision-making can prevent groupthink. Consensus doesn't mean that decisions are unanimous, but rather that everyone has the opportunity to speak and test one another's ideas: "Consensus decision-making is not just a way to reach a compromise. It is a search for the best decision through the exploration of the best of everyone's thinking. As more ideas are addressed and more potential problems discussed, a synthesis of ideas takes place and the final decision is often better than any single idea that was present at the beginning."[2]

A truly successful team is not necessarily one that lacks conflict. Rather, it is one that encourages all members to brainstorm, raise concerns, and hold one another accountable so poor or unethical decisions are not made.

[1] Nahavandi, Afsaneh. *The Art and Science of Leadership, Second Edition.* New Jersey: Prentice Hall, 2000, 87.

[2] Scholtes, Peter, Brian Joiner, and Barbara Streibel. *The Team Handbook, Second Edition.* Madison, WI: Oriel Incorporated, 1996, 4–23.

graphics they need and get your designated graphics specialist to develop the final graphics.

- *Researching.* It's a tricky problem to plan who will research project information and how and when this can be accomplished. Without some planning, individual team members may duplicate each other's effort, each finding the same information on their own.
- *Designing the document.* Early in your project, get your team to design the document: margins, type style, heading and list style, highlighting, terminology, and so on. Have each team member create a document prototype separately, and then have a group meeting to compare designs and choose one.
- *Producing the document.* Producing the final copy is no simple step. Once team members have produced their final drafts, the parts must be assembled in one complete, integrated document. Final graphics must be inserted. Getting the page breaks right may take some time. Front and back matter elements—such as title pages, covers, and tables of contents—have to be added. And you must get the document bound. See Chapter 14 for details on producing a final copy.
- *Overseeing the project.* Even your project may need a manager or overseer—someone to settle disputes and to ensure that everything is running smoothly. As a team, anticipate what disputes may arise and how to settle them. Solutions for typical problems are suggested in the next section.

Anticipating Problems in the Team Project

In any team effort, you must anticipate problems and plan how to deal with them. Think about the kinds of problems that might occur when four or five college students (who are not majoring in English or technical writing) attempt to team-write a technical document.

- *One team member ends up having too much or too little to do.* The overworked team member gets sulky and less cooperative. The underworked team member is resented by the others. What to do? Here's a solution: have team members fill out weekly project time sheets and have an overall project coordinator watch for and resolve problems. (See Figure 20-3 for examples.)
- *One team member just doesn't do her or his part—either out of laziness, personal problems, or inability.* What to do about slackers and incompetents? What if a team member has a personal crisis and can't finish the course? Develop "bylaws" that address these possibilities. Ask your instructor: if one team member doesn't produce, what will be the effect on the rest of the team?
- *Team members disagree about some aspect of the writing project and can't reach a compromise.* For example, team members may be unable to reach an agreement over whether contractions should be used (sad, but truly possible). Try getting potential arguments like these settled early and recording them in the style guide. Also, agree on a process for

Name _____
Team-Report Project: Week of _____

| | W=writing | G=graphics | P=production | |
| | R=reviewing | I=research | M=meetings | |

Date	Start	End	Code	Comments

FIGURE 20-3

Example of a project log. To ensure that team members are doing their fair share and keeping to the schedule, consider having everyone keep a project log like this one.

resolving disputes. For example, decide on a 20-minute maximum for discussion, followed by a vote, or present both sides to the instructor, who will decide.

■ *Some team members are shy and nonassertive; others, loud and aggressive.* How do you bring out those quiet members of your team who have lots to contribute? How do you keep loudmouths and bullies from taking over? Appoint a discussion leader whose responsibility is to ensure that everyone is invited to contribute and to put the overly aggressive members in their places.

Anticipating problems like these at the beginning of your team-writing project, agreeing on ways to resolve them, getting those agreements in writing, and then ensuring that everybody "buys into" those agreements can help. Build your instructor into the process as the arbiter.

HOW DO YOU TEAM-WRITE A TECHNICAL-WRITING PROJECT?

Let's put all these ideas together into a scenario for a team-writing project.

1. *Assemble and get to know your team.* Find a way to get a good mix of writing, editing, design, graphics, and technical skills for your team. Get your instructor to stage some sort of getting-to-know-you event in the classroom. Once you've formed a writing team, find out about the skills each team member has. Just for fun, give your team a name, a logo, or a slogan. You may even want to create a company profile. For examples, search online for companies like Canadian Tire and Roots.

2. *Agree on general procedures and "bylaws."* When you divide up team roles, make sure each team member has a fair share of writing to do. As a team, anticipate problems, reach agreements, and write them down. If your team is concerned about individual members doing their fair share of the work, have individual team members keep project

journals or time sheets in which they record what they do and how much time they spend doing it.

3. *Decide on your writing project.* Get together with your team to develop a project, preferably one addressing a real workplace problem. Analyze the audience, decide on a focus, and plan other details. Get these in writing, too.

4. *Do some initial research and develop an outline.* To define your writing project thoroughly and to outline it, spend some time scanning information sources, talking to experts, and brainstorming as a team. Decide on an effective way to create that outline: should everybody go off and take a stab at it separately (a tactic that brings out your quieter, less assertive teammates)? Should you get together for a big brainstorming session?

5. *Assign the team roles and tasks.* Perhaps once you've developed the rough outline, your team will be ready to decide who writes which parts of the outline and who handles which tasks. Get these in writing too.

6. *Develop a detailed schedule.* If you've assigned team roles and tasks, you can develop a schedule. (See the sample schedule in Figure 20-4.)

Individual prototypes due	October 1
Team meeting: finalize the prototype	October 1
Rough-draft style guide due	October 5
Team meeting: finalize style guide	October 5
Twice-weekly team meetings: progress & problems	October 5–26
Graphics sketches due to Jim	October 14
Rough drafts of individual sections due	October 26
Review of rough drafts due	October 28
Team meeting: discuss rough drafts, reviews	October 28
Update of style guide due from Sterlin	October 31
Revisions of rough drafts due to reviewers	November 3
Final graphics due from Jim	November 5
Completed drafts to Sterlin: final edit/proof	November 7
Team meeting: review completed draft with final graphics and editing	November 12
Completed drafts due to Julie for final production	November 15
Team meeting: inspection of completed project	November 15
Project upload due to McMurrey	November 16
Party at Julie's	November 19

FIGURE 20-4

Document project schedule. Develop a schedule with tasks, completion dates, and the names of team members who are responsible for those tasks. If you want to get fancy, try developing a Gantt chart, which shows the relationship of concurrent tasks and their different start and stop dates.

In it, include due dates for the drafts of the different sections, due dates for completed reviews, due dates for completed editing, due dates for final production, and so on. Work backward from the final due date—that date when your instructor expects you to turn in the finished project.

7. *Design the document; create a document prototype and style guide.* Agree as a team on how you want the final document to look. Create a prototype—a "dummy"—of that document. See Figure 20-5 for examples of document prototypes. In the prototype, include examples of every type of page or format: covers, title pages, tables of contents, graphics, tables, headings, lists, highlighting, notices, and so on. Agree on page size, margins, fonts, type sizes, colour, and other such issues. Make sure that all team members have a copy of the prototype to reference as they develop their parts of the document.

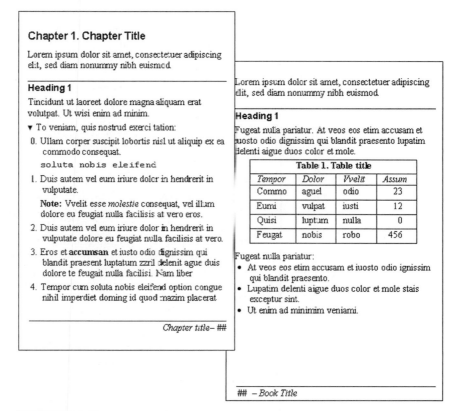

FIGURE 20-5

Sample pages from prototype for a writing project. The prototype, consisting of fake Latin text, illustrates every unique feature of the document: each unique section (title page, table of contents, body page, etc.), headings, lists, tables, graphics, and so on. These sample pages show only two body pages.

Also, develop a style guide that records team decisions about terminology; rules for punctuation, capitalization, and hyphenation; rules for italics, bold, alternate fonts, and colour; format for bulleted and numbered lists; design for headings and notices; and so on. Also record rules such as when to use digits or words for numbers in regular text; whether to use decimals or fractions; how to use abbreviations; and so on. Record these decisions along with examples illustrating them in a style guide, as shown in Figure 20-6.

8. *Write the rough drafts*. Writing projects are not neat, tidy affairs where one task stops and another starts without any overlap. When you start writing the rough drafts of your individual sections, you may need to rethink the outline, do additional research, or change the document design. These kinds of events necessitate that you get back together

---

Highlighting

1. Use bold for interface elements that function like commands (for example, the **Exit** button).
2. Use bold for menu options that get you to commands (for example, **File→Open**).
3. Use the → symbol to abbreviate menu traversal.
4. Use Courier New for sample text that users type in (for example, `myfile.doc`).
5. Use italics for variables—placeholder text for which users substitute their own information (for example, *filename*.doc).

Hyphenation

1. *Individual words*. Turn automatic hyphenation off. Do not hyphenate words except in tight places like tables or graphics.
2. *Compounds*. Mr. Hyphen (Sterlin) will keep the hyphenated-compounds list. Use only those in his list, and submit new ones to him for approval and inclusion on the list. (Hyphenate compounds only when they modify [for example, "back-up copy"], not when they act as nouns or verbs [for example, "to back up your files"]).

Terminology

1. Use only the words in **graph_project.dic**. Sterlin approves all new words for that database.
2. Use the same word for the same object, same process, or same action. No elegant variation, please!

FIGURE 20-6

Excerpt from a style guide for a team-writing project. Style guides help team writers agree on things like whether to use contractions or Latin abbreviations, how lists will be punctuated, how to handle abbreviations and numbers in text, and which terms are preferred.

with your team. For these reasons, schedule regular meetings during the rough-drafting phase—if not in person, perhaps by phone, e-mail, or Internet chat.

9. *Review each other's drafts.* Ensure that team members provide each other with good thorough reviews of their drafts. Remember that a review generally does not include picky grammar, usage, and punctuation issues. A review focuses more on content, organization, comprehension, flow, and general suitability for the audience and situation. Summarize your review comments in a memo to the writer whose section you reviewed. (See the sample review memo in Figure 20-7.) Attach the memo to the reviewed draft, which includes your markup and marginal comments.

10. *Revise and review again.* The review-and-revise phase is essential in producing any document. And it's not a once-only event. Reviewers review; writers revise; and then reviewers review again to ensure problems were fixed. Keep reviewing and revising until everyone is satisfied, or time runs out.

11. *Edit the full draft.* You must leave time between the completion of the rough drafts (including their review) and the production of the final copy for a final thorough edit of the complete document.

12. *Assemble and "produce" the final copy.* When you've got the complete document drafted, reviewed, and edited, it's time to put all the pieces together into the final copy. Now's the time to insert the final graphics and get the pagination right. It's also the time to put in the front- and back-matter elements. When you get that done, make a good clean photocopy, get the photocopy bound, and hand in the bound photocopy. (Put the original copy away for safekeeping.)

13. *Throw a party and celebrate!* Unless your team has had so many disagreements that everybody hates each other (which reflects inadequate up-front planning), get together and celebrate the completion of the project. Have some laughs over things that went wrong, and try to imagine how the problems might have been avoided. As a matter of fact, this sort of event is an actual stage in formal projects, often called a "postmortem." Team members in industry, business, and government typically go on to work on other projects together. They need to reflect on what went right and what went wrong with the project and use those insights to improve their process for the next project.

```
From hcexres36:05 2005 -0600
Date: Sun, 5 Dec 2005 15:36:04 -0600 (EST)
From: "David A. McMurrey" <hcexres@io.com>
To: julie@colltech.com
cc: xgraphic_team
Subject: Review of your section of Xgraphics HTML project
Content-Type: TEXT/PLAIN; charset=US-ASCII


Julie, your section of the guide is super! You've
done several things the rest of the team ought to
incorporate in their sections.

1. I do find places where it feels like there is too
much text—for example, in "Using Gravity and Snap."
It's not a major problem, but I'd be looking to see
if I could cut a few lines from the longer paragraphs
without sacrificing detail.

2. Your labels for the screen captures are really
nice. You'll have to show the rest of the team how
you do it.

3. You leave out generic buttons on several pages—I
think the group was in agreement that *all* pages
would have them at the bottom.

4. I notice in some areas you use italics for some
interface elements, bold for others. Our style guide
states that we wanted bold for any screen button or
similar element that makes something happen when you
click it. Maybe we need to discuss the distinction
you are thinking about here at our next meeting.
```

FIGURE 20-7
Review memo for a team-writing project. Notice that this sampling of comments focuses on contents, audience, organization, comprehension, and other such "high-level" matters.

WORKSHOP: TEAMS

Here are some additional ideas for practising the concepts, tools, and strategies in this chapter:

1. *Teamwork for a nonwriting project.* Find some nonwriting project requiring multiple individuals, such as setting up a campsite or cooking a gourmet meal for friends. Approach that project in one or both of the following ways:

- *Plan nothing!* Without any planning whatsoever, just dive in and try to get the job done. When the smoke has cleared, step back and reflect on who did what and why. Recall what problems occurred, such as tasks getting done out of order, tasks being duplicated, or people stepping on each other's toes (or turf). List the roles that were assumed by the members of your team and the steps in the process. Devise a plan for doing the same project that will ensure efficiency and effectiveness next time.
- *Plan everything!* Try to plan everything up-front. Decide who will do what and when, whether there should be an overall boss, how to resolve problems, and so on. Get everything in writing. When you've planned it to death, do the project. When you've finished the project, step back and have a "postmortem" and identify what worked and what didn't.

2. *Teamwork for a writing project.* To explore the dynamics of teamwork in a technical-writing context, find a writing project in which the actual writing has been done. For example, you will find details of a collaboration between FUN Technologies of Toronto and eBay on the FUN Technologies website at **http://www.funtechnologies.com**. This Canadian company, under its subsidiary SkillJam, provides tournament-style trivia games through eBay. Search for news or press releases on the FUN Technologies website and use them to plan other ways to announce news about the collaboration (television news, theatre ads, hot air balloons—be creative). Use the suggestions in this chapter to plan your process, assign roles, and accomplish other aspects of the project. Plan it to death; get it all in writing—remember that the point is to experience teamwork and to observe what works and what doesn't work.

PART V

Writing Tools: Mechanics and Style

Abbreviations, Symbols, and Numbers

Topics covered in this chapter include

- time travel and superluminal motion.

TIME TRAVEL
NOVA Online: Time Travel
http://www.pbs.org/wgbh/nova/time/index.html

Sci-Fi Science
http://freespace.virgin.net/steve.preston/time.html

Cambridge Relativity
http://www.damtp.cam.ac.uk/user/gr/public

Einstein: Image & Impact (from the American Institute of Physics)
http://www.aip.org/history/einstein

When you have completed this chapter, you will be able to

- use abbreviations, acronyms, and initialisms correctly in your writing;
- use symbols appropriately in your technical documents;
- create and use symbols available in Word 2003 for your technical documents;
- use accepted forms of numbers in technical writing.

In technical writing, you face numerous situations in which you must decide whether to use an abbreviation or write out the word, whether to use a symbol or the word for the symbol, and whether to use digits or words for numbers. Styles vary from field to field and profession to profession. Find a style guide for publications in your field or profession. It will show you the rules for annoying things like abbreviations, acronyms, symbols, and numbers. (See "Find a Guide" in Chapter 18.)

Here are some common examples of standards and style guides for specific fields and professions:

Symbols.com—Claims to be the world's largest online encyclopedia of graphic symbols: http://ww.symbols.com

University of Exeter. A Dictionary of Measures, Units, and Conversions: http://www.ex.ac.uk/cimt/dictunit/dictunit.htm

Electric Library. Concise Columbia Electronic Encyclopedia: http://www.encyclopedia.com

Russ Rowlett, University of North Carolina, Chapel Hill. *How Many? A Dictionary of Units of Measurement:* http://www.unc.edu/~rowlett/units/index.html

ABBREVIATIONS, ACRONYMS, AND INITIALISMS

The official difference between acronyms and initialisms is that you can pronounce acronyms (for example, AIDS, NAFTA, and NASA). "Acronym" is the term commonly used for both, while "initialism" seems to be a favourite of the hypercorrect. Here are the essential guidelines for abbreviations and acronyms.

1. Use abbreviations that are standard. Check a good general dictionary or a specialized dictionary, handbook, or style guide in your field. Don't make up abbreviations, and, in measurements, include a space between a number and its abbreviation unless your field or profession dictates otherwise.

For most work, much higher frequencies are needed such as the kilohertz (kHz) and megahertz (MHz), named after the German physicist Heinrich Rudolf Hertz.

Winnipeg Public Utility enrolled about 25 small businesses, which represent 12 percent of the total participants and account for 38 percent of its 600 kW wind turbine output.

In 1996 in some provinces, grid-connected-system owners were eligible for a tax credit of 1.6 cents per kilowatt hour for the electricity they sell back to the utility. In some eastern provinces, the credit is very low (less than $.02/kWh).

Earth's gravitational field is 1 g (9.81 m/s).

To get to Andromeda at 1 g using Newton's theory would take some 2,065 years.
(Notice that the abbreviation "g," representing gravity, is used without a period and is written with a space after the numeral.)

Our own galaxy is moving at about 600 km/s toward a distant object dubbed the "Great Attractor." This lies at a distance of 45 Mpc and has a mass approaching 5 × 10 solar masses.

2. In documents containing lots of abbreviations such as inches and feet, use the symbols ' and ":

    To build a purple-martin birdhouse, you'll need to get a 4' × 8' 1/4" sheet of plywood and a 14' 4" × 4" post.

    Cut a 25" × 25" floor from the sheet of plywood.

    Note: To get the "×" (multiplication symbol) for "by" in Microsoft Word 2003, choose **Insert→Symbol** and look in **Mathematical Operators**.

3. Watch out for abbreviations beginning with a capital letter. Words like angstrom, joule, and tesla were named after people. Therefore, according to some styles, you must use the initial cap; in others, you don't:

    Named for James P. Joule, a joule (J) is the energy expended by a force of 1 newton acting through a distance of 1 metre.

> An angstrom (Å) is a unit cf length equal to 10^{-10}
> metre; it is used to measure wavelengths of visible
> light and other forms of electromagnetic radiation.

Note: To insert the Å for angstrom, see the preceding steps, but look in Normal Text and subset Basic Latin in Microsoft Word 2003.

4. Use periods on abbreviations only if they spell a word. Usage varies; check a dictionary or style guide in your field. Acronyms and initialisms are rarely punctuated with periods, but again there are exceptions (as always). If an abbreviation ends the sentence, you only need one period:

> What would be the sense in determining that a table
> is 80 cm long if the very act of measuring it changed
> its length?

> At Winnipeg Public Utility, 25 small businesses
> account for 38 percent of its 600 kW wind turbine
> output.

> In Vancouver, British Columbia, a 30,000 sq ft office
> complex uses composting toilets and urinals for human
> waste disposal.

> Because carrots usually have a slow and relatively
> poor germination rate, they should be sown about
> 3/4 in. apart and thinned to about 11 in. apart.

5. Don't use an abbreviation if it occurs without a value:

> On the American football field, the yard is the
> primary measurement, not the metre.

> The newton was named for Sir Isaac Newton, whose
> second law of motion describes the changes that a
> force can produce in the motion of a body.

> The dyne is a unit of force in the centimetre-gram-
> second system of physical units. One dyne equals
> 0.00001 newton.

> As a unit of mechanical power, the horsepower is
> equal to 33,000 foot-pounds per minute, or 6,600
> inch-pounds per second.

6. Do not add an *s* to make abbreviations plural (but check your dictionary or style guide for the few exceptions). To show the plural of an acronym or initialism, just add *s*:

> We do not know the if the universe contains any
> closed timelike curves (CTCs), although the German
> mathematician Kurt Gödel, among others, have
> performed calculations that predict CTCs.
> *(Notice that you do not use an apostrophe on plurals of acronyms.)*

> In the United States, each state has its own regula-
> tions for labelling produce as organic, and there are
> 36 nongovernmental organizations (NGOs) that can
> certify produce as organic.

7. Don't overwhelm readers with abbreviations. For example, if an unfamiliar acronym occurs 4 times in a 6-page document, why not just write it out those 4 times rather than burdening your readers' memory?

> The kilohertz and megahertz were named after the
> German physicist Heinrich Rudolf Hertz (1857-94).
> *(No reason to use kHz or MHz here, unless you want to establish the abbreviation in parentheses.)*

> The 16,000 wind turbines in California produce 1,500
> megawatts, the equivalent of 3 to 4 large coal-fired
> plants.
> *(If this is the only occurrence of megawatts, why use the abbreviation Mw?)*

8. Always write out acronyms and unfamiliar abbreviations (placing the acronym or abbreviation in parentheses immediately after the spelled-out term) on first use. Thereafter, use the abbreviation:

> By following a closed timelike curve (CTC), we could
> meet ourselves in the past, or if the loop were large
> enough, visit our ancestors.
> *(The written-out version occurs first, followed by the acronym in parentheses. The written-out version uses lowercase—it's not a proper noun.)*

> We do not know if the universe contains any CTCs,
> though there have been several calculations,
> including one by the German mathematician Kurt Gödel,
> that predict CTCs.
> *(Notice that you do not use an apostrophe on plurals of acronyms.)*

> Internet Relay Chat (IRC) is a distributed
> client-server system, with more than a hundred
> servers scattered across the Internet.
> *(This one is a proper noun; therefore initial caps are used.)*

9. Don't use initial caps on acronyms unless they are proper nouns. NAFTA stands for "North American Free Trade Agreement"—a proper noun. ROM stands for "read-only memory"—not a proper noun.

SYMBOLS

A symbol is something like ′ (foot), ″ (inch), @ (at), # (pound), ¶ (paragraph), © (copyright), ° (degree), or Å (angstrom). Computers have made inserting symbols into regular text much easier. In Microsoft Word, choose **Insert→Symbol** and look in Normal Text, subset Basic Latin.

1. For potentially unfamiliar symbols, write the symbol and, on first use, put the name of the symbol in parentheses just after.

   To "comment out" a line in a Perl program, start the line with # (pound).

   To access your home page on a computer running Linux Apache, use the ~ (tilde) followed by your user name.

   Named after James P. Joule, a joule (J) is equal to the work done or energy expended by a force of 1 newton acting through a distance of 1 metre.

   An Å (angstrom) is a unit of length equal to 10^{-10} metre; it is used to measure wavelengths of visible light and other forms of electromagnetic radiation.

2. Avoid using # (pound) for numbered items. Just use the word followed by the numerical digit:

   The Anti-exe virus overwrites the first 8 sectors of every head and track on the hard drive starting at side 0, sector 4.

   If the software does not perform correctly, return to step 4.

   Highlighting is covered in Chapter 7.

3. Don't use a symbol unless it is next to a value:

   The primary unit of currency in the United States is the dollar.
   (No $ symbol here.)

   What's the difference between a centimetre and an inch?
   (No cm and no ″ here.)

4. If there are just a few occurrences of the symbol in the document, write out the name of the symbol instead of using the symbol.

   The ohm is the SI unit of resistance of an electrical

conductor, named after the German physicist Georg
Simon Ohm.

*(No reason to use the symbol Ω or ω, the Greek letters for omega, in this
instance. However, if you want to establish the meaning of the symbol for
later use, show the symbol and put its definition in parentheses.)*

NUMBERS

Although mathematics may be an exact science, choosing between digits
and words is not. In the technical-writing context, where precision is
important, use digits for numbers, even for numbers you've been taught to
write out (such as one through ten). But because there are so many exceptions, keep a style guide of all instances where you use or could have used
digits. (See Chapter 20 for information on style guides.)

1. Use digits for exact numbers that express an important value, even if
   they are 10 or below (this same rule applies to percentage values):

   Earth's gravitational field is 1 g (9.81 m/s).

   To get to Andromeda at 1 g using Newton's theory
   would take some 2,065 years.

   One of the problems associated with time dilation is
   that when we return from Andromeda we would have aged
   less than 4 years while the Earth would have aged
   around 4.4 million years.

   More than 85% of all viruses are boot sector (Master
   Boot Record—MBR) related viruses.

   Macro virus population diversity has gone from 1 to
   more than 800 in the last two years.

   It started with 12 "bad" files and grew to 166 by 1987.

   The Planck epoch, calculated by quantum processes as the
   earliest time that classical space—time is conceivable,
   is set at 0.0000000000000000000000000000000000000000001
   seconds.

2. Use words for nonexact, nonimportant numerical values. Obviously,
   this guideline involves judgment calls. Take a look at the following
   examples:

   For some, there are two main categories of galaxies,
   the spiral and elliptical galaxies. Others make it
   four, including lenticular and irregular galaxies.

The disk of the Milky Way has four spiral arms, and it is approximately 300 pc thick and 30 kpc in diameter. It is predominantly made up of Population I stars that tend to be blue and are reasonably young, spanning an age range between 1 million and 10 billion years.

The study of large-scale structure, currently being made by the Hubble Space Telescope, shows galaxies just a couple billion years after the Big Bang.
(Just round "ballpark" numbers here; no digits!)

Research indicates that there may be up to ten times more dark matter associated with each galaxy than the previous estimate.
(Here "ten" is an estimate—not a good spot for a digit.)

The diversity of macro viruses has gone from 1 to more than 800 in the last two years.
(The "two" years in this case is an estimated, ballpark value—not exact.)

The idea that our universe might have more than the three familiar spatial dimensions was introduced more than half a century before the advent of string theory.

3. For rounded numbers in the millions or greater, use digits followed by the word "million," "billion," and so on.

Imagine a journey to Andromeda, some 2.2 million light years away.

One of the problems associated with time dilation is that when we return from Andromeda we would have aged less than 4 years while the Earth would have aged around 4.4 million years.

To get to Andromeda at 1 g using Newton's theory would take some 2,065 years. The same journey in an Einsteinian universe, at the speed of light, would take 30,000,000 seconds, or a little under 354 days.
(The writer probably chose to use digits instead of "30 million" to make a sharp contrast with 2,065 and for emphasis.)

Each year, automobiles are responsible for some 57 million bird deaths; more than 97 million birds die by flying into plate glass; and about 1.5 million birds die from collisions with structures *(towers, stacks, bridges, and buildings).*

Businesses worldwide have lost a total of $7.6 billion in U.S. dollars in the first two quarters of 1999 at the hands of Melissa, the Explore.Zip worm and other viruses, according to a new study.

(Notice repetition of "$" and "dollars." It's essential to the meaning of the sentence to specify "in U.S. dollars" since other countries' currencies use dollars; however, if you were to remove the "$" before "7.6 billion," thinking it redundant, this could make the reader have to backtrack—we're conditioned to seeing the "$" before the number.)

4. Avoid starting a sentence with a digit; rewrite so that the digit occurs somewhere within the sentence:

   Avoid: 3960 miles is the Earth's radius.
   Revised: The Earth's radius is 3960 miles.
   Avoid: 70% of concrete mix is made up of
              aggregates.
   Revised: Aggregates constitute 70% of concrete mix.

5. Hyphenate numeric-measurement compounds; leave a space between numeric-measurement compounds:

   Heisenberg presented his discovery of the uncertainty principle and its consequences in a 14-page letter to Pauli in February 1927.

   For the Newtonian version, the power requirement is enormous, even assuming perfect efficiency. The energy required would be 5.1×10^{26} joules for a 10-ton spaceship.

6. Use digits for numbered items (but omit the #):

   The Anti-exe virus overwrites the first 8 sectors of every head and track on the hard drive starting at side 0, sector 4.

   If your software does not perform correctly, return to step 4.

   Highlighting is covered in Chapter 7.

7. Use digits for one or the other of a pair of numbers that occur side by side:

   To build the 16-plant hydroponic garden, you will need to collect 16 two-litre bottle caps.

   Panel coverage will be 36" to the weather with 1-1/4" deep major ribs every 12" and two 3/16" deep minor ribs between.

> The six 80-foot wind towers are estimated to produce 50,000 kilowatt hours (kWh) per year, or 4500 kWh per month.
>
> The specifications call for 38 six-litre biohazard containers.

8. Spell out fractions occurring by themselves without whole numbers or measurement names, unless either the numerator or the denominator is more than 10. Use digits if the fraction is associated with a measurement.

> The first sky Einstein ring is an invisible line two-ninths of the way to the top of the plot above the photon sphere.
>
> A metre is the distance light travels, in a vacuum, in 1/299792458th of a second.
> *(No "s" at the end of "th.")*
>
> Ensign wasps have three pairs of legs, two pairs of wings, and are 1/4 to 3/4 inches long with a general body shape that makes them easily distinguishable from other wasps.
> *(Use digits here because of the "inch" measurement.)*

WORKSHOP: MECHANICS

The following exercises give you some practice with the guidelines and rules presented in this appendix. For additional practice, see **http://www. powertools.nelson.com**.

1. *Abbreviations.* In the following sentences, convert the appropriate written-out words and phrases to abbreviations, acronyms, and initialisms, using the guidelines presented in this appendix—or add abbreviations, acronyms, and initialisms, as necessary. (Careful! Not all of these items should be converted to abbreviations, acronyms, or initialisms.)
   a. The CheapTech BikeLite is simply a battery-powered light source that uses light-emitting diodes to provide its light.
   b. The bike light is about 7 centimetres by 5 centimetres by 4 centimetres, and it weighs approximately 60 grams (including the battery).
   c. For example, NIST-7, a cesium clock at the National Institute of Standards and Technology, is accurate to five parts in 1015 (meaning it will lose about one second in 6 million years).
   d. For example, goldfish enjoy water temperatures of 69 degrees Fahrenheit or less.

    e. In March 1998, astronomers warned that an asteroid could come within 30,000 kilometres of Earth or even strike Earth in 2028.

    f. It's rare that asteroids are more than a kilometre across.

    g. According to Donald Yeomans, head of the near-Earth objects program office at the Jet Propulsion Laboratory, there are no known near-Earth objects that will threaten Earth in the next century.

2. *Symbols.* In the following sentences, convert the appropriate words to symbols, using the guidelines presented in this appendix. (Careful! Not all words in the following that could be converted to symbols should be converted to symbols.)

    a. For example, goldfish enjoy water temperatures of 69 degrees Fahrenheit or less.

    b. NASA has just doubled its asteroid search budget to 3 million dollars.

    c. To build the purple-martin birdhouse, you'll need to get a 4 foot by 8 foot by one-quarter inch sheet of plywood and a 4 inch by 4 inch by 14 foot cedar post, among other things.

    d. On a diamond's surface, the distance between adjacent hydrogens is about 2.5 angstroms.

    e. A micron is one millionth of a metre.

    f. Currently 95 percent of all energy produced in the world is made by one or another method of burning carbon dioxide in the atmosphere.

3. *Numbers.* In the following sentences, convert the appropriate words-for-numbers to numbers-for-words, using the guidelines presented in this appendix. (Careful! Not all words-as-numbers in the following should be converted.)

    a. In the United States today there are an estimated fifteen million people who have been diagnosed with Diabetes Mellitus.

    b. Diabetes is known as the 7th leading cause of death in the United States.

    c. Microsoft's popular software programs Word and Excel include within their hidden software code a 32-digit number, called a Globally Unique Identifier, which is transmitted to Microsoft whenever a customer registers a copy of Windows using its automated Registration Wizard.

    d. At six o'clock the five men made their way to 435 2nd Street, where they began remodeling the small house.

    e. Not until the 1999 bonfire tragedy that killed 12 students did the university seriously question whether the tradition should continue.

    f. 5'1 inches tall and only 90 pounds, the gymnast nevertheless dominated the arena.

APPENDIX B

Punctuation: Commas, Semicolons, Colons, Hyphens, Dashes, Apostrophes, and Quotation Marks

Topics covered in this section include

- computer viruses.

COMPUTER VIRUSES
Symantec
http://www.symantec.com/avcenter/global/index.html

McAfee
http://ca.mcafee.com/virusInfo/default.asp?cid=10439

Sci-Fi Science
http://freespace.virgin.net/steve.preston/time.html

GRAMMAR, PUNCTUATION, AND SPELLING
The University of Victoria's Hypertext Writer's Guide
http://web.uvic.ca/wguide

W. H. Fowler's The King's English
http://www.bartleby.com/116

Grammar, Usage, and Style links
http://www.refdesk.com/factgram.html

The Online Writing Lab at Purdue
http://owl.english.purdue.edu/handouts/grammar/index.html

Office of Public Relations, McMaster University, Writing Style Guide
http://www.mcmaster.ca/ua/opr/styleguide

When you have completed this chapter, you will be able to

- correctly punctuate your sentences;
- use Microsoft Word to create punctuation marks.

For a complete review of most grammar, usage, and style problems, see *Checkmate Pocket Guide* by Joanne Buckley (Thomson Nelson, 2005). If you are not sure which are your grammar favourites (see Appendix C), try using a sentence diagnostic such as the one available online at **http://www.powertools.nelson.com**. Also, take a look at a sampling of your papers from previous writing courses.

In any case, most writing teachers—certainly those teaching technical-writing courses—are likely to agree that the grammar and usage problems covered in the following are their "favourites."

For complete coverage of grammar, usage, and punctuation topics, see the following sources:

- The University of Victoria's Hypertext Writer's Guide: **http://web.uvic.ca/wguide**
- W. H. Fowler's *The King's English*, available at Bartleby.com: **http://www.bartleby.com/116**
- Grammar, Usage, and Style links from refdesk.com: **http://www.refdesk.com/factgram.html**
- Grammar, Punctuation, and Spelling from the Online Writing Lab at Purdue: **http://owl.english.purdue.edu/handouts/grammar/index.html**
- Office of Public Relations, McMaster University, Writing Style Guide: **http://www.mcmaster.ca/ua/opr/styleguide**

INTRODUCTORY, COMPOUND, SERIES, AND NONRESTRICTIVE COMMAS

In the technical world, where documents have multiple writers and multiple editors, all these document "co-owners" must produce some sort of stylistic consistency. For that reason, rules such as those for commas are as simple as possible.

Introductory-Element Commas

An introductory element is any word or group of words that comes before the main clause. To simplify matters, use a comma after any introductory element, no matter how few words or how short the pause. Go ahead and use a comma after words and phrases like "Today," "By tomorrow," "During the first few weeks," and "Generally" at the beginning of a sentence. Here are some examples:

> <u>Like a biological virus,</u> a computer virus invades other organisms, causing those organisms to proliferate and spread the virus.
> *(The introductory element is a simple prepositional phrase.)*

> <u>Once the virus has been executed,</u> it can exploit weak points in the Windows system.
> *(The introductory element is a dependent clause.)*

<u>Once executed,</u> a virus has free reign on all normal and high memory.
(It's only two words, but still introductory.)

<u>Typically,</u> this code will at first do little else than install the virus in high memory.
(Here is a single adverbial introductory element.)

<u>To understand antivirus programs,</u> consider the basic behaviour of known viruses.
(Here is an infinitive-phrase introductory element.)

<u>Limiting the number of initial virus infections in an organization</u> is important.
(There should be no comma after "organization"; the entire phrase is the subject of the verb "is.")

Compound-Sentence Commas

Use a comma to punctuate any compound sentence joined by a coordinating conjunction, regardless of the length of the individual clauses. A compound sentence is two or more complete sentences joined by a coordinating conjunction (*and, or, nor, but, yet, for, so*). Problems arise with those pesky sentences that look like compound sentences but are only compound predicates. Also, some compound sentences don't seem long enough, like this example: "Type your name, and press Enter." Here are some examples of the compound-sentence comma rule in action:

A virus might start reproducing right away, <u>or</u> it might lie dormant for some time until triggered by a particular event.
(The conjunction "or" occurs between two independent clauses, so use a comma.)

Virus programming does not demand special skills; there is no "black magic" about it.
(There is no conjunction between these two independent clauses. Use a semicolon, or start a new sentence.)

There are fewer boot infector viruses than file infector viruses, <u>but</u> most of virus-infection damage is caused by the boot infector viruses.
(The conjunction "but" occurs between two independent clauses here.)

The payload can alter individual figures in files or delete files.
(There should be no comma here because this is a compound verb phrase, not a compound sentence.)

```
A virus should never be assumed harmless and left on
a system.
```
(As in the preceding, there are two verbs here but only one subject. Commas not welcome!)

Series-Element Commas

A *series* of elements is a set of words occurring one after another. For example, "apples, oranges, and bananas" is a series; so is "in the den, behind the couch, under the rug." Even whole sentences can occur in a series. Punctuate series elements only if there are three or more such elements. Put a comma before the *and* occurring before the last element—it's not optional. Omitting it can cause reading comprehension problems, but including it does not. Here are some examples of the series-element comma rule:

```
A virus may infect memory, a floppy disk, a tape, or
any other type of storage.
```
(A series of four items with a comma before the "or.")

```
Once executed, a virus has free reign on the entire
memory-interrupt vector table, normal memory, and
high memory.
```
(A series of three items with a comma before the "and.")

```
Viruses can display obnoxious messages, erase files,
scramble a hard disk, cause erratic screen behaviour,
or freeze up the computer.
```
(This example has five verb phrases, each having "Viruses" as its subject.)

```
A computer virus can cause damage simply by
replicating itself and taking up scarce resources.
```
(There should be no comma after "itself" and before "and" because there are only two series elements.)

Special problems occur when you have a series of adjectives before a noun. When is it appropriate to use commas between those adjectives? Although there is probably no sure-fire rule, you can try using these two tests:

■ Try reversing the order of the adjectives. If doing so doesn't make the sentence sound strange, that's one clue that you can use commas.
■ Try putting *and* between the adjectives. If doing so doesn't make the sentence sound strange, that's another clue that you can use commas.

If you can apply both tests without making the sentence sound strange, use commas. But watch out! Don't put a comma between the last adjective and the noun. Here are some examples of the series-adjective comma:

The best protection can be accomplished by installing <u>resident antivirus</u> programs.
(You can't switch "resident" and "antivirus," so no comma is needed.)

Viruses are usually transmitted within an organization by innocent people going about their <u>normal business</u> activities.
(You can't say "business normal activities"—no comma!)

A virus is simply a program containing <u>harmful, disruptive</u> instructions.
(You can switch these two adjectives, so use a comma.)

Try to limit the number of <u>initial virus</u> infections in an organization.
(There should be no comma because you can't say "virus initial infections.")

Junkie is a <u>multipartite, memory-resident, encrypting</u> virus.
(You could probably mix and match these adjectival elements; therefore the commas are appropriate.)

Restrictive- and Nonrestrictive-Element Commas

A challenging area of comma usage involves restrictive and nonrestrictive elements. If it's restrictive, don't punctuate the element; if it is nonrestrictive, punctuate it. Here are some examples:

A virus is a code fragment <u>that copies itself into a larger program and then modifies that program</u>.
(This refers to not just any "code fragment," but one that copies itself and modifies its host.)

A partition-sector infector is a virus <u>that infects the partition record on hard disks</u>.
(This is not any old virus, but one that does a particular kind of damage.)

Viruses modify software in an uncontrolled way, <u>which can damage the software</u>.
(You could delete this clause from the sentence; that means it's nonrestrictive and takes a comma.)

The partition sector/boot sector contains a small program, <u>called the partition record/boot record</u>, that is executed each time the computer is turned on.
(The information on what it's called is just thrown in as extra, potentially useful material.)

This program, <u>like normal files infected by the file infectors</u>, can be modified by a virus and thus be infected.
(You can delete the nonrestrictive clause without causing problems to the sentence.)

```
All boot sector viruses infect disks, both floppy
and hard disk, by replacing the boot-sector program
with a copy of itself.
```
(This is just more nice-to-know information, which means it's nonrestrictive; thus commas are appropriate.)

End-of-Sentence Modifiers

A gray area in the world of punctuation involves dependent clauses and verbal phrases at the end of sentences. Two rules seem to apply: the absolute rule not to punctuate any dependent clause at the end of a sentence, and the nonrestrictive rule to punctuate only when the element is nonessential. Look at the following examples:

```
The virus then replicates itself, infecting other
programs as it reproduces.
```
(The underlined participial phrase could be deleted without harming the sense of the main clause. The main clause doesn't say much—but the phrase doesn't add anything to it.)

```
A virus can lie dormant for some time, until it's
triggered by a particular event.
```
(This is the same situation as in the preceding sentence.)

```
It is important to realize that viruses can reproduce
only if they are run.
```
(This sentence would be wrecked if the underlined dependent clause were removed. The dependent clause is essential to the meaning and the grammar of the main clause and it is restrictive; therefore, it should not be punctuated.)

```
A computer cannot become infected unless an infected
program is started on it.
```
(This is the same situation as in the preceding sentence.)

```
A virus is a computer program that copies itself when
an infected program is run.
```
(Notice how the dependent clause "restricts" the action of "copying itself." It's restrictive! No commas!)

```
A virus is inactive until the infected program is run
or boot record is read.
```
(Imagine this sentence without the underlined dependent clause—it doesn't make sense. The dependent clause is essential.)

Comma Combinations

Comma rules often combine within individual sentences, as in the following examples:

> Like a biological virus, a computer virus invades other organisms, causing those organisms to proliferate and spread the virus.
> *(This sentence has an introductory element at the beginning of the sentence and a nonrestrictive verbal phrase at the end of the sentence.)*

> Of course, DOS has the file-protection flag, set by the DOS command **attrib r** filename; however, a virus can easily modify this attribute.
> *(This is a compound sentence joined by a semicolon; the first clause contains an introductory element and a nonrestrictive element; the second contains an introductory element.)*

> They search the disk for files to infect, and when one is found, they simply change it to include the virus.
> *(Here's a compound sentence; the two independent clauses are joined by "and"; the second begins with an introductory element. Apply the introductory element rule to the second independent clause.)*

> From the resident state, a partition-infector virus keeps monitoring disk operations at all times, and if at some later time an operation on a floppy disk is detected, it can then infect it.
> *(This is a compound sentence, both clauses of which have an introductory element.)*

> When a PC starts up, the partition sector on the disk is read, and the code there is executed.
> *(This sentence begins with an introductory element—another dependent clause—followed by compound independent clauses.)*

> As early as 1916, less than a year after Einstein had formulated his equations of the general theory, the Austrian Ludwig Flamm had realized that Schwarzschild's solution to Einstein's equations actually describes a wormhole connecting two regions of flat space-time—two universes, or two parts of the same universe.
> *(This big sentence starts out with two introductory elements, followed by the main clause, followed by a nonrestrictive phrase that uses other words to restate an idea in the preceding.)*

SEMICOLONS

You can think of the semicolon as a strong comma—a comma with muscles. You can also think of it in musical terms—a shorter rest than a period. (If a period is a whole rest, the semicolon is a half- or three-quarter rest.)

1. Use a semicolon between two sentences that are not joined by a coordinating conjunction but seem so closely related that a period seems wrong or too much of a stop. (This situation causes the infamous error known as the comma splice, covered in Appendix C.)

   > Female virus writers are few and far between; so far, Sarah Gordon has encountered only five.
   > *(Notice how close these two independent clauses are—a half rest!)*

   > Appropriately used, user prompts can be valuable; however, they are frequently abused, overwhelming the user with questions or asking questions the user cannot answer.
   > *(A semicolon is commonly used when complete sentences are joined by words like "however," "therefore," and "furthermore.")*

   > Two major trends in Internet technology will have an impact on virus spread in the next few years: one is the increasing ubiquity and power of integrated mail systems; the other is the rise of mobile-program systems.
   > *(In this sentence, the semicolon joins the two sentences following the colon that explain the major trends.)*

2. Use a semicolon between sentences that are joined by a coordinating conjunction but contain other commas. Here, the semicolon acts as a stronger comma, emphasizing the point at which the two complete sentences join:

   > For $10.00, users could obtain the most up-to-date Dirty Dozen virus list; <u>and</u> for a self-addressed stamped disk mailer and disk, they could receive a current copy of the list.
   > *(To help clarify where the first independent clause ends and the next begins, a semicolon is used in front of the coordinating conjunction "and.")*

   > Often, Internet service providers already have IRC installed, available to all users; <u>but</u> if not, IRC clients are widely available on the Internet, and any user can download one.
   > *(Both independent clauses contain their commas; we need a semicolon—a comma with muscles—to mark the joining point of the two clauses.)*

Like many computer games, Sim City creates a world
that the player may manipulate; but unlike a real
game, it provides no objective.
*(Once again, this is a compound sentence, both independent clauses of
which contain commas of their own.)*

3. Use semicolons between series elements in which some of the elements
   contain their own commas—again, the semicolon acting as a strong
   comma:

In 1998, IBM researchers examined several types of
Trojan horse viruses that had been spread on the
Internet: the Trojanized PKZIP, which was widely discussed but rarely found; the Trojanized PGP, found
very rarely; Trojanized IRC scripts and clients, both
found rather frequently; applications that had been
rootkitted and systems that have been Trojanized
systems, numbering in the thousands.
*(Each of the four list items have their own internal punctuation—thus
semicolons are needed to ensure that you see where each list item ends and
another begins.)*

In his comparison of computer viruses to life, Spafford
defines "life" as having a "pattern in space-time";
being able to self-reproduce, grow, expand, evolve;
having an interdependence of parts; being able to
convert matter to energy; remaining stable under
"perturbations of the environment"; being capable of
functional interactions with the environment; and
being capable of information storage of its own self-
representation.
*(Not meant for those with "short little attention spans," this sentence
presents a phrase for each of the six characteristics. Several of the phrases
contain commas of their own, necessitating semicolons to mark the
boundaries between the six characteristics.)*

COLONS

The primary use of the colon is to punctuate the point between a lead-in
and the items introduced by that lead-in. The lead-in and the items
following it can be in the form of a regular sentence or in the form of a
numbered or bulleted list. Don't use a colon if the lead-in is not a complete sentence. Also, don't use a colon unless the items have to occur at the
end of a sentence. Here are some examples:

There are two main groups of viruses: the boot sector
and the infector of executable programs.

(The introductory element, the "lead-in," is complete in itself; use a colon.)

Two major trends in Internet technology will have an impact on virus spread in the next few years: one is the increasing ubiquity and power of integrated mail systems; the other is the rise of mobile-program systems.
(This lead-in tells you that two statements about "trends" are about to be presented.)

Honourable mentions included Stealth C, Wazzu, NPad, One Half, Parity Boot, and Ripper.
(The sentence is not complete at "included"—don't use a colon.)

The top seven viruses of 1997 were NYB, Anti-exe, Concept, Anticmos, Form.A, Junkie, and Monkey/Stoned/Empire.
(The sentence is not complete at "were"—no colon.)

This section gives a brief introduction to computer viruses: what they are, how they can spread, and what they can do.
(The lead-in sentence prepares you to hear about the contents of the introduction and is grammatically complete—use a colon!)

This section discusses what computer viruses are, how they can spread, and what they can do.
(In this version, the sentence is not complete at "discusses"—no colon!)

A computer virus can cause damage simply by replicating itself and taking up scarce resources, such as hard disk space, CPU time, or network connections.
(No colon either before or after "such as"!)

HYPHENS

Hyphenation may seem like some fiendish version of Trivial Pursuit, but careful hyphenation increases readability and comprehension. Good hyphenation practice is particularly important in technical writing. Because hyphenation usage is loaded with exceptions, writers and editors use style guides (see Chapter 20): these list every instance of hyphenation (as well as instances where hyphenation was considered but not used). The following examples illustrate common hyphenation usage rules. (For hyphenation of word breaks, see your dictionary.)

1. *Don't* hyphenate words with common prefixes such as *re-*, *anti-*, *de-*, *un-*, *mal-*, *dis-*, *co-*, and so on.

> The best strategy is to make sure that the antivirus program operates automatically.
> *(Not "anti-virus.")*

> Nonresident programs look for and deal with viruses on your entire system at one specified time.
> *(Not "Non-resident.")*

> The control on the Web page is downloaded and reinstalled every time you visit a page that uses it.
> *(Not "re-installed.")*

2. *Don't* hyphenate a compound in which the first word ends in *-ly*.

> A competently coded version of the Sharefun virus exploiting modern e-mail systems could spread very quickly.
> *(No hyphen between "competently" and "coded.")*

> Viruses can combine possibly damaging code with the ability to spread.
> *(No hyphen between "possibly" and "damaging.")*

> The area Directory X serves has a large agriculturally based population, many of whom are future AGRICON suppliers and consumers.
> *(No hyphen between "agriculturally" and "based.")*

3. Hyphenate compounds in which the words are an abbreviated version of a longer phrase or clause.

> Virus applets can open hundreds of windows rapidly on the user's display, make annoying and difficult-to-silence sounds, and try to fool the user into disclosing his user name and password.
> *(The sounds are difficult to silence.)*

> Malicious Java or ActiveX programs posing a danger to innocent users on the Web could become a more serious threat in the not-too-distant future.
> *(The future is not too distant.)*

> Virus instructions can have event-driven effects or time-driven effects.
> *(The effects are driven by time or event.)*

IBM antivirus software uses a patent-pending technology from IBM that distinguishes infected disk boot records from normal boot records.
(The technology has a patent that is pending.)

The International Computer Security Association is a for-profit corporation specializing in certification of security-related software products.
(The corporation is in business to make profits—that's a hard one!)

Password-stealing Trojan horse viruses are a much more sophisticated form of virus.
(The virus tries to steal your password.)

A platform-specific virus is one that affects either a PC or a Mac, but not both.
(The virus is specific to that platform.)

The NYB virus is a memory-resident virus.
(The virus stays resident in memory.)

The Junkie virus spreads quickly because of its ability to spread as a file-sharing virus.
(It's a virus that shares files.)

4. Hyphenate most compounds that use *self-, cross-, -like, well-,* and so on.

   Most antivirus software includes heuristic methods to detect common virus-like signatures.

   A cross-platform virus is one that can infect either a PC or Mac. Concept (Word) and Wazzu are two examples of well-known macro viruses.

5. Be careful with compounds like *back up, print out, and mix up.* If they act as adjectives or nouns, use hyphens or compound them (check a dictionary for the correct usage); if they act as verbs, don't hyphenate or compound them:

   Make sure you are using an up-to-date signature file with your antivirus program. If it isn't up to date, you will be vulnerable to new viruses.
   (Notice that the first instance of "up-to-date" modifies "signature file" whereas the second simply modifies the verb.)

6. Hyphenate number–measurement compounds when they act as modifiers:

   The four-person team of security researchers jointly unearthed a vulnerability to the virus during a brainstorming session last month in Palo Alto, California.

Plants inoculated with Rhizobium leguminosarum showed a 7-percent increase in growth compared with the noninoculated ones.

The report is based on data collected during a 12-week period on separated greywater/blackwater plumbing in an apartment complex of ten apartments.

Leaching facilities require that beds or trenches be dug 24 inches deep and filled with 6 inches of gravel, with 4-inch distribution pipes laid on the gravel and covered by 2 inches of gravel followed by 12 inches of soil.

The typical 3-pin transistor has pins for the emitter, base, and collector.

Purple-martin houses should have an 8-foot elevation above the ground and a 30-foot clearance on all sides.

7. Hyphenate adjective–noun compounds that can be misread:

Multipartite viruses are a cross between file and boot-sector viruses, infecting both files and boot sectors.
(It's not a sector virus—there is no such thing; it's a virus affecting the "boot sector.")

Microsoft uses a digital-signature technology called AuthentiCode to verify who has signed an ActiveX control.
(It's not a "signature technology" that happens to be "digital"; rather it's a "signature" that happens to be "digital." The hyphen ensures we know what modifies what.)

The fluctuations that seeded the large-scale structure of the Universe were primordial in origin, that is, associated with some of the very earliest times after the Big Bang.
(It's not a "scale structure" that happens to be "large." Even though it's not likely to be misread, the writer hyphenates this compound for readability anyway.)

8. Don't hyphenate compounds that occur after a linking verb. You may have "up-to-date virus protection," but your "virus protection is up to date."

Out-of-date antivirus software is useless. Don't let your signature files get out of date.

VRML is really just a computer language that describes three-dimensional objects. HTML has no way of addressing objects that are three dimensional.

Enhanced-reality software may provide us with more true-to-life information than our "natural" perception of reality. Not all of our perceptions are true to life.

Advanced real-time video filters may someday be able to remove wrinkles and pimples from your face! Although this is possible with programs like Adobe Photoshop, it's not yet possible in real time.

9. Avoid hyphenating an adjective–noun combination not acting as a modifier. However, hyphenate phrases like "back-up" and "print-out" when they act as nouns or adjectives. Here are some additional examples:

    Life is a pattern in space-time rather than a specific material object.
    (Just too good to pass up.)

    Netscape plug-ins raise some similar concerns about virus hazards on the World Wide Web.
    (Count on technology to wreak havoc on the English language. To prevent misreading, "plug-in" must be hyphenated when acting as a noun or adjective.)

    Some antivirus programs try to achieve an acceptable trade-off by balancing acceptable false-negative and false-positive rates.
    ("Trade-off" acts as a noun in this sentence, necessitating the hyphen.)

    Virus writers range from teenagers to college students to professionally employed grown-ups.
    (The phrase "grown-ups" doesn't make sense without a hyphen—an "up" that is "grown"?)

    To view the list of known viruses, select Virus descriptions from the Help pull-down on the main window.
    ("Pull-down" is a noun; it would be confusing if it weren't hyphenated.)

10. Watch out for compounds with punctuation that has not become established. If you cannot find a standard, just be consistent:

    As early as 1916, barely a year after Einstein had formulated his equations of the general theory, the

> Austrian Ludwig Flamm realized that Schwarzschild's solution to Einstein's equations actually describes a wormhole connecting two regions of flat space-time—two universes, two parts of the same universe.
> *(In other contexts, you'll see "space-time" and "worm hole.")*

11. Use an en dash (or hyphen) on "balanced" compounds. A balanced compound is one in which neither word is modifying the other (such as "blue–green sea" or "client–server model." Notice that the en dash is twice as long as the hyphen but half as long as the em dash. In Microsoft Word em and en dashes are created automatically. The shorter en dash is created when you type space hyphen hyphen between the text. For an em dash, type hyphen hyphen between the text, omitting the space.

DASHES

The dash is a form of punctuation similar to the comma and the parenthesis. Use it to introduce abrupt comments or to differentiate text when commas are also being used. Don't use a single hyphen as a dash. Use two hyphens, as described above, to form an em dash.

> Paris's choice—to marry Helen—like most choices, was not without its consequences.
> *(Don't use just a single hyphen to create a dash!)*

> In the remainder of this paper, we will talk about "Trojan horses" of a different kind—the digital Trojan horses users are encountering today.
> *(Come on, use a real em dash!)*

> A simple addition over all the luminous material—stars and hot gas—within the optical radius of galaxies yields a non-dynamical estimate for the mass density, Omega ~ C.005.
> *(That's more like it!)*

> A Trojan horse virus sent through e-mail will be executed as soon as the message is viewed—without any prompting.
> *(The dash here adds emphasis and dramatic effect.)*

> To suggest that computer viruses are alive also implies that some part of their environment—the computers, programs, or operating systems—also represents artificial life.
> *(These dashes act as a different form of comma. If commas were used instead, we might read this as a list of five elements—not as three examples of "their environment.")*

APOSTROPHES

Apostrophes are the endangered species of punctuation marks. Before the eighteenth century, they were scarcely used (yes, a world without apostrophes). But the correct use of apostrophes can prevent great amounts of confusion and ensure precision—something definitely needed in technical writing.

1. If the word is singular and does not end in -*s* ("employee," "computer," "disk"), add *'s* to make it possessive:

   > If the employee's personal computer is connected to the organization's network, the virus can spread throughout the organization.
   > *(One employee—one organization.)*

   > At risk are Windows users who use programs like Microsoft's Outlook and Qualcomm's Eudora, which use Microsoft's viewing software and have fairly recent versions of its Java virtual machine.
   > *(Lots of opportunities to make apostrophe mistakes here!)*

2. If the word is plural and ends in -*s* ("viruses," "computers," "disks"), add an apostrophe to the end of the word to make it possessive:

   > Political virus writers write programs that merely display a keyword such as Macedonia, their creators' names, or the name of a group as a way of marking turf.
   > *(Multiple virus creators.)*

   > If employees' personal computers are connected to their organizations' networks, viruses can spread throughout those organizations.
   > *(Multiple employees—multiple organizations.)*

3. If the word is singular but ends in -*s*, add *'s* to make it possessive (pay no attention to the styles that give you the option to add just the apostrophe):

   > Paris's choice—to marry Helen—like most choices, was not without its consequences.
   > *("Paris" is a singular noun ending in* -s; *just add an apostrophe* s *to the end of the word.)*

   > The bus's role in computer architecture is central.
   > *(Some argue that you should avoid making inanimate objects possessive. In this example, they would prefer "The role of the bus.")*

4. If the word is plural but does not end in *-s* ("geese," "men," "children"), add *'s* to the end of the word to make it possessive:

> Virus-creation kits make creating new viruses mere child's play.
> *(If you are not sure, you can rephrase it as "the play of a mere child." Therefore, the apostrophe is necessary.)*

> Children's computers are as vulnerable to virus attacks as are grown-ups'.

> The goose virus causes a computer to emit sounds resembling geese's honking.
> *(Granted, "the honking of geese" would sound better.)*

5. If you change the spelling of the word to make it plural ("pansy" → "pansies"), add an apostrophe at the end of the plural version of the word:

> Many universities' websites provide direct links to antivirus software for student and faculty use.
> *(Convert the singular word "university" to the plural "universities"; then add an apostrophe.)*

> High-tech companies' security systems will be challenged by next-generation Internet-borne viruses.
> *(Convert the singular word "company" to the plural "companies"; then add an apostrophe.)*

6. The grand exception: *its* is the possessive, and *it's* means "it is" (who made up this language anyway?)

> If you want to protect your computer against viruses, it's essential that you follow the five guidelines below.
> *(This "it's" means "it is"—use the apostrophe version.)*

> When a virus is started on a workstation, it can run any instructions that its author chooses to include.
> *(This "its" is possessive—the "author" of "it." Don't use an apostrophe.)*

> The Junkie virus spreads quickly because of its ability to spread as a file-sharing virus.
> *(This "its" is possessive—the "ability" of "it." Don't use an apostrophe.)*

> IBM tests its new antivirus software on its more than 250,000 PCs before releasing it to help ensure that problems are found and corrected.
> *(The word "its" here refers to "IBM," which is singular.)*

7. For other possessive pronouns ("yours, "hers," "theirs"), don't use an apostrophe:

> He believes that the fault for allowing the Melissa virus to spread throughout their company was hers.
> *(Don't you dare put an apostrophe between the "r" and the "s"!)*

> The responsibility for protecting your home computer is entirely yours.
> *(Don't touch that apostrophe key!)*

8. For plurals of acronyms (CPUs, CD-ROMs), don't use an apostrophe:

> IBM tests its new antivirus software on its more than 250,000 PCs before releasing it to help ensure that problems are found and corrected.
> *(It's PCs—not PC's.)*

QUOTATION MARKS

As Chapter 7 on highlighting points out, quotation marks are often used incorrectly for emphasis. Quotation marks are primarily for punctuating direct quotations; technical-writing contexts rarely require quotations. Instead, quotation marks in technical writing more commonly indicate words referred to as such or words used in unusual ways.

> For our purposes, the term "click" refers to a single click of the left mouse button. The term "double-click" refers to two quick clicks of the left mouse button.
> *(We are referring to the words "click" and "double-click" as words; we are not using them as verbs.)*

> Polymorphic viruses are well named, with "poly" meaning more than one or many and "morphic" meaning shape or body.
> *(The word "poly" is referred to as a word—actually, as a prefix.)*

> A computer "virus" is simply a program that contains unwanted instructions that change files on a computer.
> *(A computer virus is not a real virus in the original biological sense of the word.)*

> Antivirus software checks files for virus "signatures," which are identifiable byte sequences of known viruses.
> *(Viruses can't sign anything.)*

> A computer virus is a program that can "infect" other
> programs by modifying them to include a copy of itself.
> *(Computer viruses can't infect anything in the original biological sense.)*

> Virus detectors that look for these abnormal patterns
> of bytes not found in normal programs are called
> "scanners."

Note: The standard rule of punctuation of quotations is that commas and periods go inside the closing quotation mark; semicolons and colons are placed on the outside.

WORKSHOP: PUNCTUATION

The following exercises give you some practice with the punctuation rules presented in this appendix. (For additional practice, see **http://www.powertools.nelson.com**.)

1. *Introductory-element commas.* Punctuate the following sentences that have introductory elements. (Careful! Some do not have introductory elements.)
   a. In Bandelier National Monument raging fires threatened several cliff dwellings and other ancient ruins left by Native American tribes who formerly lived in the area.
   b. Donated by the nonprofit Vietnam Veterans Memorial Fund the new computer lab at a university in Hanoi will help economically disadvantaged Vietnam gain access to the World Wide Web.
   c. With an increasing number of technology-related jobs in the new economy experts fear people who lack computing skills might be left behind.
   d. This fall a project called "Home Access to the Internet and Learning" will provide low-income students with free computers and Internet access.
   e. Wheelbarrows were first used in Europe during the Middle Ages although they appear to have been common in China beginning around 230 A.D.

2. *Compound-element commas.* Punctuate the following sentences that have compound elements. (Remember that only compound sentences— compound independent clauses—are punctuated with a comma.)
   a. The 1950s have been called the "Golden Age of Science Fiction" and for the most part Hollywood's view of technology and technological process was positive and optimistic.
   b. Novelists in the 1920s and 1930s predicted much of our technology and its impact on our world and anticipated advancements such as miniaturization.

    c. Sometimes science fiction inspires science fact and a case in point involves a Texas Instruments engineer who came up with an idea for a new use of technology after watching an episode of *Deep Space Nine*.

    d. A number of books and World Wide Web sites have been written offering weird theories about the purpose of the pyramids and why they are here.

    e. Many people still believe that women are not interested in technology but women like Ada Byron Lovelace and Rear Admiral Grace Hopper are testaments to the technological abilities of women.

3. *Series-element commas.* Punctuate the following sentences that have series elements.

    a. In the 1950s science fiction movies reflected the common idea that technology brought political social and personal advancements.

    b. Admiral Hopper possessed a variety of talents: in addition to her outstanding technical skills, she was a whiz at marketing repeatedly demonstrated her business and political insight and persevered despite obstacles.

    c. A young cyber-rights activist posted criticism of Internet filtering programs on his website and accused the software developers of having a hidden political agenda.

    d. When the software developers responded to the activist's criticism, excerpts from their correspondence were posted to anti-censorship e-mail lists websites and newsgroups.

4. *Restrictive- and nonrestrictive-element commas.* Punctuate the following sentences that have nonrestrictive elements. (Careful! Don't punctuate the items with restrictive elements.)

    a. When you're holding an online conversation whether it's an e-mail exchange or a response to a discussion group posting don't forget that the other person has feelings that might be hurt by a rude or thoughtless post.

    b. Seven astronauts were killed when the space shuttle they were piloting the *Challenger* exploded early in the flight.

    c. In order to protect the air, Congress enacted the Clean Air Act of 1970 and amended it in 1977.

    d. The "digital divide" defined as the gap between people who can afford to gain access to information technology and those who cannot has the potential to further isolate uneducated and poorer people from the prosperity of the "information age."

5. *Semicolons and colons.* Punctuate the following sentences with semi-colons and colons as necessary. (Careful! Some of the sentences do not need semicolons or colons.)
   a. Even preschoolers are becoming familiar with the jargon of their generation *floppy drive, CD-ROM, mouse,* and *Web.*
   b. Some experts believe that growing up with information technology will change the personality of this generation by making them collaborators and innovators.
   c. Generation Xers are considered cynical and negative the digital generation is expected to be worldly and optimistic.
   d. This digital generation is the biggest ever they outnumber even the Baby Boomers.

6. *Commas, semicolons, colons.* Punctuate the following sentences with commas, semicolons, and colons as necessary:
   a. Cookies are small pieces of information that a website can store in your browser the website can then recognize you when you return.
   b. Website developers like cookies they can be useful in marketing online ordering and remembering passwords.
   c. Other people worry that cookies might help a website invade a user's privacy in a variety of ways by keeping a record of where the user goes, by stealing personal information, or maintaining a list of purchases.
   d. Many Internet users have heard of "cookies" they just don't have a firm idea of what this term means.
   e. While revealing personal information on the Web can sometimes bring benefits to consumers there are other situations in which people would prefer to remain anonymous.
   f. Many countries already have privacy-related regulations others will be considering whether such regulations are necessary.

7. *Hyphens.* Punctuate the following sentences with hyphens as necessary:
   a. Most technology driven companies make extensive use of the World Wide Web.
   b. Many travellers take advantage of duty free shops overseas, where they can buy products without paying taxes on them.
   c. Employees for the start up company were hand picked by the CEO.
   d. The old monitor took on an eerie shade of yellow green, which its owner found irritating to the eyes.
   e. Because the data carrying capacity of telephone lines, known as bandwidth, is low, receiving electronic data can take a long time.
   f. In 2006, an new Microsoft operating system, called Vista, arrived in computer stores.
   g. While computers are now the primary means of accessing the Internet, we're already seeing other Internet enabled devices, such

as pagers and cell phones, which can send and receive e-mail and access the Web.

8. *Dashes.* Punctuate the following sentences with dashes as necessary:
   a. Luddites a group of workingmen who rioted and destroyed new technology that they felt threatened jobs and wages named themselves after a mythical King Lud.
   b. Outbreaks of Luddism which occurred mostly in Lancashire, Cheshire, and Yorkshire, England, were harshly suppressed by the British government.
   c. Enemies of the Luddites claimed that the men were irrational that they had an unfounded fear of science and technology.
   d. However, their supporters had another viewpoint the men were defending their jobs and lifestyles from technology, which would displace them.

9. *Apostrophes.* Punctuate the following sentences with apostrophes as necessary:
   a. Its a popular myth that viruses can invade your computer when you open a piece of e-mail.
   b. In fact the viruses deadly effects happen only if you open a file that comes attached to the e-mail.
   c. Even very good virus protection programs cant protect computers from every new virus.
   d. Therefore, it is a users responsibility to be vigilant.
   e. A virus can do its dirty work only if computers owners let down their guard.

10. *Combined punctuation.* Punctuate the sentences available at **http:// www.powertools.nelson.com** with commas, semicolons, colons, hyphens, dashes, and apostrophes as necessary.

Grammar Favourites

Topics covered in this chapter include

- computer animation;
- video game design.

COMPUTER ANIMATION
Someday kids will learn grammar and usage strictly through animated games. *Sesame Street* got it started, but there's much left to do.

Imager Laboratory, University of British Columbia (Take a look at the Imager gallery in particular!)
http://www.cs.ubc.ca/nest/imager

Humber College Computer Animation course
http://postsecondary.humber.ca/11561.htm

Anna McMillan and Emily Hobson, Animation Tutorial
http://www.hotwired.com/webmonkey/multimedia/tutorials

Animation Learner's Site, provided by a former Disney animator
http://come.to/animate

Larry's Toon Institute, from Animation World Network
http://www.awn.com/tooninstitute/lessonplan/lesson.htm

VIDEO GAME DESIGN
The Art of Computer Game Design
http://www.vancouver.wsu.edu/fac/peabody/game-book/Coverpage.html

When you have completed this chapter, you will be able to

- locate and revise fragments in your technical documents;
- locate and revise comma-splice sentences in your technical documents;
- locate and revise pronoun-reference problems in your technical documents;
- locate and revise parallelism problems in your technical documents.

No doubt, most people are not likely to use the words "grammar" and "favourites" in the same breath. The grammar and usage topics covered in this appendix are "favourites" in the sense that they occur more often than others. For a complete review of most grammar, usage, and style problems, see Joanne Buckley's *Checkmate Pocket Guide* (Thomson Nelson, 2005).

If you are not sure which are your grammar favourites, try using a sentence diagnostic such the one available online at http://www.powertools. nelson.com. Also, take a look at a sampling of your papers from previous writing courses.

For complete coverage of grammar, usage, and punctuation topics, see the following websites:

- Index to Grammar Materials, University of Victoria:
  http://web2.uvcs.uvic.ca/elc/studyzone/grammar.htm
- HyperGrammar, University of Ottawa:
  http://www.uottawa.ca/academic/arts/writcent/hypergrammar/grammar.html
- Canadian University Grammar Skills:
  http://canadaonline.about.com/od/studyskills/index_a.htm
- Grammar Handbook at the Writers' Workshop, University of Illinois at Urbana-Champaign:
  http://www.english.uiuc.edu/cws/wworkshop/
- Grammar, Usage, and Style Resources, from refdesk.com:
  http://www.refdesk.com/factgram.html
- David McMurrey. Grammar & Usage Study Guides:
  http://www.powertools.nelson.com

FRAGMENTS

Fragments are "sentence wannabes" because they lack a subject or a complete verb. We tend to write fragments because we use fragments in our conversational speech. While fragments are easy enough to understand or clarify in conversation, they present potentially serious communication problems in writing. A fragment is not necessarily a short sentence. "It is" is a sentence—not a fragment! True, we don't know what "it" refers to, nor what it "is." Such a sentence might occur like this: "You may wonder whether global warming is a reality. It is." Here are some examples of fragments along with revisions:

Version with fragment	Revised version
Blasting each other to pieces in Quake or Delta Force doesn't constitute a social experience. *Unless you meet the other players afterward and share your stories.*	Blasting each other to pieces in Quake or Delta Force doesn't constitute a social experience, unless you meet the other players afterward and share your stories.
For example, fantasy is a popular setting in almost any computer game genre. *No matter whether it is an adventure, role-playing, strategy, or action game.*	For example, fantasy is a popular setting in almost any computer game genre—no matter whether it is an adventure, role-playing, strategy, or action game.
Many independent studies in various professional fields conclude that seven is the highest number of objects that a person can comfortably keep in mind at once. *A theory that applies equally to computer games as well.*	Many independent studies in various professional fields conclude that seven is the highest number of objects that a person can comfortably keep in mind at once. This theory applies equally well to computer games.
Some games violate all the guidelines for intellectual manageability and still somehow reach a wider group of players. *Civilization 2 being a good example of how successful computer games can violate "established" guidelines.*	Some games violate all the guidelines for intellectual manageability and still somehow reach a wider group of players. Civilization 2 is a good example of how successful computer games can violate "established" guidelines.
A licence with a sports league will entitle you to use the league's own logos, plus the team names, logos, and colours. *Assuming the league owns all those rights.* Of course, different leagues have different rules.	A licence with a sports league will entitle you to use the league's own logos, plus the team names, logos, and colours, assuming the league owns all those rights. Of course, different leagues have different rules.
To break into computer game design, you can and should write a fully functional demo game. *One of about 10,000 lines of C++ code with at least one and preferably several features not found in commercial games.*	To break into computer game design, you can and should write a fully functional demo game. Your demo game should consist of about 10,000 lines of C++ code with at least one and preferably several features not found in commercial games.
These days, a typical commercial game might take 100,000 lines of C++ code written by a team of 3 programmers over a period of 18 months with a budget of a million dollars. *Not something an individual trying to break into the game design business can easily accomplish.*	These days, a typical commercial game might take 100,000 lines of C++ code written by a team of 3 programmers over a period of 18 months with a budget of a million dollars. Obviously, a game of this magnitude is not something an individual trying to break into the game design business can easily accomplish.

COMMA-SPLICE SENTENCES

A comma-splice sentence is two or more complete sentences joined by a comma, but without a coordinating conjunction—that is, *and, or, nor, but, yet, so,* or *for*. The following examples show that you can fix a comma-splice sentence by (a) adding a conjunction, (b) using a semicolon between the complete sentences, (c) making each of the complete sentences a separate sentence in its own right, or (d) reducing the words to one complete sentence.

Version with comma splice	Revised version
In a role-playing game, certain icons may move the character, other icons cause the character to pick up items, rest, cast spells, and so on.	In a role-playing game, certain icons may move the character; other icons cause the character to pick up items, rest, cast spells, and so on.
In a role-playing game, enabling players to see the dice that determine the outcome of a combat is impractical, it slows down the game or takes up valuable screen space.	In a role-playing game, enabling players to see the dice that determine the outcome of a combat is impractical. It slows down the game or takes up valuable screen space.
People prefer multiplayer board and card games to solitaire games, multiplayer games are a social experience.	People prefer multiplayer board and card games to solitaire games because multiplayer games are a social experience.
In computer games, the opposite situation has prevailed, most computer games have been single-player games.	In computer games, the opposite situation has prevailed. Most computer games have been single-player games.
Using a boring game for socializing isn't exciting, get together with a couple of friends and play tic-tac-toe for an hour to see what I mean.	Using a boring game for socializing isn't exciting. Get together with a couple of friends and play tic-tac-toe for an hour to see what I mean.
There are many reasons why Civilization 2 managed to attract novice gamers, the most important is that players start with a simple, easily manageable situation (one settler unit), build the first city, and add various units and cities progressively.	There are many reasons why Civilization 2 managed to attract novice gamers. The most important is that players start with a simple, easily manageable situation (one settler unit), build the first city, and add various units and cities progressively.
To be honest, many of the science-fiction and fantasy worlds that appear in computer games aren't that creative either, they're rehashes of old ideas and borrowed genres.	To be honest, many of the science-fiction and fantasy worlds that appear in computer games aren't that creative either. They're rehashes of old ideas and borrowed genres.

PRONOUN-REFERENCE PROBLEMS

Pronoun-reference problems are the bigots and the misogynists of the sentence world—or else they just can't count. As you know, a pronoun is a word like *he, her,* or *theirs,* and it refers to nouns such as *Patrick, Jane,* or the *McMurreys.* Problems arise when the noun is human but neutral (either masculine or feminine). For example, "Everyone opened her (or his?) briefcase." Because we don't know whether these people are male or female, we mistakenly use "their." The traditional rule of using "he," "him," or "his" in these neutral situations is considered sexist writing. Of course, constructions like "she or he" and "him or her" are options, although they are awkward and pedantic. (And always putting the "he" in front of the "she" in phrases like "he or she" is also considered sexist by some.) Instead, change the noun to a plural; then references to it with "they," "them," and "their" are grammatically correct. Thus, instead of saying "Everyone opened their briefcase" or "Everyone opened his or her briefcase," you can write something like "The board members opened their briefcases."

Problems also arise when the noun is a collective thing such as the *team,* the *Orlando Magic,* the *company, Dell Corporation,* or the *Canadian Coast Guard.* Because we know these entities represent multiple people, we want to refer to them with pronouns like *they, them,* or *theirs.* The traditional grammatically correct way is to refer to such collective entities with *it* or *its.* And as the examples below illustrate, words like *any, none, each, either,* or *neither* also cause pronoun-reference problems:

Version with pronoun problem	Revised version
To help ensure that problems are found and corrected, *IBM* tests *their* new antivirus software on their more than 250,000 PCs before releasing it.	To help ensure that problems are found and corrected, *IBM* tests *its* new antivirus software on its more than 250,000 PCs before releasing it. *(Also note that it's PCs—not PC's.)*
The *customer* must be aware of the kind of software *they* are downloading and take the necessary precautions to prevent virus attacks.	*Customers* must be aware of the kind of software *they* are downloading and take the necessary precautions to prevent virus attacks.
To avoid the risk of contracting the Melissa virus, it is recommended that the network *administrator* upgrade *their* antivirus software to include detection and cleaning for W97M/Melissa.	To avoid the risk of contracting the Melissa virus, it is recommended that network *administrators* upgrade *their* antivirus software to include detection and cleaning for W97M/Melissa.
In Lebling & Blank's Zork, the game *player's* sole objective is to solve a puzzle: *they* must find objects and use them in particular ways to cause desired changes in the game state.	In Lebling & Blank's Zork, game *players'* sole objective is to solve a puzzle: *they* must find objects and use them in particular ways to cause desired changes in the game state. *(The word "players'" is a plural noun.)*

Continued

Version with pronoun problem	Revised version
To adhere to the seven-object rule, a role-playing game can confront a *player* with choices to move, rest, fight, or administrate *their* character. If the *player* chooses to fight, *they* can attack, guard, shoot, or use an item. At any level, the *player* is never faced with more than seven alternatives from which *they* must choose.	To adhere to the seven-object rule, a role-playing game can confront *players* with choices to move, rest, fight, or administrate their character. If *players* choose to fight, *they* can attack, guard, shoot, or use an item. At any level, *players* are never faced with more than seven alternatives from which *they* must choose.
Stories are inherently linear. However much *a character* may agonize over the decisions *they* make, *they* make them the same way every time we reread the story, and the outcome is always the same.	Stories are inherently linear. However much *a character* may agonize over the decisions *she or he* makes, *that character* makes them the same way every time we reread the story, and the outcome is always the same. *(Plural "characters" would be better here.)*
A game is a form of art in which a *participant,* called a "player," makes decisions in order to manage *their* resources through game tokens in the pursuit of a goal.	A game is a form of art in which *participants,* called "players," make decisions in order to manage *their* resources through game tokens in the pursuit of a goal.

PARALLELISM PROBLEMS

Sentences with parallelism problems are the psychiatric cases of the sentence world. By using different forms of grammatical phrasing, they become sentences with multiple personalities, schizophrenia, or just bad dressers. Problems with parallelism can occur any time you have two or more elements in a series. The problem involves using different types of grammatical phrasing for those items—you're supposed to use only one! For example, look at the following sentence that has series items that don't use the same style of phrasing:

Parallelism problem: In Sim City, some of the goals you can set include *building* the grandest possible megalopolis, to *maximize* how much your people love you, or *you can try designing* a city that relies solely on mass transit.

The three italicized phrases use different types of phrasing—namely, gerund phrase, infinitive phrase, and independent clause. The following table shows you some of the common types of phrasing that, when mixed, produce parallelism errors:

Phrasing type	Example
Complete sentences	One of the essential elements of a game involves decision making. Another involves managing your resources. A third essential element involves reaching a goal.
Noun clauses *(who, what, when, where, how, that)* clauses	*How you make decisions, how you manage your resources, and when you reach the goal*—these are the essential elements of games.
Participial and gerund *(-ing)* phrases	*Making decisions, managing resources,* and *reaching the goal* are the essential elements of any game.
Infinitives *(to + verb phrases)*	The essential elements of any game are *to make decisions, to manage resources,* and *to reach the goal.*
Noun phrases	*Decisions, resources,* and *goals* are the essential elements of games.

You can use practically any one type of phrasing as long as you don't mix types. Here is one good way to revise the preceding sentence:

Revised version: In Sim City, some of the goals you can set include *building* the grandest possible megalopolis, *maximizing* how much your people love you, or *designing* a city that relies solely on mass transit.

In the following parallelism problems, notice that in almost every case you can revise equally well with a different style of phrasing:

Version with parallelism problem	Revised version
As game designers, we need a way to analyze games, *what their basic elements are,* and to understand what works and what makes them interesting.	As game designers, we need a way to analyze games, to discuss their elements, and to understand what works and what makes them interesting. *(A series of three infinitive phrases)*
This guide will give you an overview of how the forum is set up, maneuvring in it, as well as methods for posting, replying, and editing messages.	This guide will give you an overview of how the forum is set up, how to maneuvre in it, and how to post, reply to, and edit messages. *(A series of three noun clauses)*
The creativity in computer sports games is found in more subtle areas: user interface design, player behaviour AI, *how character animations interact,* and intelligent audio, to name a few.	The creativity in computer sports games is found in more subtle areas: user interface design, player behaviour AI, interaction of character animation, and intelligent audio, to name a few. *(A series of four noun phrases)*
In developing a computer sports game, just consider all the events that appear in a team's annual calendar: hiring rookies, trading players, holding training camp, *exhibition games,* playing regular season games.	In developing a computer sports game, just consider all the events that appear in a team's annual calendar: hiring rookies, trading players, holding training camp, scheduling exhibition games, playing regular season games. *(A series of five gerund phrases)*
Consider the game of chess. It has few of the aspects that make games appealing: no simulation elements, *you don't have characters involved in role playing,* and little colour.	Consider the game of chess. It has few of the aspects that make games appealing: no simulation elements, no role playing, and little colour. *(A series of three noun phrases)*

WORKSHOP: GRAMMAR

As mentioned at the beginning of this appendix, we can't cover all grammar, usage, punctuation, and style problems in this book—just favourites. For complete coverage, get a grammar reference book like *Checkmate Pocket Guide* by Joanne Buckley (Thomson Nelson, 2005). To find out which are your favourites, review your past writing or use a sentence diagnostic like the one at http://www.powertools.nelson.com.

Here are some exercises to give you some practice recognizing and revising the grammar and usage problems covered in this appendix. For additional practice, see http://www.powertools.nelson.com.

1. *Fragments.* In the following, identify the fragments and revise to eliminate them:

a. At the meeting, the speaker explained how to maintain the environment within an aquarium. What types of pumps and plants are best, and how to introduce new fish to the new aquarium.

b. Not only meeting once a week to discuss schedules but also keeping in constant touch by e-mail.

c. The Internet has allowed many people access to information they never had before.

d. Despite opponents' claims that Internet privacy legislation would hinder the ability of corporations to satisfy the customers' demands.

e. Large numbers of corporations are still collecting information and tracking Internet users without the customers' consent or knowledge. Even though these corporations claim to regulate themselves.

2. *Comma splices, run-ons, and fused sentences.* In the following, identify the comma-spliced, run-on, and fused sentences, and revise to eliminate them:

a. The inconveniences of being diabetic are indisputable but the benefits of proper self-care can outweigh these inconveniences.

b. Student Bonfire workers are trained in the proper use of axes, machetes, and chain saws, however there are still many risks involved in preparing the logs.

c. At the meeting, the speaker explained how to maintain the environment within an aquarium—what types of pumps and plants are best, and how to introduce new fish to the new aquarium.

d. Privacy guidelines have been very successful in Europe, it seems logical for the United States and Canada to adopt similar guidelines for Internet privacy.

3. *Pronoun-reference problems.* In the following, identify problems with pronoun reference, and revise to eliminate them:

a. The tutorials for Microsoft Excel tables show the user where they are to click or type.

b. The World Wide Web has given the ordinary person access to information they never had before.

c. In the documentation department, they keep in constant touch by e-mail.

d. At the meeting, the speaker explained how to maintain the environment within an aquarium, what types of pumps and plants are best, and how to introduce new fish to the new aquarium.

4. *Parallelism problems.* In the following, identify problems with parallelism, and revise to eliminate them:

a. To solve the communication problem, the managers agreed to relay information about personnel changes, updates for major projects, and to make announcements aimed at the entire company through weekly meetings.

b. The judges evaluated the websites based on content, style, how interactive it was, and the quality of the graphics.

c. In a Japanese garden, designers use many techniques to ensure that the garden is attractive, as well as in harmony with its surroundings and does not sacrifice the sense of privacy.

d. Some financial magazines have warned readers about brokers who advise them to move money into variable annuities from mutual funds, retirement plans that are tax deferred, or RRSPs.

Index

Abbreviations, 103, A–3 to A–6
ABC News, 394
About.com, 382
Abstract, 322, 323
Academic, government, research-oriented
technical writers, 9
Accident reports, 28
Acronyms, A–3 to A–6
Actions, 224
Activities/exercises. *See* Workshop
Ad hominem arguments, 147
Adjustment letter, 278–280, 286–287
Administrative feasibility, 101
AJR Newslink, 393
Altavista, 386
Alternative causes, 68
Analogy, 148
Anecdotal evidence, 320
Annotated examples. *See also* Short
examples/samples
adjustment letter, 286–287
application letter, 309
cause-effect discussion, 81–82
classification, 142–143
comparison, 103–104
complaint letter, 284–285
extended definition, 137–141
feasibility proposal, 175–179
formal report, 326–335
informal report, 36–39
inquiry letter, 288–289
instructions, 63–66
memo proposal, 168–172
persuasive technical writing, 164–167
primary research report, 83–86

process document, 57–62
progress report, 181–187
progress report cover letter, 180
proposal cover letter, 173–174
recommendation report, 105–115
résumé, 310–311
review and revision, 360–363
technical description, 33–35
Apostrophe, B–16 to B–18
APA documentation style, 402–405
Appendixes
formal report, 319–320
recommendation report, 107–115
Application letter, 301–309
annotated example, 309
conclusion, 306
content strategies, 302–304
delivery mode, 306–307
detail, 303, 305–306
formatting, 307–308
how-to guide, 304–307
introduction, 302, 306
organizational strategies, 302
workshop, 308
Argumentation, 145. *See also* Persuasion
Arial, 195
Art and Science of Leadership, The (Nahavandi),
413
Ashley, Teresa, 381
Assignments. *See* Workshop
Audience and task analysis, 365–379
audience description, 371–372, 373–374
audience's background, 367
how-to guide, 370–374
instructional task analysis, 368

internal dialogue with imaginary readers, 374–375
new metaphors, 375
noninstructional task analysis, 369
process document, 59
revision, 376
who is the audience?, 366–367
workshop, 377–379
Audience description, 371–372, 373–374
Audience identifier, 21, 74
AUTHOR, 11–12

Background report, 131–134
Bandwagon effects, 147–148
Bar graph, 243
BBC, 393
Biased language, 151, 355
Biased/slanted graphics, 343
Bibliography. *See* Documentation style
Block letter format, 267, 268
Body language, 347
Bold. *See* Highlighting
Books, 389–390
Boolean operators, 384
Boolean searches, 384
Borrowed information. *See* Documentation style
Brain at Mohawk College, 382
Brainstorming, 354
Brochures, 395
Bulleted list, 211
    cause-effect discussion, 70, 81
    classification, 143
    Microsoft Word, 217
    recommendation report, 109, 114
    sample, 212
Buried information (Internet), 386
Business communications, 264–289
    adjustment letter, 278–280, 286–287
    annotated examples, 284–289
    complaint letter, 275–278, 284–285
    context, 265–266
    e-mail, 274–275
    good news/bad news, 266
    inquiry letter, 280–282, 288–289
    introduction, 265
    letter. *See* Business letter
    memo, 270–272
    paragraphs, 266

reader-first strategy, 266
    template, 272–274
    tone, 265
    workshop, 282–283
Business letter format, 267, 268
Business letters
    alignment, 269
    complimentary close, 267
    continuation pages, 269
    font, 269
    format, 267, 268
    justification, 269
    letterhead, 270
    line spacing, 269
    margins, 269
    paper, 270
    paragraph indentation, 269
    salutation, 267
    signature block, 269
    type size, 269
    type style, 269

C-SPAN, 394
Canadian Library Gateway, 390
Capitalization, 104
Categories, 125
Cause-effect discussion, 67–86
    annotated examples, 81–82, 83–86
    discussing causes and effects, 69
    examples, 70, 73
    how-to guide, 70–74
    primary research report, 75–79, 83–86
    types of causes and effects, 68–69
    workshop, 80
Caution notice, 66, 221, 226–227
CBC, 393
Cell alignment, 235
Characteristics approach, 18
Chart, 232. *See also* Graphs and charts
Checkmate Pocket Guide, B-2
Citing information sources. *See* Documentation style
City TV, 394
Classification, 125–131, 142–143. *See also* Definition and classification
Clip art, 254–255
CNN, 394
Colon, B-9 to B-10

Columbia University Libraries, 382
Comma
    combinations, B–7
    compound sentence, B–3 to B–4
    end-of-sentence modifiers, B–6
    introductory elements, B–2 to B–3
    process document, 61
    restrictive/nonrestrictive elements, B–5 to B–6
    series of elements, B–4 to B–5
Comma-splice sentence, C–4
Commands, 201
Comparison, 87–115
    annotated examples, 103–104, 105–115
    evaluation report, 101
    feasibility report, 101
    how-to guide, 88–93
    point-by-point approach, 88–90, 96–97, 103, 110
    recommendation report, 94–100, 105–115
    whole-to-whole approach, 88, 89
    workshop, 102
Complaint letter, 275–278, 284–285
Complimentary close, 267
Compound-sentence comma, B–3 to B–4
Computer literature, 6
Conceptual drawings, 251
Concession, 147, 164
Conclusion
    adjustment letter, 286
    application letter, 306
    business communications, 267
    cause-effect discussion, 74
    classification, 130
    comparison, 92
    complaint letter, 278
    extended definition, 124
    instructions, 50–51
    oral presentation, 341
    persuasion, 152, 166
    process, 45
    transmittal letter, 326
Conclusions (recommendation report), 97–98, 105–106
Conclusions summary, 97
Conditions, 224
Confidentiality, 13
Consequences, 224
Consultant technical writing, 7

Converting table to graph, 234
Converting text to table, 233
Copyright, 402
Corporate nouns, 111
Counterarguments, 151
Cover letter
    application letter. *See* Application letter
    progress report, 180
    proposal, 173–174
Crawlers, 385
Cropping illustrations, 255
Cross-referencing illustrations, 257, 258
Cue cards, 342

Danger notice, 221, 227–228
Dash, B–15
Decorative highlighting, 209
Deep Web, 386
Definition and classification, 116–143
    annotated examples, 137–141, 142–143
    categories, 125
    classification, 125–131, 142–143
    extended definition, 120–125, 137–141
    formal sentence definition, 118–120
    how-to guide (classification), 125–131
    how-to guide (extended definition), 120–125
    synonym definitions, 117–118
    technical background report, 131–134
    workshop, 134–136
Definitions section, 26
Depository Service Program website, 394
Description, 16–39
    annotated examples, 33–39
    defined, 17
    how-to guide, 18–23
    informal report, 28–31, 36–39
    part-by-part approach, 17, 18, 23
    product specifications, 23–28
    sources of, 22
    workshop, 31–32
Descriptive summary, 322, 327
Desktop-publishing tools, 225
Diagrams and schematics, 251, 253
Direct quotation, 139
Division into categories, 125
Documentation style, 400–408
    APA style, 402–405
    cause-effect discussion, 81

extended definition, 139, 141
formal report, 335
memo proposal, 171
MLA style, 405–407
primary research report, 85
progress report, 183–184
recommendation report, 107, 115
reference books, 407
table, 334
workshop, 408
Dogpile, 386
Drawings, 251, 252
Dual measurements style, 61, 103

E-journals, 393
E-mail, 274–275
Effect-by-effect discussion, 70
Either-or argument, 148
Emotional appeal, 146, 150, 164–165
Emphasis, 199, 214. *See also* Highlighting
Emphasis words, 201
Empirical research reports, 75–79
Employment-search tools. *See* Application letter;
    Résumé
Encyclopedias, 388–389
End-of-sentence modifiers, B–6
Ethics, 11–12
    anecdotal evidence, 320
    AUTHOR, 11–12
    biased language, 151
    biased/slanted graphics, 343
    groupthink, 413
    murky waters, 277
    omission, 77
    photographs, 253
    plagiarism, 403
    résumé, 307
    STC guidelines, 13
    universal language, 355
Evaluating Internet information, 387–388
Evaluation report, 93, 101
Examples. *See* Annotated examples; Short
    examples/samples
Excel
    graphs and charts, 241–244
    tables, 240–241
Excite, 386
Executive format, 99

Executive report design, 105
Executive summary, 322, 330
Extended definition, 120–125, 137–141

Fairness, 13
False analogies, 148
False causality, 148
Feasibility proposal, 175–179
Feasibility report, 93, 101
FedWorld, 395
Figure title
    creating, 257
    instructions, 65
    technical description, 33
Final conclusion, 97
Financial feasibility, 101
Finding information. *See* Information sources
First-level headings, 194
First-pass reviewing, 353–354
Flip charts, 342
Flow chart, 251, 252
Font
    business letter, 269
    headings, 195
Footnotes (table), 104
Formal report
    annotated example, 326–335
    appendixes, 319–320
    binding, 316–317
    body, 319, 332–334
    cover, 316
    displayed page numbers, 321–322
    executive summary, 322, 330
    general layout, 312–335
    information-sources list, 320
    introduction, 331
    list of figures and tables, 318–319, 329
    numbering styles, 321
    page numbering, 321–322
    table, 334
    table of contents, 318, 328
    title page, 317–318, 327
    transmittal letter, 317, 326
    workshop, 325
Formal sentence definition, 118–120
Fractions, A–11
Fragments, C–2, C–3
Freelance technical writers, 9

Full-time professional technical writers, 9
Future tense, 59

Gantt chart, 159
Gender-neutral language, 355
General encyclopedias, 388
General search engines, 386
Glossaries, 119
Good-news-first, bad-news-last strategy, 266
Google, 386
Google Groups, 386
Google News, 393
Google Scholar, 386
Government documents, 394–395
Grammar
    comma-splice sentence, C–4
    fragments, C–2, C–3
    parallelism, C–6 to C–8
    pronoun reference, C–5 to C–6
    Web sites, B–2, C–2
Graphics, 248–261. *See also* Illustrative graphics
Graphs and charts, 232–244
    biased/slanted graphics, 343
    components, 237
    convert table to graph, 234
    creating, 241–244
    designing, 236–237
    spreadsheet software, 241–244
    when used, 232
    workshop, 246–247
Groupthink, 413
Guide sites, 386

Handouts, 342–343
Hasty generalizations, 147
Hazardous materials symbols, 228–229
Heading styles, 197–198
Headings, 190–209
    comparison, 104
    creating, 197–198
    designing, 194–196
    extended definition, 138
    font, 195
    instructions, 63
    levels, 193–194
    manual approach to creation, 197
    memo, 38
    oral presentation, 347

    process document, 58
    second-level, 33, 142
    software-supplied styles, 197–198
    stacked, 142
    styles approach to creation, 198
    third-level, 33, 35, 142
    uses, 193
    what to avoid, 196
    what to do, 195–196
    word processing software, 197–198
    workshop, 207–208
Highlighting, 199–209
    character styles, 206, 207
    defined, 199
    guidelines, 209
    instructions, 64
    manual creation, 205–206
    recommendation report, 110
    résumé, 310
    scheme, 202–204
    uses, 201
    what not to do, 200
    word-processing software, 205–206
    workshop, 208
Highlighting scheme, 202–204
Honesty, 13
HotBot, 386
Houp, Kenneth, 366
How Stuff Works, 382
Hyphen, 58, B–10 to B–15
Hypothetical, projected effects, 69

ILL, 390
Illustrative graphics, 248–261
    clip art, 254–255
    conceptual drawings, 251
    cropping illustrations, 255
    cross-referencing illustrations, 257, 258
    diagrams and schematics, 251, 253
    drawing your illustrations, 255
    drawings, 251, 252
    examples of usage, 60, 66
    exporting graphics into documents, 258–259
    figure title, 257
    finding illustrations, 253
    flowchart, 251, 252
    labelling illustrations, 255
    manually cutting and pasting, 259–260

photographs, 250, 251, 253
screen capture, 254
sizing illustrations, 255
sources of borrowed graphics, 257
Web graphics, 248, 254
what should be illustrated?, 249–250
workshop, 260–261
Important points, 214
In-sentence list, 211–212
process document, 57
recommendation report, 110
sample, 213
technical description, 33
Informal report, 28–31, 36–39
Information interview, 292
Information sources, 380–399
books, 389–390
brochures, 395
encyclopedias, 388–389
evaluating Internet information, 387–388
government documents, 394–395
informal, unpublished sources, 396–397
Internet searches, 384–388
interviews, inquiries, e-mail, 396–397
librarian, 381–382
magazines and journals, 391–393
newspapers, 393
online searches, 384–388
product literature, 395, 396
questionnaires, 397–398
reference books, 388–389
surveys, 397–398
TV news broadcasts, 393–394
workshop, 398–399
Informative abstract, 322–324
Infrastructure, 17, 133
Initialisms, A–3 to A–6
Inquiry letter, 280–282, 288–289
Instructional task analysis, 368
Instructions, 46–51, 63–66
Intellectual property rights, 401–402
Interlibrary Loan (ILL), 390
Internet Public Library, 382, 389, 393
Internet searches, 384–388
Introduction
abstract, 322
adjustment letter, 280, 286
application letter, 302, 306, 309

business communications, 265
cause-effect discussion, 70, 73–74
classification, 130, 136, 142
comparison, 92, 103
complaint letter, 278
description, 21
extended definition, 124, 137
formal report, 331
informal report, 36
inquiry letter, 288
instructions, 50, 63
oral presentation, 341
persuasion, 151–152
primary research request, 79, 83
process, 45
progress report, 161, 181
recommendation report, 99–100, 107
specifications, 27
technical description, 33
transmittal letter, 326
Introductory-element comma, B–2 to B–3
Investigative, analytical reports, 29
Invisible Web, 386
Irrelevant, *ad hominem* arguments, 147
Italics. *See* Highlighting

Job search, 291–293. *See also* Application letter;
Résumé
Journals, 391–393

Keywords, 385

Lab report (primary research report), 75–79,
83–86
Label, 70
Labelled list, 212, 213
Labelling illustrations, 255
Latin abbreviations, 85
Legality, 13
Legend, 237
Letter. *See* Business letters
Letterhead, 270
LibDex, 390
Librarian, 381–382
Library of Congress, 390
Library of Congress Subject Heading, 385
Line graph, 243, 244
List, 210–218

bulleted. *See* Bulleted list
creating, 216–217
guidelines, 215
in-sentence. *See* In-sentence list
numbered. *See* Numbered list
types, 211–212
uses/benefits, 213–214
when to use, 214
workshop, 217–218
List of figures and tables, 318–319, 329
Literature review, 76
Logical appeal, 145, 150, 165
Logical fallacies, 147–148
Lone headings, 196

Magazines and journals, 391–393
Manitoba Conservation, 9
Manual highlighting, 205
Markel, Mike, 277
Marketing literature, 7
MasterFILE Premier, 392
Mechanics and style
    abbreviations, A–3 to A–6
    acronyms, A–3 to A–6
    grammar, C–1 to C–10. *See also* Grammar
    numbers, A–8 to A–11. *See also* Number
    punctuation, B–1 to B–122. *See also*
        Punctuation
    symbols, A–7 to A–8
MEL, 389
Memo, 270–272
Memo header, 36
Memo proposal, 168–172
Menu/menu-option names, 201
Meta-search engines, 386
MetaCrawler, 386
Michigan Electronic Library (MEL), 389
Microsoft Excel
    graphs and charts, 241–244
    tables, 240–241
Microsoft Excel Chart wizard, 242
Microsoft PowerPoint, 345, 346
Microsoft Word
    bulleted list, 217
    caution notice, 226–227
    character styles, 206
    cropping images, 255
    custom headings, 198

danger notice, 227–228
default heading styles, 197–198
drawing toolbar, 256
exporting graphics, 258–259
formatting controls, 205
highlighting, 205
labels (graphics), 256
lists, 216–217
notices, 226–228
number style, 322
numbered list, 216–217
page numbers, 322
paper, 270
paragraph, 315
readability statistics, 358
simple notice, 226
sizing images, 255
symbols, A–7
tables, 238–240
template, 272–274
warning notice, 227
MLA documentation style, 405–407
MLA Handbook for Writers of Research Papers,
    405
Modified block letter format, 267, 268
Modifier problems, 84
MSN, 386

Name-page system (MLA documentation style),
    405–407
Name-year system (APA documentation style),
    402–405
National Technical Information Service, 395
NBC News, 394
Nested list, 212, 213
News broadcasts, 393–394
Newspapers, 393
Noninstructional task analysis, 369
Nonrestrictive-element comma, B–5 to B–6
Northern Light, 386
Note, 221, 226
Notices, 219–230
    caution, 221, 226–227
    creating, 225–228
    danger, 221, 227–228
    elements of, 224
    examples, 221
    how to use them, 223

simple note, 221, 226
warning, 221, 227
WHMIS symbols, 229
workshop, 230
writing style, 225
Number, A–8 to A–11
ethics, 98
fractions, A–11
primary research report, 84
process document, 61
technical description, 34
Numbered list, 211
instructions, 63
Microsoft Word, 216–217
recommendation report, 108–109
sample, 212
Numeric requirements, 95

Objects (oral presentation), 342
Omission, 77
Online helps, 4–5
Online library resource pages, 390
Online newspapers, 393
Online searches, 384–388
Operational requirements, 27
Oral presentation, 336–350
body language, 347
conclusion, 341
delivery, 347–348
evaluating, 348–349
handouts, 342–343
how-to guide, 337–342
infrastructure, 339–340
introduction, 341
objects, 342
presentation software, 345, 346
purpose, 338
rehearsal, 341–342
research the topic, 339
transitions, 348
verbal headings, 347–348
visuals, 340, 342–345
workshop, 350
Oral-presentation evaluation form, 349
Oral-report visuals, 342–345
Organization-based paragraphing, 266
Organization chart, 251

Outline
oral presentation, 342
progress report, 182
Oversimplistic, either-or argument, 148
Overview list, 214

Page break, 106
Paired items, 214
Parallelism, C–6 to C–8
Part-by-part description, 17, 18, 23
Part-time technical writers, 8
Passive voice, 61
Pearsall, Thomas, 366
People finder search sites, 388
Periodical Abstracts, 392
Periodical index, 391–392
Periodicals, 391–393
Personal appeal, 146, 150, 164, 165
Persuasion, 144–187
annotated examples, 164–187
how-to guide, 148–152
logical fallacies, 147–148
progress report, 157–162, 180–187
proposal, 152–157, 168–179
Toulmin approach, 147
types of appeals, 145–147
workshop, 162–163
Photographs, 250, 251, 253
Phrase searches, 384
Pie chart, 243, 245
Placement agencies, 292
Plagiarism, 402, 403
Point-by-point comparison, 88–90, 96–97, 103, 110
Policies and procedures, 51–55
PowerPoint, 345, 346
Predicted effects, 69
Presentation software, 345, 346
Primary conclusions, 97, 105
Primary research report, 75–79, 83–86
Procedures, 51. *See also* Policies and procedures
Process, 40–66
annotated examples, 57–62, 63–66
defined, 41
how-to guide, 42–46
instructions, 46–51, 63–66
policies and procedures, 51–55
sample discussion, 46

step-by-step approach, 42, 44
Product literature, 395, 396
Product specifications, 23–28
Professionalism, 13
Progress report, 157–162, 180–187
Progress report cover letter, 180
Project log, 415
Pronoun reference, C–5 to C–6
Pronouns and corporate nouns, 111
Proposal, 152–157, 168–179
Proposal cover letter, 173–174
Proximity searches, 384
Public speaking. *See* Oral presentation
Publication Manual (APA), 402
Punctuation
   apostrophe, B–16 to B–18
   colon, B–9 to B–10
   comma, B–2 to B–7. *See also* Comma
   dash, B–15
   hyphen, B–10 to B–15
   quotation marks, B–18 to B–19
   semicolon, B–8 to B–9
   Web sites, B–2
   workshop, B–19 to B–22

Quality, 13
Queenan, John, 24
Questionnaires, 397–398
Quotation marks, B–18 to B–19
   direct quotation, 139
   process document, 59
   recommendation report, 113

Rating-based requirements, 95
Readability statistics, 358
Reader-first strategy, 266
Reader's Guide to Periodical Literature, 391
Rebuttal, 147, 164
Recommendation report, 94–100, 105–115
Recovery, 224
Redundant highlighting techniques, 209
Refdesk.com, 382, 389, 390, 393
Reference books, 388–389
Reference citations. *See* Documentation style
Reference information, 5
Reference.com, 386
Report bindings, 316–317
Report covers, 316

Report types
   accident report, 28
   background report, 131–134
   evaluation report, 101
   feasibility report, 101
   formal report, 312–335. *See also* Formal
      report
   informal report, 28–31
   investigative, analytical report, 29
   primary research report, 75–79, 83–86
   progress report, 157–162, 180–187
   proposal, 152–157, 168–179
   recommendation report, 94–100, 105–115
   site and inspection report, 28
   trip report, 28
Request for proposal (RFP), 153
Research reports, 4
Restrictive-element comma, B–5 to B–6
Résumé, 293–301
   annotated example, 310–311
   details, 297–298
   formatting, 299
   functional strategy, 297
   heading section, 298
   highlights section, 298–299
   how-to guide, 294–299
   objectives section, 298
   organizational strategy, 296–297
   reverse chronological strategy, 297
   scannable, 299–300
   Web, 300–301
   workshop, 308
Review and revision, 352–364
   annotated example, 360–363
   audience, 353
   audience and task analysis, 376
   checklist, 364
   content, 354
   document type, 355–356
   first pass, 353–354
   graphics, 357
   headings, 356
   highlighting, 357
   lists, 356
   organization, 354
   readability, 358
   second pass, 355–357
   sentence problems, 357–358

tables, graphs, charts, 356–357
technical-style problems, 358
third pass, 357–358
transitions, 354
workshop, 359
Review of literature, 76
Revision. *See* Review and revision
Ritter, Jana, 307

Salutation, 267, 284, 286, 288
Sans serif fonts, 195
Savvy Search, 386
Scannable résumé, 299–300
Scope statement, 26, 50
Screen capture, 254
Search engines, 386
Searches using truncation, 384
Second-level headings, 33, 142, 194
Second-pass reviewing, 355–357
Secondary conclusions, 97, 106
Semicolon, B–8 to B–9
Sequenced items, 214
Series-element comma, B–4 to B–5
Serif fonts, 195
Sexist language, 355
Shaw, Matthew, 360
Short examples/samples. *See also* Annotated
   examples
   audience description, 372–374
   bulleted list, 212
   business letter format, 268
   cause-effect discussion, 70
   caution notice, 221
   classification, 126, 129
   comparison, 90
   danger notice, 221
   extended definition, 120, 122
   headings, 192
   highlighting scheme, 203, 204
   in-sentence list, 213
   labelled list, 213
   nested list, 213
   note, 221
   notices, 221, 222, 224
   numbered list, 212
   part-by-part approach, 23
   persuasion, 146
   process discussion, 46

simple list, 213
specification, 24
warning notice, 221
Short-paragraphs strategy, 266
Signature block, 180, 269
Simple list, 212, 213
Simple notice, 221, 226
Simplified letter format, 267, 268
Site and inspection reports, 28
Sizing illustrations, 255
Slides, 345, 346
Social feasibility, 101
Society for Technical Communication (STC), 13
Solicited proposal, 155
Source citations. *See* Documentation style
Sources list, 133
Sources of description, 22
Sources of information. *See* Information sources
Specialized encyclopedias/reference works, 388
Specialized search engines, 386
Specifications, 23–28
Speeches. *See* Oral presentation
Spiders, 386
Spreadsheet software (Excel)
   graphs and charts, 241–244
   tables, 240–241
Stacked headings, 142, 196
STC ethical guidelines, 13
Step-by-step process discussion, 42, 44
Strategis site (Industry Canada), 395
Student activities/exercises. *See* Workshop
Style, 197, 198
Style guide, 202
Stylistic appeal, 147
Subject line
   informal report, 36
   memo proposal, 168
Subordinate headings, 195
SuDoc numbers, 394
Summaries and abstracts, 322–324
Summary table, 98–99. *See also* Table
Surveys, 397–398
Symbols, A–7 to A–8
Synonym definitions, 117–118
Synthesis, 147

Table
   comparison, 103, 104

components, 235
convert, to graph, 234
convert text to, 233
creating, 238–241
designing, 235–236
footnotes, 104
formal report, 334
informal report, 36–37
recommendation report, 112
spreadsheet software, 240–241
summary report, 98–99
when used, 232
word-processing software, 238–240
workshop, 244–246
Table of contents, 318, 328
Task analysis, 367. *See also* Audience and task
     analysis
Task pane, 345, 346
Team Handbook, The (Scholtes et al.), 413
Team projects, 409–421
     anticipate problems, 414–415
     groupthink, 413
     how-to guide, 415–419
     teams in industry, 410–412
     teams in technical-writing classroom,
          412–414
     workshop, 420–421
Technical audience, 366–367. *See also* Audience
     and task analysis
Technical background, 96
Technical background report, 131–134
Technical communication, 2–3
Technical Communication (Markel), 277
Technical description. *See* Description
Technical feasibility, 101
Technical journalism, 8
Technical journalists, 8
Technical support writing, 5
Technical texts, 4–7
Technical writers, 8–9
Technical-writing courses, 10
Telegraphic style, 225
Telescoping causes, 68
Template, 199, 272–274
The Brain at Mohawk College, 382
Third-level headings, 33, 35, 142, 194
Third-pass reviewing, 357–358
Thomas Legislative Information, 395

Thomas Register of American Manufacturers,
     395, 396
Times New Roman, 195
Title
     figure. *See* Figure title
     instructions, 63
     progress report, 181
     table, 235
     technical description, 33
Title page, 317–318, 327
Tone, 265
Tools for extended definition, 123
TotalNews, 393
Toulmin approach to persuasion, 147
Transitions
     comparison, 104
     oral presentation, 348
     process document, 58
Transmittal letter, 317, 326
Trip reports, 28
Truncation, searches using, 384
TV news broadcasts, 393–394
Two-column list, 212

Underlining. *See* Highlighting
Universal language, 355
Unsolicited proposal, 155
URLs, 201
User-entered text, 201
User guides, 4

Verb tense, 59
Verbal headings, 347–348
Visuals, 340, 342–345

Warning notice, 221, 227
Web addresses (URLs), 201
Web graphics, 248, 254. *See also* Illustrative
     graphics
Web résumé, 300–301
Web sites
     Boolean operators, 384
     company/industry information, 292
     copyright/intellectual property rights, 402
     encyclopedias, 389
     evaluating Internet information, 387
     grammar, B–2, C–2
     Internet searches, 385

search, 290, 291–292, 293
punctuation, B–2, C–2
résumés, 300
standards and style guides, A–3
subject overviews and links, 382
TV news broadcasts, 393–394
White space, 214
WHMIS symbols, 229
whois search, 388
Whole-to-whole comparison, 88, 89
WhoWhere? people finder, 388
Wikipedia, 382
Word processing software. *See* Microsoft Word
Works cited. *See* Documentation style
Workshop
abbreviations, A–11 to A–12
application letter, 308
audience and task analysis, 377–379
background report, 136
business communications, 282–283
cause-effect discussion, 80
classification, 136
comparison, 102
definition, 134–136
description, 31–32
formal report, 325
grammar, C–8 to C–10
graphs and charts, 246–247
headings, 207–208

highlighting, 208
information search, 398–399
instructions, 55–56
lists, 217–218
notices, 230
numbers, A–12
oral presentation, 350
persuasion, 162
primary research report, 80
process, 55–56
proposal, 162–163
punctuation, B–19 to B–22
recommendation report, 102
résumé, 308
review and revision, 359
source documentation, 408
symbols, A–12
tables, 244–246
teams, 420–421
technical communication, 12–14

X-axis, 237

Y-axis, 237
Yahoo, 386
Yearbook supplements to encyclopedias, 388
Yes/no requirements, 95

ZDNet, 394